Cinematic Tourist Mobilities and the Plight of Development

T0298490

It is said that movies have encroached upon social realities creating tourism enclaves based on distortions of history and heritage, or simulations that disregard both. What localities and nation-states value are discarded, suppressed, or modified beyond recognition in neoliberal markets; thus flattening out human experience, destroying natural habitats in the name of development, and putting the future of whole ecosystems at risk.

Without disregarding such developmental risks *Cinematic Tourist Mobilities and the Plight of Development* explores how, en route to any beneficial or eco-destructive development, film tourist industries co-produce atmospheres of place and culture with tourists/film fans, local activists, and nation-states. Drawing on international examples of cinematically-induced tourism and tourismophobic activism, Tzanelli demonstrates how the allegedly unilateral industry-driven 'design' of location stands at a crossroads between political structures, systems of capitalist development, and resurgent localised agency.

With an interdisciplinary methodological and epistemological portfolio connected to the new mobilities paradigm, this volume will appeal to scholars, students, and practitioners interested in tourism, migration, and urban studies in sociology, anthropology, geography, and international relations.

Rodanthi Tzanelli is Associate Professor of Cultural Sociology at the University of Leeds, UK.

Routledge Advances in Sociology

246 The Dark Side of Podemos?
Carl Schmitt's Shadow in Progressive Populism
Josh Booth and Patrick Baert

247 Intergenerational Family Relations
An Evolutionary Social Science Approach
Antti O. Tanskanen and Mirkka Danielsbacka

248 Performing Fantasy and Reality in Contemporary Culture
Anastasia Seregina

249 The Philosophy of Homelessness
Barely Being
Paul Moran and Frances Atherton

250 The Sociology of Knowledge Approach to Discourse
Investigating the Politics of Knowledge and Meaning-making
Edited by Reiner Keller, Anna-Katharina Hornidge, and Wolf J. Schünemann

251 Christianity and Sociological Theory
Reclaiming the Promise
Joseph A. Scimecca

252 Ageing, Diversity and Equality
Edited by Sue Westwood

253 Cinematic Tourist Mobilities and the Plight of Development
On Atmospheres, Affects, and Environments
Rodanthi Tzanelli

For more information about this series, please visit: www.routledge.com/Routledge-Advances-in-Sociology/book-series/SE0511

Cinematic Tourist Mobilities and the Plight of Development

On Atmospheres, Affects, and Environments

Rodanthi Tzanelli

Routledge
Taylor & Francis Group
LONDON AND NEW YORK

First published 2019 by Routledge

2 Park Square, Milton Park, Abingdon, Oxfordshire OX14 4RN
52 Vanderbilt Avenue, New York, NY 10017

Routledge is an imprint of the Taylor & Francis Group, an informa business

First issued in paperback 2020

Copyright © 2019 Rodanthi Tzanelli

The right of Rodanthi Tzanelli to be identified as author of this work has been asserted by her in accordance with sections 77 and 78 of the Copyright, Designs and Patents Act 1988.

All rights reserved. No part of this book may be reprinted or reproduced or utilised in any form or by any electronic, mechanical, or other means, now known or hereafter invented, including photocopying and recording, or in any information storage or retrieval system, without permission in writing from the publishers.

Notice:
Product or corporate names may be trademarks or registered trademarks, and are used only for identification and explanation without intent to infringe.

British Library Cataloguing-in-Publication Data
A catalogue record for this book is available from the British Library

Library of Congress Cataloging-in-Publication Data
A catalog record has been requested for this book

ISBN: 978-1-138-38867-3 (hbk)
ISBN: 978-0-367-55616-7 (pbk)

Typeset in Times New Roman
by Wearset Ltd, Boldon, Tyne and Wear

For Majid: *sine qua, non sequitur*

'True genesis is not at the beginning but at the end, and it starts to begin only when society and existence become radical, i.e. grasp their roots'.

(Bloch [1986] 1995: 1376)

'"Each attains its harmony". This harmony is not apart from balance.... This stage is referred to by the saying "Knowing the white, keep the black, and the illumination of the spirit will come of itself"'.

(*Alchemy for Women*, a practical manual on Taoist self-refinement *c.*1800s)

Contents

Illustrations

NB The maps in this book use the following symbols:

✦ Affective geographies: situating 'responses'
★ World Heritage Sites and sites of relevant resident/local or national/institutional significance
✸ Filmed sites and/or local cinematically-inspired tourist business

Acknowledgements

The book drew on particular case studies used in my previous sole-authored publications, often modifying and/or updating findings to address subsequent developments: (2007) *The Cinematic Tourist: Explorations in Globalisation, Culture and Resistance*, London and New York: Routledge (48–49, 50–51, 52, 107–108, 110); (2013) *Heritage in the Digital Era: Cinematic Tourism and the Activist Cause*, London and New York: Routledge (42, 54–55, 56, 66–67, 75, 78–79); (2014) 'Heritage entropy and tourist pilgrimage in Brave's Scotland', *Hospitality & Society*, 4 (2): 155–177; (2015) 'On *Avatar's* (2009) touring semiotechnologies: From cinematic utopias to Chinese heritage tourism', *Tourism Analysis*, 20 (3): 269–282; (2015) *Mobility, Modernity and the Slum: The Real and Virtual Journeys of* Slumdog Millionaire, New York and Abingdon: Routledge (167); (2016) '*Game of Thrones* to games of sites/sights: Framing events through cinematic transformations in Northern Ireland', in K. Hannam, M. Mostafanezhad and J.M. Rickly-Boyd, *Event Mobilities: The Politics of the Everyday and the Extraordinary*. London: Routledge, 52–67 (55–57, 60–62); (2016) *Thanatourism and Cinematic Representations of Risk: Screening the End of Tourism*, New York and Abingdon: Routledge (98–99). Permissions were granted by Intellect, Cognizant Communication and Routledge (Taylor & Francis) to reproduce this material in the present book. The maps and the photograph used in the book belong to various Wikimedia users and featured in specific map entries under Creative Commons Licensing.

Dialogues (online and onsite/in person) with Apostolos Ziakas, Maximiliano Korstanje, Adrian Favell, and Nick Emmel, as well as supervision sessions with my doctoral student, Gauthami Kamalika Jayathilaka, helped me improve the book's argument. The Routledge team's (especially Emily Brigg's and Elena Chiu's) and the Wearset team's (especially Jonathan Merrett's) support in bringing this project to completion has also been invaluable. As always, I am grateful to my partner in life, critical proof reading and 'cheat days' (pizza, curry, and pudding), Majid Yar.

Abbreviations

AD	*Angels & Demons* (director Ron Howard 2008)
ANT	Actor network theory
BJP	Bharatiya Janata Party
CAFA	*Captain America: The First Avenger* (director Joe Johnston 2011)
CAS	Complex adaptive systems
CCM	*Captain Corelli's Mandolin* (director John Madden 2001)
CGI	Computer generated imaging
CoG	*City of God* (directors Fernando Meirelles and Katja Lund 2003)
D9	*District 9* (director Neill Blomkamp 2009)
DDII	*Dirty Dancing II* (director Guy Ferland 2004)
DVC	*Da Vinci Code* (director Ron Howard 2006)
ETAG	Edinburgh Tourism Action Group
EWH	Edinburgh World Heritage
GoT	*Game of Thrones* (directors Alan Taylor, Alex Graves, David Nutter, Mark Mylod, Jeremy Podeswa, Daniel Minahan, Michelle MacLaren, Alik Sakharov, Miguel Sapochnik, Brian Kirk, Tim Van Patten, Neil Marshall, Jack Bender, David Petrarca, Daniel Sackheim, Michael Slovis and Matt Shakman, David Benioff and D.B. Weiss 2011–2019)
HES	Historic Environment Scotland
HPDH	*Harry Potter and the Deathly Hallows* (Parts I–II, director David Yates 2010–2011)
ICOMOS	International Council on Monuments and Sites
JB	*James Bond* (different directors per movie 1962–ongoing)
JoN	*Jesus of Nazareth* (director Franco Zeffirelli 1977)
LOTR	*Lord of the Rings* (director Peter Jackson, trilogy 2001–2003)
LS	*Lucky Star* (directors Yutaka Yamamoto and Yasuhiro Takemoto 2007)
MM	*Mamma Mia!* (director Phyllida Lloyd 2008)
MPCB	Maharashtra Pollution Control Board
NiR	*Nights in Rodanthe* (director George C. Wolfe 2008)
NRT	Non-representational theory

NSM	New social movements
RTDC	Rajasthan Tourism Development Corporation
SNP	Scottish National Party
SM	*Slumdog Millionaire* (directors Danny Boyle and Loveen Tandan 2008)
Soweto	South Western Township
SWFA	*Star Wars: The Force Awakens* (director J.J. Abrams 2015)
UNESCO	United Nations Educational, Scientific and Cultural Organisation
UNO	United Nations Overtourism
UNWIPO	United Nations World Intellectual Property Organisation
WR	*Whale Rider* (director Niki Carro 2002)
WTO	World Tourism Organisation

Chapter 1

Introduction

The long (28 April–1 May 2018) 2018 bank holiday weekend promised to be difficult for Venice. The beautiful World Heritage city was set to be swamped by tourist hordes once more, setting off the alarms of sustainability even louder. In response, Mayor Luigi Brugnaro proceeded to sign a decree for the implementation of 'urgent measures' concerning public safety, security and livability in the city. These involved the diversion of tourist flows heading to popular markers, such as Rialto or San Marco, and the blocking of car drivers arriving from the Italian mainland from using the one bridge that spans the lagoon, Ponte Della Libertà (Squires 25 April 2018). The arrival of some 120,000 visitors that weekend threatened to sink the city in the rising sea levels faster than climate change, so metal *tornelli* (turnstiles) were also set to regulate human and automobile traffic (Brunton 1 May 2018). Who would want to live in this chaos? The new 'Veniceland's' permanent population has experienced a dramatic dip from 190,000 at the end of the Second World War to below 55,000 souls today. Back in September 2016, the young activist group 'Generation 90' raised concerns about the effects excessive tourism has on localities in *La Serenissima* (as the city is known), which is anything but serene for those who have to live with global consumers on their doorsteps. The creative style of the protest caught the attention of international reporters, who saw for the first time angry locals pushing trolleys (a hint at the city's progressive tourist 'McDonaldization' – Ritzer 2006), while shouting in the Venetian dialect slogans such as '"*Ocio ae gambe che go el careo*" – "Watch your legs, I'm coming through with a trolley" [and] "*R-Esistiamo*" – meaning both "We exist" and "We resist"' (Squires 12 September 2016). Almost simultaneously elsewhere in Europe, in Greece and Croatia, the articulation of similar concerns called for similar measures, painting the darkest momentum in the history of tourism, in which no way forward is clear and all good futures seem impossible.

To add some academic script here, forget for a while Agamben's (1998) 'state of exception': these days Europe's beautiful cities live in a perpetual 'state of invasion'; in them, 'poor migrants' have been replaced by 'poor locals'. The term 'state of invasion', which alerts us to the cost of consumer-driven impacts on living social habitats and lifeworlds signals the Europeanisation of a postcolonial phenomenon par excellence from a Marxist perspective (see for example Ash and Turner's (1975) thesis on tourists as colonising 'golden hordes'). Significantly, it originates precisely in the twenty-first century Venetian experience of providing hospitality: commonly known as *Bollino Nero* or 'code black', the word is used today by Italians to describe motorway gridlocks (Brunton 1 May 2018). Worryingly, similar 'code blacks', which were also issued outside Europe, prompted the convention of over 60 tourism ministers and private-sector leaders in November 2017 to discuss 'the issue' at a summit co-organised by the United Nations Overtourism (UNO). In 2016 *Fodor*'s had already published the first 'No Go' list reflecting concerns that tourism was destroying the world's earthly paradises, whereas in 2017 the Galápagos Islands, the crystal-clear Boracay island shores in the Philippines and many parts of Thailand posed severe restrictions and penalties on tourist flows in an attempt by governments to combat overcrowding, littering and uncivil behaviour (Pannett 22 May 2018).

'Code Black' – a nomination of (auto) mobility control, which is also a state of immobility desired by particular groups affected by excessive tourism – acted as inspiration in my work on the ways cinematic or film (induced) tourism blocks or enables all sorts of movement in different biospheres (human and natural) and mechanospheres (the machines of the internet, filmmaking and mechanically-enabled systems of tourism-making). Stepping back again, into the field of a local vision sketched by reporters, I can add more questions: how 'real' is this catastrophic world-picture, and, in any case, who 'films' it, for whom, and with what intentions? We do not deal with 'vision' here, but the visualisation of a multisensory and affective experience of blocking and being blocked. As is the case with all products destined to enter the cycle of production-consumption, experiences of 'overtourism' (excessive touristification) and 'tourismophobia' (fear of tourism/tourists) are in fact immanent to the atmospheric design of global markets, because they belong to the ways local character absorbs or rejects the shocks of tourist globalisation.

Consequently, it is rather simplistic to decide that the press, the host city, or even I, as the book-writer alone, hold 'authorship rights' in this high drama. Many different actors and agents, activist, market and state, among others, may contribute to the realisation of this or that 'reality'. At the same time, some would argue that currently, a 'master reality' overdetermines all these productive perspectives, which has to do with systemic capitalist failures and the unchecked advance of neoliberalism (*Ocio ae gambe che go el careo! R-Esistiamo* – to 'McDonaldisation', one may add). Similar to Venice has been Spain, the by now acclaimed birthplace of terms such as 'tourism monoculture' and 'tourismophobia', which are recycled by native mass media to both communicate social discontent with the pressures linked to tourism growth and to discredit social movements and civil society groups involved in its contestation (Milano 2017). Be this as it may, barriers (*bollinos*) between human groups have to be *articulated* before they become *established* in territories, minds and hearts. Instead of chasing up solutions to such nightmares, I concentrate on what is 'written out' of such dystopian scenarios: all actors or agents contribute to productions of realities; some of them, though pretty dark in heart, action and intention, can create dystopias pointing to a source of light at the other end of the tunnel; before dismissing either producers or consumers, hosts or guests, for not living up to some version of right-wing, centrist or left-wing ideological expectation, we must study the drivers, contexts and histories of their being in the world with others. Bloch once said that humanity beholds a 'happy abyss', which encloses all sorts of 'overlooked gains', as the human longing for alternative futures is enclosed in different interpretations for 'a happy or lovable trembling at the edge of the abyss' (Daly 2013: 173). As wanderers on earth, humans are bound to both encounter or create blocks, and devise solutions to remove them. On the latter, let us try to think of ourselves as part of a world larger than us, in which nature groans under the pressures we exert upon it, then retaliates unpredictably and uncontrollably, as it surely does these days. Just to complicate things for hardcore environmentalists, let us also remember that nature's needs may also clash with some urgent human needs – a real challenge to nature-first proponents of 'sustainable solutions'.

The selection of cases of tourismophobia and overtourism this book covers are specifically connected to films featuring locations, which become popular tourist destinations precisely because of their debut in such phantasmagoric markets. On closer inspection, such development offers interesting multisensory 'glimpses' into other contemporaneous non-cinematic instances of touristification – a point reinforced by my opening example. Chapter 2 is dedicated primarily to in-depth definitions of all the main concepts used in the title. It opens with a concrete example of cinematically-induced tourist development, which is used to practically organise the book's analytical and theoretical position: first, the study is situated within existing scholarly debates on mobilities design and mobilities justice; both subjects are used in the development of an argument on the nature of well-being in contexts of hospitality. This involves the coexistence of individual and collective tourist pursuits as a form of pilgrimage to filmed sites, but also the constitutive importance of cross-cultural encounters in the collective flourishing of communities hosting cinematic tourists. Thereafter, the chapter defines the temporal (the twenty-first century) and spatial (variations of urban and rural areas, and the international spread of case studies) parameters within which the study moves, to highlight that cinematic tourism is a by-product of global mobilities in technologies, humans, ideas, expertise, but also risks. Following this statement, the chapter outlines the challenges posited by cinematically-inspired development, including heritage conservation, environmental preservation, overtourism and tourismophobia. It considers all these as highly politicised, discursive fields in which conceptions of environmental pollution, heritage guardianship, identity and belonging are produced.

Within this debate, the chapter defines 'cinematic tourism' as more-than a bundle of businesses or allegedly 'empty' popular-cultural activities: as a form of pilgrimage to foreign and home lands, which is both directed towards heritage and creates forms of heritage anew. To do this, I replace established Western scholarly definitions of the term with the Japanese notion of 'contents tourism'. Tracing its origins in an Eastern theosophy (the ancient *I Ching Book of Changes*) that transcends particular religious canons and embraces holism, contents tourism is developed in the study into a way of experiencing (giving and accepting) hospitality in foreign lands, a way of perceiving one's natural, social and cultural environment, and being in it with animate and inanimate others. This 'relational ontology', which is inspired by ecofeminism, postsecular feminist scholarship and sociologies of hope, allows pilgrims and scholars to view technologies, including those of tourist connectivities, as prerequisites for humanity and its home's (earth's) flourishing.

Following this clarification, it is stressed that contents tourism allows us to trace the ways contemporary tourist industries and localities create the atmosphere of the tourist destination. Atmospheres, one of the main themes of the book, refer to the ways place is constructed in multi-sensory ways and experienced by those who inhabit/visit it, so it has both natural, material, phenomenal and cultural dimensions. Localities also participate in the creation of atmospheres with their hospitable or inhospitable behaviour, but also their native ways of knowing and acting. On this, emphasis is placed in the pre-cognitive, affective and emotional stages of creativity in lay and postindustrial atmospheric production – another emphasis in the study. To address the organisational and lay aspects of atmosphere-making, I place choreographer Rudolf Laban's notion of *choreosophía* or communal enactment (*chorós*) of wisdom (*sophía*) alongside organised industrial *choreología*, the rational reworking (*lógos*) of lay wisdom in industrial design. Running against elitist contempt about emotion and affect as irrational, irrelevant or just auxiliary to sustainable professional cultural production, I view contents tourism as an ancient and yet modern form of mobility standing at an intersection of emotion and reason, to which business design adds little in terms of experience. My version of contents tourism, which connects the past to futures of development, allows scholars to uncover a profound *symmetry* (rather than *homology*) between design creativity in organisational cultures of consumption and communal enactments of protest against them.

Chapter 3 is a detailed methodological chapter, which also outlines the scholarly foundations involved in researching and organising the cases in this book. It begins by stressing how scholarly 'worldmaking' reflects the worldmaking of tourism experts as a collection of practices that tourism is, can be, or does to this world. In this respect, it also signposts the notion of contents tourism as both a powerful interpretative tool in scholarly research and an unconscious activity that needs to be brought into discourse (become conscious): authors produce the worlds they study, in interaction with their informants that assume different mediated forms in texts, technologies, images, and, above all, feelings. This way of knowing is not identical to the epistemological framework propagated by scholars such as Hollinshead (2007), as it points to a persistent intertwining of the emergence of knowledge (episteme) and ontology (what I call 'epistemontology'). Subsequently, the argument that atmospheric creativity has a strong pre-cognitive, affective 'life' is applied to all case studies. This is achieved with the help of non-representational theory (NRT), which attends to the significance of emotions, actor-network theory (ANT), which stresses that technological texts (e.g. interviews, recordings of events) connect humans, machines and nature in interpretations of concrete events, and complex adaptive systems theory (CAS), which stresses the ways human agency has become entangled in complex systems involving technologies, natural and landscape ecologies. Such ANT entanglements of things, animals, environments and technologies place human beings in a 'cultural economy' that exceeds the rationale of monetarisation (e.g. giving and taking money from tourists), because it involves conceptions of being hospitable with (caring for) one's cultural and natural habitats.

The notion of 'care' is expanded on methodologically and epistemologically: postindustrial tourist development, tourist guests and host communities have their own ways of caring for destinations (we call them sustainability, heritage guardianship and so forth), but scholars also have a way of caring for all of them. The notion of 'atmospheric attunement' is developed to also account for the scholar's multisensory apprehension of the studied social and natural fields and their inhabitants. At the same time, it is noted that attunement is important for the industrial and lay production of atmospheres: all subjects have particular ways of experiencing the world, which are accounted for in this chapter. This experiential methodological tool is coupled with the rational CAS model of analysis, which involves the production of digital mapping, a more detached way of understanding the studied subject through particular case studies. This involves the mapping of important areas for communities in touristified areas, and the matching of such 'spots' with activist mobilities against cinematic tourist development (activist concentration spots). Rather than considering this mapping as a Foucaultian tool of 'sorting' and 'disciplining', I posit it as a Derridian and Arendtian gateway into different affective worlds.

Subsequently, the chapter announces the uses of the *I Ching* theosophy of movement (which is similar to Laban's *choreosophía*) as the most ancient surviving variation of epistemontology and methodology. *I Ching*'s perfect matching with my modern investigative social scientific tools (ANT, CAS, and NRT) also validates my adoption of the genealogy of contents tourism as an alternative framework for investigating contemporary cinematic tourism and activism. The chapter concludes with a matching exposition of Laban's and *I Ching*'s approaches, which I use to create ways of investigating atmospheres in touristified locations ('field-worlds'). I argue that atmospheres are constantly (re)constituted with the help of scenarios of movement for tourists and locals (their 'scriptural basis' – as in a movie script), their (infra)structures and materialities (their 'architectonics' – how the destination is constructed or staged), and their invisible perimeters, boundaries and borders, within which all subjects move (the 'kinesphere', and its ethnographic extensions, the 'kinesfield'). This tripartite distribution of field-world mobilities matches data visualisation (digital mapping) at an experiential level.

Chapter 4 extends the innovative use of *I Ching* theosophy as a technology of interpretation of material and emotional movement (e-motions) to a methodical presentation of case studies (the design of particular atmospheres in particular film-induced tourism contexts). It sets aside classifications of film-induced or cinematic tourism in terms of consumption behaviours and, following Nick Couldry's work, adopts the notion of religious and non-religious (popular cultural or 'popcultural') pilgrimage as a supra-category of technological mobility enclosing different motivations, affects and practices. Couldry's thesis is modified however, because the chapter proceeds to note that, in addition to any individual motivations, cinematic pilgrims share an objective and purpose: not visitations to filmed sites as purposeless consumption, but *the spatialisation of moods we associate with healing.* More specifically, generic notions of consumer disorientation, which may guide influential theses, such as Bauman's work on tourism and vagabondage, are modified by theory and example.

Theoretically, the chapter adopts *I Ching* expositions of atmospheric production as a way of understanding different popular-cultural pathways to healing. Different occasions of cinematic tourism development, often intertwined with heritage visitation, are attuned with *I Ching*'s ancient teaching about ways of being in the world with others, which promote a holistic improvement of the human soul, mind and body, in harmony with the animate and inanimate environment ('ecoaesthetics'). This ecoaesthetics inspires a series of interpretative 'signs' in my research ('hexagrams' and 'trigrams'), which allow me to present different pilgrimages into local and cinematic atmospheres. I use light, darkness, and various blends of both, as well as earth, water, and fire, as my primary hexagrams to explain how atmospheres are designed. My primary trigrams are script, architectonics, and kinesphere (see Chapter 3 summary above). Various combinations between my social-scientific hexagrams and trigrams construct a theoretical basis for tourism mobility that does not conform to business classifications of movement, but uses their design in its organisation. Using the logic of business design problematises practices of touristification, in preparation for the shocks of the following chapter.

Chapter 5 shifts focus to the ways localities, nation-states, or international activist networks, collaborating with either of them, respond to cinematic touristification in critical or violent ways. Whereas it commences with a detailed analysis of postcolonial and decolonial literature on domination, which addresses the exclusion of native knowledge from both the management of tourist mobilities and the technological conservation of the environment, it notes the limitations of both as too anthropocentric and politically partial to address the actual costs of capitalist development, which in the context of the Anthropocene and climate change, point to globally mobile risks. In tandem, it proposes that the notion of 'technological hubris', often attributed to world centres of development and their experts, should also be applied to proponents of local wisdom and their global networks (for example, activist cultures). All in all, the chapter scrutinises native and global–local enactments of protest in particular ecosystemic and cultural contexts.

The argument put forth is that, because most of these protests or mere expressions of discontent do not conform to traditional scholarly takes on social movements, to study them, one needs to devise a new classification of 'responses' to touristification. Three types of response are identified, which allow me to analyse a series of cases: 'epistemic misalignment' is rarely openly violent, but is regulated by a combative-adaptive response to development, which usually occurs in postcolonial contexts; 'hostipitality' can be more hostile and widespread, as it often focuses on ethnonational belonging and ritual expulsion of tourists as strangers; 'postindustrial disobedience' promotes labour disputes in cinematic tourist contexts into its focus, when they are usually manifestations of identity battles. Drawing on Laban's 'choreutics' again, the chapter suggests that we consider these responses in terms of (lay) design and atmospheres. Using the same tools employed in the previous chapter to explore postindustrial productions of cinematic tourism (e.g. *I Ching* as a social scientific tool), it argues that these 'responses' need to be studied as affective manifestations of a rather animated and turbulent native dialogue with tourist industries and tourists. Through this dialogue, which first takes place in the non-representational domain (that is, in culturally-conditioned affective reaction), localities and national centres restage their own atmospheric narratives for guests and themselves. This restaging marks the passage from non-representation to representation and turns Western technologies ('making' one's own 'image' as in a movie to serve one's objectives) into tools for native development, with various results.

The concluding chapter takes a step back to assess the benefits and pitfalls of cinematic tourist development in a hyperglobalised world plagued by human-made environmental degradation, climate change and unprecedented collective identity transformations. These mobile situations, which are constitutive of the ways social science scholars discuss the dawn of the Anthropocene, expose the limitations of human nature when it comes to turning the principle of hope for a better future into sustainable action. The chapter highlights that, in addition to any generic capitalist imperatives, conflicts between business and local, national and global activist networks are based on the urge to smash and replace the opponent's 'image' (perspective and prestige). This propensity to 'iconoclasm' reduces the possibility to find common ground so as to press ahead with changes that will secure a trouble-free future for humanity and its natural home, earth. Only the development of the skill to attune to other voices by all sides, and the creation of new scientific laboratories inclusive of both professional and native knowledge, can avert dark futures.

Chapter 2

On touring the world

An epistemontological frame

Phantasmagoric palimpsests: twenty-first-century cinematic tourist atmospheres

We keep on dreaming while awake in our contemporary worlds, which are steeped in phantasmagoric machineries. The observation echoes Walter Benjamin's (2002) wanderings in the arcades of capitalism, one of the most widely discussed scholarly *flâneries* in critical theory. Between the publication of his essays and today, the experience of dreaming complexified at both ends of production and consumption: today, we dream of things that never existed in real life, so our dreams have lost their Freudian referents to a solid autobiographical libido (Baudrillard 1973, 1994). Our contemporary worlds are wonders engineered by technological Muses, human and cyborg demi-gods inhabiting urban enclaves. In these spaces of flow, new systems of imagination emerge and new environments are invented for tourists to traverse, which are superimposed on real landscapes and natural habitats. Standing just a click away for the tourist who can afford to reach them, these new fantastic worlds form uneasy cohabitations with what existed in their stead for the land's inhabitants. Every time we dream, the capitalist machinery produces a new phantasmagoria to satisfy our desires; every time we take a journey to our dreamland, another world dies or changes beyond recognition.

Such stories of layering of worlds upon other worlds – commonly known as 'palimpsests' – fit most mobile situations connected to cinematic touristification. Take for example what happened to the Croatian city of Dubrovnik: featuring as 'King's Landing' in the popular TV series *Game of Thrones* (directors Alan Taylor, Alex Graves, David Nutter, Mark Mylod, Jeremy Podeswa, Daniel Minahan, Michelle MacLaren, Alik Sakharov, Miguel Sapochnik, Brian Kirk, Tim Van Patten, Neil Marshall, Jack Bender, David Petrarca, Daniel Sackheim, Michael Slovis and Matt Shakman, David Benioff and D.B. Weiss 2011–2019 – *GoT*), a cinematic adaptation of George R.R. Martin's novels, induced a palimpsestic process in tourist consumption. Its stunning Gothic and Baroque architecture (Dubrovnik's old town and surrounding areas outside city walls are World Heritage sites of outstanding 'artistic, urbanistic, cultural and historical value' – ICOMOS 2015: 4) and its beautiful Dalmatian coasts, are increasingly overlaid by a make-believe plot populating its sites with dragons, direwolves and royal dynasties. Of course, all places change, together with the needs of those who inhabit them. Here change is introduced from without, by technological means and with no explicit consent: in the cybersphere, Dubrovnik continues to be advertised as a beautiful natural location and a World Heritage destination, but it features more and more amongst the *GoT* must-see bundles of fantastic locations (Phelan 29 April 2014). Indeed, cinematic fans climb today its City Walls and walk its circumference not for a panoramic view of the Adriatic Sea, but to see Fort Lovrijenac, a.k.a. the 'Red Keep' and 'Backwater Bay', from which they watched Myrcella Baratheon shipped off to 'Dorne' in the filmed series. Others walk up and down the Jesuit Stairs off St. Dominka Street, where Cercei Lannister took the infamous walk of atonement, or buy 'shame bells' from a nearby souvenir shop, if they wish to immerse themselves in the full simulation. They all see Dubrovnik through a cinematic lens, which has added yet another (hyper-)real level to their perception of its environments.

This engineering game of make-believe has not merely altered the location's Gothic ambience, it also caused a spontaneous alteration in its affective landscapes, including those of hospitality. We must lend an ear to rumours: apparently, the 'walk of shame' down the Jesuit Stairs almost did not happen, because the Dubrovnik Church was reluctant to participate in 'such a blatant display of nudity near its holy halls' (Taylor 13 August 2017). This should have also raised alarm bells for the global *GoT* network of tourist destinations (Dubrovnik features among a group of filmed locations scattered across Europe and beyond), but it did not, so things took their own course: in 2017, Dubrovnik featured next to Barcelona amongst those European cities in which waves of tourismophobia surged, to expel visitors, who allegedly polluted places with their very presence.

It is true that fans of the show flock into the city every year: it is still cheaper to visit because the Croatian currency is still outside the Euro. Dubrovnik enjoys good economic returns from these mobilities: studies conducted by the Zagreb Institute of Economics indicate a surge in visitations to the filmed locales, with the number of cinematic fans-tourists as high as 60,000 a year (Godfrey 11 August 2017). There is, however, an evident misalignment between economic remuneration and the plea to live in a clean or not overcrowded environment. I intend to focus on such misalignments between the technological development of new atmospheres for places and the affective atmospheres mobility changes in them induce. As the example suggests, we deal with the emergence of complex systems of production (what I explore as 'staging'), consumption and response/reaction (what I explore as 'performance') to touristification, which cannot be studied individually without having in mind the ways they interact. Drawing on complexity theory, I endeavour to explore overlappings and crosscuttings of different systems of being, belonging and creating, including the anthropological, the ecological/natural and the technological in twenty-first century contexts of cinematic touristification.

At a first stage, I deal with the spatiotemporal staging of mobilities as a practice of designing lifescapes. Postindustrial design is invariably controlled from 'above', the sites of political and economic power, through partnerships of multinational corporations and states, which manage the circulation of resources (Bærenholdt 2013). However, as Jensen notes (2013: 5, 2014: 15), mobilities are acted 'from below' by people engaging in everyday interactions – an observation certainly applying to design in cinematic tourist destinations. Nonetheless, a comprehensive holistic approach must also consider those who inhabit redesigned environments. This introduces questions of mobility injustice to the picture, pertaining to the capacity of staging to mobilise local human and nonhuman resources as passive objects, rather than active subjects. For Sheller (2012a: 199–200) mobility justice refers to a modality raising questions of who is able to access and appropriate mobility capital, and how broadly capabilities of movement are extended throughout a social system. I will extend this definition of movement capability so as to include natural environments and nonhumans in it. Considering 'localities' and 'communities' (on which I deliberate in Chapter 3), as well as their natural environments as actants or agents in a holistic ecosystem also suggests that we extend Jensen's analysis of mobilities design (Chapter 4), so as to cover variations of what we know in tourism and hospitality studies as 'hosts'. Indeed, as I proceed to argue in the penultimate chapter (Chapter 5), the hosts respond to tourist development in various *styles*, thus producing 'counter-designs', or polemically appropriating those of the newcomers: creative industries such as tourism and film.

Hence, in a second stage, I look into the styles or modes of such counter-designs in the making as blends of lay knowledge and/or organised protest, which posit alternatives to the lifestyles and imperatives of global capitalist structuration. We could posit such rebellious self-changes as by-products of modernism, which Berman (2010: 16) understands as manifestations of 'loosely grouped' values and visions of the world with the advent of twentieth-century modernisation. However, I wish to refrain from devising rigid epochal divisions of human history and memory, which are based mostly on European and Western experiences. Without discarding the knowledge they contributed to humanity, I prefer to connect such counter-modes to *modism* (a speculation on ways in the world) or, better, *tropism* (the nature of being in the world with others) existing even outside modernist structures in multiple variations. *Trópos* from *tropē* (*τροπή*: 'style with velocity'), equips humans with manners that are both visible and invisible, perceptible and imperceptible to the naked eye: it produces and affirms 'character', which endures the attacks of positivism (because it can be physically examined sometimes in embodied habits – Neurath 1983: 60), while also retaining immense and undivided interest amongst phenomenologists (because it communicates affects, emotions and the pursuit of counter-worlds we desire to realise). Close to Bourdieu's (1984) '*habitus*', character is one of the primary *loci* of my atmospheric investigation into revolutions for two reasons: on the one hand, its manifestations allow me to *feel and understand* how collectivities behave unconsciously; on the other, its conscious manipulation and misuse by postindustrial creators, nation-states or communities themselves in highly volatile environments, helps me consider the ways rebellious groups 'experience truth' in *naked* ways. Character both encapsulates elusive atmospheric movements of human nature in particular directions (*trópos*) and exposes the style of this experience as a potentially marketable product in consumption domains, such as those of film and tourism ('selling native style off to the higher bidder' while hiding the ignominy the seller experiences). Marx would have approached this nakedness as the stripping of an aura from the subject's being in the world (Berman 2010: 105–107, 115–116). However, as I endeavour to show by example, the movement of character into and out of markets can also become an affirming experience that unexpectedly produces new characters and styles, or allows disempowered groups to transcend structural impositions. Seeing beyond the economic imperative, encounters with development are bound to change the one set to be developed, but not always in expected and designed ways: most importantly, its effects transcend economics, turning culture into a domain of experiential conflict.

Mobilities design and mobilities justice are emerging subject areas within the 'new mobilities paradigm', which claims interdisciplinarity and amasses methodological tools from different social scientific and humanist fields questioning their own anthropocentric roots. With an explicit focus on post-Wallersteinian systems connected to ANT and an *epistemontological* repertoire (e.g. knowledge/knowing intertwined with becoming) connected to NRT, both areas share an interest in redefining how and from where intentions emanate in a system so that design and the redistribution of 'goods' across sociocultural fields can secure better life prospects for all (D'Sa 1999; Fennell 2009). Indeed, a broad understanding of the 'good life' invites considerations of the ways mobilities, such as tourism, and socially embedded, collective skills, such as hospitality are afforded in different parts of the world. These questions are framed and answered differently by different scholarly constituencies, which do not always communicate well. A coherent epistemontological framing of such clashes would invite careful considerations of the perspectives each constituency holds, including those that claim to be critical over other epistemologies, such as those guiding postcolonial and decolonial studies. Above all, however, the present study produces new analysis of the ways various stakeholders, beneficiaries and human/non-human agents interact in a particular field (see Chapter 3 on the notion of the 'kinesfield') increasingly known as film-induced (Beeton 2005, 2016) or cinematic tourism (Tzanelli 2007).

Although this field has been expanding on the study of film-induced tourism as a novel global business, with various scholars exploring questions of popular consumption but also community development, there is less consideration of questions of 'sustainability' as a problem, rather than a given. The field's connection to media studies might obstruct such investigations, when scholars disregard histories of technology (the philosophy of craft), as well as its relationship to technicity (skill) and human *téchnes* or arts (Ingold 2011: 294–311; Tzanelli 2016a). I aspire to address some of these gaps from a mobilities paradigm perspective as a sociocultural theorist with an interest in the popular and the everyday. However, I do not want to add more to the fast-growing pile of studies on film-induced tourism business, but to outline the broader ethical implications of 'sustaining' it as a leisure activity. Conceptions of sustainability turn my attention to potential sites of production and consumption: cities and the countryside.

Cities and countrysides: toward a new cinematic tourist mobilities paradigm

The popular and the everyday are recurring themes in the sociology of consumption, which focuses on the city as a phantasmagoric factory, and increasingly edges towards immaterial forms of labour and the symbolic production of goods (Cronin and Hetherington 2008; Richards 2011, 2014; Richards and Wilson 2006). Similar observations reappear in tourism studies with a special focus on urban tourism, innovating on analyses of advertising, production and marketing (Law 2002: 53–55; Cronin 2010: 44). Between practices of consumption favouring the urban cool and existential calls to devise ways to escape from the urban cages of modernity, a romantic appreciation of the countryside reinstated itself. However, clocks cannot turn back: the immaculate countryside that could lift the spirits through practices of leisurely walking, photographing and rites of holiday-making often revealed itself as the simulacrum of a golden age that probably never existed as such (Urry 1995). What are today's countrysides, if not the highly networked suburban enclaves of urban commuters who have to venture into city centres for work? Nowadays, even for scholars, any division between the country and the city sits on a quicksand that absorbs conceptual constants as soon as they are formed.

The social basis of this complication was noted almost half a century ago by cultural theorist Raymond Williams, who, sizes and characters of villages in his observations aside, noted the existence of different forms of settlement between the traditional opposites of country and city, including suburbs, dormitory towns, shantytowns and industrial estates (Williams [1973] 2016: 2). Towards the end of *The Country and the City* he concludes:

> People have often said 'the city' when they meant capitalism or bureaucracy or centralized power, while 'the country' … has at times meant everything from independence to deprivation, and from the powers of an active imagination to forms of release from consciousness.
>
> (Ibid.: 418)

Williams' influential book was written in an era dominated by the rise of profitable representations in capitalist systems of mobility, when countrysides and cities were still moving in time through networks of terrestrially-embedded relationships. The proliferation of simulatory regimes in twenty-first century capitalist contexts has altered both the geopolitical coordinates in which such networks thrive or die, and the nature of social relationships and experiences they produce. It also introduced new social and cultural challenges, including those pertaining to the ways relationships between representations and simulations impact on network formations. These days we must also examine how terrestriality and virtuality interact in sociocultural terms to produce those mobilities discussed in this study: media-induced tourism.

These issues assert the presence of new sociocultural complexities transcending the borders of the nation-state, a social network or a single fixed cluster of representations of place and culture. More to the point, place-making in media-induced tourism and the tourist industry's worldmaking systems (Hollinshead 2009a; Hollinshead *et al.* 2009) are implicated in ever-shifting formations of place. 'Place' in contemporary media-induced tourism can include or enclose as diverse things as the space-bound heritage of a region or nation (Egberts 2017); an *exurbs* or territory geographically adjacent to and economically codependent with a city, but designed in terms of lifestyle as a village (McKenzie 1996; Weaver 2005); a theme park area within a city simulating old ways of life or old colonised lifeworlds (Clavé 2007; Whatt 2010); or even a touristified slum, which figures as a segregated, exoticised sociocultural sphere within a city (Tzanelli 2015a). Take now all these examples and consider how they figure in digital tourist business. The cybersphere, where tourist capitalism thrives today, superimposes itself onto such terrestrial variations and many more, whereas the potential of online representations and simulations may also feed back into other place-making systems, such as that of the cinema. In conclusion, new technological complexities require an adjustment in our perspective.

Of course, in *The Country and the City* Williams already notes that the 'escalators' of industrialisation and modernisation led to the disappearance of 'organic community' and 'unspoilt nature', and a nostalgic turn to the representation of pristine socialities and landscapes in political, social and artistic discourse (Williams [1973] 2016: 12–27). In addition, he debates the simultaneous emergence of a 'pastoral delightful', in which rural life is whitewashed of its hardships, and the rise of the gaze of scientists and tourists, which would eventually colonise rural lifeworlds ideologically, economically and materially (ibid.: 27–30; Urry 1990, 1995). But he could not have foreseen the complete demotion of nostalgia for rural utopias to the realm of representation with the scientiation of pastorality in the context of climate change or overtourism. Nowadays, extra-urban 'nature' and the rural sublime operate as picture postcards in the hands of cultural industries, such as film, tourism and their digital extensions (Bell and Lyall 2002: 189–190). Having joined profit-making and consumption practices in tourism as scopic propositions (on the 'picturesque' see Williams [1973] 2016: 184–185; Duncan 1999), they have been separated from the scientised mission of alleviating climate change or mediating on ecosystemic resilience.

The picturesque, which is a mode of aesthetic appreciation of the natural world mostly associated with tourism consumption (Carlson 2000: 4–5), remains dependent upon the artificial framing of landscape and not an awareness of the 'fragility or biodiversity of certain "unscenic" natural environments' (Todd 2009: 164).

Such conflicts of appreciative regimes are acted out even in transnational policy frameworks of heritage conservation. Take for example UNESCO's use of the term 'outstanding natural beauty' (2012: 6, 10–19) in its framing of heritage landscapes (see Hepburn [1966] 2004 on art, nature and framing). As Hepburn (1995: 65) notes, regardless of whether we wish to defend such areas against degradation, we must examine our account of the appreciation of beauty and how 'its value can be set alongside competing and vociferously promoted values involved in industry, commerce and urban expansion'. The isolation of the term from such contexts leaves the door of interpretation open for all constituencies, whereas its separation from notions of an unscenic, but ecosystemically vital aesthetic, also allows for unregulated industrial exploitation. Incidentally, the picturesque has been constitutive of colonial articulations of spatial organisation that created familiarity for the European tourist gaze in the place of the inhospitable vastness of countries such as South Africa (van Eaden 2007: 122–123). Its contribution to the emergence of the global theme park industry via international Expos featuring Oriental specimens (human, flora and fauna) both in Europe and the United States (Carlton 1994: 26–45) has been pivotal. These less mobile spaces of twentieth-century leisure started their life in the ludic spheres of the wandering circus and the carnival. In line with dominant Orientalist themes, the nomadic entrepreneurs of such ventures often used picturesque imagery in which 'exotic human beings [were] integrated with a presumably defining and overtly limiting décor' (Nochlin 1991: 50–51).

All in all, systems of consumption and ecosystemic resilience feature as enemies in dominant debates on the futures all sentient inhabitants of the earth might be facing. As I explain in Chapter 5, not only do constructions of this relationship as hostile or even impossible by local or translocal interest groups stand at the heart of responses to cinematic touristification, their discursive nature *literally* suggests a backward-looking orientation of society to a golden age (Williams [1973] 2016: 51; Herzfeld 2005: 149). At the same time, the glorification of nomadic metaphysics in some policy-making regimes 'has little time for notions of attachment to place, and revels in notions of flow, flux and dynamism' (Cresswell 2006: 26). The backward-looking discourse clashes with the futural orientation of science addressing both environmental sustainability and the resilience displayed by systems of human mobility, including (tourist) labour. In addition, it has knock-on effects on the formation of moral economies in cinematic tourismophobic situations, especially when the disaffected groups begin to articulate demands that may prove to be environmentally, socially or culturally incompatible. But least we label all polemic responses to (cinematic) tourist development 'tourismophobia', we must remember that all systems faced with impending changes are of a *machetic* (from *máchōmai* (*μάχωμαι*): to struggle) nature (Urry 2003, 2005b). The vitalist properties of such struggles for survival call for respect of tacit knowledge and wisdom alongside science, rather than the former's replacement by the latter – a suggestion that introduces in this study's epistemontological tools the notion of *choreosophía* or choreutics (circular dance formation) of insight. There will be more adjustments of this model to consider with regards to struggles for survival in a neovitalist analytical framework below. We cannot ignore that the *machetic* principle adheres to vitalism, which celebrates the 'bio' in diversity, with as catastrophic consequences such as those recorded in histories of genocide and deforestation.

The *machetic* principle of systems is more evident in market environments, which operate according to evolutionary imperatives and tend to eliminate what their dominant players consider weak elements in them (Heilbroner 1999: Chapter 4). From an anthropocentric perspective, those labelled 'weak' retort as well as they can, and a battle of survival and/or recognition ensues; 'responses' or 'feedback' apply also to nature, with which we cannot negotiate. However, this principle alone cannot explain the orchestration of mobilities in sociocultural and natural environments: in them we also need to address the will to (self-)presentation, representation and simulation. Relaying one's presence in the world (representation – Nora 1989), crafting their own identity performance on social stages (self-presentation – Goffman 1987) and inventing realities without real referents (simulation – Baudrillard 1973, 1975) are both lay contemporary practices and the bread and butter of the postindustrial machines of film, the internet and tourism. Similar connections were made in critical scholarship a long time ago, but there has been less transference of such scholarship into cinematic tourism (Tzanelli 2007: Chapter 1). The original critical scholarship itself is less interested in the phenomenological dimensions of these issues as such and more in the functional-structural role they acquire in markets. The gap is justified by pragmatic regional needs, but, ironically, there is still no organised cross-national statistical analysis of what film/media tourism contributes to localities, nation-states or cross-border regions. We can get a glimpse from a recent study conducted by VisitBritain (February 2018: 4) – but only just: in its profiling of international tourists,

- Overall, 6% of respondents indicated they had previously visited a film/TV location on holiday and that this was the main reason for them choosing the visit the destination. A further 9% said a film/TV location had had some influence in the destination previously visited for a holiday. In total, 20% have visited a film or TV location whilst on holiday abroad.
- Of those who have previously visited the UK at some stage in the past, a higher proportion (31%) had visited a film location on holiday, vs. 15% who had not visited the UK before. (NB they did not necessarily visit the film/TV location while on their trip to the UK.)

- Almost all markets in the study had high proportions of respondents say they had or would be interested in visiting a film or TV location – the highest markets to do so were China, India and South Korea. In total, either 78% either had or would be interested in doing so.
- Of those who indicated they had visited a film or TV location on holiday, 29% said a film or TV location was the main reason for selecting the holiday destination. This rises to 33% amongst those who have previously visited the UK.
- Amongst respondents who had not previously visited a film or TV location on holiday, but indicated they would be interested, 11% said a film or TV location would be the main reason for choosing a holiday destination. However, a further three out of five respondents said a film or TV location would have some influence on destination choice.
- Within each market surveyed, at least 50% of all respondents who had not previously visited a film or TV location on holiday said a film or TV location would have some influence on their decision to take a holiday to a specific destination.

In 2015, Creative England, which works in partnership with the British Film Commission to promote England internationally and provide a free film office service to productions filming in England outside London, and Visit England, which is responsible for tourism generation, to create investment, jobs and profile, had also conducted similar studies. Its report had indicated that 36.1% of all international tourists and 11.6% of all domestic tourists surveyed on site at six locations 'can be defined as core screen tourists – i.e. a screen production was the primary motivator for their visit' (Olsberg SPI 4 March 2015: 1). It was concluded that some sites that featured in films attract day-spend value from international visitors of up to £1.6 million annually, and domestic core screen tourists of up to £4.3 million over the same time span. Overall, it was noted that 'international core screen tourism is valued in the range of *£100 million–£140 million* for the rest of England in 2014' (ibid., emphasis in text). The numbers are not insignificant and remain compatible with the fact that the country has in the last decade or so served as filming grounds for such successful TV series and film franchises as *Star Wars: The Force Awakens* (director J.J. Abrams 2015 – *SWFA*), *Harry Potter and the Deathly Hallows* (Parts I and II, director David Yates 2010 and 2011 – *HPDH*), *Spectre* (director Sam Mendes 2015), *Captain America: The First Avenger* (director Joe Johnston 2011 – *CAFA*), *Broadchurch* (directors James Strong and Euros Lyn 2013–2017), and many more examined later (see analysis by Doward 26 December 2015).

However, numbers and film tourism categories need to be complemented with phenomenological content: reflections on design, the structure of tourist experience, the nature of host reception and development, and much more. To complement or replace structuralist functionalism with phenomenology in practice, and to think about the ways people as producers and consumers experience the roles in which they find themselves within the constraints imposed by markets, one has to go the extra mile: to consider how role-crafting, role-playing and role-watching inform and are informed by the lived environments in which all these activities take place. Otherwise put, one has to reflect on the ways the ecosystemic contexts in which such roles are embedded actually bring not just the roles, but our whole sentient being to life (Thrift 2007). Understanding this 'being with' in the ecosystem forms my principal epistemontological hypothesis.

At first, this seems irrelevant for the study of film-induced or cinematic tourism, but on a second inspection, ones realises that it informs its postindustrial form and content. From my perspective, which was born out of a critical take on occulocentrism, revamped from Urry (2002) and Larsen's work (Urry and Larsen 2011), I discussed previously 'cinematic tourism' and the 'cinematic tourist' as ideal types of mobility. I identified four types of 'cinematic tourist' and respective 'cinematic tourisms' in:

> a Representations/simulations of tourist mobilities within cinematic texts
> b The act and performance of film viewing and interpretation
> c Virtual travels (web surfing) and constructions of 'tourist' online
> d Film viewing that transforms into embodied visits of the cinematic stage.
>
> (Tzanelli 2013: 4)

Beeton (2016: 45–46) follows a similar schema, while also shedding light on other nuances I discussed in the same study, including mobilities we know as pilgrimage and celebrity film tourism. But I am not interested in marketing taxonomies of mobility; instead, I note the lack of epistemontological interrogations in business studies, popular culture and management research. Generally, markets are interested in such interrogations only if they yield profit, while keeping the peace in contexts of mobility. All the same, some rudimentary connections made to imagination and memory (Reijnders 2011) and the collective experience of fandom (Connell and Meyer 2009; Connell 2012) could feed into phenomenological fields, as well as a critical connection of those to market imperatives.

Let me begin afresh then, by viewing cinematic tourism as a technological system that *relays* natural and human ecosystems. The idea of relaying goes beyond the practice of representation populating media studies, because it concerns the ways a blending of the art of filmmaking with the crafts of engineering redefines the content of life. When such a process informs technological systems of mobility, we find that a correspondence begins to form between artificial and living worlds. This correspondence – and increasing interdependence in mobility practices, such as cinematic tourism – is what I call, after Stiegler (2011), 'schematisation'. Schematisation structures consciousness in a cinematographic style, allowing for both selection and forgetting of pasts, objects and experiences, so that they form a *dérushage* or montage, complete with materialised ploys and bodily performances. Conceptions of consciousness extend beyond that of the human mind, because, once in motion, schematisation is animated across actors and networks. In other words, technology produces ecosystems, in which humans, animals and nature become reorganised or staged constantly – for, practically, both life and the artifice of technology exist in constant flux.

In anthropocentric philosophies of science, which follow the project of Enlightenment (against religion but *for* capitalist development), the first call for a sustainable future is to design a scheme that 'draws together the increasingly marked ecological, biomedical and cybernetic interests that are charting the course of Humanity 2.0' (Fuller 2012: 122). The scheme does not transcend set possibilities, because its epistemological foundations are found in the hermeneutics of Enlightenment. This is not so with the neovitalist philosophies of becoming, which can work with such 'interests', but only to carve alternative futures. Here I recall my previous musings on the city and the country, which occupy a central role in the staging of nature and culture as atmospheric 'quasi-things' (Dufrenne [1953] 1973; Böhme 1993, 1995). It is easier to accept that urban life exists in motion, but what about (self-)schematisations of the countryside, this elusive *topos* of innocence? Whereas neovitalists would consider staging as an always-already ecological and cybernetic project, they would also urge us to discover alternative possibilities for the future in the ways it enables us to reimagine biodiversity in artistic styles (see Tzanelli 2017: Chapter 2 on 'imagineering'). The technological project of retrieving something that was never there as such contradicts the argument that schematisations 'engender a gigantic hole, a *loss* of connection with the past' (Stiegler 2011: 75): cinematic technologies allegedly 'rescue', but actually create locations and notions of home(-land), thus partaking in (re-)definitions of what is handed down to new generations as 'heritage'.

The concept of 'heritage' has a turbulent European genealogy, which connects practices of property demarcation, guardianship and bloodline in exclusionary ways (Tzanelli 2013: Chapter 1). Anthropocentric patterns of demarcation and exclusion from the 'goods' of the earth and society have a phenomenal basis in Judeo-Christian religious systems, so they do not provide the whole story. For an in-depth exploration of film-induced or cinematic tourism in relation to alternative backgrounds, we can shift emphasis to the term's Japanese equivalent, 'contents tourism' (*kontentsu tsūrizumu*), which underwent a process of adaptation into Western systems of thought, only after the country's first contact with the British and the twentieth-century American colonisation of Japanese markets. Apparently a loanword from English, the term refers to 'information that has been produced and edited in some form, and brings enjoyment when it is consumed' (Seaton *et al.* 2016: 4). Apparently, when the term was first used in the 1990s popular cultural production in Japanese cities (the main cultural industrial hubs), it referred to the multiple usage of storylines, characters, locations and other elements across different media formats, such as books, comics, films and computer games for consumption. Despite Japanese adaptation to the West, this would also promote a different definition of popular culture from the one we find in Western contexts: the Western significance placed on media format (see McLuhan's (1964) thesis that 'the medium is the message') took a back seat in classifications of creativity vis-à-vis *kontentsu*. This posits a problem: if the medium is not the creative element in contents, but fixity of meaning across media formats produces unique artwork, then we must search for the locus of creativity elsewhere, even outside the narrow confines of the fully-formed domain of popular culture.

This is the point from which we enter phenomenology: wrongly considered as a straightforward derivative of the English word 'tourism', *tsūrizumu* is a standardised translation of *kankō*, whose etymology derives from *I Ching* (The Book of Changes), one of the five classics of ancient Chinese philosophy. The two characters for *kankō* are 'see' and 'light', commonly referring to 'seeing the light of the country and thereby making oneself useful as a guest of the king' (Seaton *et al.* 2016: 3). From here, we can also create phenomenological links with systems of automobility and modern technology at large: *kankō* entered the Japanese lexicon in 1855, when a steamship was named *Kankō-Maru*, and in the twentieth century it became the standard translation for tourism. Hence, flows of technology with the help of nature participated in conceptions of travel movement at an early stage. Note now that in Japanese culture 'light' connects to notions of land, hospitality and monarchy as structural elements in definitions of Japanese-ness. Indeed, today 'land' in contents tourism is considered to be part of visiting heritage sites and sights (Seaton and Yamamura 2015: 2–3), so vision and light are connected in some scholarship in banal (Europeanised/Westernised) ways (note for example the absence in most discussions of the notion of 'inner vision' in Zen Buddhism). However, to analyse this relationship of 'land', 'light' and 'sight' with 'heritage contents', we need to account for the technologisation of Japanese popular culture (anime, manga) in terms of schematisation. This would prompt us to consider conceptions of the world from a Japanese stance, as an animate human sphere (lifeworld) and a metaphysical terrain (of the mind and ancestral spirits). Such links were affected by the process of modernisation, but never eliminated – rather, they split into forms of atmospheric attraction for the tourist visitor and private domains of communication with ancestral memory for the native.

Indeed, we could use Urry's (2004) observation that dark tourism signals a shift from (home) land to (abstracted) landscape in capitalist contexts as a starting point, but issue a few correctives along the way – for, as becomes obvious later, I do not intend to adopt the argument of globalisation theorists, that we live in a 'flat world'. Significantly, the argument found massive appeal amongst the new twentieth-first century breed of Japanese artists-entrepreneurs, such as Takashi Murakami and Yoshitomo Nara, who embraced the so-called 'Web 2.0 moment', according to which complex ideas or feelings are much better communicated through imagery and instant-impact design to the masses (Favell 2011: 63–64). However, such imaginaries of growth in a world *en route* to degrowth, suit better the lifestyles of urbanite middle classes such as those to whom Friedman (2005), the *New York Times* columnist and writer of the original 'superflat' thesis, belongs. The thesis leaves out of the picture, in which such art politics thrives, non-urban or minoritarian imaginaries of 'being with', while overlooking the cultural-political edge of this overlooking – issues I address in this book. As Sheller (2011: 2) cautions, mobilities theory is (or at least should be) sceptical towards epochal conceptualisations (flatness overtaking diversity), suggesting instead a set of questions, theories, and methodologies in the place of totalising descriptions. At the same time, not only do we need to challenge the rigidity of binaries of mobility/stasis (Bissell and Fuller 2011; Massumi 2015, 2017; Merriman 2012, 2018), we must also acknowledge that movements and becomings, including those of the cognitive and affective type, 'are below and above the threshold of perception' (Deleuze and Guattari 1987: 281).

The significance of the 'world' in contents tourism is also not explored sufficiently and in context – having recourse to conceptions of 'sites of memory' (Nora 1989), 'imagination' (Reijnders 2011) or 'site' (McCannell 1979) is not sufficient but necessary. Japanese conceptions of the world do two jobs in contents tourism at the same time: they spatio-temporalise tourism mobility to content sites, while pluralising the quality of motion/action itself (it can involve physical, technologically mediated or spiritual 'travel', in multiple combinations). The Japanese word for 'world' is *sekai* (世界), a rendition of the 'global', which would normally permit its user to generate links to conceptions of globalisation. Yet, this is still reductive. We may note that *sekai* is produced from a merger of two kanji (世 and 界), both individually signifying 'world'. The first kanji is used in words referring to social bonding, such as *seken* (世: society) and *sedai* (世代: generation), but it is also included in conceptions of spiritual realms, such as *kono yo* (この世: the world/realm of the living) and *ano yo* (あの世: the world/realm of the dead). The second kanji is a reference to a delimiting boundary or the presence of plural 'worlds/realms'. Its modern usage in terms such as *makai* (魔界: the world of the demons), *reikai* (霊界: the world of spirits), *tenkai* (天界: heaven), but also *gyoukai* (業界: business world, industry), *seikai* (政界: world of politics) or *gakkai* (学界: the academic world) delineates its generic epistemological significance, bringing back into focus notions of vision, 'enlightenment' and knowledge that we associate with Zen Buddhism (see for example the derivative term *shikai*: field of vision). The second kanji activates one's definitional and deductive faculties: different worlds have their own boundaries, which we must identify so that we arrive at a clear understanding and definition (*genkai*: delineation) of different realms/worlds.

The overall conclusion is revealing: the two kanjis together produce the 'world' as a potential group of tangibles (sites, locales), but mostly intangible (spiritual, metaphysical and normative) states and activities (thinking, writing, legislating and working) in different ontological contexts (living or dying/be dead). Their ability to delineate (second kanji) states of *being and activity* serves as an *enlightening tool* for those who comprehend and legislate on social membership in a variety of groups. Though sadly ignored in Western analyses of contents or cinematic tourism, it is difficult to find a better rendition of lay epistemontology than this. Also, though at first compatible with commercial creativity, and useful for the operation of global transaction, we cannot completely identify the practice of Western industrial 'worldmaking' we find in the works of Hollinshead (2009) with *sekai*'s process of worldliness across multiple realms. The tourism-making expert of *gyoukai* is a Western specimen transplanted into one particular world that came into being with Japanese modernisation. His or her postindustrial elective affinity with business was followed by an exclusion of other 'worlds' and 'visions', consigned to the realm of the 'inside', the so-called *honne* of Japanese culture (Graburn 2012). In this respect, the argument that contents tourism generally endorses or reproduces memory sites is wrong: postindustrial tourist activity is a process of forgetting the multiplicity of Japanese histories and cultural biographies so as to create them anew. Also, the suggestion that in tourism or pilgrimage to contents, imagination and creativity are involved needs both synchronic and diachronic qualification on the basis of who does the imagining and under what conditions. We may conclude that the historical trajectory of the term and its development into a form of popular culture has more lessons to teach than those proffered by film-induced, media and cinematic tourist scholars operating within European and Western academic domains. The revelation that schematisation is a process amassing animate and inanimate actants in the system to relay life within, on the screen, then back within, but through performances (cinematic tourism as a popular culture), instantiates circularity as affirmation that we are being alive in a system larger than us.

The tourist as the primary subject of mobility also deserves a word here. It would be inaccurate to attribute the effects of schematisation exclusively to postindustrial or host creativity: both parties 'stage authenticity' even in simulatory regimes (MacCannell 1973, 1989; Wang 1999, 2000). The embodied/cognitive/affective nexus of such actions makes up for a performance not always carried out consciously, as some scholars have suggested (MacCannell 2001; Urry and Larsen 2011), but semi-consciously, in the middle of a so-called 'phaneroscopic cycle' (Peirce 1992, 1998). This is when experiences of mobility are sensuously recorded in a cinematographic-like style by subjects-participants, but still not granted with stable meanings (or indeed images) in the conscious. The affective quality of this so-called 'secondness' of comprehension is quintessential for the production of tourism as a form of pilgrimage *en route* to acquiring a particular quality of agency, which is not rooted in an oppositional imagination but adheres to ideas of respecting subjective encounters with the world (Braidotti 2008: 2). Tourist pilgrimage is pragmatically conceptualised in terms of performative and embodied action, but also a semantic field of movement and as a metaphor (Coleman and Eade 2004: 16–18).

As an all-encompassing metaphor, pilgrimage points to understandings of absolute hospitality, of being accepted as a friend or a guest in need. This conceptualisation of the tourist subject, which is not a-political, retains a normative dimension, in the sense that the subject's journeys through different cultural spheres *ought to respect* the other/host in all their human, floral, faunal and technical diversity. Any existential tincture this might have had in the tradition of Bauman's (1996) disoriented subject of modernity gives way to a phenomenological certainty that the journey itself will become a meaningful experience: a true pilgrimage. Endowed with rich symbolic significance (Adler 2002: 27), any such journey can begin as a mundane road trip, but its destination or the process of travel as personal hardship (an adventure), allows it to acquire religious or postsecular meanings (Eade 1992) corresponding to Peirce's 'thirdness' of the phaneroscopic cycle: the journey makes sense now as a story. Incidentally, this journey can also commence or remain in the participant's mind, as today cybertourists represent powerful prosumers in international tourist markets (Prideaux 2002; Germann Molz 2012). Ever since the publication of Paul Fussell's *Abroad* (1980), scholars have been discussing unfortunate dichotomisations of travel and tourism in terms of progression from the authenticity of exploration to the falsity of simulacra (see Wang 2000 on constructivism). Such problematic splits consolidated the pairing of embodied pilgrimage/travel with purposeful movement towards a sacred (personal or collective) centre, discarding tourist experience, especially of the virtual (internet or cinematic) type as too commercialised to be honest, wholesome and authentic, and hence contribute to the preservation of human freedom (from capitalism). The idea of cinematic tourism as frivolous 'popcultural pilgrimage' (Couldry 2003; Gyimóthy *et al.* 2015) or as commoditised pilgrimage to a 'mediated centre' with no soul (Couldry 2003b) is problematic in the sense that, for most contemporary subjects, life unfurls in the interstices of terrestrial and virtual worlds, in terms of information-gathering, creating and disseminating knowledge. As the cybersphere exerts influence on the shape of human lifeworlds (it produces locations, amongst other things), we should consider it as one of the living and evolving systems of technology: a 'mechanosphere'.

To sum up then: the notion of 'contents', which can include both heritage sites and sites and artefacts brought to life through technological advancement (as in film-induced or internet-induced tourism) or technical practice (craftmaking) extends our understanding of interactions between technology and embodied experience (terrestrial mobilities of travel) to the phenomenological field. This field is sidelined in business-inspired taxonomies of film-induced tourism, or demoted to explorations of mobility motivation. In cultural studies scholarship, the same field is filtered through reductive understandings of tourism as popular pleasure, with distinctive ocular practices enhanced by the media. Neither side considers the ways such contemporary schematisations have trajectories within particular historical contexts of mobility in which they produce holistic lifeworlds. Moreover, there is no consideration of the global potential such lifeworlds may acquire, because academic establishments are mostly trapped in Western epistemologies, whereas those who object to them can become equally trapped in an oppositional imagination degenerating into hatred. The following section explores some of these tensions in the form of 'schools of thought', looking specifically at how 'heritage' is manipulated by them in the discursive field.

Western/European practice on the bar? Heritage and the holistic plea for life

In the previous section I discussed at length genealogies and cultural or economic interpellations of the city and the countryside. Among my concerns has been the ways such interpellations in market domains and lay imaginaries of place are beginning to interact in favour of further unregulated commoditisation of lifeworlds. This discussion was often conflated with the role of technology in the acceleration of lifestyles and a corresponding decline of well-being standards. The connection is spurious, if not dangerous: not only does it discard centuries of creativity, invention and innovation, it reinstates a fascistic belief in the good peasant life that surely had (has) its own serious shortcomings. Speculations that we move faster and faster may also be too zealous to accept as factual. First, 'social acceleration' (Rosa 2013) necessitates perspectival analysis, because every new generation is conceiving of its own movement as historically unprecedented (Vostal *et al.* 2018: 2). Second, the politics of speed need not be automatically associated with conservatism, authoritarianism or, indeed, neoliberalism, thus being cast as uncritical towards capitalist modernity (Duffy 2009). Finally, and most importantly for the present study, artistic blends between natural and scientific/technological environments will not necessarily consign our social and cultural lifeworlds to some dark pit of Enlightenment rationality. Popular amongst scholars influenced especially by the arguments of early critical theory (Ellul 1964; Böhme 2008, 2017; Bauman 2007, 2008), such pessimistic prognostications should not be confused with critical mobilities thinking, which 'works with both problems and potentials' (Jensen 2014: 46). These pessimistic theses require a great deal of applied testing, and although this study cannot provide such extensive evidence, it can at least point to an obvious elective association between prognostications of social death and technological creativity in their arguments.

Pronouncements of social death often acquire the best seat in the theatre of life politics, with prospects to be promoted to protagonists in the play of 'heritage': the human future and the future of our whole planet. This suggests that the temporal ecologies of natural and scientific/technological environments involved in the production of heritage tropes, recurring themes of enunciation, are embroiled in a battle of 'definition of the very thing' (Lefebvre [1992] 2015). Let me explain at length here, for, heritage and inheritance are contested fields of sociocultural practice: early on in modernity, an enduring conceptual scaffolding was built that opposed heritage to legacy, while aligning the former with ethno-racial versus civic belonging. However, late capitalist structuration often brought the two opposing forces closer than expected, with the former defending recognition of inheriting and circulating goods, ideas and humans on the basis of ethno-national affiliation and the latter affirming property possession on legal grounds (Tzanelli 2013: 2; see also Giddens 1990 on modernity and structuration). We may say that heritage and legacy are the two coins of mobility in late capitalist environments.

In this study I endeavour to adopt a more relational, non-anthropocentric perspective, which examines the replacement of humans as subjects and objects in heritage and legacy with planet earth. I use Ingold's (2011) identification of five terms in the policy lexicon associated with definitions of indigeneity (ancestry, generation, substance, memory and land) to suggest the need for a purposive shift of ecological discourse from a 'genealogical' to a 'relational' model. Genealogical models of identity consolidate a-historical takes of ancestral history as nature, see transmissions of tradition as predetermined and of biogenetic substance and turn ancestral experience into the necrotic stuff of 'cultural memory', while using 'land' as mere surface to be occupied, rather than bringing its inhabitants 'into being' (ibid.: 133). By contrast, relational models consider people's experience of inhabiting the land as a never-ending, transformative process of engaging with it and human and non-human beings (ibid.). Whereas the first model subtracts time from holistic ecologies of being and belonging, the later reintroduces it as a form of relational agency. In this book, I demote my previous thesis on heritage (Tzanelli 2013) to a subsection of this argument, to which I intend to shift perspective. To address 'the perpetual state of war that capitalism makes' to our planet (Stengers 2015: 23), necessitates an urgent decolonisation of our imagination that does not simply focus on issues of racism and imperialism, but considers varieties of 'microfascism' that regulate human attitudes towards fellow humans and the environment (Blencowe 2016: 26; Deleuze and Guattari 1983; Nederveen Pieterse and Parekh 1995; Stengers 2012). Such microfacisms lead to a certain future scholars call 'ecocide' (Broswimmer 2002: 103; Korstanje and George 2015: 22).

By way of clarification here, throughout the book I will refer to 'heritage tropes' in methodological terms, as recurring narratives of ownership over landscape and intangible assemblages (myths, music and history), which different interest groups in the social field negotiate: creative industries of film, tourist industries, localities and nation-states, but also even tourists, who can bestow novel meanings upon the visited 'sites'. The crystallisation or contestation of such tropes may point to communicative gaps between visitor and host, hospitality and protest or general tourismophobia, which are recorded in media circuits. Highlighting such recurring tropes – especially those focusing on what is perceived of as overtourism or environmental damage – evokes Bateson's (1973, 1980) suggestion that patterns of thought (and action) contribute to the formation or solution of external problems. In other words, I am not interested in the truthfulness of such reports of hostility or otherwise, but the ontological power they exert over the generation of 'social issues' such as overtourism in zones developed into cinematic tourist destinations. I am, of course, aware of the presence of other hypotheses and arguments: for example, realist accounts of such issues may stress that little time is spent on discussing how the colonisation of the cultural sphere by politics exerts power over such interpretations a priori anyway, or how it actually affects the rhythms of cultural spheres (Pels 2003). At the other end of the analytical spectrum and within social scientific environments, it is claimed that there is little investigation into the complex interaction between the latest mutation of capitalism (what Böhme (2017) calls 'aesthetic capitalism') and the real intentions or effects of creative industries' responses to the 'fear of a fast planet' (Glezos 2012: 1–16). To such (hypo-)theses one may respond that postindustrial creativity produces its own 'unintended consequences' (Capra 2002: 77–81; Merton 1936: 895; Giddens 1984: 281–286, 1987, 1990, 1991), thus setting in motion new hermeneutic cycles in business (Bramwell and Lane 1993), new social reactions in nation-states and localities and new processes of cultural adaptation in all (Tarde [1890] 2001; Latour 2004; Barry and Thrift 2007).

Discussions of adaptation have also featured in anthropocentric narratives of capitalist growth that focus on the nature of today's 'Empire'. Hardt and Negri's (2000) work suggests that imperialism and colonialism reached their end when they began to obstruct global capitalist growth. In their place, the world saw the emergence of global markets, whose sole objective became to control the constitutive desires of the 'multitude' – a term associated with the commercial bourgeois societies of an increasingly nationalised Europe (Korstanje 2018a: 7). However, as today the power of nation-states has declined (or, according to others, became intertwined with that of market mobilities), taking with it the idea of a single world centre, postcolonial production has ceased to require an 'open borders' policy of market expansion: there is no longer an 'outside' world to conquer, only globally spread and ever-shifting networks of capital (Hardt and Negri 2004). The result is still uneven development of the world, but its nature is, much like contemporary capitalism's, not territorial but immaterial. Unlike Hardt and Negri, Castro-Gómez (2007) and Walter Mignolo (2000, 2009) argue that this thesis does not account for the darker side of modernity, a lasting epistemological hegemony of European empires over all other world cultures (a notion they conflate with the world economy). This hegemony was achieved within a single world system when the scientific revolution of the Enlightenment opposed theological domination, but not capitalism. For them, because coloniality is the other side of modernity, postcoloniality should be considered the structural counterpart of the postmodern world that Hardt and Negri discuss. Empire, which is still based on this scientific revolution, will not bring the end of coloniality but its postmodern organisation. If so, Hardt and Negri's obscuring of the dark side of Empire remains Eurocentric, because it fails to recognise the colonial tools on which it was built.

Regardless of their oppositional nature, both theses discard holistic investigations of the growth of world systems of hegemony: for them the 'world' is the property of humans, who are its sole masters. But there are also some exceptions: Colombian anthropologist Arturo Escobar (1995) has explained that the notion of biodiversity, the value of conservation and the repression of non-occidental systems of knowledge have entered the global vocabulary of 'sustainable development', which thus ceased to be measured by material standards and focused instead on the promotion of human aptitudes and experiences. These observations certainly posit the need to reconnect human with non-human ecologies: cinematic tourist growth is both anthropocentric, uneven across regions and potentially damaging for ecosystems, not just because it consolidates the production of human capital at the expense of other forms of capital, but also ignores how capital-exchange is the vehicle of late capitalist heritage-legacy mobilities. Smith-Nonini (2017) effectively considers the interlacing of growing climate-related health problems worldwide, the false hopes generated by emission reductions during the recession for lower consumption trends and a conflation of growth in production with growth in profits in the 'developed world' to highlight the difficulties social scientists face in assessing complex systems of mobility. We are back to speculations on mainly assessments of 'benefits' from (cinematic) tourist consumption by global business, which often 'omit' to disclose or answer to arguments that capitalism cannot lead to exponential growth, or how non-mitigation on limited stocks or impacts on human welfare will have dire consequences for our fragile ecosystems (Mitchell 2011; Huber 2013; Urry 2013).

The elephant in the room is the definition of 'sustainability' as a bundle of co-dependent forms of social, economic and political flourishing. It is telling, for example, that in an exploratory review of indicators in sustainable tourism commissioned by the English Tourism Intelligence Unit, optimal use of environmental resources and respect for the sociocultural authenticity of host communities are tied to the maintenance of 'viable, long-term economic operations, providing socioeconomic benefits to all stakeholders' so as to ensure fair distribution of 'stable employment and income-earning opportunities and social services to host communities, and [contribute] to poverty alleviation' (10 October 2011: 3). Likewise, the official definition's co-dependency on forms of capital, with the economic as dominant amongst them, promotes a particular version of development on which creative industries (film and tourism) rely. This version is largely anthropocentric – note, for example, that the UK Tourism Intelligence Unit review recognises the environment among the four key stakeholder groups to engage in the management of tourism, by which it refers to environmental organisations (ibid.: 6). We may only add that Chapter 40 of Agenda 21 signed in Rio de Janeiro within the framework of the United Nations Conference on Environment and Development (1992) views humans 'as users and carriers of information' in sustainable development (Castro-Gómez 2007: 438). Sustainability with regards to biodiversity and the management of genetic resources has also become the focus of multi-national corporations, which wish to secure intellectual property rights, especially in the 'developing' and 'under-developed' regions of the world. Such battles over material resources are reflected in policies concerning immaterial products, considered in the United

Nations World Intellectual Property Organisation (UNWIPO) as creations and innovations of the human intellect (ibid.). However, at the same time, sustainability's anthropocentric definition of progressive and unfettered development ('development that meets the needs of the present without compromising the ability of future generations to meet their own needs' – World Commission on Environment and Development 1987: 37, also known as the Brundtland Report, in Phillips 2015: 55) bypasses the degree or quality of the process.

For the purposes of this study, it helps to focus the definition on the interplay between the maintenance of pro-ecosystemic values and the support of technological creativity (e.g. staging cinematic tourist environments) with a view to support fragile posthuman ecosystems. It is also important to note that, for a global evaluation of bioproperties in post-Fordist mobility contexts, such as that of cinematic tourism, we must not merely discard Hardt and Negri's hegemony of immaterial work and Mignolo and Casto-Gőmez's emphasis on economic and cognitive restructuring in postcolonial regions in a zealous fit of counter-argumentation. The book's focus on atmospheric design calls for considerations of the ways material and immaterial *loci* turn into sites of local, national or international heritage, so notions of immaterial labour are essential, but their historic depth, with all its (dis-)continuities cannot be discarded. Generally, we deal with a highly charged discursive field, in which ideas of positive or negative action for ecosystemic conservation are constantly negotiated (Robinson 2004). This discursive manipulation is reflected in the World Tourism Organisation's (WTO) cautioning note that all sustainability indicators for the development of destinations are 'not an end in themselves, but rather signals of important trends and changes, a catalyst for discussion on future plans, risks to the destination, and impacts on what is important to all' (2004: 463). As the Anthropocene or era of human domination over built and natural environments has reached its apogee, the preceding age of the Holocene or ecosystemic interconnection beyond a dominant 'human agency' has become more of an activist and nostalgic multisite in our sociocultural imaginations – a phenomenon immediately connected to the rise of New Social Movements (NSM) (Delanty 2013: 157). The rise of new complexity postulates across different disciplines prompts scholars to explore the ways new systemic properties are affected by ever-shifting associations between their components, a task demanding extra attention to spatiotemporal contexts of change (Meadows 2008; Byrne and Callaghan 2014).

Postcolonial and decolonial arguments are still useful in this study, because I eventually shift focus to varieties of NSM led by stakeholders in touristified environments, who see themselves as disenfranchised or disaffected because of capitalist development. Notably, however, I also use 'social movements' in a much broader sense than that adopted by academic experts in the field, so as to encapsulate responses to development of much less hostile tones or widespread effect to register in the field, but of significant historical depth. The current scholarly trend focuses on definitions of tourismophobia, which are invariably connected to the current European crisis in affected cities, such as Barcelona in

Spain (Quaglieri Domínguez and Scarnato 2017: 111), when in fact we deal with a global crisis inducing the broadcasting of movements. For the particular purposes of the present study, wherever it occurs (and this is debatable), 'tourismophobia' can only be placed in a network of affective 'motions' as a consequence of something that preceded its manifestation: overtourism, the spiralling of capitalist accumulation out of control, or climate change and environmental degradation.

However, we arrange such 'events' in spatial terms, the temporal Anthropocenic context remains a constant. It is important to view such protestations or 'responses', as I term them, however mundane, as constitutive of 'events': eruptions and disruptions of the flow of time and everyday life (Hannam *et al.* 2016: 5–6). Another observation to make is that tourismophobia and technophobia can become inseparable components in the 'field' of such affective motions – a conflation that also reappears in academic critiques of the new mobilities paradigm (Korstanje 2018a: 8–9, 12–13). Indeed, tourismophobia connects to calls to respect the natural, built/heritage or human/social environment, which is perceived to be under threat by external forces: technologies of mobility such as film industries, or their digital extensions, tourism and the new human and material mobilities these induce (resort development, littering, emissions and new consumption practices such as neotribal rituals in filmed locations). In turn, the native plea for 'respect' often becomes inseparable from discourses of ecosystemic resilience – incidentally, the offspring of post-Second World War development of space science, American anti-communist geopolitics and confused embrace of cornucopian capitalist progress (Martel 2017: Chapter 12). This is also the history of positivist implementation of modernisation theory, which called for eradication of native knowledge and lifeworlds in the name of development (Meadows *et al.* 1972; Meadows 2008).

There is a counter-thesis to account for, according to which creative industries contributing to such cinematic touristification policies attempt to engage in a form of structural-scientific revolution of sorts (Kuhn 1970; Hjarvad 2008). The emerging 'paradigm' such development puts forth concerns the creative extrapolation of an imaginative world from a movie plot and its transformation into a tourist lifeworld. This consideration occupies space in Chapter 4, where I turn to the production of atmospheres in such touristified locations. Hence, as a whole, the book debates different habitats and discourses of revolution – note, for example, how another scholarly constituency would argue (as per Habermas 1989) that tourismophobic movements are concerned with developing Enlightenment's unfinished project of betterment and justice. It is perhaps futile to prioritise their programmatic statements and more productive to explore their atmospheres, and how these clash with or reproduce those of creative industries. This focuses the investigation on existing and emerging lifeworlds and systems of cognition in terms of processes (e.g. Capra 1996), rather than stiff structures, thus making more space for an analysis of networked connections between them (Capra and Luisi 2014). In some cases, atmospheres run almost parallel lives with those of 'tourist imaginaries', the way places outside one's primary residence, where leisure activities happen, are imagined by individuals or social groups (Gravari-Barbas and Graburn 2012). More importantly, it seems that both tourist imaginaries and atmospheres are used by tourism workers and the trade's professional elites (i.e. designers of destinations) as transcultural frames that demonstrate cultural uniqueness, when situated in a particular location (Salazar 2010).

However, there are also three fundamental differences between tourist atmospheres and tourist imaginaries: whereas both spatialise experiences, the latter are always rooted in the pictorial world (they are representational and based on images of place) (see Salazar 2009: 49–50, 2012: 864–865), whereas the former often stem from, or may reside in the emotional world, which is non-representational; although both involve performances, for atmospheres these form the effects of affective non-representation, and they may even signal their transformation into novel imaginaries of place (I explore this phenomenon in Chapter 5 in atmospheric resistances to touristification that eventually transform into a movie-like imaginary of place – the point at which non-representation leads to schematisation, hence self-representation); finally, whereas in tourist imaginaries we deal with marketable manipulations of the exotic and the strange involving some form of 'taming' (everything acquires a softer feel – Salazar and Graburn 2016), in tourist atmospheres we deal with their amplification (a point I discuss in the Chapter 4 with regards to the role of the detective and horror genres in cinematic tourism). As a conclusion on these comparisons, I note that tourist imaginaries appeal to some fixed notion of aesthetics, which atmospheres may challenge with their ethereal and malleable quality. Staying true to a holistic *eco*aesthetics, my thesis draws upon dance philosopher and choreographer Rudolf Laban's '*choreosophía*', an ancient Greek word referring to circular communal enactments (*chorós*) of wisdom (*sophía*) (see also Laban's ([1966] 2011: ii) blurred etymology). A rudimentary description of *choreosophía* led Laban to define the word as 'the wisdom to be found through the study of all phenomena of circles existing in nature and life', which he traced back to the divine protectorate of the arts in Sicily (the cult of Muses) and the development of mathematics by the Pythagorean community of philosophers (ibid.).

Laban attributed these creations to a watertight system of knowledge managed by the ancient Greek empire of knowledge. However, deliberations on the constant 'flow of life' in circumcircles, the notion of rebirth and the emotional/cognitive appreciation of creativity as a divine gift were present in ancient religions and civilisations other than the Greek, including the Islamic, the Buddist and the Zoroastian. Laban notes that circles connect to shapes we find in nature and the very conception of life, as well as its roots in magic 'shared by peoples in early stages of civilisation' (ibid.), letting his audiences wonder if he has consigned non-European civilisational products to lesser developmental orders. Setting aside these ambiguities, I note his significant observation that the circle played a vital role in articulations of mentality, mood and feeling. This is what I explore under the rubric of 'atmosphere': a material, affective and cognitive rendition of experiencing the world as natural and built environment around us, which in contemporary economic and sociocultural contexts is mediated in blends of 'divine' artistic inspiration and science. I intend to distribute the application of this broad definition across the planes of postindustrial tourist production (urban design hubs) and sites of resistance (in which design is an emergent theme).

For the site of postindustrial production, I mobilise Mikel Dufrenne's elaborations on the ways the perceived world of art (film) expresses bundles of spatio-temporal relations – what he terms an 'expressed world'. This world overflows, or, better, replaces the representational content of the aesthetic object with a quality we cannot immediately convey, but which communicates itself in arousing a feeling' (Dufrenne [1953] 1973: 178). This is the atmosphere or 'luminescensce of meaning' (ibid.: 188) on which tourist industries forge connections with the worlds of cinemas. The omnipresence of mediation in contemporary cinematic tourist consumption, which turned *choreosophía* to *choreología*, the rational sense-making (*lógos*) of circular communal enactments (*chorós*), produced 'a kind of grammar and syntax of the language of movement, dealing not only with the outer form of movement but also with its mental and emotional content' (Laban [1966] 2011: viii). I argue that the design of tourist mobilities in filmed locations, or locations rumoured to have been filmed or inspired movie plots and picture, is a *choreologic* product (what would normally amount to Derrida's (1997: 234) notion of the 'closure of representation'). However, in practice, the finished grammatical and syntactical product exists only when placed in an eternal pendulum-like or circular movement that leads its students to a new *choreosophía.* In trying to grasp the expressive content of filmed locations, the postindustrial enterprise of design discloses 'an unpopulated world, one which is only the promise of a world' that acts as 'a prelude to [novel] knowledge' (Dufrenne [1953] 1973: 183). In this respect, the cinematic-tourist design of mobilities in actual and imagined sites creates atmospheric 'ecstasies' of locations sensed only through the bodily presence of tourists in them (Böhme 1993: 122).

The circular or pendulum-like movement also manifests itself in responses to postindustrial development or their corresponding social movements. Nevertheless, the atmospheric quality of them need not be a completely delocalised phenomenon, as scholars of the subject suggest (Della Porta and Diani 2006: 146–147). The 'quasi-objective feeling' (Böhme 2006: 16) that fills in the space of objection, contestation or protest, and which emanates from the assembling of human, non-human or discursive bodies (Stewart 2007) contributes both to the formation of new subjectivities (humans assuming their place in an environmental larger than their needs) and new collective identities (an affective (re-)claiming of landscape). Berman (2010: 19) recognises the impeding transformations of modernity in the way Marx wishes to make humans feel the atmosphere of revolutions through extravagant imagery such as volcanic eruptions, abysses and crushing gravitational forces. Significantly, the mobilisation of physicalism clashes with his conviction that 'all that is solid melts into air', making nevertheless 'men [*sic*] forced to face with sober senses the real conditions of their lives and their relations with their fellow men [*sic*]' (Marx in Berman 2010: 89). The sentence packs several contradictory or highly contestable statements: that modernity is fluid and changeable, but overlaid by fixed material conditions; that humans use their senses to perceive one, fixed reality despite modernity's unstable atmospheric irradiation; that a climate of what he calls elsewhere 'drunkenness' can produce 'sober' subjects, who shunt aside emotions and comprehend their situation logically. This ambiguity, which places atmospheres of revolution between a materialist and a (neo-)vitalist phenomenological imagination (Anderson 2009: 77–79) impacts on perceptions of heritage. Such turbulent atmospheres shape for example norms and practices of (in-)hospitality in the developed locations, so we cannot ignore them because they are perceived as quasi-things. It is, therefore, paramount to examine how psychological and cognitive movements of intentional and accidental nature comingle in local responses to development to shape the social and cultural environment towards which they were originally directed as discourses (Kahneman 2011; Tzanelli 2011). This realisation necessitates serious engagement with non-representational epistemologies and ontologies that I explore in the following chapter (Thrift 2004, 2007).

The phenomenological basis of non-representational theory transcends Williams' ([1973] 2016: 64–65) 'structure of feeling', which is based on ideas of a happier past order, innocence or pure nature – pure nostalgia, in other words. Because affects can reside in, emanate from or affect human and non-human actants in a network, one must consider a variety of materialities and effective conditions that are not orientated towards the past. In Chapter 5 the clash between atmospheres of hospitality (promoted by creative industries) and inhospitality (induced by movements geared towards reclaiming space and forms of heritage from global consumption) provides a rudimentary binary opposition on which one may assume that relational ontologies emerge and, together with them, a new relational emotional landscape does too. At the same time, if not careful, one may make this opposition as problematic as the old dictum that colonised peoples need lifting out of their own ignorance and barbarism. Therefore, across Chapters 4 and 5 I adopt a more investigative perspective, considering whether either side can actually be hinged on Enlightenment traditions of communicative rationality, or post-Enlightenment traditions considering the creativity of emotion and experience so as to produce a different orientation towards the future (e.g. not as the past of humanity, something we immediately associate with Enlightenment temporalities). In this respect, non-representation facilitates investigations into becomings and ways of knowing that emerge beyond rational decision-making. As I now explain in Chapter 3, experiencing reality at the microlevel depends on the observer's and their observed object's orientation in time and space – a schema feeding into the researcher's relative theorisation of experience (Morin 2008: 20–21).

Chapter 3

Attuning and aligning

Synaesthesia and the making of worlds

An ecoaesthetics of worldmaking in cinematic pilgrimage

In the previous chapter I explained why I did not design this study from the stance of a Baumanesque tourist subject, and cast doubts over suggestions that all actual cinematic tourists simply conform to this ideal type. Instead, I side with a recalibrated Baumanesque pilgrim, who is nevertheless attuned to the world around her/him. One may argue that this observation amounts to little more than a personal truism that can neither sustain a methodology nor support a solid epistemological structure. Indeed, the same voice could note that, if we require a reliable tourist/observer/social scientist to lead this study's design, we should resort to Keith Hollinshead's notion of 'worldmaking', as a collection of practices that tourism is, can be, or does to this world, a governing '*force majeure* in our lives and across our small and large long-run communities of being' replete with axiological content (Hollinshead *et al.* 2009: 428). From this definition, we can extract a professional agent, able to appropriate the iconography of place, by re-naturalising it as a largely 'innocent' and 'artisanal' place that plays into the hands of policy statescraft. Note that Hollinshead is openly critical of this type: as the mythomoteur of places (e.g. the maker of a place's constitutive ethnonational myth – Smith 1986), he says, this ideal type's function ends up erasing visions of cultural life and 'vistas of local/regional/provincial being' not fitting into his or her design (Hollinshead 2009a: 526). I agree with Hollinshead (and Smith) on this essentially reductive function of the state/designer (see Tzanelli 2008b), who may be formalistically replicated by the working scholar: the methodological craft may exclude alternative versions of place and culture that cannot fit into the objectives of design (Tzanelli 2017: 48–49). My approach seeks to minimise the ways our scholarly representationalism is superimposed onto that of our critiqued worldmaking forces. It therefore wishes to contribute to a growing field of '*eco*aesthetics', which combines perceptions of the environment with processes of appreciation in both material and phenomenal ways (McCormack 2008: 369). This blend of material and phenomenal inception makes space for the recognition and care of all beings in equal stead, so its promotion to a 'project' retains some utopian qualities.

Our craft is both social and scientific, as is that of tourism makers, so let me begin by hypothesising that, in practice, science and society are inseparable, with the former constantly reinvigorating its existence by adapting its strategy to achieve its goals to the needs and expectations of its audiences (Latour 1988: 28). Thus, to successfully enact a worldmaking journey that addresses most actors in the world(s), I have to do two things at the same time: the first involves engaging with the more-than or non-representational aspects of their visions, which have sensory (sights, voices, smells, tastes and more), as well as embodied/cognitive/emotional extensions (affects, feelings and emotions). The second point has to do with granting symbolic space ('chapter(s)') to each constituency or stakeholder, something which implies their minimal taxonomic grouping ('types' of stakeholders/actors and agents). Again, my non-representational approach may subsequently blur the picture (Merleau-Ponty 1962, 1964, 1965; Gibson 1966; Thrift 2004, 2007), because it refutes the idea of pre-given intentionalities (groups knowing exactly what they do, to what end and why at all times) and hence that of fixed actor/s agents, to which Hollinshead refers. The complexity of this task may induce anxiety: a book that commences with cinematic tourist development as its core theme but proceeds to connect this to issues of ecosystemic flourishing with technological contributions amidst human protests against both, appears to be unfocused – why not focus on either of these issues exclusively?

Against such critiques, I stress that the study presents us with at least one island of order standing at the boundary of chaos: what seems to drive chaotic 'flows' from chapter to chapter, just highlights systemic splinterings and bifurcations, each of them dealing with the perspectives of one or more networked groups of agents, actants and actors in the system (Urry 2005b: 5–6). This strategy has consequences for the nature of the book's original problem: every chapter presents its focus as more pressing and fundamental than the original or previous one, even though all chapters, questions and themes will be resolved with the means used in the original proposal (Latour 1988: 68–69). This book is, in short, both an exposition and an exposure of the messy nature of all world-makings: policy, scholarly and lay. Because none of these microsystems or 'environments' enjoys facticity, they are all approached via this book's epistem-ontological performances. Such chaotic orchestration of research thrives on contingent correlations of action, which shift the weight of causal claims 'from inferential statistics to sociological concepts and theories which link together recurring motifs into a symphonic narrative' (Halford and Savage 2017: 1139).

It helps to recognise that the ways projects are framed cannot be excised from their articulator's cognition, which, nevertheless is influenced by his or her experience of 'being in the world', but *with the world* (Merleau-Ponty 1962: 225; Ingold 2011: 262–267; Archer 1995, 2008; Haraway 2008). In this respect, the book's ecofeminist framing is a reflection of both my own subjective becoming and my sociocultural environment's diverse feedbacks and changes. My experience of participation in extensive virtual and terrestrial networks of theory and analysis already suggests my scholarly identity as a thing in motion, shaped by trials and errors: I am one of the many scholarly worldmakers on the move (Elliott and Urry 2010). I view the making of tourism in a similar fashion as a blend of arts, practices and experiments – what Pickering terms the 'mangle', a perspectival platform whereof science, technology and society interact, and so do their distinctive and diverse temporalities. Pickering's project 'seek[s] a real-time understanding of [scientific] practice' (1995: 3) – a tall order, when the social scientist is asked to record and reflect upon processes in motion to produce interpretations. Pickering indicates the intention to examine intersections of temporalities as they unfold, rather than retrospectively or historically (Vostal *et al.* 2018). Particular attention is called in examinations of failures (what he calls 'resistances') and adaptations (what he calls 'accommodations'), as well as the dialectic motion between the two.

An enlarged interpretation of worldmaking in cinematic tourist contexts of mobility prompts me to also reconsider the world around us, not as piles of inanimate things, but a phenomenon whereby materiality is internal to its inhabitants and not an inert space to traverse or use (Serres 1995; Latour 2005; Thrift 2007; Alaimo 2012; Phillips 2015). From this conceptualisation follows an aesthetics whereby beauty does not exist as 'a thing or quality', but 'a kind of communication' that may either prompt its holders to live in ways enabling others to live as cocreators of meaning (see Phillips 2015: 61 on artmaking) or authority to generate 'sustainable' biopolitical regimes (Tzanelli 2016a). The two ends encapsulate understandings of generosity and distribution respectively, generating a cultural economy concerning the recognition of beings in the world (O'Neill 1999; Fraser and Honneth 2003). However, the notion of 'economy' is not a structural unity imposing itself on non-human nature but a realm constituted through human practices and non-human performances. As Braun (2006, 2008) and Mitchell (2008) explain, we should stop thinking about the economy as something that exists separately from human and non-human systems, onto which humans introduce changes, and consider how it is made up of mundane interactions and everyday things. This observation bears extra significance, if we are reminded that this book studies various forms of creativity but also 'feedback' from natural habitats, the built environment and human communities, in places staged by cultural industries for tourists.

Meaning cocreation appears to be lost in a study based on audiovisual and textual materials, only if we disregard the ways its textual surfaces and informants (actors and agents in the system of meaning) allow the researcher to resurrect dying worlds through sounds that lost their fixed meaning (Shklovsky *et al.* 1919: 13). However, this method of 'defamiliarisation' or 'enstrangement', which aims to awaken the mind from its unconsciously repetitive stylistics, by attacking the subject's habitual automation of perception, does not 'reveal nature' or the 'very face of reality', as Kandinsky (1979: 105), the Bergsonian

Formalists (Shklovsky *et al.* 1919: 5) and Foucaultian urban theorists (Hasse 2011: 52) would argue. Its value rests with nurturing in us the ability to consider all these worlds we or the powers that be tend to kill unconsciously, in favour of fixing social and cultural meaning. But more on the ways such recovery overlays systemic interpretation later. For the moment, it helps to note that defamiliarisation detaches traditional takes on the phenomenology of perception and the study of behavioural structure we find in scholars such as Merleau-Ponty (1962, 1965) from existentialism or the tyranny of occulocentrism. The new focus is how perception emerges out of encounters in ways involving ad hoc multisensory aesthetic appreciations of the world we make on the move – what Ingold (2000: 497) identifies as both lay and expert 'exercises on possible narration'. This is what I term 'synaesthesia', a multisensory process that reintroduces non-human actants in systems of perception and becoming. Unlike Ingold (2011: 158), however, I do not consider sensations as private and individual vis-à-vis representations, which he considers as public and social, but place the two in a continuum. This is not because humans as social beings receive sensory education for the whole duration of their lives, but because they can only assess sensory inputs in relation to their environment, therefore considering relevant outputs as orchestrated aesthetic narratives: what we hear, see, taste or smell are shaped collectively as aesthetic experiences, resulting in our aesthetic education.

When it comes to aesthetic analysis, we are faced with the challenge of perceptive inclusion: a book on collisions and collusions between renditions of the 'city' and the 'country' necessitates attunement to more-than-human voices, materialities and their temporal matrixes. In fact, attunement *as a method* refers to more than ways of listening or scopic regimes, because it promotes 'rhythm' to a way of mapping spatiotemporal fluctuations, transpositions and relocations of humans, animals, nature and 'things', such as buildings, technologies and technics (see Lefebvre 1992 [2015] on rhythmanalysis; Fraser *et al.* 2005: 3 on vitalism). Even the Germanic notion of *Stimmung*, which is translated as 'harmony' in Heideggerian analyses, is often used to convey dissonance and tension (Wallrup 2015). Such ambivalence also resonates with different approaches to sociosystemic/ecosystemic resilience as the ability lifeworlds have to absorb disturbance and maintain stability (a Western-centric perspective – Habermas 1989), or reorganise and thoroughly adapt to dominant difference (a more (post-)colonial tendency – Tzanelli 2015a). The second perspective speaks of the ability to find, make connections and be open to new cultural tunes (Kagan 2010b: 1098) – a process some associate with artmaking (Kagan 2011) and others with policy deliberations on utopia as the good life (Levitas 2013a, 2013b). Brigstocke and Noorani (2016) discern four broad traditions of scholarship on attunement: Kant's mediation between the human faculties of imagination and understanding, the preconscious disposition to our environment, an embodied relationality endowing us with empathy and a transient connectivity with uncanny or uncertain situations relating to pasts, presents or futures (also

Ingold 2011: 148–150). Their schema is based on Guattari's (2000) critique of anthropocentrism in environmental, social and mental ecologies, to propose 'forms of creative listening to more-than-human life and material agency' (Brigstocke and Noorani 2016: 2). Their programmatic statement thus looks to recovering those voices and phantoms not granted with authority or presence in authorial scripts of the world and are instead considered 'out of tune' (Ahmed 2014). The same programmatic statement echoes postcolonial and decolonial sociologies, but limits its field of activity to subjected human communities (de Sousa Santos 1995, 1999).

The tuneless or out of tune is often represented as dark and fathomless, but also horrifically sublime and desired. Its eerie qualities are seen as other-than-white, feminine and natural, and all three are associated with notions of wild or unrefined heritage in need of two opposing interventions: sculpting/adapting and preserving/conserving. It is not coincidental that places haunted by ethnic memories or natural habitats, in which folk traditions are rhizomatically embedded, occupy such a central place in films and computer generated imaging (CGI) as modified landscapes, or that they are marketed as must-see pristine tourist destinations in their original form. Both interventions are quintessentially connected to definitions of dark tourism because of their qualities of intimacy (Lennon and Foley 2000: Chapter 1), the ability to speak of the originality and authenticity of one's motherly natural hearth – therefore, both are associated with myths of origins and becomings (Tolia-Kelly 2008, 2010). There is extensive literature on dark tourism as visitations to sites of disaster, war, suffering and ethnic heritage with an anthropocentric focus (e.g. see Dann 2001), addressing their political extensions better than their phenomenological ones. Early on in modern European history, the alleged natural darkness of such places of intimacy was posited as the polar opposite of light or *lumen*, the Cartesian source of outer, scientific knowledge (Ingold 2011: 256). Associations of dark tourism as national or humanity's heritage with Northern European Enlightenment traditions of artificial light (Jay 1993: 29–30) invite us to explore the strange, enchanting and 'horrific' (Anderson *et al.* 2012: 213) angles of authorial attunement in cinematic tourist contexts, endorsing Brigstoke and Noorani's urgency to perform a neovitalist analysis. This makes space for analysis of mobilities of spiritual practices and feminist materialisms or indigenous connections to the natural world, where urban design dominates both filmmaking practices and emergent touristic rituals (Anderson 2014; Braidotti 2013; Tzanelli 2013, 2015a, 2015b, 2015c). Nonetheless, as 'systems of mobility', tourist and creative industries also add their own attunements to the environments on which they intervene (Sheller and Urry 2004). This suggests that the researcher develops 'an adaptive gaze' to fluid spatiotemporal scales of production within these places and environments (Simus 2008: 70), and/or a 'musical ear' of sorts, to perceive 'the competitions, symbioses, interferences [and] overlaps of themes in one same symphonic stream, where the brutal mind will only recognize one single theme surrounded by noise' (Kagan 2010b: 1098).

Dark tourism should not be confused with what Phillips (2015) discusses as 'zombie environmentalism', although its practical manifestations in certain contexts of consumption and academic production the two may overlap. Overlaps would include pointless attraction to forms of darkness such as pollution as 'sexy', social retreatism following the embrace of environmental catastrophism, or a general uncaring attitude towards the other (ibid.: 59). These links could also lead us to conceptions of conspicuous overconsumption of post-Fordist undertones (Featherstone 1991; Harvey 1989; Soper 2007, 2008), of which many localities today seem to accuse cinematic tourism and tourists. Incidentally, the terms 'community' and 'locality' are as malleable as those of 'site' and 'place', so any investigations of accusations have to be treated with attention to the maker of the news. Meethan (2001: 61) has already noted that such terms may distract from 'the intense complexity or micro-politics that all sides are inevitably imbricated within and shaped by' in tourist encounters. To recover the experiential aspects of this complexity we must pay particular attention to the role of contingency in the ways media tourism connects specific places to global networks, but also the modes of communal interpretation of media events, which may be less local than they seem to be at first (Delanty 2013: 149, 173–175; Urry 2014: 189; Robertson 1992; Nederveen Pieterse 2009).

Such observations certainly echo the certainty that cities and the countryside are ideal types in our work that merit unpacking, destabilising notions of place. Laban suggests helpfully that the conception of space as a locality, in which changes take place, should not be separated from movement, even in particular moments in time and happenings, because movement 'is a continuous flux within the locality itself, this being a fundamental aspect of space' ([1966] 2011: 4). This flux is even more prominent in tourist situations characterised by host-guest conflicts, especially in urban settings, where locality and globality readily commingle. Urban scholar Ole Jensen (2014: 50) developed Laban's concept of 'ballet' ([1966] 2011: 30) to consider the language of embodied micro-interactions in the 'dynamosphere' or sphere of social action, effectively introducing the emergence of the ephemeral local beyond fixed neighbourhoods. He focuses specifically on urban development, so his ballet refers to eukinetic (good movements) and dyskenetic (bad movement) interactions in the city (ibid.). I will be discussing mobile interactions in the field of cinematic tourist hospitality in similar terms, but as a vocabulary of collective action. Both Jensen and Laban's ballet and dynamosphere agree with discussions on the production of eurythmic social organisation that Lefebvre introduced in urban studies ([1992] 2015). In particular, all three scholars use music as more-than a metaphor, to explore issues of social interaction. A hidden binding force behind such analyses is the ways civility emerges in situ, as a way of being with others in the social field – what Nobert Elias discussed as a civilising process in his history of manners (Elias 1978). This is a useful observation in discussions of tourism mobilities and in social protests alike.

Ingold (2011: 151) also notes that categorical oppositions between indigenous and non-indigenous populations or natives and settlers are the product of colonial taxonomy, which rests on the genealogical rationale: land is a surface to be occupied and lifeworlds are countries people traverse and to which they bring endowments of generation as the serial replacement of abstracted beings. Significantly, local, national, and regional takes on such categorical oppositions sustain a battle of metanarratives on issues of heritage ownership and use (it seems that, to date, 'incredulity' (Lyotard 1984) towards them has not ceased to exist altogether). In other words, 'locals' and 'indigenous people' may self-interpellate so that they claim land ownership and therefore sole control over the spoils of cinematic tourist development, thus labelling industries and tourists as trespassers to legitimate the war they wage against both. It is clear that we should not confuse such versions of tourismophobia with the logic of Green Movements, such as ecofeminism and holism (Capra and Spretnak 1984; Harding 2012). As much as it is uncritical to attribute reactions to tourism development to a uniform and sentient 'locality', free from the influence of diverse external interests, we must be mindful of discrepancies within an allegedly uniform 'oppositional imagination' (Cocks 1989). Another danger stemming from such confusions would be the declaration that authentic experience (e.g. living and working in overtouristified zones) can only be articulated by 'localities', effectively shutting down the generation of social scientific knowledge by scholars, or the illumination of those aspects of culture locals try to conceal from public view (Harding 1992: 178–180; Herzfeld 2005: 61).

To those practices of discourse-making, we should add a third-order one that we find in media platforms – what this book focuses on, after all. The notion of discursive construction and analysis has been overused in media communication studies, both in its Gramscian and Foucaultian variations (Fairclough 1992; Wodak 2015): the press constructs realities that appeal either to hegemonic interests, or to ever-shifting networks of power, diffusing its effects across living communities. Although the latter model matches contemporary complexities better, it merits modification to address the presence of overlapping ecologies in the study, including media flows of news, physical ecologies of movement (landscapes and natural sites) and symbolic but embodied movements (styles of protest) (Vannini *et al.* 2009: 466). The interaction of different ecological mobilities suggests a dialogical schema of analysis, in which discourse is better understood as the emergent property of virtual and terrestrial sites (Urry 2008; Dennis and Urry 2009). We are back, therefore, to my original suggestion that knowledge about the subject of this study is contextually emergent, which constitutes the theme of the following section on practice.

A primer in epistemontological investigation

The well-known European proponent of the principle of hope, Ernest Bloch, spoke in his work about ways of overcoming the 'ontology of the Not Yet', in which objective possibilities and aspirations of becoming create so-called '*entelchies*' (an end enclosed within the process of becoming). At least in the case of humans, hoping to become better involves *docta spes* or educated hope, which involves a great deal of cognitive, emotional and physical labour to the point of no return to starting points, hence a sort of optimistic nihilism in their overall commitment to the future (Bloch [1986] 1995: 1130–1131). Much like Hannah Arendt's (1958) *Homo Faber* or working human, Bloch's human actor strives to imbue her/his nature with purpose, through different forms of labour. But Bloch also attempted to resolve this problematic dualism between informed speculation (philosophising about the human condition) and social action (doing things), so as to both naturalise humans and humanise nature. The speculative materialism of the 'Not Yet' led him to study Christianity, Cabbalism, and Gnosticism as religious systems, in which he recognised significant overlaps between Marxist apocalyptic thought, Nietzschean understandings of desire and metaphysically informed traditions of rebellion. Importantly, he was convinced that human nature retrieves itself from the surplus of its existence, which is to be traced in things that make little rational sense at first (such as dreams, belief, and faith). Such inexplicable 'dark moments' also wipe away strict divisions between ontology ('being human') and epistemology (knowledge of one's humanity and its place in the world) (Thompson 2013: 84). The ultimate darkness of the moment, he argued, is to be found in the fear (and trauma) of collective and individual death, which can only be countered by cultivating a certainty, against all odds, that humans are in the process of attaining a liveable future. Replacing the Apollonian economist inevitablism with a Dionysian vitalistic possibility, human investment in hope against all odds produces radical futures (ibid.: 91).

The cosmic clash of Dionysian joy and spontaneity with Apollonian restraint and rational planning stand at the heart of histories of wellbeing, from travel, leisure and tourism, to institutionally organised welfare policies. In pessimistic Marxist tales of development, such as those proffered in the beautifully crafted story of Faust by Berman, they are set to expose the impossibility of the human subjects to stabilise notions of the good life, leading to circles of calamitous self-development, development of communities and mastery of nature. Berman's tragic allegory personalises this world-historical trauma via Goethe's protagonist, whom he uses to provide a Marxist reading of the plight of modernity. His take on development, which views culture and morality through economics, takes the hero on a journey with three distinctive phases. As a 'dreamer', who lives metamorphosis only in his head and does not share ideas with others, Faust desires change so much that he contemplates suicide. The torment lasts until Mephistopheles materialises with the promise to resolve his personal paradoxes, which stem from clashes between the limiting comforts of his childhood and the radical revolution haunting his dreams. As a 'lover', he turns his interest to others he knew best in his early years but now approaches as a stranger, with the certainty that he can improve their lives by sharing his ideas and longings. However, his lover, Gretchen, a much younger villager embodying ways of being he has transcended, becomes the victim of his desire: stranded between her effort to catch up with him and to cope with the surveillance, resentment and open rage from her family and friends, she meets her death. In the last stage, as 'developers', a grieving and guilty Faust and his devilish advisor reach point zero, from where they can only implement ideas of building a better future at any cost. However, even Mephistopheles cannot catch up at this stage with his former apprentice, who has transformed into the duality of tyranny for workers and himself, willing to drive everybody to death to achieve his plan. Having exhausted the devil, Faust now turns to the source of absolute power, the Emperor, who will provide him with all means to realise his dreams. Here Berman (ibid.: 67–71) adds an interesting subplot to his story, which features an old couple embodying the ways of absolute hospitality and kindness we also saw in innocent Gretchen, who refuse to follow the Faustian tide of change and do not move out after the developer's way. His decision to eradicate them introduces the feminised spectres of Need, Want, Guilt and Care into his life, which he struggles to exorcise. The last exorcism, of Care, strikes him blind, thus forcing him to confront his own darkness.

Berman's reading of *Faust* is supposed to remind us that the deepest horrors of development can stem from the noblest motives of our utopian dreams – a point he proceeds to elucidate further, by showing how at certain moments in human history, even radical socialist planning has pushed developing societies into the darkest pit (ibid.: 72). Hence, grand plans and narratives are dangerous for the world, and we would do better to stick to particular issues we can solve in context. Helpfully for the methodological framework of this study, he cautions us that, paradoxically, in an era of accelerated globalisation only the most extravagant and systematic 'thinking big' can open up channels for 'thinking small' (ibid.: 83). I use this note of caution every time I am confronted with big data for big solutions in cinematic overtourism, so that I consider contexts of development – a resolution better matched by mobilities theory, which focuses on various forms of ethnographic analysis. My aim is not to point to solutions as a developer/policy maker, but, more modestly, to point to causes of grief as a dreamer and lover as an inquisitive researcher. However, I also cannot follow Berman's dogmatic pessimism, which is total and inescapable. Although he speaks several truths to the contemporary developer, the key to unlocking his box of pessimism lies in his reproduction of the trope/*tropē* of Romanticism, which Goethe followed when he decided to drive especially his heroine, Gretchen, to death. The paradox Berman omits from his Faustian analysis, which he claims to be suitable for contemporary situations, is that developing may create pathways to forms of small freedom.

Indeed, Berman's Faust is typical of the patriarchal national developer, who eradicates social difference by conforming it to the canon of heritage – much like the macho gaze of the local, who renders its services to tourist performance (Ateljevic and Hall 2007). It is telling that he identifies in Gretchen and the old couple Faust eliminates the values of hospitality, thus matching contemporary scholarship's sojourns on the question of gendered labour (Lynch *et al.* 2007: 128; Paolucci 1998), but endows Faust with the skills of surveillance and self-surveillance contemporary scholarship identifies in contexts of overconsumption and migration alike (Urry 2002, 2005; Bauman and Lyon 2013). Ironically, the tragic ending of these three characters falls into a decades-old fallacy shared by social scientists and humanities scholars, who refuse to acknowledge that hospitality as more-than commercial exchange can take place both within commercial and non-commercial contexts (Germann Molz and Gibson 2007; Lashley *et al.* 2007; Lashley and Morrison 2000), hence, it can involve both market-based and nonmarket-based consumption practices and experiences (see Tzanelli 2007, 2008). Paradoxically then, Berman's tragedy of development is concomitant with the plight of keeping a European/Western macho heritage alive – a quintessentially Romantic trope/*tropē* that even the oppressed groups learn to follow in sociocultural contexts (see reflections in Tzanelli 2011, 2013). In the following chapters, I craft an alternative Gretchen, who is highly mobile, a pilgrim who uses her non-European Asian heritage to change things, but does so in popular cultural contexts. My pilgrim's path is not straightforward or problem-free – indeed, she stumbles upon successive realisations of her growing power to change human and non-human worlds around her, reminiscent of Berman's Faustian allegory. However, her own path is also one of potentialities that heritage occludes, by treating communities and localities as 'objects' of development. My Gretchen's 'popular culture' is, therefore, an answer to Berman's (2010: 128) critique of Arendt's weak continuities between public life/spectatorship and action, because it cautions developers to not develop cinematic privatopias, where these are not wanted. As I endeavour to explain, Arendt's *Homo Faber* works synaesthetically on development or degrowth, and she should be taken very seriously, if critically at times. The slowness of her vision should not obey heritage proper's shortcomings, but the principles of hope and care that nevertheless do not reject the benefits of technological fastness uncritically or care's theological conundrums (see also Ateljevic 2009 on transmodernity and tourist worldmaking).

Bloch's analysis of religion is key to understanding how humans make a necessity out of contingency in their dealings with the world. Might we be able to push this argument farther to consider humans in and with the world, in all its animate and inanimate forms? And how can we counter his Eurocentric focus when it comes to teleology? To answer these questions in the context of my study, I base my entire epistemontological and methodological portfolio on the ancient repository of Chinese wisdom, which informs non-representational systems and mobility systems, but is hardly ever acknowledged in contemporary scholarship in these fields or in Blochian studies of hope, which bear significance in discussions of tourist development for hosts and guests. *I Ching*, also dubbed as *The Book of Changes*, is the most ancient classic text of Chinese civilisation. Wisely considered as a basic guide for conscious living, it entertained interpretations in Chinese Buddhist, Reality Taoism, Confucian and even Sufi schools of thought, whereas subsequently, in postclassical periods it was connected to the spiritual, political and cultural development of China and other

East Asian nations (Cleary 1994: vii). Despite their topical differences, both the Buddhist interpretation, which was produced in the seventeenth century by Chinese Buddhist *Chih-hsu Qu-I* (1566–1655) in a period of extensive political and social turmoil, and its Taoist equivalent, which was written in 1796 by Taoist adept *Liu I-ming*, also during times of severe crisis, share a belief in the restoration of balance between human mind and body and the celestial universe; an emphasis on the development of interpretation of natural and social phenomena as a skill assisting in the interpreter's self-realisation; and an elevation of adaptability to the pedestal of highest values. Chinese Buddhism was appropriated into military organisation and state governance (a theme running across Christian and Muslim religions and even influencing medieval and early modern Japanese organisation through the promotion of charismatic personalities of populist potential – ibid.: viii). In a similar vein, Reality Taoism concentrated on the advancement of 'sciences of human development', which considered divination (one of the manifold functions of *I Ching* over the centuries) as a framework for contemplative practices involving the analysis of situations (Cleary 1986: 5). This focus, which effectively outlines the principles and conditions of giving and receiving advice, is today associated with cultures of policy-making expertise (Rose 1999) and (social) scientific paradigm-making (Kuhn 1970).

There have been other points of convergence between Buddhist and Taoist readings of the *I Ching*, which are important for the design of this book. Notably, for example, the Buddhist emphasis on achieving mental opening and benevolence with the help of study, constant incantation of the name of the Buddha of Compassion (*mantraydna*) and yoga exercise for the former (Cleary 1994: xi) matches the Taoist emphasis on the 'sciences' of observation and understanding for a harmonious human development (Cleary 1986: 5). Both *mantra* recitation, and attunement to the environment and the compassionate gaze, ear and nose, feed into my epistemontologies and methodologies. However, it is the old Taoist concern with harmonisation of celestial with human time (or nature with culture) to achieve a complete understanding of the 'anatomy of events' in phenomenological/existentialist terms (ibid.: 7–8) that mirrors precisely today's scientific (and my) application of systems theory into the futures of both human nature and the environment. Not only is receptivity to reality connected for Taoists to the creative nature of silence as the stilling of personal dispositions (habitus, cultural nature – otherwise, rectifying imbalances between *yin* and *yang*) and a selectivity to act, it favours the human quality to deal adaptively and effectively with change (ibid.: 9–10, 21). Even my promised ecofeminist relational ontology connects to ancient Chinese wisdom. Indeed, the Taoist manifesto on adaptation owes much to a practical manual by a noted nineteenth century female adept (*Alchemy for Women*), who proposed that 'self-refinement' as the Taoist practice of overcoming the impulsive self to 'become' (represented by the non-discursive, 'dark side' of the mind), involves emptying the self instead so as to achieve a definitive climax of 'spirit illumination' (ibid.: 12–13). In other words, to perceive the eternal and temporal laws of change without the interference of subjectivity, the subject has to achieve a balance between rest and movement – two states today informing global cultures of leisure and travel (Fullagar *et al.* 2012; Howard 2012). We are back to the Blochian question of how we can achieve a Dionysian state of radicalism, when societies move towards ever more stringent forms of Apollonian rational self-regulation (Korstanje 2009: 54; Daly 2013: 177; Isaac and Platenkamp 2018).

Cast into our contemporary social scientific vocabularies on epistemontological formations of the subject, capitalist accumulation, and climate change, these ancient scripts yield surprisingly topical pedagogical value: the critical social-scientific cultures of climate change suggest that excessive global consumption and rising carbon emissions enhance the 'gravedigging cultures' of capitalism (an imbalance between *yin* and *yang*, prompted by a careless human attitude towards the environment and other ecosystems), especially in urban enclaves of the world (Urry 2011b: 209). Mindful of the fact that, as a dynamic, human-made system, capitalism is always characterised by disequilibrium, the adjacent school of degrowth proposes a complete dissociation ('emptying of the self') from capitalism, its 'new mobility complexes' (e.g. technologies of travel, communication or play/leisure – Elliott and Urry 2010; Urry 2007, 2008, 2011a) and neoliberal ideology (e.g. reduction in working hours, antimaterialism, increased benefits for local/host populations – Andriotis 2014: 40–41), so that the human race and its home, earth, start anew (D'Alisa *et al.* 2015; Martinez-Alier 2015; Paulson 2015; Şorman 2015). Finally, the elephant in the room, which this study illuminates with poignancy, is the pressures exercised upon communities inhabiting national and international peripheries to achieve a hasty form of self-refinement, which may leave them disorientated, even though more 'refined' (see also Nederveen Pieterse 2006 on 'cosmetic cosmopolitanism'). On all these fields, *I Ching* theosophy achieves more than allegorical or metaphorical equivalence: *it is the origins of systems and mobility theory from a more anthropocentric perspective.* Evidently, then, my focus on cultures of pilgrimage aims to reintroduce a meta-theological key into all these sociocultural scientific debates, while staying true to *I Ching*'s historical disconnection from particular religious-ideological systems (for, subsequently, I show how such systems contribute to more attitudinal and economic imbalances). As an initiative, my project attempts to build into the world ways of being that connect to ancient cultures of pilgrimage by fusing and adapting them to contemporary needs and desires (Nünning and Nünning 2010).

Selecting methods and epistemic tools to investigate these interconnected processes and phenomena pushes the researcher to think outside narrow disciplinary boxes, while trying to avoid the dangers of abstraction, reductionism and (Cartesian) dualism (Smith-Nonini 2017: 688). Employing CAS theory to examine ad hoc systemic transformations that result in experiential changes for actors dwelling in the system, acknowledges the multiplicity and fragmentation of social and cultural realities in the era of globalisation and hypermobility, while highlighting the limits of expertise, where interdisciplinary work can more easily spot the 'hidden obvious' (Morin 2008: 4; Byrne and Callaghan 2014: 38; Tzanelli 2015a: 26, 32. 131). At the same time, CAS theory needs to factor in how neoliberal ideology has transferred the power of professionals and local politicians to make aesthetic judgements mostly to developers and users (Maitland and Smith 2009: 183). Although Smith-Nonini (2017: 689) is adamant that complexity thinking represents a break with positivism, in that she regards the accumulation of alleged knowledge gained empirically as problematic 'Newtonian formalism' and hierarchy, complete rejection of any factual basis in a research project, even in terms of materially-based perception, may discard positive contributions of scientific authority altogether. Certainly, one must be mindful of systems/complexity theory's normative framing, which may place agency or power formation in a determinist cage, if not counterbalanced by hermeneutic methodologies (Jirón 2011: 50; Fuller 2011).

There is an evident inclination in this study to employ qualitative methodologies that support meaning as something always specific to the environment and resting on contingency. However, this is complemented with research into tropes (the equivalent of *mantras*), patterns of discourse on key concepts such as resilience or sustainability, so quantified analysis is not sidelined (Tzanelli 2015a: 22, 27, 60, 2017: 12, 96, 131; Halford and Savage 2017: 1135, 1137). An evident diversion from qualitative methods hostile to positivist evaluation is found in the acknowledgment that emergent assemblages informing action (e.g. complaints about overtourism in certain areas) proliferate conceptions of topography and heritage location. Mining social conversations that are recorded online to locate this phenomenon in the everyday lives of millions of people is increasingly associated with big data social science that currently entertains interest in the academy and commerce alike (Halford and Savage 2017: 1133; Langlois *et al.* 2015). This immediately calls for forms of mapping, which overlay cinematic touristified areas with areas and spots most popular with tourists and most valued by localities or institutions. The overall methodological design uses particular cases and examples to test theories of mobility, therefore providing opportunities for accountability (Gänshirt 2007: 25 in Jensen 2014: 26). Evidently then, I do not wish to reject the usefulness of visualisation, only to use it to counter ideologies of visualism in excessive consumption milieus (Halford and Savage 2017: 1139; see also Büscher 2006).

Büscher, Urry and Witchger (2011: 8–12) include among mobile methods both practices of mapping real places and capturing their atmospheres – two suggestions that I combine in this study. Below, I analyse what I discern as the architectonic component of atmospheres, thus reintroducing environmental perceptions into the study. Methodologically speaking, this component considers movement, the physical or cognitive/affective as living architecture, a series of emplacements of feeling or bodies in changing cohesions (Laban [1966] 2011: 5). My mapping tries to encapsulate living and moving atmospheres in space, in what Laban (ibid.) poetically names 'trace-forms', while also recording their accompanying action moods or 'shadow-forms' (ibid.: 65–66). Incidentally, the appeal to ocular methodologies does not contradict my non-representational framework or its decolonial dimensions, it just acknowledges that, because tourism mobilities are Western phenomena, research cannot merely reject Western paradigms in practice. In any case, my mapping extends beyond the visual field, not simply in Merleau-Ponty's footsteps, but in blended Eurasian phenomenologies of multisensory appreciation of the world, and of feeling, emotion and affect (see also Tolia-Kelly 2008). Detecting and mapping affects and emotions in living spheres of action is challenging, but their shadows can be captured through the implementation of techniques of incremental development: like music, they have overtones and sound fluctuations. Affects and emotions, which are supposed to be unrefined responses to situations in Taoist thought, are useful evaluative vehicles in studying the withdrawal of hospitality and the emergence of hostile responses to touristification. Such blended methodologies engage systems thinking in a critical dialogue with humanist paradigms, acknowledging that CAS theory is suitable for both highlighting the partiality of knowledge and introducing neovitalism into social thinking (Urry 2003, 2005a, 2005b).

Spotting the 'hidden obvious' – what I discussed above as NRT's ability to bring to light systemic changes at the experiential level – is often debated as 'emergence' (Byrne and Callaghan 2014: 356–358). Whether this concerns the ways a film industry represents landscapes, online tourist business debates spectacular filmed locations, or localities perceive themselves vis-à-vis such decisions, such changes in the system can have serious ontological effects that change or harden old motifs in identities and collective subjectivities (see Tzanelli 2016b: 28–55 on entropy). Practically speaking, the method of ad hoc investigation, which would presumably render a project with grounded ethnographic style, is replaced with the *ex post facto* retrieval of particular key moments of adaptation or change, as these are recorded in press and digital sites. The result is a blend of temporalities that mangles social scientific practice *à la* Pickering (1995) and looks once more to *I Ching*'s blending and separation of multiple temporal frameworks. Mangling acknowledges that encapsulations of temporal authenticity are ethnographic fictions, in that researchers always rework 'facts' (a key CAS admission). The researcher's spatiotemporal distance from key reported events still allows for dispassionate appraisals of the behaviours a system can exhibit in past contexts – again, regardless of whether the focus is on democratic politics, cultural diversity or ecosystemic biodiversity (Smith-Nonini 2017: 690). Even the idea of biodiversity as something existing out there, a priori, awaiting measurement, disregards the fact that discursive assemblages of practices, humans or technologies may actually produce novel perceptions of environmental space (Lorimer 2006: 540 in Braun 2008: 672).

However, techniques of data visualisation in mapping provide limited information on attunement (a principal pursuit in Confucian, Sufist, Taoist and Buddhist readings of *I Ching*). It is essential to devise a model of data analysis that acknowledges and debates the performative aspects of tourist mobilities and the local/regional/global responses they induce, which match expertise to local habitus. Such a model has to address at least three aspects of movement, while allowing the researcher to view inner and outer experiences and effects of mobility on a continuum (Hasse 2011: 55). Since Bruno Latour's (1987; 1993) observations on the immutabilty of mobiles, research on infrastructures, technical objects and embodied practices has proliferated in the social sciences, with scholars also interrogating dualisms in movement more critically (Bissel 2007; Bissell and Fuller 2009; Tzanelli 2015a, 2016b). More importantly, scholars began to examine more extensively embodied, kinaesthetic and sensory geographies of movement or dwelling (Fuller 2005; Parikka 2011), while also thinking about their place in media ecologies in more sociological ways (de Souza e Silva and Sutko 2010; de Souza e Silva and Frith 2011; de Souza e Silva and Sheller 2014). It is, therefore, important to complement data visualisation in a study that addresses the experiential aspects of mobility, with notes on the latter, without resorting to tired binary schemas of mobility/immobility. There are important interplays of materialities and affects, bodily and ethereal movements in the fields in which we move – but how can we encapsulate them for our studied subjects and ourselves?

We need to return to my modifications of Hollinshead *et al.*'s (2009) observations on worldmaking to craft an analytical model of attunement. Heretofore, I argue that the world practically exists in our impressions of the environment, which we apprehend with the help of our body and via various collaborations of our senses with the environment and our subject of study (human/non-human assemblages). Different senses afford comparable modes of engagement and apprehension of our *field-world*, to propose a new term, this slice of the world, in which we move, structure ourselves and interact with other beings and things as human beings. However, different senses are not equivalent but complementary, hence, our environment or field-world is intertwined with the field of the sensible, which is pre-objectively given (Merleau-Ponty 1962; Gibson 1966). I do not seek to attribute to scholars a privileged order of perception: our subjects, both human and non-human, also move in a field-world, which is constituted through social and habitual practice (contra Archer's (2000) anthropocentricism; see also Bourdieu 1977, 1984, 1993). Indeed, their field-worlds, as is the case with ours and their interactions, are constantly (re-)constituted with the help of scenarios of movement (their 'scriptural basis'), their (infra-)structures and materialities (their 'architectonics'), and their invisible perimeters, boundaries and borders, within which we move (the 'kinesphere', and its ethnographic extensions, the 'kinesfield'). This tripartite distribution of field-world mobilities matches data visualisation at an experiential level. I now proceed to unpack each of these modes of movement.

The scriptural basis

The scripts I explore are not identical to traditional products of literature, although they share in their sources of imagination. For example, in Chapter 4, which considers organisational designs of cinematic tourist destinations, traditional conceptions of the novel as a 'knowable community', with its writer(s) 'offer[ing] to show people and their relationships in essentially … communicable ways' (Williams [1973] 2016: 239), are revised in digital investigations into cinematic tourist advertising. The 'authors' of such digital texts are difficult to trace, as authorship is, properly speaking, a set of qualities or attributes bestowed upon visited places and cultures by discourses emanating contingently. Detaching understandings of agency from liberal humanistic understandings of intention, reason or will as parts of individual property, allows for a collection of sources for this study, which are not fixed on locating intentionality and specific authors. 'Authorship' as the true location of power (to enunciate places) and 'agency' as the true location of subjective change (to design places) (Hollinshead *et al.* 2009: 429) are destabilised in most cases, because they both to come life in particular contexts. For the present study, it is easier to pinpoint the collective actors of this digital advertising, whether these are independent business, national tourist organisations or, increasingly, a blend of both. Of primary importance in such collective mobilisations is the notion of the 'assemblage', which combines the ideas of layering or coming together with that of agency or the capacity to produce effect (Callon and Law 1995; Law and Hassard 1999; Braun 2008).

Here I depart from Hollinshead's (2009b: 530–531) recognition of the state as the primary 'authority' in tourism, and attribute instead the creative power of representation and simulation to cumulative media processes across time and spaces (Lash and Urry 1994). Neoliberalism has ensured that states are, at best, one of the principal players in the kinesphere, in which scripts can be rewritten or adapted to the needs of the moment. For this reason only, I cannot ignore Zelinsky's (2006) call to enact a sort of 'palaeontology' of media analysis, which denies credibility to progress-orientated conceptions of cultural change or a belief that representations and simulations of place in cinematic tourism emanate from fixed sources of power and develop linearly in media channels. However, because this study acknowledges that cinematic tourism at large develops on network capital that spreads across regions or nations with the help of technology (Larsen and Urry 2008), I cannot adopt a humanistic perspective of media involvement in tourism, which would sideline the 'lifeness' of the artefact. Network capital is sustained by specific assemblages of humans and non-humans entrailed in performative ontological events: no network or assemblage has a predetermined form prior to the ways people and things engage practically (Deleuze and Guattari 1987; Stiegler 1998; Szerszynski *et al.* 2003). Thus, I acknowledge that place and culture in media channels acquire temporal qualities through processes of 'enframing', which make technology a 'world-forming process' (Žižek 2014: 31; Knorr Cetina 1999). This means that, by always being mediated, humans belong physically and ontologically to the technological environment as much as they are part of a human-nature system. Ultimately, mediation does not construct reality, it transforms it, thus constantly enacting new interpretative cycles in social and cultural contexts. We are back to the study's core neovitalist argument, according to which the studied media-human-natural systems exist in the kinesphere as multi-agential forces (Kemper and Zylinska 2012: 40).

Through particular scriptural examples, I endeavour to show how postindustrial design of places of the cinematic imagination (e.g. see Reijnders 2011) can sell contemporary hypermobile styles of consumption, while still trying to resurrect rural utopias. As I mentioned above, such utopias retain particular ethnic and gendered qualities, which re-enchant ideas of noble wilderness, sublimation, and intimacy. These scriptural principles persist even where visitors/tourists are invited to immerse themselves in urban cinematic field-worlds that murder these sites of intimacy. This is so because the relevant touristic rituals serve to illuminate and mourn intimacy's absences, therefore cultivating the need to re-enchant place (Roberts 2012: 23–25). Significantly, as I mentioned before, similar principles inform some responses to development, in which the 'local way of life' or a holistic aesthetic of place are elevated to ideals. In short, scriptural stylistics reveal a lot about how field-worlds are structured and restructured from the perspectives of formal and lay designers.

Architectonics

The aforementioned exposition invites analysis of the second aspect of atmospheric design: 'architectonics'. Literally speaking, architectonics points to the governance (*arché*) of creative construction (*tektoniké* or building coupled with *téchne* or art). As a creative enterprise, modern architectonics became a form of dwelling landscape, or producing a 'chronicle of life and dwelling' in the world (Adam 1998: 54). I will use the term to refer to how multiple modes of (ways of imagining, inventing, and creating) and structures in (from animal and natural habitats to buildings and whole cities) the world appear to us materially. At first, this seems to come close to Nelson Goodman's (1978) notion of 'worldmaking', which is based on the predicament that neither are we able to encapsulate the world as such, nor can we ever know that it exists as a uniform or fragmented totality, or as plural totalities. For Goodman the human mind can only capture world versions, ways the world is, or symbolic systems that attain several forms via language, dancing, pictures or other symbols and symbolisation processes. In reality, my approach differs significantly, because it discards the idea of the mind as a computer in a body, and prioritises perception as an exploratory activity within the environment, which is not producing representations and symbols, but guiding beings in their field-world (Gibson 1966). However, architectonics also exerts a peculiar 'graphic', representational effect on the field-world, which 'locals' view as external to it: an intrusion by creative industries. Here we see a convergence between the experiential and the sociocultural levels, which is addressed in Chapter 4.

Practically speaking, in terms of architectonics, I focus on the ways environments are built in tourism or destroyed/challenged/reshaped by activism and local complaint (a theme close to Schumpeter's ([1942] 1975) notion of 'creative destruction' but with a cultural life beyond economics), so I must heed Ingold's identification of human designs as constructs of the imagination 'prior to their realisation in the material' (Ingold 1986: 40–45), which are distinctive from animal constructions (Ingold 2011: 175). Architectonics in cinematic tourism refers to destination areas imagined, then designed as physical *loci* of simulations of fictional landscapes and lifeworlds, or representations of actual historic, country or urban sites in films, TV series, comics and literature. For cinematic tourist architectonics to be realised, designers must appeal to the art of *skenografía*, or stage design of an illusion (Tzanelli 2012: 292), which brings to life spaces with mood. Indeed, perceptions of architecture as 'surface design' or 'stage painting' (Böhme 2017: 93) invoke connections to both the still art of painting and the moving ones of film and theatre. However, it would be incorrect to think of the tourist/visitor's engagement with these stages as modes of speculation. Embodied and visual connections enable participation in this play of make-believe, thus not representing a field-world or a group of things, but showing how these come to be within the field-world: 'how the world becomes a world' in the stage (see Merleau-Ponty 1964: 181). We cannot assume, as Böhme does in his critical argument, that visitors see illusions, rather, they see according to the staging, thus participating in it in pleasurable, playful ways (ibid.: 1964; Edensor 2001: 64; Urry and Larsen 2011: 193–194; MacCannell 2001; Schiller 2004).

I will not follow Ingold's (2011: 166) rejection of the emergence of novel perceptions from imagination and present 'creative acts of discovery' as their sole source. From the designer's perspective, novel perceptions of the environment can be the works of imagination (Tzanelli 2017: 34), especially when tourism design is based on simulations, which refer to non-realities or what cannot be discovered. The tourist, who bases their creativity on stimuli and information 'available to anyone attuned to pick [them] up' (ibid.), is more likely to discover things already out there, in the environment, but the ways in which they will rework them in the kinesphere may also involve imagining alternative possibilities. In other words, tourist affordances in the kinesphere should not be solely connected to practical action and existing 'objects' and 'events' in the environment (Gibson 1979: 127–143), but extended so as to include the working of the faculty of imagination, from which one may even try to engineer the impossible. This is more likely to happen in the mobilisation of creative arts, such as film, for the reinvention of physical as tourist sites. Significantly, as I explain later, the imaginative production of atmospheres without a pregiven referent in the environment is absent in reactions to cinematic tourism, especially in the case of social movements, which tend to borrow from already existing lifeworld scripts. Here I want to stress that cinematic tourist architectonics, which delineate the domain of both joint practical activities and individual pilgrimages, cannot be confused with the physical world of nature (ibid.: 8).

Kinesphere (and kinesfield)

A definition of the kinesphere is essential, because I reposition Rudolf Laban's original monadic definition within collective mobility contexts. My kinesphere is not abstracted space 'out there', a physical domain or a natural environment, nor is it a particular location perceived by individual subjects, although it can interact with all these, shaping their collective perception. This has methodological consequences, because the researcher cannot fall back on traditional divisions between an 'etic' or 'objective' account and an 'emic' or 'subjective' apprehension and analysis of the field (I will elaborate on this by using the master concept's sibling, 'kinesfield' below). Where, epistemologically, such divisions turn the world into constructions of the field/environment by design (what designers perform in tourist locations), methodologically, they postulate some clear-cut division between apprehension, perception and narrative. Where Merleau-Ponty (1962: 82) sees the body as the vehicle of being in the world involved in a 'definite environment', I see the body/soul/mind complex as embedded in it, and thus producing accounts of it in both tourist and activist contexts. For Laban, the kinesphere is 'personal space, the sphere around the body whose periphery is reached at all limbs' length, with the rest of space outside it figuring as not our personal world' ([1966] 2011: 10, 29). Much like other artists preoccupied with phenomenologies of dance, including Wassily Kandinsky, for whom the body of the jumping dancer could be translated into the language of shapes, such as circles and lines (1979: 42), Laban is interested in finding ways to marry bodily presence and materiality with the phenomenological aspects of human experience. Contrariwise, my rereading of Laban's term is filtered through urban studies discussing the segmentation and zonification of space in the city (Harvey 1985, 2000, 2006), but also the transformation processes of urban polyrhythmia into a studied object (Lefebvre [1992] 2015). However, my concept is also practically applied to non-urban cases of touristification and resistance, because all practices of differentiation from which it is conceived have structurally homologous equivalents in the (contrived versions of the) countryside. As Macnaughten and Urry (2000: 169) remind us, affordances that stem from reciprocities between the environment and the organism, derive from how people are kinaesthetically active within their world. Given that I focus on specific worlds of consumption and resistance to consumption, the kinesphere is theoretically applicable across urban and rural/marine environments, with all the appropriate adaptations to them.

The kinesphere is a sphere of performance, especially when it comes to tourism mobilities and social movements (see also Bærenholdt *et al.* 2004 on tourist performances). It is a sphere in which subjects move in the rhythm of different tasks, which are recognised by their communities as leisure or activism. Such performances do, of course, rely on fully structured (by human interaction) landscapes that afford movements of humans and animals, wherein both emerge as corporeal forms in temporal frames (Connerton 1989). For Ingold (2011:

194–198), this temporality also inheres in patterns of dwelling activities, which he calls the 'taskscape', a category of mobility that is both scientific, natural, material and social. But is this measurement of task or activity social scientific or just scientific? Sorokin and Merton (1937) for example, observed that labour is measured in units of astronomically-calibrated clock time, providing for some a notion of objectivised time of performance. However, it helps to note that performance in physics includes socially useful conceptions of time: work done per unit in time, which ultimately evaluates human activity by the *manner*, rather than the outcome of the execution (Marcuse 1955: 44). Applied to leisure activities, such as tourism or film-watching, and re-enacted in filmed sites and situations, the performance principle is valued according to critical theorists as a social achievement vis-à-vis its efficiency to produce, consume or experience (Böhme 2017: 45). Although, phenomenologically, tourist performances of this sort do belong to an external frame, they are registered in tasks visitors to sites perform, while tending to one another. Applied to sociocultural protest, the performance principle connects to the cultures of petition and lobbying it resides within and nurtures, thus revealing a lot about the protesters' cultural styles and observations on their opponents' styles (Della Porta and Diani 2006: 110–111). Indeed, both in Ingold's (2011) observations on dwelling and in Lefebvre's ([1992] 2015) thesis on rhythmanalysis, the body cannot be pure object confronting tasks, but is the very subject of performance.

It also helps to stress again that the kinesphere involves ontological dwellings exceeding those attributed to human subjects. On this, I consider critically Ingold's (2011: 217) note that, whereas the image of the globe appeals to the environmentalist principles of ecocentrism, the image of the sphere is anthropocentric through and through. From an ANT perspective, this suggestion leaves much to be desired: not only does it assume that non-humans do not reside in spheres, it could potentially consolidate the role of experts as outsiders, rather than participants of experiences in a biosphere or lifeworld to which they are not native. It also, nonetheless, as Ingold (2011: 218) himself notes, conceals the fact that both positions presuppose the existence of one big environment identified with the order of nature. Thus, it is better if we consider the kinesphere – or 'kinespheres' – in this study by simply removing the human subject from the centre of everything. To complicate things further, because the present study has an environmental angle to account for, the narrative of multiple environments has to connect the kinesphere to the globe, where globalisation takes place – put otherwise, to connect the experiential to the political (for, all epistemontological becomings are registered in sociopolitical contexts with all their experiential hues, after all). Ingold (2011: 210–212) suggests that the image of the globe was deployed in geopolitical contexts early on in modern histories of the West and Europe, but its connection to the environment is more recent. All the same, the globe is heavily loaded with practices of contemplation, seeing from without, rather than experiencing from within.

To demarcate the domain of lived experience Ingold uses the notion of 'sphere', a softer perception of the environment that can be apprehended in multisensory ways (ibid.). Historically, the globe adhered to a colonial image of the environment awaiting occupation, so it was always perceived of as an invasion into supposed privacy (Holton 2005; Sloterdijk 2009; Inglis 2010; Tzanelli 2015b, 2016). It has been argued that this geometrics of space, which invites looking at and therefore subjecting alterity to a Western occulocentric canon, has to be replaced with a spherological poetics, which can account for the native experience. However, I argue that this historical perspective should not be applied to contemporary tourist mobilities singlehandedly, even though there are disquieting connections to be made. There are many spheres to account for in cinematic tourist contexts, and a straightforward equation of modifications of the native environment with destruction presumes a world already constituted through archaic natural and/or human forces, not a world in motion – a spectacle, rather than a pliable phenomenon. Paradoxically, therefore, this anti-globalist narrative mirrors the imperialist attitude to patronise native lifestyles, displacing them into some premodern utopic sphere. Otherwise put, if we adopt this 'cultural imperialist' argument, we do not treat the world as lived-in environment, full of interconnections within and across other environments, but resort to scopic practices, in which nothing changes, unless a source of governance dictates change. Even the artifice of technology should be reconsidered as part of the lived sphere, as I explain by example in the following chapter.

All the aforementioned clarifications connect to understandings of the kinesfield, which is the field of academic production. There, the body is indeed still the subject of perception as part of the studied environment, so the kinesfield it inhabits is a generative field constituted by the totality of organism–environment (Ingold 2011: 200). However, the academic subject/body (e.g. the researcher) has to produce a field of study, which can never be accounted for as emic/objective. As a result, the study's multiple 'environments' are made meaningful through the act of observation and narrative, which is nevertheless already part of the larger world to which the observer belongs. Despite any appeals to objectivity or exteriority, ethnographic and webthnographic scholars cannot truly observe from without. All the researcher can do, in terms of intervention, is to enhance or intensify the atmospheres (s)he studies: arrange light, texts and architectonic movements (Dufrenne ([1953] 1973; Böhme 2006), as well as affective narratives and embodied performances that are already there (Stewart 2007). This power to orchestrate 'animates all dynamic transactions that take place between the body and the environment', as choreographer Gretchen Schiller notes (2008: 433). My use of the term 'kinesfield' should be attributed to her reading of Laban, as a field whereby bodily movement is placed within particular spatiotemporal conditions of the environment, replete with atmospheres, social events, and cultural attunements. I apply the principles of the kinesfield throughout the rest of the book, but especially in Chapter 5, where social movements and cultural responses to cinematic touristification may also produce dynamic and palpable spaces.

In the first chapter I promised to promote an alternative style of movement in the world from that of the disorientated Baumanesque tourist. To discharge this task, I have to craft trajectories in time and space for the two principal ideal groups of the study: cinematic tourists and cinematic hosts. Occasionally, these trajectories intersect with those of other actants and human agents in field-worlds, collective or not (states, tourist organisations, business), so I also make space for these crossovers, because atmospheres are always relationally produced. To relay these mobilities, I take cues from the ways both principal groups become involved in activities that form the (in-)hospitable relationships in which they become implicated. I endeavour to discuss visitor and host taskscapes in two separate chapters and in mapped/carved trajectories that are not of my own inspiration. In the following chapter, which examines cinematic tourism, I outline both ways that postindustrial experts design cinematic journeys and ways that cinematic tourist designs emanate spontaneously from some lay performances of touring filmed locations. In Chapter 5, which focuses on host taskscapes, I explore the styles of activist mobilisation against cinematic touristification, hence ad hoc designs of being in the world with others. There is explicit Taoist symmetry between Chapter 4 and 5 in terms of design, which nevertheless does not extend to the study's final conclusions. But let us first consider the ways cinematic tourism develops places into locations of consumption and play.

Chapter 4

Mobile design

A purposeful pilgrimage into cinematic tourist sites

Carving mobilities: a preliminary statement

The retro is back in fashion, to the discomfort of some critical theorists (Korstanje 2018a: 17–23). Engagement with retro cultures erodes civic participation according to these arguments, which wage wars against an imagined fixation upon the past, a 'retrotopia' resulting in sociocultural anaestheticisation (Bauman 2016). Much like its equally notorious partner, kitsch, retro can be consigned to unconscious memory by theorists. The unconscious is replete with unpleasantries human subjects prefer to expunge, so retro memories surface in the conscious social sphere only as anodyne consumables (on kitsch and retro see Holliday and Potts 2012: 21, 72). Might this be too absolute a conclusion to reach? As Schäfer (2018: ix) notes, popular imaginaries of mobility can only be explored when we place their pasts and histories in a dialogical relation to contemporary conditions. Such pasts have multiple routes and roots, which carry on living in the present rhizomatically, hence, substantively, but never in their original state. Instead, as constantly renewed entities in holistic environments inhabited by humans, animals and machines, they carve new paths to the future. Add now to this the so-called 'postmodern' turn to simulation, whereby retro is replaced with hyperrealities of the big screen and the television, with cinematic audiences surfing filmed sites, then visiting locations the cinematic machine had previously modified almost beyond recognition. This complexity contributes to rebranding place but also recreating locations and identities, ultimately blending situated and simulated pasts with deterritorialised presents in a new atmospheric magma. Welcome to our post-retrotopian field-worlds: the worlds of pastiche and *bricolage* from cinematically adapted novels, real heritage sites, refashioned architectural materialities and auratic mobilities. In these field-worlds, rhizomes rarely disappear; more often they become entangled with new blooming breeds and creeping ivies to create the eeriest gardens on our planet, neither wholly human, nor fully natural.

In this chapter I do not intend to follow the established taxonomic rationale of cinematic tourist scholarship, only to provide a constructive answer to anti-retrotopic proponents. I could summarise this thus: the ways retro or kitsch are postindustrially manufactured does not mirror their adaptation in different socio-cultural spheres at all times (see Appadurai 1986 on the social life of things). In addition, the unmistakable governmental shift from societies of surveillance to societies of control, which made power more fluid and decentralised (e.g. see Deleuze 1995; Lacey 2005; Urry 2007, 2011a), did not succeed in making cinematic pilgrims/*flâneurs* invisible human quantities to host communities. Complex control systems can and are emulated by any of these communities, which gather information about visitor profiles on site, thus amassing the means and information to replace indifferent fascination with guilt and social involvement (for more see Chapter 5; Basu 2012; Dyson 2012; Meschkank 2011, 2012; Tzanelli 2015a). At the same time, however, the very ritual of mobility through cinematic sites and products is generative of new meanings and experiences that exceed their manufactured atmospheres (on tourism as transformative praxis see Edensor 2001: 60; Graburn 2001: 151; Bærenholdt *et al.* 2004; Larsen *et al.* 2006; Crouch 2009). Isin (2017: 506), who primarily sees performed citizenship in 'how people stage creative and transformative resistances and articulate claims' can be applied at both ends of the host-guest relationship.

Drawing on Simmel's *Metropolis and Mental Life* ([1903] 1997: 180) one may make an additional note on the ways atmosphere, as this is enveloped in conceptions of urban life, encompasses sets of impressions reflecting the characteristic diversity of the city's dwellers and *flâneurs*. Given that today we experience an accelerated pluralisation of cities and ruralities, I also consider Simmel's observations in non-urban contexts. Furthermore, to modify Simmelian theory, rituals of mobility through manufactured sites may also point to a more collective response to processes of touristification, which do not promote purposeless consumption, but *the spatialisation of moods we associate with healing.* Setting aside the fact that such metaphors risk associating a unilateral monetarisation of pleasure with the destination's needs for a 'cultural lift' (Connell 2006), cinematic tourist pilgrimages resemble the ways some cultures of medical tourism attend to the tourist-patient's body, so that they also heal the soul (Dillette *et al.* 2017). From a healing perspective, cinematic tourist pilgrimages can figure as a feeling of presence (Böhme 2016), which is located between subjectivity, objectivity and the world. This enmeshes it to spatialised extensions of atmospheres coproduced by visitors (Schmitz 1993: 33 in Hasse 2011: 58–60).

These observations have implications for the design of the chapter. First, by using the principles of *I Ching* theosophy, to which contents tourism traces its origins, I proffer a fusion of technical cultural horizons (East meets West through multiple adaptations of atmospheric perspective). The emphasis on technical fusion suggests that even schematisations can take the form of an event, rather than a predetermined 'design', thus assuming the mantle of contingency 'the whole way down, rather than covering over or reducing contingency' (Mackenzie 2003: 4–6, 2002). Psychic Enlightenment as healing stands at the heart of many versions of *I Ching* on which I draw to organise tourist performances (but not 'invent' their style). Technics refer both to the style of interpretation (as in

Buddhist theosophy) and the subjects' communications with nature (as in Taoist theosophy) as a sort of environmentally-adduced hermeneutics (as in Confucianism). Delanty (2009) promotes a similar fusion of horizons in his deliberations on cosmopolitanism, while adducing that privileging one particular register of meaning ('western explanatory concepts or non-western concepts' – Delanty 2015: 375) is not sound cosmopolitan practice (or, I would add, cultural-sociological methodology). However, his perspective is anthropocentric, so he has little to say about ecoaesthetic connectivities. For me, technical meeting points between different worlds and provinces of meaning rest on the principles of combined human and non-human mobilities, with an emphasis not only on the holistic improvement of the human soul, mind and body, but also its harmonious and respectful existence in the animate and inanimate environment (Singh 2012: 214, 218, 223).

Such movements also depend on a greater ensemble of things dwelling in the system of tourist mobility, including inanimate and natural actants, so any interpretive performance is overdetermined by them. The idea stands next to my post-retrotopic or hyperreal theory and case studies, suggesting a healing fusion of atmospheric horizons with a long history. Drawing on Latour's (1993) claim that we have never been modern, I proceed to explain that the phenomenological essence of our cinematic journeys, *their atmospheric core*, is as ancient as those rituals of self-fulfilment described by the interpreters of the *I Ching* canon. At the same time, my premises cannot be technophobic or antimodernist (if so, how can one enact mobilities based on cinematic technology?), nor can they aim to snatch the trophy of innovation from today's postindustrial creators. Equipped with the tools of interdisciplinary (in dialogue with other disciplines) and transdisciplinary (in dialogue with the third sector, such as business initiatives in design) sociology, I use my knives to shape paths, not kill mobile entities in the tourist field-world.

In what follows, I use a series of 'hexagram' and 'trigram'-like atmospheric components (*I Ching's* tools of interpretation of events) from established cinematic tourist design to investigate cinematic tourist mobilities in different parts of the world. The elusiveness of atmospheres necessitates a shift to the pictorial and material world, through which they are mediated or 'extended', so that we can capture them in a study. Given that my principal investigation is into design, I use light, darkness and various blends of both, as well as earth, water and fire, as my primary hexagrams to explain how atmospheres are *designed* – hence, brought into audiovisual discourse. My primary trigrams were outlined at the end of Chapter 3 as script, architectonics and kinesphere. Various combinations between my social scientific hexagrams and trigrams construct a theoretical basis for tourism mobility that does not obey business imperatives, but uses organisational design in its construction all the same.

Poly-graphic design: a selection of case studies

Light and darkness

The retro and the simulacrum are ubiquitous in cinematic tourist design. Contemporary urban environments hold extensive records of the major twentieth and twenty-first century shifts from a 'Culture 1.0' model of development based on patronage, to a 'Culture 2.0' one based on creative activities supplanting the whole urban economy, and finally, 'Culture 3.0', in which networked cultural audiences manipulate creative content provided by the cities (Sacco 2011; Richards 2011; Ashworth and Page 2011; Urry and Larsen 2011). The latest phase brings contemporary transformations of contents tourism to the fore, as a force set to define new symbolic economies based on atmospheres (Pine and Gilmore 1999; Zukin 1995, 2010; Yue 2006; Richards 2010). Indeed, atmospheric sources of illumination, which circulated in different ethnoreligious narratives for millennia, are now used to define urban tourist milieus, especially those connected to filmmaking. The Christian allegory of divine light might have shed its religious content in contemporary technological innovations, but kept all its sensory connotations in urban environments, to advertise cities as beautiful utopias, capable of inciting joy and enthusiasm (Hasse 2011: 63). The Buddhist notion of Enlightenment (Cleary 1994) and Taoism's acknowledgment that the 'workings of Heaven' only allow humans to harmonise their life experiences with the design of the universe (Cleary 1986), produce analogous utopias, which are also traced in the Islamic scriptures regarding the paradisiac atonement of religious subjects (Asad 2009: 118, 277).

By the same token, however, the notion of darkness, which even the Realist Taoist canon recognises as the non-discursive 'dark side' of the mind (Cleary 1986: 12), contributes to contemporary urban illuminations. Cinematic cities in which tourist trajectories follow the steps of film heroes and heroines enmesh both light and darkness in the journeys, thus proving that the vertical sublime of skyscrapers and the deadlocks of claustrophobic alleyways bring into focus the myth of a horrifically beautiful location for sale to global tourist gazes (Tzanelli 2016b: 33; Lyall and Bell 2002). The darkness of the creative city generates atmospheric nuances, which are phenomenologically effective for the tourist experience. Much like Foucault's observation on the idea of the 'exterior' as an abyss beyond the rationalistic orders of thinking and experiencing (Hasse 2011: 63, fn. 30), darkness embedded in cinematic scripts and their corresponding tourist architectonics exposes the limitations of seeing rationally while walking through filmed sites. There are many ways to design dark journeys in the cinematic city, from which I present three examples: the first cluster prompts tourists to adopt the scriptural role of the detective; the second to embrace the poetics of communal kinesphere with an architectonic journey in the intimate city; and the third to prioritise inner movement towards healing by embodied performance.

Cluster I

Consider the recent revamping of Bergen in the style of the Nesbø-inspired *The Snowman* (director Tomas Alfredson 2017), a Scandi-noir steeped in cold whiteness under a grim sky. Previously known as 'the gateway to the Norwegian fjords', the city of Bergen now prepares for film fan tourists, who wish to visit locations in and around it, but especially the popular Vidden hiking trail between the Ulkriken and Floyen mountains, where the film's horrific murders take place. Although in 2017 the city invested in a national bid to put Bergen back on the European cultural map 'as a destination for more than just stately Saga cruise daytrippers or devotees of BBC4's hit Scandinavian dramas', the waterfront Bryggen district, which is a World Heritage Site, recently crossed by Michael Fassbender as detective Harry Hole, is set to receive more cinematic tourist visitors (Thorpe 15 August 2017). There is an ongoing clash of design in the background: on the one hand, media industries promote the film's scriptural tourist potential, on the other the Bergen administration prioritises heritage pathways to development, which lead to the suppression of more mundane or vernacular forms of creativity favouring experiment (Borén and Young 2013: 1801). Experimental cinematic tourist development can, and does draw on such immediately available phenomena as the romantic atmosphere of the fog, the gaslight or the cabs, and above all, the eccentric sharp mind of the detective that sociologists recognise in Kracauer ([1960] 1997), Benjamin (1983, 2006) and Simmel's ([1903] 1997) writings on the city.

Let me stress once more that atmosphere is endowed with the emanation of emotionally rich experiences in material contexts. The scriptural potential of *The Snowman* marries easily with the natural atmospheric environment of Bergen, which, in turn, makes space for the opaque complexity of modern life represented by crime (Williams [1973] 2016: 327, 239). While cinematic tourist visitors are invited to adopt the gaze of the knowing detective, they are also endowed with the knowledge of the misogynistic murderer, the eye of horror, that knows where and how all crimes are committed (Clover 1994). The juxtaposition of the act of touring as the opening world of education and play, to the act of murdering as manifestation of barbarity associated with wild, barely accessible natural environments (Williams [1973] 2016: 381) dissolves, leaving the visitor with a complex feeling of pleasing and inquisitive dread. This emotional journey has a name in sociologies of deviance: 'edgework'. Usually, edgework is taken to include a wide range of voluntary risk-taking behaviours that negotiate 'the boundary between chaos and order' and which 'all involve a clearly observable threat to one's physical or mental well-being or of one's sense of an ordered existence' (Lyng 1990: 855, 857). However, it has a less well-acknowledged affective side, which extends beyond sports and other outdoor activities, in which participants risk physical injury. Certainly, cinematic tourism belongs to the realm of controlled emotional edges, which are prominent in contemporary systems of leisure (Korstanje 2011), but such self-guarding is never fool proof. Sociological genealogies of edgework associate it with cultures of overconsumption, insecurity and existential crisis, which may have no place in cinematic tourist performances as such. All the same, the concept is useful in investigating how safely designed trips into emotional chaos allow such fans an alternative journey, which resembles the objective of *I Ching* meditation to test and adjust one's response to an (in)hospitable world.

The detective's scriptural presence is embedded in complex architectonic formations in other cases, where local heritage and popular culture entertain a more amiable relationship. This is present in Ystad's configurations in tourist design connected to the highly popular *Wallander* novels (ten detective novels by Henning Mankell) and films. Since 2004, 34 movies starring Krister Henriksson as the main character (Kurt Wallander) were produced in Ystad, whereas since 2008, 12 episodes were produced by Left Bank Pictures, BBC and Yellow Bird with Kenneth Branagh as Kurt Wallander (Ystads Commun 1, undated). Other Northern European cities also promote connections between detective films and tourism: for example, Amsterdam has its own two-hour Baantjer walk tour to locations from the popular *Baantjer* TV series (directors Pollo de Pimentel, Will Koopman, Anne van der Linden and 16 more), which is organised by a local tourist company. In fact, every year, around 3,000 tourists from the Netherlands, Belgium and France get to know the old centre of Amsterdam in this way (Reijnders 2010b). However, the case of *Wallander* presents us with a more concerted public-private management of tourism. Visit Sweden, Sweden's official website for tourism and travel information, keenly advertises the town both for its 'fascinating history, top-class museums and art galleries, 40 km of sandy beaches and gorgeous rolling Skåne countryside on its doorstep' and its contribution to the films figuring the famous inspector. Prompting tourists to visit the Film Museum Cineteket, which organises *Wallander* tours, and Ystad Studios, Scandinavia's largest film studio, it assumes an agential worldmaking role in cinematic tourism, where authority is actually controlled by corporate media (Hollinshead 2007).

The tours blend the stories' script with local heritage markers, thus taking visitors through a journey embedded in local landscapes (Ystads Commun 2, undated). As a result, they produce a map of mobility through local dark sites/sights (see Lennon and Foley 2000; Croy and Smith 2005; Stone 2006, 2013; Biran *et al.* 2011 on dark tourism and heritage), which are framed by the diagnostic tools of police work (a modern version of *I Ching* interpretation). Regardless of whether such dark locations are heritage sites, their mediated versions do not merely generate 'place markers' in the form of images (e.g. MacCannell 1989), but moods connected to cinematically-derived atmospheric 'tinctures' (Böhme 1993: 121–122). It has even been suggested that detective film tourism hinges upon the marketisation of erstwhile 'guilty landscapes' (those of the concentration camp), which is denuded of history's emotional burden, so as to cater for pleasure (Reijnders 2010b). Yet, I would stress that the movies themselves inject into the filmed sites new emotional content, which can be as rich as their predecessors'. Generally, all filmed sites, but especially those featuring crimes, are overlaid with potent shadow-forms, which assist in choreographies of tourist movement (Laban [1966] 2011: 55). Thus, Ystad's places as physical sites participate in the staging of a constellation of feelings connected to the aura of a particular work of art: the *Wallander* novels/films (see Böhme's (1993: 117) reading of Walter Benjamin).

It is also important to note that, at least in the case of Kenneth Branagh's filmic trilogy, such feelings do not haunt the body in unlocatable ways, but can be and are associated with Ystad's harbour, where a dead body appears in the movies, the country's grim midwinter landscapes, where the stories were filmed, and the pervasive loneliness of the Swedish horizon as a whole (on an actual tourist account see Eames 26 May 2016). Ystad thus stands as an atmospheric extension of the phlegmatic Swedish character, which assumes a civilised veneer through its insertion into global tourist performances and creative industries (Elias 1978). This is how location as country, land and ethnic character are produced, and then reinterpreted in tourist atmospheres, which hinge upon cinematic ecoaesthetics. If we are to follow Reijnders (2009) in the case of *Wallander*, and Cateridge (2015) in the case of the Oxford cinematic tours based on *Inspector Morse* (1987–2000), detective narratives develop a topophilic affiliation with place, which extends to practices of deep mapping on social media, such as Flickr and Google Maps, where tourists can subsequently plan their own visits. Cateridge's analysis of such lay cartographic designs of detective cinematic pilgrimages presents cyberphere as an atmospheric extension of embodied tourist performances in what I have termed the kinesphere (see Chapter 3). Lay digital pilgrimages resemble the ways professional designers make 'manufactured landscapes' stand for lived experience in motion, so we should treat their digital modifications in the same way one would treat any landscape as the outcome of human tasks accumulated in time to generate modes of dwelling (Heidegger 1971).

The observation could apply to the numerous maps of fictional worlds of *The Lord of the Rings* (director Peter Jackson 2001–2003 – *LOTR*) and *GoT*, but also those of *James Bond* (1962–ongoing – *JB*). Note how mapping company Esri UK created after the release of *Spectre* (director Sam Mendes 2015) an interactive map showing every location visited by 007 since *Dr No* (director Terence Young 1962) was released, in which 146 visits made to 49 countries were recorded (Cosslett 26 October 2015). The map, which was advertised in the British press, suggested a dark popcultural design of the British agent's travel across different countries, cultures and continents, thus connecting physical to cognitive-emotional tourist mobilities. The large-scale *GoT* map of Kingdoms, which physically redraws three continents (Europe, parts of Africa and Asia, with parts of the Arctic Ocean implicitly included in the design) is also an interesting exercise in fusions of imaginary with real imperial geographies, given that these parts of the world were colonised by different empires in ancient (ancient Greek, Roman), medieval (Byzantine, Ottoman) and modern times (Spanish,

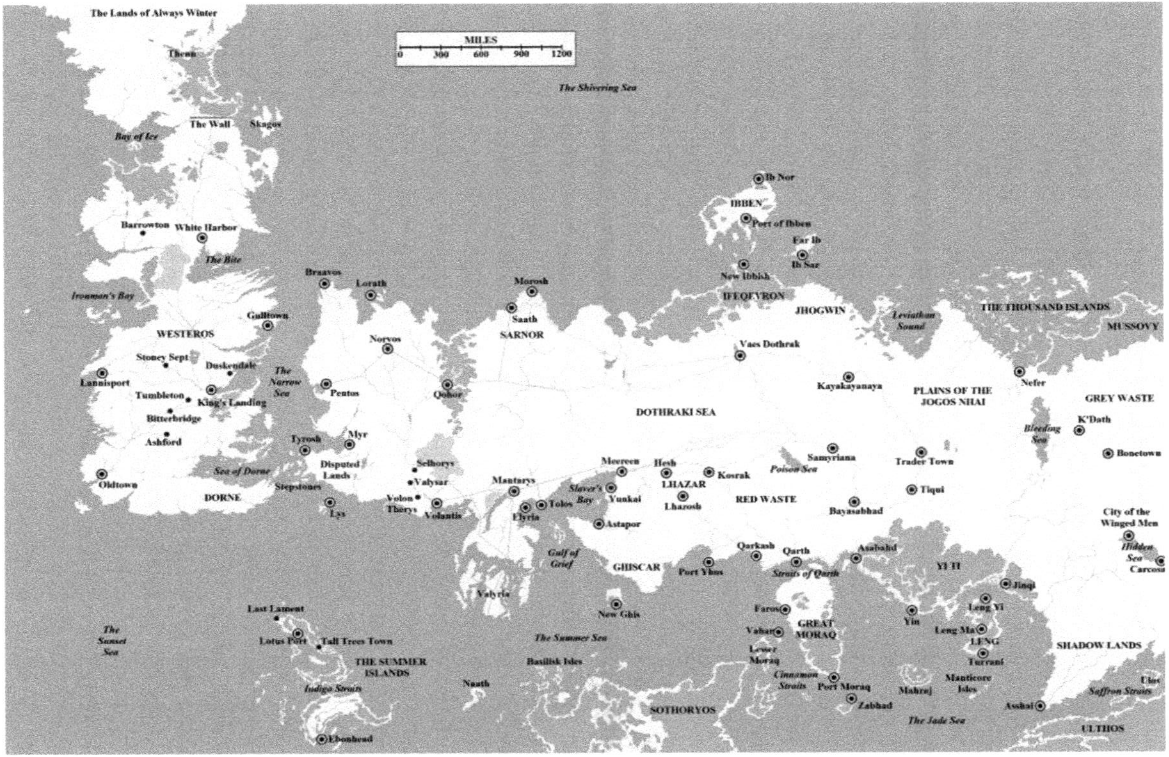

Figure 4.1 *GoT* world map and cities.

Map credit: awoiaf.westeros.org, Wikimedia Creative Commons Attribution-Share Alike 4.0 International Licensing.

British, French and more). This kind of popcultural worldmapping, which overwrites successive histories of colonialism, replaces actual national borders cinematic pilgrims have to cross to visit filmed sites with those of fictional civilisations, which are nevertheless designed on the basis of actual geographies of power (Hollinshead and Suleman 2018: 203, 212). I return to this point through examples from Northern Ireland. For the moment, I note that such *GoT* worldmappings interact with professional tourist worldmakings in atmospheric registers, because they are based on versions of dark (heritage) tourism.

Intriguingly, the *GoT* map's imaginary world brings real geographical controversies regarding map design to the fore. Of significance in discussions of worldmapping in heritage representations has been a clash between the 'Mercator' and 'Gall-Peters' Map Projections. A cylindrical projection of the world by Flemish geographer/cartographer Gerardus Mercator in 1569, the former design became a standard seafaring medium in nautical navigations due to its successful representation of constant course lines ('loxodromes'), and despite its distortion of landmasses in latitudes further away from the Equator (i.e. Greenland and Antarctica appears much larger in relation to Central Africa). To achieve the cylindrical design on which Mercator's projection is based, East–West and North–East scales are stretched, so that distances appear *conformal* (of the same form reminiscent of the Bergsonian formalist tradition – see Chapter 3), thus almost eliminating Polar Regions. It was claimed that shrinking landmass sizes near the Equator (compared to those of Europe and North America, which the Projection magnified) supported representations of the corresponding countries (coincidentally, mostly marked in real politics as 'underdeveloped' or 'marginal') as less significant. Thus, the argument connected spatial perceptions to forms of power that eradicate particular forms of epistemontology.

In more recent years, the idea of unrolling the cylinder so as to provide a planar map (see Snyder 1987; 1997) has been applied to online street mapping services such as OpenStreetMap, Google Maps and MapQuest, despite the Mercator's obvious scale variation, because it was deemed better-suited for interactive purposes than other models (Barcelona Field Studies Centre 2018). And yet, Mercator-inspired street mappings enlarge vision at the centre of the image, blurring peripheral environs. This brings into being a neat rendition of the original Labanian subject's kinespheric movement, with the prescription of blinkers, ensuring that his/her movement itself produces knowledge *while on the move*, in a typical Gibsonian fashion (Ingold 2011: 228–231; see also Chapter 3). Notably, maps based on the Gall-Peters Projection, which are rectangular, are claimed to relay the correct sizes of all areas relative to each other, but achieve this by distorting regions anyway (especially the Polar Regions). The Gall-Peters Projection is used in mappings of areas by UNESCO and in British schools (Higgins 2009), as well as by charities such as Oxfam and the National Council of Churches, so we could easily connect it to the ideologically suspect projects of imperialism, heritage conservation or 'development' at large. The model, which was first introduced by clergyman James Gall in 1855 as the 'orthographic' projection of distances between parallels, but not taken up by geographic communities before German filmmaker Arno Peter's 1973 publication of a version of it, was presented as a corrective of the Mercator Projector's defects (i.e. its promotion of a form of 'cartographic imperialism' – see also Crampton 1994; Monmonier 2004). However, critics have remarked that the only completely undistorted areas in it are the mid latitudes, in which Peters' homeland (Germany) is situated, at the expense of those occupied by less technologically advanced nations (Robinson 1985).

Thus, both models/projections view representation as a prerequisite for human perception, not considering the uses of mapping by different groups and in different 'habitats of meaning', or indeed the very epistemontological conundrum in the social sciences. The *GoT* map, which, as a vista (a 'semienclosure' or 'set of unhidden surfaces ... what is seen from here, with the proviso that "here" is not a point but an extended region' or world – Gibson 1979: 198) is a complete distortion of the real world as globe, adopts a playful attitude towards its key plot's ('archplot' – McKee 1999: 3–4, 41–42) headquarters: thus, a conformal projection between the eastern Shadow Lands and the western Westeros appeals to atmospheric projections of darkness and light, while nevertheless still displacing the home (Westeros) of powerful dynasties from the map's centre, which is populated by the Dothraki Sea. The enlargement of Dothraki regions nicely matches the increased significance of its political personalities in the story (especially Khaleesi Daeneris Targaryen's ascent to power). As an imaginative wayfaring medium, the map employs vectors of projection 'that serve to transmit the total composition [of fictional lifeworlds] from a now exteriorised world to the recesses of the mind' (Ingold 2015: 74). Hence, the Mercator paradigm of experiential travel and the Gall-Peter's unrecognised field of intimacy in its design (how can it be that the filmmaker's own homeland is accurately represented in it?) enter an uneasy pact in its field-world philosophy. By employing actual political controversy as fiction, the *GoT* map inverts the Mercator/Gall-Peters focus on realist depictions of a 'world out there', asking a simple question: are not all worlds variations of our 'being in the (a) world', after all?

Cluster 2

Juxtapositions of light and darkness guide India's project of branding and urban regeneration, which is adopted by independent business. However, where branding strategies capitalise on notions of incredibility (Incredible India) and light (Shining India) (Geary 2013), hence fascination (Schmid *et al.* 2011: 7–8), a more involved community project of reaching out to strangers emerges. This project stresses that administrative corruption and its consequences, poverty and suffering, might overdetermine everyday life, but are just the 'darkness of the moment'. Note how this critical reversal of official branding policies, which intensified in Mumbai with the international tourist influx after the release of *Slumdog Millionaire* (directors Danny Boyle and Loveen Tandan 2008 – *SM*) facilitated a narrative of resilience of the disenfranchised hosts (slum communities) in the face of multiple anthroposcenic changes. The slum of Dharavi, in which many *SM* scenes were shot, especially designed its own self-presentation to tourists with help from local tour operators, Reality Tours. The fear that touring a place like Dharavi could turn for visitors into 'education' (Richardson 22 January 2009), a narcissistic project of self-betterment we associate with the intrusion of nineteenth-century European middle-classes into London and Paris' shantytowns (Holdnak and Holland 1996; Seaton 2012; Freire Medeiros 2012), was also turned into a 'weapon for the weak'. Slum self-advertising involved press discussion of Dharavi's 10,000 small-scale industries (with an estimated $665 million in annual revenue), the presence of less crime in slums than the rest of the city 'because there is a sense of community' (Sesser 21 February 2009), and, above all, a strong local involvement in India's disorganised environmental policies. As Duff (2010: 88) notes, any affective environment 'is an expression of the social ties that form its foundation', so such commentary is central to the slum's lay tourist design (see also Chapter 5). Central to that has been the recurring featuring on and off line, in community and artistic activist projects, of the slum's recycling area, where 'old ink vats, cooking oil containers and paint tints were being returned to gleaming perfection, while scraps of trashed plastic were converted into pristine pellets and twisted aluminium was returned to ingots' (Richardson 22 January 2009).

Soot, dirt and darkness cater for zombie environmentalists at best, and factions set to exploit poor communities in their political programmes at worst. In 2011 the Ministry of Environment and Forests introduced a series of E-waste Management and Handling Rules that placed the disposal burden solely on producers and consumers, making the function of Mumbai's *kabadiwallahs* (*dalit* ragpickers) in Dharavi and elsewhere a necessity (Lobo 11 August 2013). Whereas Mumbai in particular has 17 dismantlers/recyclers listed on the Maharashtra Pollution Control Board (MPCB) site, the actual collection and disposal/dismantling is left to such scavengers and ecologically aware companies. There is a whole system of informal waste disposal in place, passing through *kabadiwallahs*, who handle toxic lead and cadmium without any health and safety precautions, to piles in Deonar landfill, where all sort of retardants release toxins into the groundwater, or, when incinerated, into air. Lack of national surveys on e-waste and general waste, and no real enforcement of e-rules, explains why the '13th Compound', Dharavi's pit in which all electronic waste is dumped, thrives locally and is dignified in the national and internal press. In fact, other cities, such as Chennai in Madras, adopted similar private-public initiatives not too long ago (Moore 23 August 2013).

Here, urban landscape acts as a polyrhythmic composition of processes 'whose pulse varies from erratic flutter of leaves to the measured lift and clash of tectonic plates' (Ingold 2001: 201). At all times, however, we cannot but consider the relationship between urban aesthetics and philosophies of design as one concerning the human experience of cities. Social structure and ideology need to be factored into our analysis in combination with phenomenological takes on urban lifeworlds or field-worlds, so that we think of place and culture holistically. In Dharavi's case, the involvement of many agents in the '13th Compound' includes political parties at both extremist ends, striving to secure the votes of slumdwellers. In political ecologic terms, the recycling project is a manifestation of 'contested urbanism' (Boano *et al.* 2013), a situation whereby the urban realm turns into a battleground between top-down and bottom-up forces that exercise spatial, political and social resistance. Engel's 'romantic anti-urbanism' stressing the prevalence of anomie and alienation in the city brushes against older images of the metropolis as a monster with million heads and eyes (Williams [1973] 2016: 310–311) or the locus of terror and insecurity (Cochrane 2004; Bauman 2008).

It is such tropes of fear that lay and official Dharavi narratives of a 'place to play' seek to eliminate, so that a sense of commitment to human development and the environment are communicated to slum visitors (Thibaud 2011: 209). The presence of a recurring community trope in press observations, tourist testimonials and local narratives (see Dyson 2012; Diekmann and Hannam 2012; Tzanelli 2015a; Hannam and Diekmann 2016), confirms that slum tourism hinges upon aestheticisations of industrial modernity's material traces (Edensor 2005a). In opposition to the tightly regulated tourist enclaves of globally sanctioned heritage such as the Taj Mahal (Edensor 1998: 45–53), which also featured in *SM*, slums are living places on the social margins, which can accommodate transgressive and playful activities (Sheller and Urry 2004: 7–8). Slums stand between the dark industries of modernity and the bright past of rural utopias, so they appeal to the urban tourists' appetite for nostalgic consumption. Thus, we must provide a social contextualisation of such atmospheric nuances (Tolia-Kelly 2006; Rose *et al.* 2010), which reportedly play on visitor anticipation: both on the official website of Reality Tours and those of other activist organisations (see Tzanelli 2015a) as well as during on-site tours, increasingly managed by native labour, Dharavi's hopeful atmospheric kinesfield relies on *SM's* 'viewing field' (Thibaud 2011). This field of vision is in fact emotionally mediated (Merleau-Ponty 1962), and places *dalit kabadiwallahs* into the cinematic slumdog's role (Jamal as *SM's* hero), so as to transform the disinterested visitor into a volunteer tourist, who donates to the slum's developmental projects. This process of atmospheric attunement employs the entire gamut of 'lightness' and 'darkness', which, alongside the visitors' olfactory and auditory participation in Dharavi's taskscapes (on which see example 3 below), colours and tinctures the environs (Böhme 1993: 121; Thibaud 2011: 211; Edensor 2012: 1106). However, the messages' orientations to an international visitor audience also challenge sociocultural exclusions within the Indian nation. This happens subtly through the assignment of critique to the task of moviemaking: online, everything is executed by an allegedly disinterested filmmaker, striving to achieve the technical mastery of light and sound, while, at all times, (s)he manages the 'technical shaping of materiality' (Böhme 2010: 29).

Of course, constructive orchestrations of tonality in lighting shape the feeling of space and alter the sensory and perceptual (including emotional) pathways on which meaning relies (Thrift 2009). A similar technique of 'brightening up' the life of host communities in slum tourism is shared by activist and business groups in the case of *City of God* (directors Fernando Meirelles and Katja Lund 2003 – *CoG*) in Rocinha, Rio de Janeiro. Much like *SM*, *CoG* introduced a tourist influx into the filmed slum communities. UK NGO Tourism Concern put the number of tourists visiting Rocinha at 'around 40,000 visitors per year, making it the fourth most visited "attraction" in Rio' (Cheded 17 January 2018). Nevertheless, we may compare and contrast Rio on Watch, another NGO's discussion of *favela* interpellations in tourism, with Bravietour's, one of the many tour operators and destination management companies based in Rio de Janeiro, which capitalise on Rocinha's cinematic glamorisation, to revise polemic argumentation. Where the latter advertises 'social project tours' into the shantytown's filmed locations to assist different local groups 'gain back their dignity' (Bravietour 2018), the former uses multiple interviews with international tourists to stress how visiting filmed *favelas* helps dispel negative stereotyping and reinstate the image of solidary ordinariness in them (van Rompu 6 May 2017). There will be more extensive analysis of slum activism in the following chapter. Here I want to focus on this unacknowledged structural affinity between business and activist design, which is supposed to be sorted at the level of function and intention (resistance to interpellation and social exclusion for activism versus profit-making for business), only it is not.

A dip into their shared atmospheric aesthetics is instructive: there is no doubt that, as ethnographies of relevant onsite tours suggest (Freire Medeiros 2011), *favela* tourism hinges upon the dark realist aesthetics employed in slum movies so as to invert them. Cinematic aesthetics amplify in visitors' affective perceptions of the vertiginous chaos of such places, 'not as exemplars of the purposeful accelerated turmoil of the great rushing modern metropolis, but as a confusing *bricolage* of the uncivilized and unregulated materiality of whatever was to hand' (Jaguaribe and Hetherington 2004: 156). However, online itineraries of the slum and You Tube recordings of tourist pilgrimages in Rocinha readjust such architectonic designs of slumming, especially with regards to 'predisposed routines, emotions and movements' (Adey 2008: 444). Generally, through physical and virtual travels, the unknown crime-ridden *favela* encloses both controlled risk and a deep sense of adventure, 'the opportunity of acting as a concerned citizen (by supposedly contributing to the economic development of a poor area) and … a beautiful view of the city captured from above' (Freire Medeiros 2011: 22). However, the technical inversion of this horrific sublime, which, like *SM's* tourism, recovers pastoral rurality in the city, eliminates the darkness of crime. All tourists are left with is a community (or communities) trying to make ends meet in a harsh, neoliberal jungle.

In turn, this calls for a softer version of edgework in the design of tourist mobilities that sociologies of deviance associate with gendered performances of emotional risk-taking. One may stress that the scriptural emphasis on detective work in the enactment of tourist mobilities in the previous section is often associated with the accruement of masculine capital ('being brave' – for compatible comparisons between detective movie scripts and tourist mobilities see also Reijnders 2010a), whereas the volunteer tourist 'edge' of *favela* mobilities combines the minimisation of personal risk from crime with affective and emotional exposures of the needy private self to a community of peers ('being compassionate' – on gendered edgework, risk and volunteer work see Lois 2001, 2005; Campbell 2005; Laurendeau 2008). This is not highlighted so much to remind that edgework was made narrowly useful in conceptualisations of 'the unique experience of white, middle class, adult males' (Lyng 2005: 11), as to stress that the design of the *favela* experience introduces the role of emotion in the accruement of embodied skills we associate with moral responsibility (Newmahr 2011). In such lay (local tour labour), activist (national and international NGOs) and business designs, 'light' facilitates unauthorised fusions of thought, emotion and sensation, which manifest in further aural blends, between those who want to know (the tourist subject) and those to whom this desire is applied (the host object) (Griffero 2014: 77). Such epistemontologies are omnipresent in cultures of spirituality we find in religious pilgrimage (Evers Rosander 2004: 70; Nikolaisen 2004: 90–92). However, I endeavour to establish their presence also in more banal versions of spirituality connected to bodily wellness in film tourism mobilities.

Cluster 3

Although light is associated with personal enlightenment in ancient Asian religions, contemporary recreational cultures that view the body as an extension of the soul have turned it into an essential aspect of the cult of self-identity (Featherstone 1991; Giddens 1991; Schilling 2003). This has not erased its incorporation into imaginaries of environmental conservation and community ethics, nor has it eliminated its contribution to individual and collective cultures of ecoaesthetic responsibility. This is obvious in cinematic tourist designs both in urban and rural or marine contexts, where light is strongly connected to slow pilgrimage into filmed cultures. This slowness, which stands between Arendt's (1958) utopian *Homo Faber*, the slow and plodding human worker who moves social life, and a Confucian/Taoist scientific philosophy of *I Ching* that encapsulates the 'essence' of the celestial mind (Cleary 1986: 16–17), unveil the metaphysical properties of atmospheric illumination in tourism.

SM's mobilisation in travel itineraries in Mumbai by tour operators, who displace the movie story so that they develop for visitors a kinesfield informed by blends of Indian mysticism and Western mobilities, is instructive. By advertising a variety of pilgrimages to mobile situations vaguely alluded to in the film (e.g. Salim and Jamal as children engaging in bike races), local companies, such as Reality Tours, are in fact promoting native practices of *deshatan* or slow travel

(Singh 2009). However, this practice is extended to the employment of environmentally-friendly automobility or velomobility – that is, the profound sociocultural dimensions of riding a bicycle, such as those associated with tours to local amenities instead of cinematic phantasmagorias (Furness 2010; Aldred and Jungnickel 2012). Blends of technics are prominent in this business: thus, although Reality Tours invites visitors to select the option of 'Sightseeing by Car', reproducing Baudrillard's (1988) driver and Eco's (1987) consumers, who enjoy landscape through their windscreen, it also offers a 'Bicycle Tour' as an ecofriendly alternative for those who wish to enjoy 'the cool weather of the early morning', while watching 'some devotees performing puja … jog or do yoga before the heat of the day arrives' (Reality Tours, 'Bicycle Tour', undated).

Likewise, Viator (undated), a Trip Advisor Company, has been running bicycle tours in the city. Including Chhatrapati Shivaji Terminus (CST), India's busiest railway station and UNESCO World Heritage Site featuring in *SM*, the tour prompts visitors to 'explore this eclectic city at a leisurely pace' while riding the bike and on-foot, by fleeting visits to local markets, bazaars, and flower shops. Online comments by customers describe their *flânerie* enthusiastically for its intimacy and authenticity, which we tend to associate with non-representational engagement. Of course, cycling has figured as a potential resolution to the problems of the car system, which constricts the autonomy of mobility (Fincham 2006), and does not promote the production of a commons (Freudental-Pedersen 2015) or any naturally creative ways of 'performing the city' (Jones 2005). On the contrary, cycling contributes to the production of ecofriendly assemblages, which include humans and machines (Jensen 2014: 99–101). Such performances, which are also proposed in tourist websites hosting narratives connected to *SM*, construct 'shadow maps' of Mumbai, which are or can be performed by cyclists (Duncombe 1997: 59 in Furness 2014: 322; Jensen 2010).

Interestingly, their design hits the right ethnoreligious notes, because it epitomises especially Hindu values of non-violence towards animals and plants (Singh 2002). Note also how this peaceful ecoaesthetics, which connects to *punya* or the accumulation of material/religious merit (what we might perceive from a Western viewpoint as the promotion of atmospheric sustainability), is complemented with the provision of opportunities to acquire *moksha* (the kind of spiritual merit that liberates humans from the cycle of birth and death). This liberation, which can only be achieved with a holistic commitment to one's pilgrimage through yoga exercise (Singh 2012: 219), approximates some Western forms of privatised utopian achievement to train the body through spiritually-rich exercise. Such novel forms of healing are associated with wellness as an enterprise combining physical health with mental activity through meditation, 'all built around taking responsibility for ones [*sic*] health and embedded … in environmental sensitivity' (ibid.: 223). In these designs, hopeless and overbearing mobilities in the city (Williams [1973] 2016: 321), including those that pollute the environment and the human soul, are banished with the help of a purposeful embodied quality we find both in sports and the ascetic rituals of pilgrimage (Adler 1989, 1992, 2002).

There are also less openly spiritual kinaesthetic designs in cinematic tourism that support healing via similar experiential pathways. In some cases, guests' ignorance of local custom is bliss and amplifies satisfaction: thus, for example, the excessive projection of Greek island/folk dance styles in *Captain Corelli's Mandolin* (director John Madden 2001 – *CCM*), which was based on a concoction of actual traditional dance forms by the film's choreographer, found variable lay mimicries in taverns on Kefalonia for the entertainment of foreign visitors (Tzanelli 2007: 114–115). Though largely followed by scornful comments (in Greek) regarding the visitors' lack of proper knowledge on folk custom (a trend I examine in more detail in the following chapter in the Indian context), such lay 'staged authenticities' (MacCannell 1973) certainly contributed to ad hoc participation of guests/tavern customers in lay orchestrations of dance events with cinematic connections (Herzfeld 2001: 289). Such lay enactments of atmospheres of *kéfi* or mirth, which were built as simulations of a simulation (e.g. *CCM*'s heroes dancing non-existent Greek dances) hide from public (visitor) view how the male Greek body of the underpaid waiter communicates the affective atmospheres of the 'Greek body politic', which excels in grandstanding and the accumulation of prestige (Cowan 1990).

There have been more professional cultures of this type in cinematic tourist design, which transform the original notion of the kinesphere as an area existing at the dancing limbs' length (Laban [1966] 2011: 10) into the sphere in which tourist mobilities are performed (see Chapter 3). Advertising dance classes with reference to particular films, such as *Dirty Dancing II* (director Guy Ferland 2004 – *DDII*), which inspired several dance schools in the UK and elsewhere to offer Latin American lessons by reference to the cinematic heroine's romantic experience in Havana (Tzanelli 2007: 134–140), proffers an alternative route to affective atmospheres of passion or even what Malbon (1999) calls 'ecstasy'. The idea of studying exotic embodied capital so as to incorporate the other's embodied 'essence' is a quintessential component of atmospheric consumption, when sexual attributes and ethnic characteristics are deemed to cater for the same experience. Not only is embodied sensuality valuable as an oriental fantasy, it endows the Western tourist/apprentice's unlimited desire' with 'deep generative energies' (Said 1978: 188). The atmospheric formula works so well, that it finds several mutations in similar markets. Healing the body through purposeful movement in tourist settings is prominent, for example, in a new online map launched by VisitScotland, which details Scottish filming locations used by Bollywood films so that it boosts film tourism from India. Films such as Edinburgh-set *Mausam* (2011) and the Loch Ness-based thriller *Three: Love Lies Betrayal* (2009), feature in *The Bollywood Scotland Map* which was sponsored by Qatar Airways (The Location Guide 20 January 2015), with a view to connecting landscape representations to embodied non-representations or, simply put, the affective environments of films (the atmosphere of the thriller and the drama).

It is worth stressing that, much like the Western *salsero/salsera*'s propensity to abstract choreutic *ecstasis* at first, until (s)he masters the exotic body's 'essence' (and enter the secular stage of *punya*, so to speak), VisitScotland's constructivist aesthetics, which focuses on the picturesque of Scottish nature, clashes with Bollywood (kin-)aesthetics. Bollywood scripts consider the story's hero/heroine as an acculturated actor in a natural/cultural network, in which (s)he is expected to tell stories with his/her body. Based on the ancient northern Indian dance-form of *kathak*, which was subsequently mobilised in twentieth century Sanskrit drama and theatre, and thereafter in European Orientalist choreographies (Gassner 2002: 453), postmodern Bollywood performances are 'dance-events' in the Labanian sense. In dance-events limbs, complete with instrumental props, such as bells, orchestrate a musical narrative 'in harmony with the strokes of the accompanying percussion instruments' – so much so, that the body tells the story in deeply affective ways (Tzanelli 2015a: 98). There is an atmospheric disharmony in the Scottish enterprise, which desires to attract Indians to the country. Associating dance-sound more with the atmospheric intensity of cityscapes, which European *flâneurs*/pilgrims find incongruous with the serenity of landscape pilgrimage (Bell and Lyal 2002: 33), it sidelines soundscape ambience in favour of its 'paratexts' (e.g. environments or their graphic layouts, as in maps – Dufrenne 1953 [1973]: 32; Griffero 2014: 84–87). I elaborate on variations of paratext in the following chapter, where I examine 'epistemic misalignments', a difficulty hosts and guests encounter in sharing aesthetic context, because their experience of hospitality is structured differently (Germann Molz 2007: 67).

Ice and water

An interesting staging of Mediterranean atmospheres emerged through more contingent collaborations between lay tourist performances and professional design in the case of Skopelos, the fictional island of '*Kalokaíri*' in *Mamma Mia!* (director Phyllida Lloyd 2008 – *MM*). The cinematic plot's focus on a wedding, which was partly filmed in the remote chapel of Agios Ioannis, served as a 'dark spot', a site with unrecorded genealogy that can be manipulated, reinterpreted and remembered by different visitors (Rojek 1993: 147). Only thanks to *MM* it currently entertains global digital exposure in tourist circuits, including business networks catering for film fans (see for example Skopelos Net 2018). It is built on the top of a sea rock at a height of 100 metres and can be visited by boat from Skiathos via a 20-minute car drive from the town of Glossa down a winding road, then up some 200 steps carved into rock. Although there is no record of the chapel's construction, local history connects it to a resident's dream of a woman prompting him to go to the top of the rock with other residents and search for an icon. Hence, Agios Ioannis acquires tourist value as a 'nostalgic black spot' (following the digital tale of the moving icon), as a filmed site (following *MM's* narrative) or even as a sort of 'vertical pilgrimage'

Despite their transgressive role, the ephemeral communities of travel also assert the certainty of social structure: we always return to 'normalcy' and assume our place in everyday orders after our journeys (Graburn 1977). As geographers and sociologists of sexuality have noted, queer sexual experiences have become an integral part of the transitory spaces queer subjects tend to inhabit and in which they form solidarities (Knopp 2007: 23). Film artscapes (Appadurai 1990), imaginary formations of artistic creativity and marketing, sustain and are sustained by queerscapes in global tourist settings such as those of the Northern Sporades (on neighbouring Skiathos and art see Tzanelli 2011: Chapter 4). These technologically-mediated transformations may perform community-building along the lines of touristic 'neonomadism', loose and ephemeral community formations during travel (D'Andrea 2006; Delanty 2013). Agios Ioannis and its fictional small beach are framed in *MM* as such a queer synaesthetic experience – what with Streep and Brosnan's clumsy but endearing singing at its entrance, or Colin Firth's (one of Sophie's potential fathers) pronounced 'camp' persona in the same and other scenes. Indeed, Skopelos Travel (2018) advertises the chapel as a cinematic tourist marker (MacCannell 1989) in a synaesthetic fashion, noting that there 'was performed the most moving scene of the film, when Meryl's Streep character Donna sings the emotional ballad "The Winner Takes It All" to Pierce's Brosnan character Sam'. Homosexual tourist mobilities are expected to contribute to the wedding market on islands significantly over the next decade (Poon 2009). However, the marketing of *MM* wedding tourism is still affected by heteronormative expectations, as only heterosexual couples make it to online advertising (e.g. see Style Me Pretty Europe 2018; see also Bell and Valentine 1995; Hubbard 2008). Thus, *MM's* virtual presence recycles heteronormative expectations through omission, shaping touristified spaces, transient socialities and their affective atmospheres (Tzanelli 2017b). Such atmospheric conditioning betrays a symbolic acclimatisation of social performance to the spatiotemporal conditions of the Greek island environment, stressing how *MM's 'choromediated tourist space'* is palpable and dynamic (Schiller 2008: 432–433, emphasis mine).

Such choromediations develop in the border zones of contemporary urban civilisation, on islands already culturally touched by touristification, but only just. The changes are recorded in their atmospheric attunement to romantic urbanite desire for folk ways of being, which are materially registered in architecture. Again, the Greek *MM* example is instructive of the effects such preference for the traditional architectural style has in the actual built environment. Only a couple of years after the release of the film, Skopeliote property prices soared to £120,000 for 'traditional' townhouses and £200,000 for villas. Northern Sporadiotes pride themselves on their meticulous preservation of Pelion-style architecture that grants the region with a unique flair other islands have lost. However, global tourist networks' advertising magnified all signposts on the *MM* trail, prioritising popcultural pilgrimage over cultural tourism of this sort. Undoubtedly, there is an uneasy architectural coexistence of the traditional with the popcultural on the island, if we account for the fact that Brosnan's flip-flops were reportedly retrieved from his villa and nailed to the wall of a local travel agent for tourist inspection (Fryer 31 July 2009). The trend's actual significance can only be evaluated if we note that cultures of dwelling are in fact searches for the right atmosphere – an atmosphere guaranteeing protection and privacy to satisfy one's sociocultural needs. In other words, the atmospheric staging of second homes or tourist apartments on the island of *MM* was bound to encroach upon its domestic environments (Hall 1966: 133; Griffero 2014: 96; Herzfeld 1987) in ways tourist reporting detects but cannot fully address. Much like the family tourist gaze, which takes pleasure in creating domestic memory-stories resembling personalised postcards (Bærenholdt *et al.* 2004: 91), this domestic affect aspires to preserve architectural intimacy. However, such architectural encroachments are far from unusual in cinematic touristification – we will, for example, find them again in the population of Kefalonia with *CCM*-inspired 'Villa Pelagía' complexes in honour of the fictional Greek heroine of the film (Tzanelli 2007: 94).

Thus, we may say that the spaces that films turn into 'dramaturgical landscapes' for tourist play are managed by people or institutions acting as playwrights, directors and stage crew, so to speak (Edensor 2001; Hollinshead 2002; Tzanelli 2011). The presence of the aquatic element in these spaces especially activates affects of pleasure and playful activities we tend to associate with the beach, a socially defined zone appropriate for specific patterns of interaction, and the shore, a 'liminal time-out' zone in postindustrial imaginations (Shields 1991: 85). As the aforementioned examples prove, the clientele for cinematically-inspired second homes is informed by a fundamental dichotomy: they are either 'romantic gazers', favouring privacy and uniqueness, or 'mass' ones, favouring orgiastic indulgence in crowd activities (Urry 1990). Both gazes, which are in fact metaphors for different types of synaesthetic engagement with location, depend on blends of aquatic and cultural architectonics. Such atmospheric 'tincturing' through environmental and material constellations (sea and architectural structure – Böhme 1993: 121) was present in the tourist marketing of 'Serenity' or 'The Inn at Rodanthe', as the filmed house was named in the 2008 movie *Nights in Rodanthe* (director George C. Wolfe – *NiR*) based on Nicholas Sparks' popular novel. Today a beautiful oceanfront vacation rental located in the small Hatteras Island village of Rodanthe on the Outer Banks of North Carolina, the Inn was originally thought lost to the natural elements (coastal storms, hurricanes and erosion by ocean waves) because of its official neglect (Sun Reality undated). Its 2010 restoration (its new owners, Ben and Debra Huss, who described themselves as 'extreme fans' of the *NiR*, replicated the interior and exterior of the movie, even utilising original props from the movie set (Hooked on Houses undated)) and move from its original site by Expert House Movers, managed to recreate the same 'laid-back mobilities' we often associate with family-based holidaymaking (Bærenholdt *et al.* 2004: 126). This is a stark example of how a domospheric romance can be created from hyperreal scratch, a novel and a film. The area's serene atmosphere appeals to the pilgrim's search for intimacy, rather than straightforward group-performed popcultural tourism.

At the other end of this atmospheric arrangement stands democratised cinematic consumption, which turns unknown paradisiac beaches into international tourist destinations. *The Beach* (director Danny Boyle 2000) has had such an effect on the island of Phi Phi Leh, in the Krabi region of Thailand. The news of the movie's filming saw international Leonardo Di Caprio fans flocking into the area, thus turning it into a proxy of Phuket, which had been swamped by Western backpackers aspiring to 'live like the locals' long before these developments (Westerhausen 2002: 6). Such young and hippy-like travellers, who are identified as Thailand's subcultural enclaves (ibid.: 24, 57), are a far cry from the more affluent, often middle-class tourist clientele of *Rodanthe*. Back in 1999 and during filming, they were identified with *The Beach's* production company and crew as the source of environmental and ethnonational pollution and degradation by activist groups in a familiar cultural imperialist style (Tzanelli 2007: 47–56). Despite protests against unregulated popcultural waves of touristification, the island moved on to become an international film fan destination, especially for those enjoying the idea of consuming pristine blue waters and the near-Edenic serenity of Thai nature. During such adventurous journeys, the oneiric quality of cinematic, televisual, photographic and artistic representations or paintings of such Orientalist *topoi* (Edensor 2012: 1107) is replaced with direct somatosensory encounters with a world of blue and green, which can only be 'the real thing' (Thibaud 2011: 211).

However, on this occasion, the 'technical shaping of materiality' (Böhme 2010: 29) went too far, and in 2018 Maya Bay, the famous beach of the movie on Koh Phi Leh, was closed to tourists in an attempt by authorities 'to reverse decades of damage done to the region's marine environment' (Coldwell 14 February 2018). With about 5,000 visitors a day, most of whom travel by boat from Phuket or Koh Phi, thus contributing to fuel pollution, as well as constant littering by insensitive visitors, Maya Bay and the whole area's coral reef population has dwindled to the point of extinction. There will be more discussion on Krabi's cinematic overtourism in Chapter 5. Here it is more appropriate to note that lack of regulation over the hybrid complexes facilitating mobility to and from the island may erase, rather than enhance its atmospheric environs (Thibaud 2011: 210). Despite online tourist business' 'constructive orchestration of tonality' for the two cinematically famous islands (Thrift 2008: 92), the erosion of actual local textures and sensory experiences travellers tend to associate with aquatic-island utopias (Sheller 2004) is slowly becoming a certainty.

We saw how detective dramas amplify the feeling of atmospheric darkness. But here I am not interested in the hexagram of light as such, only its illumination of ice, as both a somatosensory experience we associate with cold climates and landscapes of the North and an allegory of emotional alienation. The case of *Frozen* (directors Chris Buck and Jennifer Lee 2013), the Disney 3D-animated fairytale inspired by Hans Christian Andersen's *Snow Queen*, is an interesting example of how local atmospheres are manufactured synaesthetically. The world of *Frozen* is populated with princesses, trolls, snow, sky-high mountains, magic tricks, and picturesque views that its makers found in Norway. Norwegian natural landscapes, architecture, and fauna were deemed perfect inspirations for a movie discussing the relationship between two sisters, their falling out, and reunification. Natural, affective, and architectural architectonics were thus blended in its making: the plot takes place in the fictitious town of Arendelle, an allegedly typical Norwegian town. In fact, it was speculated that Arendelle, 'with all those fishermen, storekeepers, wooden buildings and fussy harbor, seems to be Bergen in the world of animated films', whereas the design of its castle 'looked like that of medieval stave churches in the country' (Tamara June 2017). At the same time, it was noted that the name of the mythical town, is architecturally and linguistically associated with Oslo (the Norwegian town of Arendal is located in the county of Aust-Agder, to the southwest of the Norwegian capital, Oslo (The Disney Wiki 2018)).

The film's creators were inspired by Norwegian and Sami cultures: trolls, Viking ships, a hot spring, Fjord horses, clothes preserved in Oslo's Norsk Folkemuseum and traditional food, such as lutefisk (Lee 23 September 2013). Other inspirations included Fetsund Lenser, the 200-year-old timber processing plant-turned-museum along the Glomma River, in which small black wooden structures were used as spaces to store ice before electricity and as wood warehouses; the snowy peaks and valleys of the town Røros, which turned into the beautiful white landscapes of *Frozen*; the arctic archipelago of Svalbard, and Northern Norway, where one can see the Aurora Borealis (Condé Nast Traveller 2018). In this respect, cinematic tourist design drew on architectonic conceptions of a particular 'Nordic Lighting' (Sørensen and Haug 2012) – a term conveying the natural light in Scandinavian countries, which guides actual lighting practices. The term is constitutive of a movement of 'claiming authenticity' across Scandinavian countries, which brought together intangible (atmospheres) and tangible/material forms of heritage (e.g. 'Nordic cuisine'), practices and policies (e.g. 'Nordic design' or 'welfare model') (Bille 2013). Especially on the back of cinematic tourist successes such as that of *Brave* (directors Mark Andrews and Brenda Chapman 2012) in Scotland, which I examine later, the Norwegian tourist industry prepared to surf on the market effects provided by the movie (ThorNews 5 December 2013).

Indeed, tourism picked up specifically in the remote Lofoten Islands of the Arctic Circle, known for their pretty fishing villages, snow-capped peaks, and traditional homely architecture (Kitching 10 August 2016). The icy atmospheres of *The Snowman's* Bergen melted in the intimacy of these beautiful lifeworlds: much like the children's fascination with the ephemerality of snowflake structures, which also inspired the film, the cosiness of such snowy village structures illuminated Swedish cultural intimacy (e.g. Herzfeld 2005). Notably, such appeals to tradition can draw on both neighbouring national heritage tropes and generic tropes of Nordic design: thus, tourist providers such as Condé Nast

Traveller (2018) use on their website blends of shadows, darkness and light to showcase Norwegian landmarks that inspired *Frozen*, and so does The Fairy Tale Traveler (Sandvik 24 July 2014), which uses photographs of misty and mysterious landscapes. Again, light and water commingle in the design of a 'unique' Norwegian aesthetics. However, one may note that the same dimness of light is important in Danish home designs, which promote *hygge* or cosiness, a feeling of informality and relaxation allegedly guiding Danish social behaviour and structure (Linnett 2011). Dimed lighting signifies *hyggelys* or cosy-light (Bille 2013: 5) – something communicated with candles that can allow one to slow down and relax. The ecstatic role of lighting technologies shapes perceptions of the visited environment, activating pilgrimage (Böhme 1995: 155). Running against brightness as the marker of a clinically clean home, shadowy flickering, the warm glow from the subdued light and the accompanying smell of flame from a fireplace orchestrate intimacy (Bille 2013: 8). The same atmospheric narrative is registered in the advertising of locations that inspired the TV show *Vikings* (director Michael Hirst 2013–ongoing). Tourist providers promote visits to Lofotr Museum in the Lofoten Islands because of the show, which used the design of the only surviving chieftain long house in Borg, Lofoten, as Ragnar Lothbrok's home (Thompson 18 February 2016).

In the case of *Frozen* this atmospheric trope of intimacy is reengineered in collaborations between Visit Norway and Disney: in a relevant exhibition at Disney World in Florida, the film's stage was moved to Epcot's Norway Pavilion, where a scaled-down replica of the Gol Stave Church area that inspired the film was constructed. The *Frozen* attractions formed an extension of the same area, and were set to resemble a traditional, Norwegian village (Visit Norway 2018). Backed by Disney Imagineering, the recreation turned heritage forms we associate with dark tourism into a family entertainment project, in line with an integrated 'Nordic design' movement, in which wellbeing and cinematic entertainment become integrated into national heritage. However, at the same time, its practice of displaying 'exotic nativeness' (Nochlin 1991) formed continuations with colonial histories of the theme park industry (Clavé 2007; Whatt 2010) that generally inform the post-tourist gaze of McDisneyisation (Ritzer and Liska 1997: 97–99). The transposition of Norwegian village atmospheres to an American phantasmagoric city is a significant moment for Norwegian film tourism, which, much like art exhibitions (see Lai 2004), enables ethnic heritage to travel the world.

Land and earth

It is as difficult to associate the picturesque with the atmospheric as it is to identify a sentimental-synaesthetic 'halo' in pictorial art, which incorporates aural signs (music or sounds) orientated towards the cinematic pilgrim's 'felt-body' (Griffero 2014: 83): how can we stabilise links between sound and emotions? Here the notion of cinematic schematisation comes to the rescue of atmospheric design of tourist destinations, when these are mediated on the internet. Digital mediations of cinematic tourism mobilise the ways cinematic art allows us to apprehend locations from a privileged angle – that is, understand *how atmospheres should be treated by the pilgrim.* Therefore, websites mediating filmed locations do not 'expose' atmospheres (these are already embedded in the original cinematic work of art), but, while communicating and expressing nothing, allow us to learn about the experiences we can have (ibid.: 84). All the same, it is easy for postindustrial design to overlay place-memories with photographic snapshots, forgetting their affective histories, and even easier to mobilise such affective repositories to yield profit. This practice, which guides the design of 'guilty landscapes', to recall Reijnders (2010b) once more, proves highly effective in filmed locations that once hosted war, genocide and civil conflict. It is worth presenting a few examples from each of these categories' contribution to atmospheric production. The hexagramic signification of these categories connects to notions of national land, 'earth' that is transformed into a tourist landscape (Urry 2006; Williams [1973] 2016), when it is devoid of its poignant history.

The case of *CCM* is an immediately available example of this process, because the film and the novel from which it was adapted (Louis de Bernières' *Captain Corelli's Mandolin* (1997)) delved into the Second World War's forgotten pasts. Set in 1944, the script narrates against the foreground of a love story between an Italian soldier and a Kefalonian woman, the massacre of a whole Italian Division camped on the beautiful island of Kefalonia, Greece, by the Germans. The broader historical background is that of Greece's Axis Occupation, the blossoming of Greek resistance, and civil strife between the Greek communist fighters of EAM/ELAS (National Liberation Front/Greek People's Liberation Army) and anti-communist forces. The spread of Germanophobia after the end of the war to the domains of popular culture (Huyssen 2000), including filmmaking, certainly contributed to what Huyssen (2003: 30–31) identified as the 'inflation of memory as a way to redemption' – a practice even the German nation sought to implement in its negotiation of the recent past (Tzanelli 2011: Chapter 2). Indeed, the whole idea of historical redemption was supposed to be achieved through eroticism and love as affective manifestations of a counterworld the modern German nation yearned to enter (Huyssen 2003: 31–32). Not only did the politics of guilt, love, and redemption guide the film's plot, which lamented the destruction of Kefalonia's peaceful multicultural utopia (Italian occupiers coexisting with natives), it was injected into *CCM*-inspired heritage tourism. Today mostly performed as a disorganised form of pilgrimage by the victorious side (Britons), less so by Italians (see Tzanelli 2004), such dark tourism retains the hexagramic qualities of land/earth. One can retrieve several online British testimonials of visits to the monument erected for the *Acqui* division of Italian soldiers murdered by Germans (see, for example, Trip Advisor 'Memorial Acqui Division' 2018). Situated outside Argostoli, the capital of Kefalonia, the monument connects to *CCM's* scriptural basis. The testimonials themselves produce a unique design of this dark spot, generating orientations, kinetic suggestions, and markings we associate with affective atmospheres. The recurring suggestion in them that encounters with the cold monument induce feelings of sadness point to the 'metaphorical sonority' of its structure (Griffero 2014: 95): the depth and exuberance of its architectonics. If anything, sadness is an emotion that emanates from a long affective process, which can include guilt and love for the loss of a perfect counterworld we associate with 'artificial vacation worlds, such as theme parks ... often modelled directly after film subjects, with a "narrative" orientation' (Hennig 2002: 173).

The 'theme park' effect is paramount for the maintenance of atmospheric affect as well as its imagological attunement to tourist consumption. An example of such manipulation of memory embedded in land is the case of *District 9* (director Neill Blomkamp 2009 – *D9*), a science fiction satire of apartheid's corruption and racism. Causing its own controversy in Johannesburg, where it was mostly filmed (see Chapter 5), the film is on its way to producing a fusion of slumming with cultural (heritage) tourism. Jaya Travel & Tours (2017) is an online provider of tours to filmed locations, which has already designed its *D9* tour to key filmed sites and sites associated with South African memory. These include inner areas of Johannesburg that were included in the film's aerial shots, the Apartheid Museum, which documents the history and horrible practices of apartheid through 22 individual exhibits, Constitution Hill, a Boer fort eventually turned into a prison for famous dissidents, such as Nelson Mandela, Soweto (South African Township), the city's mega-slum, where *D9* scenes were shot and Mandela's house-museum is located (Jaya Travel & Tours, 2017).

We may compare artistic intentionality and cinematic touristification, to ascertain the extent to which Blomkamp's distant shots match the digital tourist gaze's. *D9*'s city stands for the world 'at a glance' (Larsen 2001: 80), but where distant cosmopolitan spectatorship is also allowed to listen to inequalities and pervasive racism. Its cinematic slumming is intentionally based on apprehending Johannesburg's worldly space 'from above', when the filmmaker tries to objectify divisions as geometrical schemata (Sloterdijk 2009). The observer's slumming transforms *technik* or 'technicity' into a progressive hermeneutics (Massey 1993, 1994, 2005), because his/her distant camera eye sweeps the spectacular city at night, repositing darkness as corrupt development, whereas the shantytown's overwhelmingly daytime shots better *expose* the state of poverty (Tzanelli 2016b: 69). To some extent, the strategy of the tourist provider borrows from *D9's* architectonics of distance. It posits the popcultural/heritage tourist as a gazer, and also equips them with modernity's quintessential scientific technique of 'on-screen dollying' (Lundberg *et al.* 2017), a mechanical eye which allows them to inspect the filmed heritage sites from all possible angles and 'afar' (Szerzynski and Urry 2006). Where Blomkamp dulls images, the tourist entrepreneur brightens them up, just so they bring land/heritage into sharp focus. Much like the urban planner and the surgeon, popcultural tourists are empowered with the option of dissecting, disinfecting and beautifying sites of suffering and 'heritage that hurts' (Uzzell and Ballantyne 1998; Sather-Wagstaff 2011) so that they welcome global clientele. Where art's intentionality is rendered theatrically obvious in a Brechtian fashion, its appropriation by online business endorses a more open hermeneutics (Moscardo and Ballantyne 2008), which potentially dissociates tourist performances of museum visitation, sightseeing and slumming from atmospheric darkness. The choice is displaced on to the 'onlooker', who may feel abhorred, guilty or simply amused by the 'exhibits'.

However, it would be incorrect to associate the theme park effect exclusively with tourist providers or the cybersphere. Manipulations of memory and transformations of land into landscape can also be the effect of collective performances in locations associated with filmmaking. Whether we choose to term 'staged' (MacCannell 1973, 1989), or in the case of cinematic simulation, 'simulated authenticities' (see Herzfeld 2005: 6–8 on 'simulacra of sociality'), or specifically in postcolonial contexts 'mimicry' (Bhabha 1994; Hollinshead 1998), such performances result in a bottom-up form of self-advertising, which contributes to the creation of new tourist markets. The practice could be critiqued as an offshoot of neoliberalism, but I reserve this for the chapter's conclusion. Focusing specifically on hexagramic productions of atmosphere conducive to landscape pilgrimage, we can turn attention to the unique case of *Avatar* (director James Cameron 2009). The film, which was based on CGI, featured an elegiac farewell to colonised lands and cultures in a science fiction allegory. However, the film's picture designers sought inspiration for the fictional landscapes of these lands ('Pandora'), which is supposed to be on another planet humans set out to conquer and exploit, on earthly paradises. Specifically, they identified an appropriate design for the film's simulated 'Hallelujah' or 'Floating Mountains' (an important marker in 'Pandora's' fictional environment) in the natural structure of the 16 Southern Sky mountains in Zhangjiajie, China.

The selection of this location complements the environmentalist subtext of the movie: the destruction of alien ecosystems by militarised humans – a neocolonial allegory of thanatourism or dark tourism. China is notorious for its 'floating populations', as migrant labourers from other countries and the countryside into cities are known (Luo *et al.* 2017). The fact that such non-citizens are forced to live in deprivation and abuse, transforms *Avatar's* story into an allegory of environmental racism (Tzanelli 2016b: 29; Blanton 2011). Indeed, the film's pictorial design, which borrows amply from the European traditions of painting, and an elegiac music, which borrows from non-European indigenous traditions (Tzanelli 2015b), produce a synaesthetic atmosphere of loss and mourning of utopian harmony between human beings regardless of ethnic origins and nature. As Degen *et al.* (2010: 5) have noted on CGIs, 'they are far from "disembodied texts" … instead, they are laboriously materialised in order to depict … specific embodied regimes and affective sensory experiences to appeal to … consumers'. Despite their iconic origins, *Avatar*'s CGI formations of an alien lifeworld produce a universalism that assumes 'a singular western sensibility'.

Most cinematic tourism commences with the encapsulation of the natural and sociocultural dimensions of landscapes around the world – an act tapping into questions of national and international definitions of tangible and intangible heritage (Hudson and Ritchie 2006). *Avatar* publicised an array of issues regarding the ways new media routes reinvent cultural roots through simulated signposting (MacCannell 1989; Clifford 1997). Such *onomatopoeia*, or poetics (making) of naming and claiming (Barthes 1993), hybridises forms originating in Enlightenment divides between culture and technology (Wiggershaus 1994: 202–203; Tribe 2007: 10). *Avatar's* Hallelujah namemaking and tourist ontogenesis have effectively been hooked on to a real visual topography in provincial mountainous China, in Hunan Province: the renaming of Southern Sky Column in Zhangjiajie as 'Hallelujah' after the 'Floating' Pandora Mountains is an example of global image mobility that partakes in tourism growth (Anders 14 January 2010). Zhangjiajie National Forest Park is China's first national forest park (est. 1982) and part of the Wulingyuan Scenic Area, which in 1992 was officially recognised as a UNESCO World Heritage Site on the basis of criterion vii. This criterion includes 'superlative natural phenomena or areas of exceptional natural beauty and aesthetic importance' (UNESCO List undated). The aesthetic significance of this spot was pivotal in the construction of *Avatar's* own artscape but also its reappropriation in China. After achieving World Heritage status, in 2001 the location was approved by the Ministry of Land and Resources as Zhangjiajie Sandstone Peak 1 Forest National Geopark (3,600 km^2–1,400 square miles). In 2004, Zhangjiajie Geopark 2 was listed as a UNESCO Global Geopark (English Zhangjiajie Tourism 24 December 2010). It seems that this landscape's aesthetic validation by a transnational organisation also strengthened its chances of achieving national recognition. But there are limits to what can be achieved via such foreign channels, which are purposely geared towards conservation of idyllic rural imagery as a form of global and national heritage. Protectionist discourses can also limit the inclusion of communities to other developmental pathways such as that of cinematic tourism (Croy and Buchmann 2009). This brews an almost unavoidable miscommunication between transnational organisations (UNESCO) with national strands, and national centres with their peripheries during policy-making processes that lead to the consolidation of one decision over plural needs. The Zhangjiajie region had to learn to speak a global 'idiom' so as to enhance its status as a tourist destination, and had to do this fast.

The 3,544 ft Southern Sky Column allegedly figured as the main inspiration for *Avatar's* magical 'floating peaks' after a Hollywood photographer's visit and photographing tour in 2008, prompting a national park spokesman to explain that 'many pictures become prototypes for various elements in the "Avatar" movie, including the 'Hallelujah Mountains' (Mail Foreign Service 27 January 2010). This comment could be in response to feared cinematic tourist influx in a conservation area. In any case, its wide reproduction in Chinese-backed press suggests that it was important. Western media also presented Cameron and *Avatar's* production designers claiming that the inspiration was drawn from similar mountainous formations from around the world, including those in the Hunan Province. Cameron claimed that about 60% of the film consists of CGI elements, with the remaining 40% involving traditional miniatures and live action (Thompson 9 January 2007). Actual inspiration for the film aside, the Zhangjiajie landmark generated a debate specific to tourism development, with Cameron's visit to Beijing in 2009 used as proof of global recognition by the Chinese centre. Journalistic sources suggested that during his visit to Beijing, Cameron recalled sending his crew to the beautiful site in 2008 to select scenery and take pictures: 'All we had to do was simply recreate Huangshan Mountain 12 [Southern Sky column] in outer space' (Renjie 24 December 2009).

Notably, Cameron's praise during his visit in Beijing for one of China's foremost metropolitan artists, director Yimou Zhang (*Hero* 2002; *House of Flying Daggers* 2004) already suggests *Avatar's* iconic link to metropolitan manipulations of Chinese art. Zhang made recourse repeatedly to the great Chinese traditions of theatre, painting and poetry in his movie-making and became globally renowned for his ability to combine moving image with techniques of 'making still life' on the big screen (Tzanelli 2013: 134). The pillar-like formations of Zhangjiajie that are seen throughout the Zhangjiajie Geopark are a distinct hallmark of Chinese landscape, and can be found in many ancient Chinese paintings, so their re-mobilisation in new Chinese heritage discourse after *Avatar's* global success is an expected consequence (on national implications of such image-formation see Hudson and Ritchie 2006). Such cinematic enterprise secures for national artworks a glamorous place in global artscapes. Yet, in such moments it is in fact the human groups largely understood as the original custodians of this artwork that have to re-claim a place in the global chronicles of heritage. Thereafter, either by strategy or by necessity a hybrid form of self-narration emerges to reinstate their lost original, authentic status in the eyes of foreign and national spectators. Tourist flows provide the minimum guarantee for such status renewal – but only if the 'claimants' exercise their creative agency.

The Tujia people of *Avatar's* photographed areas populate the Wuling range of western Hunan province and some parts of the south-eastern Hunan. The original connection of their language to the Chinese-Tibetan system has been mostly lost due to state practices of assimilation. Contra Western considerations of working-classness as 'dissonant heritage', Chinese communist rhetoric glorifies the country's postindustrial modernity, but in practice not its rural equivalents. In 10 January 2010 hundreds of Zhangjiajie locals launched in ethnic Tujia costumes an official ceremony to rename the mountains of the region after *Avatar's* 'Hallelujah Mountains' (Agarwal 26 January 2010). This marks an agential shift from the production of a movie's simulated authentic stage to 'staged authenticity' rituals informed by set ethno-national traditions quite independently from the actions of *Avatar's* makers (MacCannell 1989: Chapter 1; Tzanelli 2007: Chapter 3). The dramaturgical event accounted for a 'polytopia of views' (Ziakas 2016), with the potential to eventually integrate different or even antithetical perspectives on the atmospheric origins of the same product (a film).

However, the event's local nature should not confuse us about its adapting rationale: its propensity to 'globalise' local nature matched perfectly that adopted by the Japan Tourism Agency and Japan's Ministry of Economy, Trade and Industry following the success of *Lucky Star* (directors Yutaka Yamamoto and Yasuhiro Takemoto 2007 – *LS*), a TV series based on the four-frame manga series by Yoshimizu Kagami that made the town of Washimiya a tourist destination. Coordination between them and the local Commerce and Industry Association of Washimiya, ensured that anime pilgrims to the filmed locales and the town's filmed Washinomiya Temple contributed to local development, by attending organised *LS* events and consuming relevant designed souvenirs connected to Japanese cultural practices (Yamamura 2015). Therefore, despite film's scriptural 'lightness' (a focus on the everyday lives of four girls), the event's poly-topic nature brought together fan, local and national concerns over cinematic touristification. Significantly, *LS*-informed contents tourism enmeshed notions of land as national property, given that the series parked a debate on copyright regulation of anime/manga artwork (ibid.: 70–72, 74). In addition, the on-foot anime pilgrimages to the town's filmed sites were calibrated to fit Japanese practices of *mikoshi* (a local traditional festival involving the temple's portable Shinto Shrine) decorated with anime characters – an innovation that gained international attention in the 2010 Japan Day Expo in Shanghai (ibid.: 68–69).

A similar initiative that marked the prelude of Beijing 2008 Olympic Games was staged in Guilin by Olympics director Yimou Zhang, who used performers dressed in ethnic costumes for the Opening Ceremony. There is a hidden link to *Avatar's* appropriation by ethnic minority tourism agents there: even today, the Tujia colourful costumes and peoples figure on international travel websites connected to Beijing 2008 as beautiful, if actually marginalised, Chinese specimens (see Beijing International Travel Website undated). Zhangjiajie's performative reproduction of this artistic metropolitan initiative makes sense as a form of social poetics that ensures the global trade in ethnic fixities, where mobility is deemed to be 'better' organised by the national centre (Herzfeld 2005). Filtering Zhang's ethnic narratives through Western simulated tales of natural wilderness granted the act with some extra authenticity. It can be debated who actually made the decisions for this global performance: in Hunan the municipal government was prompted to adopt the slogan 'Pandora is far but Zhangjiajie is near' to induce tourism in the region (BBC 26 January 2010). The invitation was deliberately designed to connect the Southern Sky Column to *Avatar* imagery for a global tourist audience, and to Cameron's recognition of Zhang's cinematic iconography for domestic tourists (on destination image management see Iwashita 2006; Croy 2010: 23). Li Ping, an official with the Zhangjiajie branch of the China International Travel Service made sure that global reporting included a note on the 25-minute *Avatar* shots in the region, thus amplifying the fabulist capital of the Chinese region.

Although the Zhangjiajie scenic spot in the newly baptised 'Hallelujah' area is a protected area in need of novel global advertising, ideoscapal and mediascapal clashes were almost inevitable in a capitalist node shared by so many different interest groups. A local rumour that developed into global gossip suggested that *Avatar's* later withdrawal from Chinese cinemas aimed to make way for domestic films such as *Confucius* (director Hu Mei 2010) that silenced state practices of forced land evictions in China. *Avatar's* civilisational allegory invoked these social dramas in the story's 'Na'vi people's' downfall to the altar of technological postmodernity, constructing links between Western and Eastern ideological circuits reminiscent of other cinematic successes. It is understandable why Zhangjiajie regional groups opted to ally with Western cinematic apparatuses: as practice and policy, this blended image-making was possible at this stage outside the national domain. The Zhangjiajie town is characterised by undeveloped land and river transportation, and its mountainous terrain makes cultivation difficult. Notably, it has been labelled 'the Land of the Savage Southern Minority' since the earliest recorded history, whereas additional derogative descriptors, such as those of the 'Wuling Rude People' and 'Tujia Rude People' remain indicative of discriminatory views held against the regional culture. *Avatar's* 'cool' design made possible a shift away from such derogative views, providing the metropolis with new incentives to support Zhangjiajie's global tourist profile. Given Zhangjiajie's UNESCO status, China's metropolitan priority has been to nominate the region as a natural heritage destination (Harrison 2005). *Avatar's* mobile technologies and nostalgic atmospheres complemented this with a different vision of heritage, based on audiovisual thanatourisms inspired by European memory and Hollywood cinema. Borrowing from UNESCO's aestheticisation of nature and *Avatar's* exoticisation of humanoid types, the Wuling/Tujia groups proceeded to stage their heritage in the fashion of a mega-event. In this 'event', some largely unknown variations of national character (an alternative, atmospheric conception of 'nature') claimed a place on the global tourist stage.

Seeing past environmental racism, notions of landscape as the technical extrapolation of land communicate with how we perceive the spatiotemporal aspects of our environment. This '*eco*phenomenological' approach, in which, in the European aesthetics of Immanuel Kant and Alexander Baumgarten, 'experience' is always, at least partly aesthetic, the human body and its sensory pathways act as *fulcra* (Chandler 2011: 555). It is obvious by now that, when we discuss the mediation of cinematic tourist experience by tourist business, we cannot exclude the internet, in which nature figures as a form of human otherness domesticated through perception and appreciation (Böhme 1992: 90). Our engagement with the natural landscapes that comprise national heritage on the web is a visually conditioned extension of the real landscapes 'out there'. Such '*ecstasies*' produce forms of thinking based on 'emotion as motion' (Thrift 2004: 60), which is connected to the character of the landscapes: their fables, legends and cinematic mediations. Cinematic tourist design often capitalises on such *animot* (human/non-human) ecstasies to induce or market tourism.

Let me explain through the development of tourism mobilities from *Brave*, a Pixar/Disney animated film about a young Scottish princess' coming of age. *Brave's* tourist worldmakers had to first calibrate an image of Scotland 'free from drug-abuse, midges and depressing B&Bs' (Carrell 2012) that global audiences knew from Danny Boyle's realist *Shallow Grave* (1995) and *Trainspotting* (1996), which featured Kelly MacDonald in her debut as a sexually active schoolgirl. The battle for impressions appeared to be imagological (rationally and logically connected to images) then, and attached to a utopianism, which harbours images of a 'national nature': an atmospheric variation. Especially for less powerful players in global politics, such enterprise wins only when it is harmonised with commonly endorsed ideas of civilisation and progress. Perhaps the most revealing statement in this context has been the Scottish National Party's (SNP) previous First Minister Alex Salmond's depiction of Scotland as 'a land of major opportunity', open for business and – above all – civilised. 'We have a long and impressive track record in life sciences, sciences, technology and creative industries developing an environment where ingenuity and innovation can create jobs and wealth for Scotland', he stressed (BBC – Scotland Business 2012).

Although renouncing the old Christian *conditio humana*, in which paradise is an ordered garden, Salmond's nationalist-socialist version of a modern Scottish paradise supports Pixar's myth of unspoilt nature and ennobled native habitus (Scottish voices, amply recruited in the making of *Brave*). But on the realist plane, the SNP's tourism policies have to openly refute this utopia as a counterworld to modern everyday existence and tourist consumption (Henning 2002: 183–184). Urry's (2004) observations on the death of places suggest in our case a carefully planned return to normative connections between the significant dead in Scottish society (heroes, places of legendary battles or ritual – *Brave's* narrative *modus vivendi*) and the living (professional labour-seekers in the context of Brexit and recession). Walter observes that dark tourism ought to be located in genealogical discourse,

> the kind of relationships that the living have at dark tourism sites … within the family of institutions in which the living relate to death and the dead; and … the function such sites may play for society as much as for individuals.
>
> (2009: 49)

Not only does this apply to the Scottish pilgrimages of *Brave*'s artists, it frames VisitScotland's and Adventures by Disney Tour's (one of the most powerful private *Brave* tourist operators) digital and terrestrial tourist initiatives. Although not strictly framed as a dark tourist project, *Brave*-driven nationalist-corporate enterprise is based on a moral economic contract (Sayer 2000; 2003) between globalised pilgrims to ancient Scottish sites and Scottish 'nature' – all the surviving shrines of pre-modern times that excessive industrial progress and ecological erosion now threaten to destroy.

Building on Thrift's (2004b) distinction between different modes of 'natural order' that constitute the background to human life, Urry (2007: 159) distinguishes three such backgrounds, including the natural world, the artificial world of the industrial revolution, and the virtual world of computer software and hardware. Although the third background allows for the articulation of the first world in these websites, the second is consigned to the pit of hell – for, industry is the enemy of bucolic landscapes and sounds on which *Brave*'s utopian Scotland is based. Especially where combined audiovisual technologies are involved in these articulations (Edensor 2005a), a tourist synaesthete, whose senses (*aesthesis*) are coordinated (*syn*) to perceive and understand the world, is interpellated with the help of various 'authorized' discourses (Urry and Larsen 2011: 19). These include education *à la* Grand Tour, group solidarity within the tourist group, pleasure and play, heritage and memory, as well as nation. The last discourse has been identified by theorists of national identity (McCrone *et al.* 1995) as pivotal in the advertising of Scotland as a brand, the more general role of establishing lineage as identity and the development of heritage-conservation tourism as part of a cultural nationalism programme via institutions such as the National Trust of Scotland. The discourse of 'nation' becomes enmeshed into those of tourist play and memory, which are nevertheless connected to a particular version of group solidarity of universal appeal: the family idea(-l).

Nowhere is this synergy between nation and tourist business firmer than in the case of music. Much like *CCM's* reinvention of native melody, *Brave's* musicscape (following Schafer's (1994) 'soundscape' here) crafts listening as an experience of perceptive dislocation 'able to give shape to a sensible space that marks the extension of our sensibility' (Griffero 2014: 84–85), thus also honing our affective attachments. However, music *is* land turned into landscape, if we consider its colouring by native tones, to borrow a synaesthetic pun as a metaphor. *Brave*'s music was composed by Patrick Doyle, who travelled to Scotland for research and inspiration, and is performed by the London Symphony Orchestra with Celtic instruments such as bagpipes, a solo fiddle, Celtic harps, flutes and the *bodhrán*, with an electronically treated dulcimer and cimbalom to give it a more contemporary feel. Doyle deliberately employed classic Scottish dance rhythms such as reels, jigs and strathspeys to 'not only serve the action but keep it authentic' (PRNewswire 2012). The composer's research even included trips to the Hebrides to listen to unaccompanied Gaelic psalm singing. He subsequently played recordings of the haunting sound to the film's producers. 'I want to make it accessible but to honour the Celtic traditions if I can', he said (Cornwell 2011). Although neither Adventures by Disney nor VisitScotland reproduce Doyle's artwork, they do have recourse to the ways particular instruments, 'tools', represent national forms (lands) and content (storytelling). Thus *Brave* heritage marketing is enabled through *technopoesis*, 'the totality of practices and processes of "self-making" available to a community and embodied in the artefacts, techniques and technologies available to a culture' (Hand and Sandywell 2002: 208) by various social groups for the promotion of disparate causes.

However, in the era of digital reproduction, *technopoesis* – a term signifying the human mastery of nature – can be both kinship-based and transnational in context (Tzanelli 2013a: Chapter 1).

Notably, VisitScotland's main Library webpage does not match text with music. Instead, we leave the first page (populated with the main *Brave* royal family characters) to enter a virtual stage (a curtain embellished with the royal coat of arms, a lion symbolising Scottish monarchy) with four directions (North, South, East, West). At this stage, we are in a globular world, rather than a kinesphere, where Scotland exists as geometric space. From these so-called 'magical areas', one is dedicated to 'landscapes' and leads (via a virtual image of Scottish landscape) to five important destinations (including castles, lochs and glens). Although not based on still photography but a video with haunting pipe music, the visual narrative blends distant shots of monuments with close-ups of Scottish nature (especially lake flora floating on deep blue waters that are illuminated by hints of sun). Now we enter a peculiar limbo, where we can at least apprehend the sphere of 'Scottish identity' and form an *eco*aesthetic impression of it, if only 'from afar'. Communicating the purity of Scottish landscape, the shots merely replicate location photographs that populate the Library's 'Itineraries' section. Scott's View, the Luss and the Road to the Isles via Fort William are narrated as images fixed in time – or better, *timeless lucid narratives* of place in green, sky blue, snow white and reddish-brown autumnal colours. This is the bright eternal Scot-*land*, the photographs suggest, which does not even need the cinematic sounds to shine.

But Scotland's *Brave* tourist clientele demands a blend of heritage purity with cinematic simulation. Thus, the US advert that figures on VisitScotland (2012b) under 'extras' alongside *Brave*'s trailer reiterates the place's 'beauty', 'magical feel' and 'braveness' (for, as Andrews explains, 'you had to be strong and brave to settle in this rugged place'). Prompting the global mobile synaesthete to visit the castles, coasts, flora and fauna that a godly cameraman encapsulates from above, voices from the film's artistic contingent (Mark Andrews, Kelly MacDonald, Kevin McKidd and executive producer Lasseter) suggest *Brave* as 'a love letter to Scotland' (by its migrant artists). The viewings of the video on YouTube (2012) reached 44,623 as of 17 May 2018, but the clip is connected to VisitScotland's site, and hence this sample does not represent its true global reach. The rooted epistemontological community's artwork is backed by a music, in which only Doyle's otherworldly flute survives, with no evident supporting digital instrument. Just like its inspiration from the long list of the advert's concluding credits of landscapes, and just like its human voices' natural connection to the land, the music is pure and sublime so as to induce the right normative emotions for global consumers of sublimation.

Unlike VisitScotland's sober musical gamut, Adventures by Disney's video on 'Scotland Vacations' combines images of a young white family running in fields and castle routes under a blended symphony of instruments. Closer to the spirit of Doyle's emotional articulation, it prompts the synaesthete to 'be in awe together, adventure together … from the rich history of Edinburgh to the rugged Highlands'. On the one hand, this reinstates the idea of mobile family networks, people travelling and enjoying together in tourist sites and sights, reproducing banal socialities and performances in new spaces (Haldrup and Larsen 2003). On the other, the clip's discourse on 'timeless [Scottish] traditions' – repeated in some *Brave* e-itineraries – is replaced with specific travels in time and space, which match Kirschenblatt-Gimblett's (1997) heritage time. Just like its associated video clip, Adventures by Disney's digital textual discourse is an exercise in advertising Scotland's sublime landscape, tailored nevertheless to the needs of family groups seeking 'safe' breath-taking adventures that enlarge the soul (Bendix 2002) and feed mobile subjects with a sense of (be-)longing for harmony. But images of Disney's generic family blend into particular human and natural 'landscapes' along the way, crafting a 'demediated mediation' (Strain 2003) of Scottish heritage. Regardless of the music's 'corruption' by technology (or not), the articulation of heritage as landscape is achieved in the nationalist-capitalist mindscapes of global cyberspheres. In these cyberspheres perception becomes the mode of bodily presence in given surroundings, allowing the synaesthete to relate to the world. This mode of engagement relates to physiognomy, atmosphere, and disposition or feeling. Instead of considering on-site phenomenological and digital mathematical space as unbridgeable, we can consider how they may intermingle in experience: 'one perceives objects as presented in space from the perspective of bodily presence' (Chandler 2011: 557).

Although both websites encourage a form of daydreaming or mind travelling as a prerequisite for the tourist's concrete movement through space (Löfgren 1999: 7), VisitScotland's itineraries certainly tie this imagined mobility to western artistic creations (Ingold 2010). *Brave*'s plot is an exercise in what Eliade (1989) identified as the power of myth to craft eternal entities that live outside time. Nevertheless, the film's conception as a fairytale *bricolage* could easily be connected to concrete locales by tourism specialists and national propagandists – albeit for different reasons. Merida's story folklorises a real struggle for (Scottish) independence that belongs to the nation's spiritual realm. At the same time, it synchronises this with a generic western 'civilising process' (Elias 1982), in which tourist and digital mobilities prevail. Unsurprisingly, *Brave*'s nationalist-capitalist node was legitimated with the help of a migrating narrative: a fairytale. Although, like the Grimm Brothers' and Andersen's fairy tales, the stories can be traced as far as South East Asia and the Middle East (Hemme 2005: 72; Tzanelli 2011: 94–95), today they are associated with nationalised and universalised ideal(-s) of modern European cultural unity.

VisitScotland's visual-virtual foregrounding of travel itineraries in the country with Merida's image is a nominalising practice: those who name Scotland a *Brave* mythical land can claim it, alongside its tourist revenues and the international recognition these create. All itineraries are advertised on VisitScotland's website in a nodal webpage but can be printed out individually like tourist brochures; most of them have Merida at the top left of the page with an appropriate caption. Divided into six sections (Clans and Cultures, Wildlife and Nature, Castles and Royalty, Myths and Legends, Landscapes and Forests and Ancient Scotland), all *Brave* itineraries seem to lead to the same end: this land's culture is a natural gift its epistemontological communities help Scotland to share with global visitors, families and modern pilgrims. Digital declarations that 'the spirit of the clan is still alive … across Scotland and thanks to Scottish immigrants' (VisitScotland, 'Clans and Culture' 2012b) reiterate an SNP 'third way' of pronouncing one's identity as a mobile rooted subject. This connects to global phenomena of individualisation (Giddens 1991), whereby the migrant can act as pilgrim to a 'homeland' they hardly know but can adopt through genealogical exploration and archiving processes. I return to this in the chapter's atmospheric discussion on 'fire'.

The connection of humans and lands into dead landscapes is also present in the section on 'Lands and Forests', which 'inspired writers, painters and filmmakers for generations' (VisitScotland 2012b). As is the case with other European counties, in Scotland the forest has been traditionalised through folk and high popular literature (the romantic *litterateur* Walter Scott's reference on the website is indicative), thus paving the way for the modern romantic gaze of tourist industries, which 'rely on symbols as information' (Hemme 2005: 77; Urry and Larsen 2011: 18). Mediating the Scottish forest through a contemporary animated tale helps the disembodied VisitScotland narrator to avoid the clichéd romanticism that turns forest journeys into 'family kitsch' (Hemme 2005: 80), adopting instead the idealised Adventures by Disney family that photographs their own tourist experiences (Larsen 2005). Presenting the forest as another version of the imposing fortress and castle structures that 'have the power to fire the imagination – and there's undoubtedly a little bit of each of these in Brave's Castle DunBroch' (see 'Castles and Royalty' in VisitScotland 2012b) constructs Scotland's 'mediated centre' (Couldry 2003b) for cinematic tourist visitors and heritage tourists. This 'centre' is rooted in Scotland's history but becomes mobile and centrifugal in individual tourist narratives of the visited sites (Cohen 1996: 93).

The thrill of communing with the dead of glorious national pasts in order to turn the clock back and forth as the heritage industry pleases, has a peculiar twist in *Brave*'s case. The movie is supposed to be a simulacrum, but it is based on longstanding artistic representations of the Scottish 'picturesque' (Seaton 1998). We cannot study its filmed sites directly, but, as is the case with the *LOTR* cinematic trilogy, we can infer photographic connections to real landscapes from what the movie industry wants us to know about its sites of inspiration (Croy 2011: 160; Tzanelli 2013; Beeton 2016). Professional photography is tightly connected to heritage reproduction: not only were field visits in search of the 'right' locales widely advertised by Scottish artists as a mystical return to family roots, they also allowed both Adventures by Disney and VisitScotland to cater for US and Canadian tourists at such diverse locales as Kingsmill Hotel in Inverness, Edinburgh's Balmoral Hotel and Cuilin Hills Hotel in Skye (McKenzie

9 September 2013). In this system of tourist services, two 'ancient' sites appear to act as nodal cinematic referents: Dunnottar Castle and the Calanais Stone Circle. Whereas the former is placed by VisitScotland's tourist suggestions under 'Myths and Legend', rather than 'Castles', the latter figures under 'Ancient Scotland' – a section prompting travellers to 'follow the trail' of 'these prehistoric stones', just like Merida's quest to 'change her fate' led her to 'a mysterious ring of stones'. Significantly, most photographs from 'Myths and Legends' (a section foregrounded by a Merida surrounded by her three siblings as cursed black bears) play with chiaroscuro techniques: they employ dark shades or colourless snow-white tones to communicate the country's haunting by (marketable) evil spirits that tourists can see and enjoy as spectacles. If Dunnottar figures, alongside Loch Ness and Rosslyn Chapel, as 'Scotland's most haunted Castle [and] spiritual home to many apparitions' ('Myths and Legends' in VisitScotland 2012b), Calanais' explicit connection to ancient religious rituals promises a unique thanatourist journey to the nation's prehistoric origins.

Unlike Adventures by Disney's holiday package (Itinerary: Day 6), where Dunnottar and the Callanish visit are placed amongst banal consumption practices such as a pub-style lunch on the Isle of Lewis, VisitScotland's narrative of antiquity is based on this type of 'hauntology' (the presence of versions of the past in narrations of the present (Derrida 1994)) on which cinematic scripts are based. Whereas Disney's phantasmagoric narrative of tourism is marketed as an eight-day family vacation, with some filmed highlights, VisitScotland's narrative also functions as a pilgrimage to the country's endless, but clearly delineated, past. The visual communication of paranormal landscapes via shading and tonality of professional photography is absent on Adventures by Disney Tours' front page, which figures a castle in earthly colours and young tourists running over a bridge. Dark tones and shading appear in a single grey photograph of the Callanish Stones. Such images communicate the idea that Scottish pasts might also have a dark depth that tourist industries can transform into an adventure. Even a visit to Loch Ness can turn into a banal canoeing adventure, as a relevant photograph of tourists battling the lake's dark and rough waters suggests. 'Mystery' is reduced to colour and camera techniques conventionally associated with the horror movie genre: this demonstrates (*monstrare*: to show, reveal) the horror of an unknown 'picture' of a situation, which is hidden from the spectator's lucid gaze (Wood 1986), but does so in the safe space of a cinematic (tourist) auditorium. The suggestion is that the cinematic tourist should not be afraid of the photographic dark and should just confront it as an alternative adventure encounter with wild Scottish environments.

Even then, one cannot bypass the fact that Adventures by Disney's Day 2 itinerary includes a visit to the National Museum to introduce the Chess(-men) of Lewis that Merida played with Elinor in the movie, followed by one to Dovecot Studios to discover the craft of tapestry-making to 'take home your very own bobbin as a souvenir' (Adventures by Disney Tours 2013). Heritage serves as the backstage of the stranger's experiential journey, but the knowledge that she/he enters sacred sites of embodied and naturalised tradition flags the presence of a moral contract with the host. Whereas within the nation the craft of tapestry may communicate social cohesion in the face of unprecedented global change, externally it is addressed to the ephemeral community of (Merida's cinematic) tourists as a souvenir, providing novel 'path[s] of integration between guest and guest, host and host, guest and host, or tourist and destination' (Hume 2013: 2–3). Securing a piece of tapestry from one's visited destination (one of Adventures by Disney tours offers) is one thing, but knowing via media advertising (of the 'Great Tapestry Project') that this piece of personal travel memory connects to Scotland's ancient traditions is another. The guest, the tourist family, takes back to their own home a magical piece of Scottish storytelling, which (as *Brave*'s plot suggests) connects a personal journey to the host nation's great journey through time: the ancient treasure that binds the (national) family, just as Merida's stitching of a torn tapestry cures her mother and the Kingdom's clan divisions. Both journeys appeal to Kirschenblatt-Gimblett's (1997) manipulation of heritage time in tourism, allowing the craft of tapestry to be ennobled as a national art that can be serialised and sold to visiting strangers (on 'serial vision' analysis see Jensen 2014: 68–70). By the same token, the visitor's immersion in Céilidh dancing and bagpipe music, or Day 7's private archery lessons, allow for synaesthetic performances that appeal to Scottish visions of the eternal nation-family, even when they functionally serve a different purpose (tourist consumption).

Thus, cinematic tourist design seems to adopt a blended method for creating atmospheres that Böhme (1993) discusses when he conceives of 'staged materiality' as appealing to the pure appearance of building materials. This particular trend of postindustrial production of atmospheres by design is ultimately blended into pregiven environments, which, in digitally choromediated spaces are taken to follow similar lines to those of designed environments. Distinguishing between human and natural design in the present context of the global ecological crisis is problematic, not only because 'environments can be anthropogenic without being objects of human design' (Chandler 2011: 560), but the notion of conservation has acquired a new partner in digital sustainability (Gretzel *et al.* 2015; Lamsfus *et al.* 2015). The elephant in the room is that the vast majority of cinematic tourist destinations in Scotland, and, as I proceed to show, Northern Ireland, are parts of the countryside. Therefore, the role of the internet in postindustrial design thrives on a performative contradiction: selling 'from afar' rescues the environmental sublime, but, at a later stage in the tourist cycle (Butler 2006) potentially contributes to environmental degradation and ultimately, tourism decline. For many cinematic tourism scholars this signals a turn from *eco*aesthetics to *eco*criticism – a turn prominent in some responses to such development, as I explain in Chapter 5.

Such inherent contradiction is embedded in *GoT* tourism to filmed locations in Northern Ireland. As mentioned in the section on 'light', the TV series' locations are scattered across different countries, but here I focus on Northern Ireland specifically. The source novels' (George R.R. Martin's popular fantasy novels, *A Song of Ice and Fire* (1996-ongoing)) fictional characters and the selection of actors and filmed sites were not random but constitutive of the literary plot's dark character as well as its association with blends of ethno-national habitus (e.g. a 'propensity to conflict and feud'). At the same time, this association did not turn the literary-come-cinematic narrative from a simulation to straightforward representation of 'real events'. It is better to consider *GoT* as an allegory from which regions in need of economic bolstering benefit. Frederic Jameson's original claim that 'all [third-world] cultural productions ... are necessarily allegorical, and in a very specific way: they are to be read as ... national allegories, even when ... their forms develop out of predominantly western machineries of representation' (Jameson 1986: 67) needs to be tailored to Martin's and the *GoT* screenwriters' (D. Benioff, D.B. Weiss, J.R.R. Martin) historical and fictional hybridisations. It is better if we consider allegory as an offshoot of new global complexities (Urry 2003), in that it disseminates ethnically rooted narratives outside their cradle, in global market networks. Such neoliberalisation processes should not be projected onto artistic creativity uncritically, but placed amongst successive hermeneutic chains by different agents and digital actants in a disorganised socio-economic map, where different mobilities are designed and staged (Lash and Urry 1987; Jensen 2013, 2014). In line with Lash and Urry (1994) we may argue that, in the case of Northern Ireland, a potential hermeneutic chaos was stabilised due to the global recession. I return to this below.

Martin's novels, which follow the violent dynastic struggles among the families of the Seven Kingdoms of Westeros to control the Iron Throne, certainly resemble conventional family friction. However, their inception from fusions of true events and characters from European history (Holland 24 March 2013) (including the English War of Roses (1455–1485), the adventures of Isabella of France's (1295–1358) family or the uses of the Byzantine 'Greek Fire' in anti-Islamic warfare) produced an artistic displacement of times – what Foucault (1986) called *heterotopia*. This temporal displacement is accompanied by a spatial one – a common practice in location-hunting for films with no real or accessible sites (Bolan 2010) that is endorsed by the deterritorialised Internet, where relevant cinematic holidays are sold. For the first season exterior scenes were shot at Sandy Brae in the Mourne Mountains (the 'Oriental' Vaes Dothrak), Castle Ward (Winterfell), Cairncastle (Lord Stark's execution site), Magheramorne quarry (Castle Black) and Shane's Castle (tourney grounds) (Josh 1 April 2012), all in Northern Ireland; Doune Castle near Stirling in Scotland (exterior Winterfell scenes) – already 'a place of pilgrimage for movie fans after it featured as Castle Anthrax in the 1975 film Monty Python and the Holy Grail' (BBC 23 October 2009); finally, Malta and Morocco (the southern scenes). The second season moved the southern setting from Malta to Croatia (Dubrovnik), whereas 'Frostfangs' and the 'Fist of First Men' were filmed in Iceland. The third season returned to Morocco to film the scenes of the city of Essaouira and Daenery's (the exotic Dothraki Queen) Essos stay (Phelan 29 April 2014).

The overt association of Northern Ireland with ancestral origins is matched in this place-assortment with sites standing symbolically or physically at the margins of European 'civilisation', as a, by now old, but still potent 'Orientalist' discourse would purport (Said 1978). Hence, *GoT*'s narrative node is based on a peculiar Oriental-European cultural fusion. Martin's and his cinematic companions' critical take is based on a discursive *bricolage* of realist approaches to violence – what with Morocco's crypto-Islamic identity, or Irish associations with a crippling civil war and terrorism in the British postcolonial context. Conflict is explicitly relocated in the exotic domain of mystical pasts, castles, rock formations, deserts, and nomadic people who happen to marry exiled princesses, determined to claim back their place in civilised parts of the world. The play on the cultural as 'structural hybridisation' based on imaginary civilisational borders and crossings (Nederveen Pieterse 1997) finds a synaesthetic extension in composer Djawadi's use of decidedly non-medieval renditions of songs from the series source novels by noted Indie bands. German-Iranian Djawadi claimed that he was inspired to write the main title music by an early version of the series' computer-animated title sequence, but the music's use in key moments of the main characters' lives certainly turned it into part of the series' central scenario of adventure, scheming, murder and horror (Savas 22 December 2012). Its contrapuntal theme can be likened to Said's contrapuntal epistemology (Chowdry 2007), which sets different worldviews side-by-side to highlight meeting points. Such artistic hermeneutics were complemented by the maintenance of regional, especially Northern and Southern English, accents in cinematic dialogue, to denote spatialised difference as a form of ethnic habitus (Tzanelli 2007).

The selection of Northern Ireland as a sort of heterotopic area in the form of landscape markers signifies the borderland of European civility. Cinematically or technologically the province encloses both Eastern and Western influences (music, accents, aristocratic nomadic characters) and produces a mobility vortex (e.g. Hannam *et al.* 2006; Sheller and Urry 2006; Tzanelli 2013), into which artistic technology sucks numerous histories about the actual filmed places. At the level of literary-cinematic narrative, Northern Ireland fits a centuries-old 'political bill', whereby first Celtic flows produced ancestral traces of Northern *British* heritage. Subsequently, these became enmeshed into regional anticolonial struggles that past medieval and early modern times would solidify as a religious-nationalist split between pro-British Protestants and anticolonial separatist Catholics. The infamous 'Troubles' that intensified the conflict between Unionists and Loyalists over the constitutional status of Northern Ireland lasted between the late 1960s and the 1998 'Good Friday Agreement', further sinking the island into blood and pushing Irish populations to (self-)exile (McKittrick *et al.* 2007).

Such coerced mobilities produced representations of Irishness globally – something of relevance for this study. Historical research has highlighted that, especially the colonial era and periods of transatlantic Irish migration, consolidated the image of the mobile Irish subject/vagabond as non-European, 'black' (Curtis 1971) – a nominalisation the Irish Protestant elites projected onto

Catholic populations to consolidate their superiority and participation in British postcolonial nation-building. Interestingly, this 'bill' is nicely matched in *GoT*'s instance by the selection of Balkan sites for filming, which were also implicated in genocidal processes of ethnogenesis, first with the collapse of the Ottoman Empire (in the early 1900s) and then with the demise of communist influence (in the 1990s). The ubiquitous use of 'Balkanisation' in global politics as byword for unresolved civil conflict is firmly connected to the region: the Balkans have been repeatedly discussed as indicative of Orientalist tendencies and alleged civilisational clashes with 'Europe proper' (Todorova 1997). The addition of Maltese locations does not deviate from this theme, as the island is geographically distant from well-known European cultural centres and politically connected to histories of British colonisation: its rugged landscape, medieval ruins, and Mediterranean climate make it picturesque in a dark and natural fashion.

Evidently, then, we deal with a highly complex case of events, which, while circulating in historical and mythical proveniences, change meaning and function (Hannam *et al.* 2016: 8). The extraordinary (*GoT*'s magic, political intrigue, and illicit love scenarios) is reconfigured into the everyday and back again into the political realm – for, globally Northern Irish sites are overdetermined by the island's dark histories. Perhaps currently *GoT* informs 'geographically specific formations of … narratives about mobility and mobile practices' (Cresswell 2010: 17) from a fictional stance. Yet, Ireland is the site of ethnonational memories; even mythical narratives of national formation survive primarily in realist contexts – for, 'it is always through [a] process of interpretation' that cultures 'are kept alive' (Bleicher 1980: 225). We should consider *GoT*'s fictional *lieux* as clever modifications of Northern Irish histories of conflict – an abstraction of real *milieux de mémoire* (Nora 1989) in the province. Northern Ireland may be unrecognisable from the outside as Ned Stark's ancestral home, but the popular knowledge that it mythically served as the site in which a 'fictional family' met its end is vital (a *lieu d'imagination* – Reijnders 2011). Its exchange with Croatian locations in the second season ('King's Landing might be the single most important location in the entire show, and it has to look right', explained Co-Executive Producer David Benioff (Josh, 1 April 2012) turns an assortment of locations from Europe's geographical margins into a single mythical site of disaster. By audiovisual means, the Northern Irish locations partake in *GoT*'s 'mediated centre' – the filmed places that the process of spectacularisation turn into a 'sacred' popular domain (Couldry 2003a, 2003b). The plot's sorcery background suggests that there is darkness in family feuds – a perfect accompaniment to the tourist staples that the Northern Irish Tourist Board wishes to offer to global cinematic tourist clientele.

As is the case with any sociological analysis, the analytical may subsume the normative discourse, but in line with my preliminary statement in Chapters 2 and 3, I prioritise the former: due to the global prevalence of e-tourist initiatives, Northern Ireland's *GoT* 'tourist governmobilities' work through technological and institutional forms of self-government, through objects and digitised relations (Bærenholdt 2013: 29; Urry 2007). Perhaps Northern Ireland has been globally earmarked as a dark site of terrorism and civil strife, but its new mythical acquisitions can help it claim back its stolen prestige in another 'meaning province', so to speak (Graml 2004: 149; Tzanelli 2013: 57). The 'nature' and 'character' of a place can be modified with the help of new technologies of governance/mobility, in other words. To this end, even the persistence of darkness as part of the filmed places' aesthetic branding and design was subjected to allegories of a bright paradisiac landscape, ready to be consumed by cinematic tourists, on-foot and in cyberspace.

Today the gap between digitisation of cinematic narratives, real filmed landscapes in *GoT* and the political discourse of Northern Ireland as an image-place are principally mastered in the cyberspace, where Irish *GoT* filmed locations are advertised by disparate stakeholders, regional-national and international. There, the series' musical background disappears and, save vision, all other human senses find little use. We need to bear in mind that landscapes have always been (re-)produced at the intersection of tourism with (visual and informational-communicational) technologies of mobility – a phenomenon more systematised in the current context of e-tourism or 'smart tourism' (Germann Molz 2012: 39). In any case, *GoT*'s dark family narrative node and the global financial profile of its cinematic networks, terminate, so to speak, in a Belfast studio and the province's e-tourist providers. This phenomenon is part of global mobility channels that connect locative media to international phantasmagoric communication centres, such as Hollywood and Los Angeles' city of bits (de Souza e Silva and Frith 2011; de Souza e Silva and Sheller 2014). The interpretative power of these locative apparatuses follows more powerful global governmobilities that promise regional regeneration (Wang 1999: 351).

What we receive visually in *GoT* tourist websites is a series of landscapes as naturalised signs, ready to be granted meaning by web designers, who are interested in generating profit more than preserving history. Again, Urry's discussion of 'places that die' (2004: 208) applies in this e-tourist context. This shift suggests that representations as such matter less than the ways they are produced, conserved or modified (Mitchell 1994). Controlled by national centres, such hermeneutics of place valorise culture in the technological spaces of late modernity, where imagined communities circulate ideas and customs for global consumption. But when we deal with both external advertising pressures (to enhance Northern Ireland's network capital) and international business collaborations, the death of place (the obliteration of its histories and cosmological moorings) can also give birth to (apropos Cosgrove 1998: 2) 'landscape ideas-as-ideals'. This does not merely denote a way of seeing-as-inhabiting material environments with the assistance of technologies of mobility but also encloses the utopian possibility to produce new memories of place as culture. Welcome to the field-worlds of our alleged postmodernity.

Lest we uncritically endorse neoliberal profiteering, it must be noted that the digital modifications of *GoT* actually filmed environments conform to the

Western European principles of the picturesque, according to which landscapes matter principally as forms. Yet, by returning to the original sources of the series' visual inspiration (i.e. the 'real landscapes' of individual *GoT* episodes), especially Northern Irish e-tourist providers also capitalise on the alleged 'essence' of these places. Amongst them, *GoT*'s Dragonstone (Downhill Beach, Londonderry), is discussed in Discover Northern Ireland.com (2014) as 'one of the most iconic locations … on the Causeway Coast … home to Mussenden – a tiny temple perched dramatically on a 120 ft cliff top, high above the Atlantic Ocean'. The spot is close to a conservation area and is also advertised as ideal for a 'family day out'. Connected to scenes of revenge and vendetta, Carrick-a-Rede, Larrybane and Antrim are also officially advertised for their 'special Scientific Interest: unique geology, flora and fauna'. This is especially significant for Carrick-a-Rede, which is located near Giant's Causeway, Antrim – a geological formation that resulted from a volcanic eruption 60 million years ago. The filmed site is discussed as 'focal point of a designated Area of Outstanding Natural Beauty [that] has attracted visitors for centuries' (Discover Northern Ireland.com 2014). It must be noted that a great part of the Giant's Causeway and Causeway Coast World Heritage Site is today owned and managed by the National Trust. However, the recognition of the Coast as World Heritage Site in 1986, as a national nature reserve in 1987 by the Department of the Environment for Northern Ireland, and as the fourth greatest natural wonder in the United Kingdom (Northern Ireland Tourist Board 18 August 2008), form a peculiar couple with the area's recent cinematic glamour. One wonders whose 'community heritage' is advertised – and to what ends.

Such unresolved questions are constitutive of *GoT*'s digital mobilities, which promote analogical classification of ideals: nature and landscaped 'physiognomies' (e.g. unusual geological formations) behave *like* natural human bonds we find in families. Their ecosystemic management conforms with and reproduces the biopolitics (Foucault 1997) of the nation-state (the management of its populations) while simultaneously turning this into the handmaiden of governmobilities (the global management of naturalised ethnic character). There is no mention of the Troubles online, only of the archaic legends of these sites, scientific information on geographical formations and even their management, in some cases, by proper scientific institutions (Giddens 2009; Urry 2011). The 'scientisation' of such Northern Irish landscapes transcends the imperatives of nationalism, as it responds to international-institutional calls. But such calls also enable the restoration of nature in the cybersphere's meaning province, were *GoT*'s cinematic reality matters less than its recuperation as a Northern Irish ecosystem. At the same time, such 'recuperation' assists with historical healing.

A narrative identical to Discover Northern Ireland's figures on Tourism Ireland's (2014) website, where it is stated that 'of course, aside from the fantasy landscapes, there's a good reason why Northern Ireland was picked by *GoT* location scouts. There are castles everywhere; incredible structures that catapult you right to the heart of the mythical land of Westeros', confirming the province's 'breath-taking natural beauty'. Much like natural habitats, the idea of mystical structures acts as an atmospheric fluctuation in a given place, arousing a faint shiver or overwhelming and paralysing the subject. This atmosphere 'clings' according to Otto (1936: 12), to old religious monuments and buildings, and penetrates the mind, until the soul resumes its 'profane' non-religious mood of everyday experience. Turning 'dark' land into 'bright' landscape is a difficult process, which requires local-national orchestrations with the flow of global markets. Note that Tourism Ireland was established under the framework of the Belfast Agreement of 'Good Friday' on April 1998, to increase tourism to Ireland as a whole. The institution has worked closely 'with its sister agencies on the island of Ireland, particularly in the development of this website, Fáilte Ireland, the national tourism development authority of the Republic of Ireland, and the Northern Ireland Tourist Board' (Tourism Ireland 2 April 2014). The harmonisation of the website's discourse on the *GoT* locations with that of Discover Northern Ireland is also in agreement with postcolonial and post-nationalist tourism policies. Agreement is achieved digitally by forgetting political disagreements in order to enable global tourist mobilities.

Therefore, it is more accurate to argue that the governmobile ethos of such websites is geared towards the mastery, packaging and international promotion of Northern Irish landscapes as the only part of 'Irish character', habitus and history worthy of salvation from oblivion. Although clearly implicated in Northern Irish political intrigues, this move is constitutive of post-industrial ecological movements that haunted Western modernity with the condemnation of humans to rootlessness and eternal mobility (Bauman 1996, 2000; Urry 2007; Cresswell 2010). The occulocentric techniques of these websites enable potential film tourists to accept death as a spectacle that stands outside their own experiences – to spectate the mask or image of the 'dead King' from afar, as distant cosmopolitans (Szerszynski and Urry 2006) with little affective engagement with local 'troubles'. This aesthetic emphasis on the distant picturesque corresponds to the American poet William Cullen Bryant's (1817) coining of 'thanatopsis' to denote contemplation about one's own death through the eyes of others, while entertaining relief for avoiding it, at least temporarily. Thus, instead of considering thanatopsis as part of the dark tourist's fascination with other people's death, we may view it as the mechanism with which new technologies use consumerist prerogatives to enable prospective clientele to enjoy the gift of life (Tzanelli 2016a).

The promise of this gift is actualised through visual representations of tourism in filmed sites – as is the case with independent Belfast company 'Game of Thrones Tours' (2014), which warns prospective cinematic tourists that 'in Ireland, Winter is never far away. Winter is always coming, almost every day'. The likeness of rugged Irish climate-landscape to Martin's mythical domains allows for the transformation of thanatourist simulation into embodied performance for those who are not 'faint-hearted' (ibid.) and not interested in history's troubled events. Needless to add that such independent websites, which link the technologised phantasmagoric city (of Belfast and Dublin) to the 'dark' countryside (Williams [1973] 2016) still work in harmony with nationalist interests that wish to obliterate unpalatable 'events'. Hence, a truly holistic scholarly appraisal of the movement from *eco*aesthetics to *eco*criticism cannot be limited to environmental problems: what is at stake is the habitual *and* biological nature of the world humans inhabit. Clashes between biospheres and biopolitics constitute one of the nodal spots of the problem.

The biopolitical recalibration of filmed locations as representative of different national characters is a common practice in competitive global financescapes, in which artistic creativity is subsumed by profitmaking (Lazzarato 2004, 2013). With *The Da Vinci Code* (director Ron Howard 2006 – *DVC*) as the earliest and most influential example, one can now account for a recurring phenomenon, in which the heterotopic scriptural basis of cinematic stories connects to the polytopic staging of cinematic tourism (Ziakas 2016). Aside from the *DVC*, which was filmed in such geopolitically dispersed locations as the Louvre, Saint-Sulpice and the Chartres Cathedral in Paris, Rennes le Château in Aude, the Last Supper and the Sforza Castle in Italy, Rosslyn Chapel in Edinburgh, the Temple Church, Westminster Abbey in London and Lincoln Cathedral (today all figuring as both heritage and cinematic tourist locations), *Vikings* and *GoT* produced spatially dispersed networks of capital, which streamlined ethnically fixed atmospheres into global channels of consumption.

The *Vikings* series mobilised histories and traditions, as well as natural environments from Iceland, Denmark and Ireland in their architectonic (for film photography) and scriptural (for history) design, prompting the corresponding countries and independent tourist operators to respond with cinematic tourist advertising. Conceptions of land were important in this enterprise: the journey of the cinematic character Hafna Flóki – Raven Flóki on the black sand beaches in Iceland (Vatnsfjörður fjord on the south coast of the Westfjords) in the fifth season, corresponded to the Icelandic The Book of Settlements (*Landnáma*), in which the Norwegian settler names the place 'land of ice': Ísland (Iceland Magazine 3 March 2017). The island had an economy mostly based on fishing the global recession put this under serious threat, so the arrival of cinematic tourism was welcome. Less than a year before *Vikings*, the influx of *GoT* fans, who wanted to visit filmed locations on the island, prompted changes in the ways tourism is managed in ecofriendly ways (Davies 30 May 2016). In Norway, the series prompted a broader form of image management also applicable to national tourism branding, with the establishment of Scandinavia's first government-funded training course on how to live like a Viking, one who does not rape, plunder, and display racist attitudes. Central to this initiative has been the country's Second World War experience and subsequent hosting of the Nobel Peace Prize (Higgins 17 September 2015). Danish heritage tourism has also experienced a boom due to the series: whereas the Viking Ship Museum of Roskilde has seen ticket sales soar, the Fyrkat Viking Centre has been visited by more American tourists than ever before, who try to verify Ragnar Lothbrok's historic existence (BBC News 18 May 2018). In all these cases we note that the darkness of distant pasts of plunder and invasion is subsumed by the architectonics of land, which is transformed into an educational tool for visitors (Cohen 2011).

Despite the dispersal of historical events across different European countries, with the exception of indoor shots in Ashford Studios, most of the series was filmed outdoors in the stunning Irish county of Wicklow, where the fictional Norwegian village of Kattegat came to life 'with just a touch of CGI' (McCarthy 18 February 2016). At the start of 2018, the filmed sites (Luggala Estate in the Wicklow Mountains, the Devil's Glen in Ashford, Newcastle, Silver Strand and Brittas Bay Beach, the Avoca Mines and the Blessington Lakes) featured as backdrops of an exhibition ('Vikings in Focus') at the Mermaid Arts Centre in Bray, to help fans and the film industry place the sites on the map (Miller 23 February 2018). Long before that, *Vikings* tour development had become a profitable business, with international companies such as Crystal Travel and Tour (2018) offering an '8 Day Viking Tour of Ireland Itinerary', including fan pilgrimages to the filmed sites, areas in which archaeological discoveries of Viking presence were established, the Viking Cork City and the west coastline (featuring the charming little fishing towns of Skibereen and Clonakilty, a Viking King's seat in the Rock of Cashel, a themed cruise to Athlone Castle and a Dublin visit). Its blend of urban-rural sites followed the example set by *GoT* Northern Ireland tours and film tourism itineraries more generally (Couldry 2003; Beeton 2016), which cater simultaneously for heritage tourists, ecotourists and media pilgrims. Significantly, the iteration of blended CGI-natural landscapes in the series and the tourist industries' advertising of them, confirms what Degen *et al.* (2010: 16) note in another (urban) case study: that digital technology has not only had a role in the development of morphogenetic architecture most famously espoused by Hadid or Gehry, it also allowed the production of 'life-like simulations of materials, light effects and temporal changes in representations of projected architectural environments'.

The examples help us reach the conclusion that the land/heritage the cinematic machine turns into landscape, may act as a transnational capitalist node, which is however reappropriated by individual regions or nations as unique 'network capital' (Larsen and Urry 2008; Tzanelli 2013). The filmed sites' atmospheric mobilities are enabled by such capitalist 'nodes' (Virilio 21 October 1984: 156), in which interconnections of policies (tourism industries) and practices (filmmaking) craft novel versions of Orientalism. The difference between the old colony-focused versions Edward Said (1978) examined in his work and the new, often European-based ones is based on a peculiar recalibration of the 'exotic'. The new exotic emanates from postindustrial uses of the former 'world-centre's' multiple national pasts, which yield atmospheric *bricolages*, neither fully Eastern, nor fully Western, but allegedly 'cosmopolitan' (Delanty 2009). In realist terms, this enterprise is offshoot of an experiment we call 'disorganized capitalism', in which the decentralisation of modes of production, the pluralisation of advertising and the manipulation of cultural signs dominate how we consume the world (Urry 2007: 212; Harvey 1999; Lash and Urry 1987, 1994).

Fire

However, capital mobility and node assemblage are also connected to phenomenologies of place and cultural belonging. For this I turn attention to the study's last hexagram, 'fire', which has both material and auratic qualities painfully recalled in the heavy consequences of the Promethean theft of knowledge. In some cinematic texts knowledge is stolen by women, who promise the re-enchantment of a world in which everybody dreams alone the dark of 'an enormous night' (Bloch 2006: 148). Because fire illuminates the dark, women who want to alter the world's atmospheric qualities are marked as both transgressors of a divine order, who have to be burned, and goddesses, who have to be worshipped. The same binary antithesis is reproduced by cinematic tourist technologies, which alter the properties of nature in filmed settings in order to glamourise it. Of course, stories about the 'profanation' of nature and the feminine, in which progress becomes irrevocably associated with control and technocratic barbarism (Böhme 2008: 116–119), also have a long activist academic history (Shiva 1993). The paradox of such technologically informed design is that it attempts to re-enchant manufactured (mediated in film) environments, by inducing experiences of being 'shaken by the extraordinary that lives amid the everyday' (Bennett 2001: 2). Blencowe (2016: 28) sees in the feminist figure of nature as enchantress an aesthetic 'centered on affirmation, diversity, and interconnection'. This vibrant aesthetic, which affirms the immanent creative capacities of earthly entanglement, mystery and wonder in the 'here and now', also sustains the emotional life of ecofeminist politics. It is this aesthetic that stems from aspects of *Outlander*'s literary and TV plot, and enables touristic design and filmmaking to connect affectively. The plot's ecological attunement, which centres on ecofeminist spirituality, also connects healing (Claire as the 'White Witch' of the story) to the craft of ecstasy (the witches drug themselves and perform an ecstatic dance around the stones – a scene which figures in every episode's opening credits like a *mantra*). Scriptural connections of ecofeminism to drug use reveal how the figure of the enchantress merges popular cultural imaginaries of the pharmacist, who can either beautify or poison, with that of the mendicant, which Bauman sees as a disenfranchised migrant. The merger manifests itself in an atmospheric parable of ecstasy, in which a new figure emerges: this is the magical figure of the *alítissa* or pilgrim/ascete, who wanders the world (*aláomai*), until she fulfils her purpose in life, by turning life into a moving picture, dead and alive at once (Belting 2011: 86; Tzanelli 2016b: 55). The use of the camera as a communicative vehicle or portal, transforms all the non-representational experiences of the journey into images and then imaginaries of place. It helps to remember then that all travel designs are the products of a radical adaptation of perspective, an epistemontological state that commences with the medium of drug (*aláomai* is a passive verb form denoting how one *is made* to wonder *with the help* of something).

This is a form of dark tourism that does not appeal to battlefield events, but a common heritage of knowledge-making and knowledge-breaking. Critical theorists such Adorno and Horkheimer (1991) associated this with the advent of the Enlightenment in enchanting myths, however, neither of them had much to say about phenomenologies of pilgrimage. Much like the atmosphere of the uncanny Heidegger calls *Stimmung* or subject-object boundedness (Heidegger 1962), experiences of dark tourism of this sort are constellations of people and things, or 'ecstasies of the thing': the way the thing (or event) qualitatively and sensuously stands out from itself (Böhme 1993: 121). Such atmospheric ecstasies do not stem from the architectural character of the city, but appeal to philosophical utopias of lived experience we associate with the countryside as the site of emotional intimacy, security and homeliness (Giffero 2014: 93, 95). It is, of course, the same rural utopian promise to heal the trauma of homelessness that we find in more negative affective manifestations of identity or the need to belong to an imagined community (Laachir 2007) – a theme properly addressed in the following chapter. Being 'spirit with matter' (Starhawk 1999: 38), healing can only be activated through kinaesthesia or multisensory movement in the environment (Böhme 2006) – which is why its manifestations in fan tourist rituals always involve some form of pilgrimage to filmed sites scripturally demarcated as 'holy'.

Indeed, even the inconclusive task of locating the stones granting passage to a bygone era or world, which is followed these days also by *Outlander* fans online and on-site, translates into a purifying ritual for the cinematic ascete. We encounter the recognition of a similar atmospheric boundedness in cinematic pilgrimages inspired by the *DVC*, which draw on scriptural dynamics: many cinematic fans follow eccentric British researcher, Sir Leigh Teabing's certainty that Sarah, persecuted by the Church, can put an end to 'suffering of the poor, those of different colour and women', when they visit Rosslyn Chapel, whereas others visit the Louvre's inverted Pyramid, where Mary Magdalene's body allegedly rests. The healing capacity of these two female martyrs has produced a constant stream of female tourists enacting their own photographic witchcraft in front of the alleged tomb, which has evolved from a mundane tourist ritual to a technology for transforming attention (Stengers 2012). The paradox of this design is that, although it was never conceived of outside the structures of 'capitalist sorcery' (Pignarre and Stengers 2011), it retained its life-affirming ecofeminist qualities.

As explained above, it is suggestive that, in terms of design, such rituals of paying respects to the female transgressors of divine order are almost always part of a specific synecdoche of action: recovering nature *and* verifying one's progeny. Significantly, *DVC*, *Brave* and *Outlander* cinematic pilgrimages feed into the content of a centuries-old Scottish identity, hence, they are built into the structures of performing a past diasporic tourists hardly ever experienced in everyday life. Thus, the entwining of genealogical locatability with cinematic pilgrimage brings the mnemonic role of ruins in the Scottish Highland landscape into popular cultural designs of identity (Basu 2000). Design entails in this case the cultivation of desire for a past destined to open a liminal rift between collectively-endowed *lieux de mémoire* (Nora 1989) and personalised *lieux d' imagination* (Reijnders 2011), where 'popcultural' pilgrimage can thrive. Such design, which is increasingly encouraged by the official Scottish tourist organisation, VisitScotland, commences online with a generic invitation to

> trace your family tree back in time, discover the occupations that kept your ancestors busy, find out more about your clan and then plan the holiday of a lifetime, where you can visit the towns and streets where your ancestors once walked.
>
> (VisitScotland 2018)

Nevertheless, the cinematic tourist connections begin to amplify, once this Scottish tourist organisation joins ever-expanding business networks, which may not be based in the country.

Where VisitScotland Chairman Mike Cantlay recognises that collaboration with the Forestry Commission, Scottish Natural Heritage and the National Trust can consolidate engagement with the family market in the case of *Brave*, which is also set to benefit other businesses, Disney Pixar and its tourist arm contribute to the dissemination of heritage markers around Scotland in their specialised cinematic tours (Weldon 18 March 2012). Likewise, the *Outlander* effect is visible in activities coordinated by The Scottish Ancestral Tourism Group, which includes representatives from the Scottish Government, local authorities, Scotland's People, Association of Highland Clans and Societies, individual genealogists and specialist tour operators, Historic Environment Scotland, National Trust for Scotland, Scottish Tourism Alliance and Scottish Enterprise. Emma Chalmers, owner of Mary's Meanders, noted that tourists joining their *Outlander* tour usually do some ancestry research in advance and are keen to explore their family roots. 'Everyone coming from the USA and Canada knows their clan and once they get here and realise much of the heritage is still intact, they want to come back again and explore further' (VisitScotland 6 August 2016). The whole enterprise mirrors what independent websites have created as a guide to the '*Outlander* Family Tree' (Fremont 10 September 2017; Fandom Wikia undated), thus bringing together contents tourism pilgrimage with heritage cultures. The endeavour originates in the film's scriptural content: Claire's historical investigations and her family's 'lived experiences' represent the two opposing visualisations of belonging, with the dendritic imagery of genealogy as a method of learning 'from outside' and 'above', and the so-called 'rhizomatic' (Deleuze and Guattari 1988: 15) or 'progenerative' one (Ingold 2011: 140) as the paradigm of interlacing humans with their environment so as to achieve growth and self-knowledge 'from below' and the 'inside'. The rhizomatic rendition of one's life-world, whereby roots are cast and spread in non-predetermined ways and directions, contrasts with the genealogical enterprise promoted by film-tourism as a mode of disengaged consumption of one's genealogical history. One may argue that, paradoxically, the film-induced genealogical enterprise fixes persons in the lifeworld, while they are on the move, as it divorces knowledge from lived experience. However, even genealogical self-ethnographies can generate new rhizomes, turning tourism into a new sphere of nurture, replete with new emplacements in new networks of trails or life-lines or communities of digital or terrestrial genealogists. Since knowledge is not received by ancestors prior to its application, objects, and subjects of memory cannot pre-exist remembering. Such forgeries also apply to local reactions to modifications of the lived environment by cinematic tourist industries.

The panoramic picture to which such endeavours belong is also instructive: the orchestration of tourism mobilities in the deterritorialised kinesphere of the internet exemplifies the troubling connection between the genealogical model and Western modernity by reverting intimate filmic narratives of origins to the taxonomic principles of the genealogical tree. Basu (2004), who stressed that such genealogical journeys (commonly known as 'homecoming' among the global Scottish diaspora) are connected to the 'foundational trauma' of clan uprooting from the Highland Scots' old country in ways similar to those of the African-American and North-American Jewish diasporas (Kugelmass 1992, 1996), resorts to Clifford's (1997) 'roots/routes' schema to study them. However, the liminal rift cinematic tourism introduces into this type of ancestor pilgrimage suggests that a new or modified analytical framework may be necessary to understand the phenomenon's popular cultural nature. The unlikely combination of genealogical with popular cultural pilgrimages better connects to ideas of 'returns' to a non-existent land of birth (Clifford 2013). The idea of a home, to which one cannot return, certainly conforms to the phenomenological nature of cyberspace, which is supposed to lead to actual places – only it does not always do that. The incompleteness of the journey (e.g. Germann Molz 2007: 74), which is resolved only scripturally, by securing documents that verify one's ancestry at best, is emblematic of what Augé (2008) discusses as the non-places of contemporary capitalist markets. One may observe then that the real gratification from the popular-pilgrimage rite rests in the journey itself, especially when it is undertaken by families with young children. 'Popcultural journeys' of this type (Gyimóthy *et al.* 2015) turn emotions of loss, which are difficult to communicate, into memories of sharing family experiences in photographs and other representational registers for the decades to come (e.g. see Haldrup and Larsen 2003; Larsen 2005; Larsen *et al.* 2006).

Feelings of loss are almost always part of genealogical journeys. Deleuze and Guattari's (1987: 18–20) discussion of the modern uses of tree diagrams as constitutive of hierarchies of control and taxonomic division certainly finds biblical connections with the tree of knowledge and evil in the Garden of Eden. In specific disciplinary contexts such as that of anthropology, the genealogical method also led scholars, such as W.H.R. River to upend the tree, placing its roots at the top and thus erasing its image as a living entity. This 'dendritic geometry', in which persons are reduced to points and lines, says nothing about their place in the world, because the schema endows personhood by mere genealogical connection. The selfsame separation may divorce time from being, transforming genealogical points and branches into persons (Ingold 2011: 134–136). But of course, the collapse of a *relationship* into *relatedness* can become generative of new relationships in fleeting encounters of a touristic nature: where such separations of the descent-line from the life-line can feed into ethnonational prejudice or racism in national domains, their transposition to mobile domains of tourism leads to the abolition of the past in favour of one's present biography. In fact, the thrill of being inspired to find one's ancestry because of a movie or a TV series, which endows the split of intergenerational transmission of knowledge from environmentally situated experience, introduces a technical ecology into the picture, in which remembering is about retrieving from the pre-existing cabinet of memory like an autonomous hermeneut, rather than a historic object (see also Morinis 1992 on the power of interpretation in pilgrimage).

The *DVC* phenomenon of pilgrimage mobility is instructive. On the one hand, its script naturally fit into the spirit of already established events like Homecoming Scotland (2009), which the international Scottish diaspora from New Zealand, Australia, Canada, and the USA attended to reconnect with its roots in the manner of heritage tourism. On the other, like *Braveheart* (director Mel Gibson 1995) before it, and *Brave* (2013) since, it brought together depictions of land and heritage (e.g. in the scenes shot in Rosslyn Chapel near Edinburgh), to induce a desire for 'return to roots' and belonging, more characteristic of conventional heritage tourism (Martin-Jones 2014). More importantly, however, the design of such cinematic pilgrimages must be attributed to entrepreneurs and artists of Scottish diasporic ancestry. Such artists/entrepreneurs signal the accelerated hybridisation of taste that has become characteristic of 'the new middle classes and their cultural and social practices arising in the context of migration and diaspora and the new modernities of the "emerging markets"' (Nederveen Pieterse 2004: 88; Favell *et al.* 2008). Such markets hybridise even the search for ancestral roots, turning them instead into holistic journeys to old religions. For the *DVC* specifically, a striking example is Sacred Earth Journeys (2006), a travel business website (est. 1994) located in Canada which advertised extensively combined tours to Paris, London and Edinburgh under the care of Mark Amaru Pinkham, author of *The Guardians of the Holy Grail*, 'Templar Knight' and 'co-director of the North American branch of The International Order of Gnostic Templars' founded by himself and his wife. Pinkham, who is a devoted traveller to India and other countries and has studied the Hindu scriptures and the Theosophists of India who wrote on the secret history of earth, links with Andean esoteric societies and the occult (incidentally, he had previously led an expedition in search of a secret monastery in the Andes *à la DVC*). At the time of the *DVC*'s release, he was advertising his Scottish ancestry, which allegedly dated back to Prince Henry St. Clair, whose family built Rosslyn Chapel. His activities after the release of the film included the delivery of lectures on the history mobilised by the author of the *DVC* novel, Dan Brown in the film on location, thus bestowing the tour with the aura of erudition and authority through lineage (Tzanelli 2013: 81).

Currently, Pinkham runs a series of mystic journeys to such diverse countries and heritage sites as California, Greece and Peru (Sacred Sites Journeys 2018). His Orientalist style involves the appropriation of cultural signs, histories and identities of ancient Eastern civilisations, and their treatment as environments that can be managed in mystical rituals akin to those of the cult of Gaia (Argyrou 2005). His autobiographical record establishes his professional cultural capital (Bourdieu 1993: 77; Giddens 1987) and celebrity aura as historically connected to popular beliefs in royal divinity (Rojek 2001: 13). Indeed, Pinkham's hazy genealogical connection to Arthurian legend replaces old auratic authorial frames with the postmodern discourse of experiential tourism (Earl 2008: 409). Hence, his business style exemplifies the transformative power new technologies and the markets they create have on cultural traditions: by merging elements from different religious traditions, his enterprise produces a new 'cultural grammar' (Nederveen Pieterse 2004: 54–55). Capital accumulation aside, we observe how Pinkham's 'fantrepreneurship' (Lundberg and Ziakas 2018) transforms atmospheres of mysticism into tourism imaginaries based on conceptions of an Oriental utopia (Salazar and Graburn 2014). Where usually such fan event organisers encourage cocreation processes in contexts of fandom and cinematic neotribalism (e.g. the *DVC* phenomenon), Pinkham's genealogical celebrity status allows him to present tours as an experience catered by an expert. On this occasion, then, genealogical abstraction facilitates the privatisation of an Orientalist utopia based on metaphysical atmospheres of *Stimmung*.

A similar cultural grammar was mobilised by the artistic contingent involved in the filming of *Brave*, and VisitScotland, to advertise Scottish land as a biographical source, although dismissing the affective connection of artists and tourist worldmakers to it would be wrong. Hence, first, enquiring into the roots of *Brave*'s travel discourse prompts one to investigate the role of the film's Scottish 'epistemontological community' of artists in the design of its tourist atmospheres.

> Brave is an amazing magical adventure with larger than life characters – including Scotland itself. During our research, we learnt that everything in Scotland tells a story – every stone, tree, mountain – which is why we are so proud that this beautiful country is the backdrop of our film

said director Mark Andrews (VisitScotland 2012a). This backdrop reinstates an imagined Scottish community defying territorial borders and reborn in animated characters fronting artistic subjects with native roots but global routes. Fire is an appropriate hexagram in this case of atmospheric emanation, because it highlights the paradoxical relationship between mobilities and immobilities, where social groups are involved. Diken (2010) suggests that fire is a metaphor of radical sociopolitical change, because it is associated with temporal 'emergency breaks'. At the same time, we may think of fire as the nihilist marker of terrorism, which tourist hosts may associate with their guests, including film crews (Tzanelli 2011). The fear that such newcomers wish to eradicate identity rests on a paradox, when filmmakers are in fact native cosmopolitans, as is the case with *Brave*'s artistic contingent. The pyric qualities of such groups do not obstruct mobility, on the contrary, they accelerate it, while simultaneously reproducing local narratives of identity. Andrews, whose ancestors came from Torridon, Wester Ross, declares an interest in King Arthur and European history, which as a young reader led him 'up into Scotland' – 'but as you can tell it was so long ago that I lost the accent' (McKenzie 2 July 2012). Thus legitimating his new pilgrimage as a professional traveller, he reappears in other interviews with US producer Katherine Sarafian working on and promoting the film in Scotland. Sarafian said she had an impression of what Scotland would be like before her visit but 'didn't fully understand the special connection that the people have with the land – their sense of place.... Driving up to Inverness and seeing the landscape again was very emotional' (McKenzie 2 July 2012).

Other members of *Brave*'s artistic contingent, such as actor Kevin McKidd (Lord MacGuffin and young MacGuffin in the film), who grew up in Elgin (Moray), follow in Andrews' steps. McKidd declares being delighted that Pixar's young MacGuffin spoke Doric, 'the Scots' dialect of north-east Scotland' and his grandfather's language (McKenzie 2 July 2012). According to other reports, all were keen to contribute their own Scottish words to the script – 'hence the inclusion of manky, gammy, numptie and hurdies. Kelly Macdonald even utters that Scottish legend "jings, crivvens, help maboab"' (McLean 29 June 2012). By immersing themselves literally and literarily in Scottish landscapes, 'swimming in lochs and rolling in heather', the creative team produced a lavish Scotland. Even artists of non-Scottish origins, such as the art director for set, scenery and characters Tia Kratter, spoke of the finished product as close to one's heart, 'a labour of love':

> I marched up and down the Royal Mile, gathering every swatch of tartan I could find.... We went up the east coast and found our castle – Dunottar Castle. We looked at standing stones and lochs and moss and heather and we lay down in it to get a real sense of what it was like.
>
> (McLean 29 June 2012)

Embodied verisimilitude aside, *Brave*'s authenticity stems from artistic pilgrimage to beautiful lands.

It is not coincidental that the issue of stereotyping entered global public discourse, or that *Brave*'s filmmakers and actors – especially Scots, whose voices were used in the film, such as Kelly MacDonald – responded that the story captured the reality of Caledonia. Craig Ferguson's (Lord Macintosh) claim that stereotypes oscillating between those of the 'noble warrior poet' and the 'angry, belligerent drunk' have a 'basis in fact' (Yang undated), suggests an apparently crude sell-out on Scottish cultural specificity. This might miss a disjunction between what is deemed to be useful to share with the world and what can damage the national image in global cinematic tourist markets, if disseminated to those who cannot read the 'small print'. Yet, the external recognition of some embodied aspects of Scottish cultural identity that 'are considered a source of external embarrassment but nevertheless provide insiders with their assurance of common sociality' (Herzfeld 2005: 3) is still a form of global recognition. This phenomenon hosts a variety of contradictory opportunities for communities *en route* to change – most notably, the urge to cover up the true faces of sociality, which in reality are just simulacra anyway, butts heads with an increased awareness that all social structures and habits have to be used 'with sensibility' (in Mills' (1959: 17) terms) to secure communal wellbeing. In this respect, the furore around Merida's 'glammed up' version on Disney's website (Child 13 May 2013) matches verifications by professional historians that the cinematic characters' appearance and the landscape's attractive ruggedness project verisimilitude – even if '[they] only reflect the Highlands … peddled abroad since Queen Victoria … a bare … land, inhabited by wild men in kilts' (Barnett 20 August 2012). Backed by Oscar-winning director Chapman, Change.org's petition calling upon the studio to restore the character's 'more realistic' origins gathered over 200,000 signatures, forcing Disney to remove Merida's revamped version from its site (Child 16 May 2013). And yet, upon closer inspection, the action's feminist statement preys on centuries-old feminisations of colonised land, which nationalist discourse subsequently sacralised so as to demarcate national time from the conqueror's time (Anderson 2006: 195).

It helps to remember that touristic *Brave* references online endorse the selfsame travel performances that visitors enact in terrestrial tours to Scotland (Friedberg 1995: 67). Although such 'illustrative seeing' allows virtual and terrestrial tourists to match cinematic images with their own understanding of them (Benjamin 2002: 419), the original story's appeal to female emancipation overdetermines the story's 'arrow of time'. Supported by its own slingshot holder (a young agency ready to be independent), the arrow points to Scottish nature. This nature is perennial, like natural landscapes and ecosystems, but also presented as a medieval being created out of nowhere (*ex nihilo*) – hence, humanly historicised. This networked self-creation of Scotland as an animated land does not entail that we deal with mere simulated landscape. The film's central scenario or 'archplot' communicates with real developments in Scottish self-narration, including that promoted by the 'Great Tapestry of Scotland', a 160-panel long textile artwork depicting 420 years of history handstitched by 1,000 volunteers. The inspiration for the tapestry, which was on show at the Scottish Parliament an[illegible] ublic display at Cockenzie House and the Gardens in East Lothian in [illegible] ngs to an epistemontological community with ancestral roots in the [illegible] uding artist Andrew Crummy, stitch coordinator Dorie Wilkie and [illegible] nder McCall Smith (Harrison 18 October 2013). The project's advertising as a coordinated 'arts and crafts' initiative echoes the function of the tapestry in Disney's fairytale: the magical restoration of 'family' unity, the realisation that the love between mother and child survives generational conflict. The use of previously underappreciated crafts in the media by a *belles artes* group helps turn them into glamourous folklore. It is part of a process of nationalising the unknown, know-how crafts 'associated with the emergence of national consciousness and glorified as the repository of ancient skills' (Herzfeld 2004: 5). Thus, even if Pixar's intentions were to craft an innocent fairytale, entering Scotland's political minefield was bound to alter the artistic project's meaning and intentions. By appealing to embodied character and connecting it to national lands, *Brave*'s cinematic discourse opened wide a door to populist appropriations of its content.

The following chapter highlights further how the clash between dendritic and rhizomatic belonging guiding artistic epistemontological communities is reflected in various communities' political-cultural claims to heritage. Suffice it to mention that, when it comes to the design of tourism mobilities, prominent artists are treated, or often treat themselves, as legitimate manipulators of the ethnic atmospheres they use in their artwork. This attitude has theoretical implications: it suggests that claims over and tropes of experiential authenticity cannot be considered as Foucaultian *fulcra,* nor can we dismiss their place in affective field-worlds. In such field-worlds we deal with human and non-human relationships, therefore with *questions of hospitality*, for which phenomenology proper, as is propagated in the works of Derrida, and philosophies of hope stemming from Bloch's writings, are more appropriate epistemontological tools than those of Foucaultian epistemology. Even the researcher, whose primary role is to understand (*epístatai*), cannot completely avoid precognitive/affective (hence ontological) change. As a note, the phenomenon of claiming heritage by professional worldmakers manifests itself in such different cinematic tourist contexts as those of the *LOTR*, where Peter Jackson figured next to native tourist entrepreneurs and senior political functionaries as a native proponent of the shiny (New Zealandish, of course) Hobbitton utopia film pilgrims visit from all over the world (Peaslee 2010; 2011; Tzanelli 2013: Chapter 2), and of *SM,* where Mumbai-born and UK-resident author of *The Satanic Verses* Salman Rushdie and Indian author and political activist Suzanna Arundhati Roy, contested the glamorisation of the slum in new cinematic tourist cultures (Tzanelli 2015a: 169–172). Such diametrically opposite habits of protest are claims to belonging to what occasionally proves to be a counterworld, far removed from the rough native realities. In addition, it is not uncommon for the style of these claims to counter processes of native becoming, or modify those further, without necessarily altering native adaptations to new transcultural realities.

The island of order(-ing): freedoms and burdens in Orientalisation

By way of conclusion, I will make an awkward observation about my *I Ching* methodology, to issue a word of caution to all of us, who think and write about the impact of filmmaking on tourism development. I confidently commenced this study by designing an epistemontological and methodological portfolio, akin to that we associate with the new mobilities paradigm, out of the plural interpretative frameworks of this ancient work. This certainly facilitated ways of reading events and actions in different contexts of media-induced (film and the internet) tourism. However, by devising an alternative schema of reading such mobilities, I gradually slipped into the garments of artistic and tourist worldmakers – nay, I became one of them. Of course, associations of 'travel proper' with authenticity and positive values must always be treated with suspicion, because they normalise notions of mobility and freedom, prioritising the very notion of travel hardship over the arrival at a certain destination (O'Reilly 2005). However, it would be equally problematic to ignore how I, the *I Ching* pilgrim, may serve as the mediator of the exoticised discourses that representational industries, such as film regularly use to domesticate otherness – especially, but not exclusively in post-colonial settings (Huggan 2001). Such mediations of the travel exotic included in the present chapter's narrative a series of 'banal worldmaking instillments', where I, as the 'articulating actor or projecting agency [became] complicit with others from the past or from the present' (Hollinshead and Suleman 2018: 203) engaged, even unconsciously, in the design of the examined filmed destinations as Orientalist dollhouses, divested of native life and history. Generally speaking, treating pilgrimage-like cinematic *flâneries* as European, Western or romanticised processes (Wolff 1993; Kaplan 1996; Sutherland 2014) produces a metaphysics of flux that may 'inadvertently play into some of the most damaging hegemonic ideals of the network society' (Sutherland 2013: 7). The progressive Orientalisation of European and other world histories in such worldmaking contexts, which either endorse the cosmopolitanism of actual tourists uncritically (for discussion see Hollinshead 1998: 121; Haldrup and Larsen 2010: 76, 80; Salazar 2017: 188–189), or tend to rely on an ontological realism that flattens out difference (Sutherland 2013: 10), suggests the rewriting of the past for futures unhelpful to localities. And there is more: my newly discovered power to nominate atmospheres is usually constitutive of the experience of alienation from the field-worlds I studied – a phenomenon replicating the ordeal that native professional worldmakers may undergo in contemporary neoliberal contexts. The realisation that what starts as a committed pilgrimage potentially enables commercialisation is the very conundrum of cinematic tourist development.

When brought to discourse, the conundrum induces guilt, occasionally urging cinematic tourist designers/pilgrims to rectify their manners, by becoming more involved in local matters. The shift from individualist travel to activist filmmaking or scholarship, if we treat scholars of the subject also as designers, produces an array of contradictory discourses of professional mobility in the public spheres of travel and tourism. Such contradictions turn the idea of tourism as entertainment or wellbeing into an act of welfare directed towards others, often destroying the original objective of mobility. Berlant (2011: 226–227), who reminds us that the affective nature of public spheres often prevents their participants from fulfilling their innermost desires, is instructive: cinematic artists or tourism policy-makers with affective connections to 'developing' communities are simply a *different* type of citizen from them, so they can hear, indeed fully relate to their cause, but *cannot fully partake in it, like them* – if anything, such total identification would eradicate their being in the world altogether. This unlikely scenario of being another by forsaking oneself is nothing short of a fundamentalist occurrence, because it flattens out difference in the name of some perverted justice or equality project. At the same time, it is needless to add that designing atmospheres and developing locations into tourist destinations can go wrong in all sorts of ways. Thereafter, a process of scapegoating alienates professional creators (native or not) more, casting them as postindustrial 'traitors' to the community they thought they could support with their profession.

What happens, then, when a hopeful process becomes a programme that does not fulfil human desires for betterment – when host societies (or, specifically, communities in developing cinematic tourist spots) see little or no positive change in their circumstances? Note that the trope of 'failure' is as subjective as any anthropocentric project may be, and emanates from circumstances, contexts and those who enunciate them: localities, the press, the national centre or independent capitalist business. In short, it may be unwise to discuss the withdrawal of hopeful horizons of expectations exclusively on realist grounds (Merriman 2018: 4) or, alternatively, mere phenomenological circumstances. Badiou, who speaks of a 'crisis of negation' certainly encapsulates this slide into negativity and nothingness that we associate with recurring world economic and cultural limbos (Thompson 2013: 97–99), but he sidelines the polytopic nature of the crisis' subjective interpretation. Instead of fixating upon the economic crisis as a metanarrative of negation, I examine such 'zero points' for various world societies that host cinematic tourism contextually. Significantly, the reorganisation of their being in the world with others (humans, nature and artefacts) is *only* supplemented by religious eschatologies (nihilism or *ressentiment*); the actual core *mantra* of their action, however localised, is geared towards apprehending the events of touristification contingently. This means that, despite any possible objections, the nature of desire for collective self-realisation has already shifted alongside the locality or nation-state's material and cultural development (Archer 1995): the guests have changed the hosts in barely perceptible, but significant ways.

Chapter 5

The 'hubris of the zero point'

Three responses

Towards a choreutics of ecosocial action

We live in an era wherein human observers cannot be observed any more. Consider for a moment how postcolonial or decolonial perspectives, such those proffered by Walter Mignolo (2000, 2011), Buonaventura de Sousa Santos (2007) and Santiago Castro-Gómez (2007; Castro-Gómez and Martin 2002), are both anthropocentric and peculiarly fixated upon vision as the primary epistemic source. Like most theories of liberation that reject fascistic constrictions to growth (e.g. Dussel 1985), these perspectives detect the roots of the problem in human communicative *blindness*. Much like Bauman (Bauman and Lyon 2013), Bloch (1990: 145) laments how our hypermobile modernity has led to the emergence of a citadel culture subjecting everyone to a state of emergency, and eventually turning discourses of paranoia and rights retrenchment into a self-sustaining ideology of security. Of course, with *humanitas* as a small part of living ecosystems in need of protection, the present study must consider the argument set forth by these philosophers to inspect the human condition first, but not stop there. For them, to achieve true decolonisation of previously occupied territories and minds, proponents of 'liberation' have to reach a definitive rejection of 'being told' what and who they are from the epistemic privileges of the zero point, where all decisions are made on behalf of others. However, the human condition is part of a posthuman ecology, so such decision-making must be managed otherwise, if it is to be truly democratic. Although earth's last four centuries have been full of zero points, the twentieth-first century in particular has seen the colonisation of lifeworlds and ecosystems by non-imperial human machines. Consider how the circulation of expert discourses focusing on earth's epochal progression may be managed by independent business and regional administrative regimes in equal measure (Klein 2007: 21–22; Urry 2011: 149, 165). Although the rest of humanity assumes the role of a seamless audience, even professional experts cannot claim any certainty over the course of natural events. The concept-makers who work in a small fraction of business proclaiming its awareness of ecological and social inequality, also find that they have to plough their way through a vast dark forest of 'sigillary signs', unfulfilled symbols that may encapsulate a desired image of how things might be (Daly 2013: 165–166). It seems that, as a species, we have reached a zero point of knowledge shared by transnational experts of postindustrial complexes and the rest of humans, who, in all the hierarchical inequalities they suffer, still form the earth's absolute monarch.

Of course, to ignore sociocultural asymmetries in any actual setting in favour of perspectival considerations of the ways humans exercise agency over non-humans and nature is easier said than done. Human sentience and morality are still mostly assumed absent from all other life forms – in any case, action over perceived injustices is perceived and dealt with by humans. We have already spent some time exploring the implications of immaterial and material production and consumption in the previous chapter. I explained that, although the entire cycle of labour and leisurely practices in cinematic tourist contexts focuses on 'recovering' (but actually recreating) actor-network rituals in the mechanosphere of terrestrial and virtual travels, the primary division between hosts and guests and labourers and consumers within it persists with a vengeance. This polarisation is used by various constituencies to raise claims over land that has turned into touristified landscape, ignoring the by now common knowledge that the earth is not our property, but our home. The problem with developing is that it always leads to a tighter policing of landscapes, which are constructed as if 'in need' of sustainable guardianship. It is not uncommon for discourses of overtourism or uncivil tourist behaviour to begin to plague these developed sites, or to incrementally come to life as serious 'issues' after press coverage (Scott *et al.* 2012; Korstanje and George 2015). The groups recognised as locals or guardians of regional heritage foster their own discourses to address the 'issue', with various good and bad outcomes (a sort of 'morphogenesis' of structure through collective social action largely ignored by Archer 2008). The host groups' rejection of 'being told' who they are and how to act by those controlling the epistemic privileges of postindustrial enterprise (i.e. the cinematic tourist worldmakers) muddies the darkness of the zero point further. There is an even worse, but not uncommon scenario to consider, which we will find in particular local responses: where claims to justice should illuminate the way to a solution, cunning, bitterness and spite are introduced instead, to sediment an inhospitable atmosphere (Daly 2013: 166). From there on, it is difficult to ascertain who commits hubris in the mobile situation and how.

This chapter makes two points: first, that established Western and/or European notions of 'professional design' always meet with alternative local ones, which can be situated even within the demarcated (but marginalised) domains of the West or Europe. This puts the very notion of design under scrutiny, suggesting first that its cinematic tourist standardisation is external to particular lifeworlds at all times, and not just in postcolonial contexts. But this is a simplistic approach, which disregards how different viewpoints interact in lived spheres, where technology, nature, humans and animals form and reform field-worlds. The second point I wish to make pertains to a radical Marxist pessimism, which either declares that situated field-worlds die under (post-)industrial impositions, or reduces them to a simile of

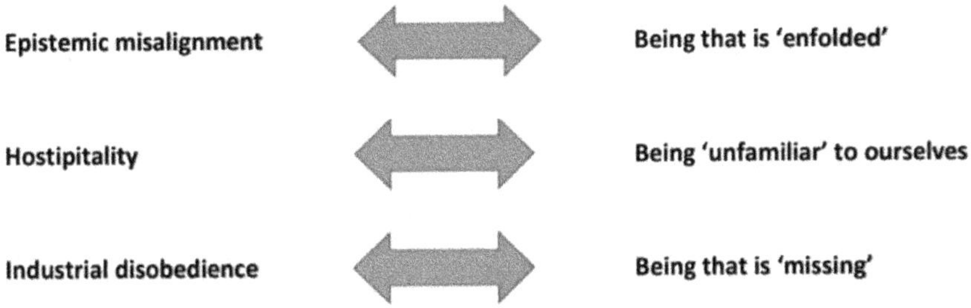

Figure 5.1 Diagram of responses to cinematic touristification.
Diagram credit: Rodanthi Tzanelli.

standardised social movements originating in or managed by the 'developed world'. If there is a radical reading of 'structural hybridisation' (Nederveen Pieterse 1997; 2004) to inject into the mobilities paradigm on sociocultural movements (Adey 2010; Cresswell 2011; Sheller 2012a), we will find it here, in the adaptive resilience displayed by local lifeworlds. As I explain in the next three sections, such adaptations may import blueprints of action but turn those into exemplary, 'authentic' local agency (on alliances and conflicts between cultural reality and structural interests see Alexander 2011: 59–62).

I look into three sociocultural movements that critique cinematic touristification, which I term 'responses' or 'modes of movement', each with its own specificity to add to this study: epistemic misalignment, hostipitality (the presence of hostility in hospitality contexts) and postindustrial disobedience. These modes or responses reflect Ernest Bloch's (2000: 200–201) 'unfulfilled states of being', the ways social groups react under enormous strain to the possibility of all sorts of systemic or lifeworld failure, including in our case the death of local ecosystems, social structures, identity and heritage with the advent of touristification. The cosmogonic changes introduced by cinematic touristification produce unbearable forms of longing for something that is 'missing', or something that has been taken away by the professional manipulators of impressions, who want to attract tourist clientele. Daly's (2013) organisation of such 'unfulfilled states' into three categories (being that is 'enfolded', being 'unfamiliar' to ourselves, and being that is 'missing') roughly overlaps with epistemic misalignment, hostipitality, and postindustrial disobedience respectively. Where epistemic misalignment suggests that host localities turn their behaviour inwards, to juxtapose established cultural modes and native affective atmospheres to cinematic touristification imports, hostipitality hinges local response to openly hostile feelings towards strangerhood and industrial disobedience confirms the desire to 'retrieve' the stolen identity through combinations of emotional and cognitive labour. The modes connect to affects as much as they may lead to theatrical performances (see Giesen 2011) – in any case, we must heed Tolia-Kelly's

(2006) and Rose *et al.*'s (2010) suggestion that we need to study particular contexts in which they occur, to establish them as cumulative historical processes of interaction between humans and places (Kobayashi *et al.* 2011). Notably, all three modes exceed the 'reactive' framework attributed to social movements (Jasper 1997): where a reaction suggests an antithetical modality we find in classical Marxist dialectics, the response fuses the practice of communal dialogics (i.e. addressing multiple perspectives to multiple 'problems' at multiple audiences – see also Bakhtin 1984: 252–253) with that of responsibility towards others in the lived environment (Honneth 1992: 119, 2007: 76). The ensued hybridisation produces *a* truth in encounters between postindustrial designers, the nation-state and local or visitor populations, which adheres to the Bakhtinian principle, because 'it exists only as a succession of mutually constructing speech events' (Metcalf 2002: 9; Gardiner 1992). Although, for analytical reasons, I treat each response as a self-contained phenomenon, in context there are cross-cuttings and fusions between all three modes.

Note again my recognition in Chapter 1 that the present study's phantasmagoric mobilities snuggle within a long history of postcolonial adaptations to contemporary capitalism: there, I stressed that cinematic/contents tourism shares much with the theme park industries we find in most 'developed' areas of the world, or in economically developed areas of countries 'in need' of development. Naturally, one may think that patronising capitalist attitudes merit the same response that localities used to address at colonisers. From there, for a locality or community of any sort, a leap to a zero point is suicidal, if performed without ropes, acrobatic planning and a clear end in sight. Likewise, whether 'addressing the issue' develops into a fully-fledged protest against tourists (see Quaglieri Domínguez and Scarnato 2017 on tourismophobia), or it is lodged peacefully in the cosmological cracks of a touristified region, it is important to know more about its scope and nature. At the same time, the scope and spread may reveal little about the response's cosmological significance: isolated episodes often disclose a lot about generalised public sentiment in the form of rumours only journalists pick up, occasionally at their personal risk. Merriman (2018) examines Deleuze and Guattari's (1987) 'molar' (highly organised, easily represented and expressed and aligned with state or non-state actors) and 'molecular' assemblages (disorganised, vital, operating below the threshold of perception and associated with 'becomings') in the new mobilities paradigm. He argues that not only do they not always display differences of size, scale, substance, or perceptibility, representational ability and mode of organisation, they often overlap. This observation becomes even more important when we consider affective forces, events and encounters at the microlevel (Merriman 2012). The relational and imperceptible cultural-political entanglements (which nevertheless are not to be understood as micro-social renditions of symbolic interactionism but pre-structural events) still remain largely unacknowledged in fields such as those of cultural and political sociology in terms of their ability to affect events and futures (Deleuze 1988; Bissell 2016).

To create a flexible taxonomy of all three aforementioned modes of 'addressing the issue' in connection with the nature of the 'issue' itself, I mobilise Laban's space-movement principles again. He states that, regardless of whether it is a matter of life and death or a simple activity or task, all living organisms 'use the simplest and easiest paths in space when fighting' ([1966] 2011: 45) with objects and materials. This struggle in the environment maps an 'economy of effort' that constructs a 'dynamosphere'. This sphere encloses attitudes (Ingold's (2011) 'taskscape'), including choices of a certain path and set of affordances; above all, it involves the choice of dynamic stresses (Laban [1966] 2011: 27). Not only does the dynamosphere supplant the kinesphere with a plan of activity (the equivalent of the ways choreographies are configured in dance-movements) it relates the moving person's feeling for dynamics to spatial harmonics within 'trace-forms' or the ways particular moments in movements have accumulated in memory. Trace-forms are sedimented emotions that inform ad hoc affects in responses to cinematic touristification with various consequences.

With an eye to classical sociologies of solidarity and conflict, I filter antitourist phenomena through Laban's choreutics, equating his notion of 'dance-movements' with that of collective movements: the chapter's 'modes' or 'responses'. Each of these responses-movements is shadowed by particular emotional formations that appeal to specific forms of solidarity and conflict. Laban's ([1966] 2011: 84–85) valuable observation that the four, principal trace-forms collapse in spiraloid curves or 'coiling around an axial line', like DNA, suggests that such movements-responses seek to affirm biopolitical belonging (Tzanelli 2013: 25–26). Put simply, the three responses map cognitive, affective and embodied dynamics of the ways in which communities appear to respond to cinematic touristification in ecosystemic contexts. Starting from the mode displaying the least stressors, but not necessarily the least problematic nature, I escalate the analysis to larger processes we associate with globalised spaces of discontent, which I connect to nationalised notions of heritage and land, flows of immaterial production and global labour mobilities. My mapping of modes/responses follows the physical and cognitive movements of the participants in the response to determine how courses of action ('stressor applications') are imprinted in the environment (i.e. cinematic tourist or heritage sites). Such imprints or trace-forms preserve biographical records of remembering and experiencing places as heritage or 'home'.

Epistemic misalignment

The mode of misalignment is found in postcolonial situations of consumption in which tourist mobilities from the First World are the dominant economic and cultural reality, hence, it shares much with the study of decolonial movements around the world. However, its nature is rarely openly violent in cinematic tourist contexts: we can imagine it as part of a mode of adaptation, managed by the repression of damaging emotions of *ressentiment* and hurt, before erupting into violence or turning into organised protest in post-Fordist contexts of consumption (Tzanelli 2011). I draw inspiration from Walter Mignolo's (2009) thesis on 'epistemic disobedience' to proffer a modified argument about the ways native regimes of knowledge survive and are conveyed in contemporary contexts of cinematic tourist production and consumption. As Mignolo contends, geopolitical configurations of a uniform world in colonial and postcolonial contexts set by racial classifications – equivalent to Ingold's (2011) conception of the sphereless globe of Western epistemic rationality – are the product of the colonial gaze. The 'knowing' Western or European subject maps the world and enunciates the problems that inflict its 'underdeveloped' regions, which, unsurprisingly, coincide with 'Third World' colonised regions. The primary division between 'First World' science (based on a philosophy of progress engineered by rational technological means) and 'Third World' indigenous or aboriginal 'wisdom' (an unrefined diamond of perception in need of processing by reliable experts) does away with local or regional lifeworlds' intrinsic value (Mignolo 2000, 2002). Mignolo invites scholars, and implicitly also policy-makers, to attempt a delinking between politics and episteme, but also decolonising and decolonial knowledge, so that they assist in the emergence of democratic, just societies, where the colonial claws ravaged situated knowledge, and local lifeworlds were replaced by colonial systems of thought (Mignolo 1999). Orientalised formations of *ánthropos* or the human being aspiring to (self-)perfection from an epistemic privilege, both matched ancient and Renaissance ideals of a disembodied generic *humanitas* (Tzanelli 2008b: Chapters 7 and 8) and modern globalist formations of the world as geometric space, a surface ready to be traversed, explored and occupied, but never experienced on its own terms (Tzanelli 2016b).

Mignolo's proposition attacks the rules by which scholarship on these domains is conducted, because it never questions the assumptions on which knowledge is produced – notably, that the knower is implicated in the formation of knowledge from the outset, while she or he is always in the privileged position to evaluate phenomena (see also Alatas (2004) on decolonial knowledge production and the alleged feebleness of the native mind). Like others, he resorts to cosmological investigations, which should lead scholars to remove all theological and philosophical presuppositions from the cultural and political picture, so that silenced voices are heard. Indeed, like scholars such as Chatterjee (1998) and Chakrabarty (2000), who identified in subaltern or peripheral modernities the future of subjugated lifeworlds, he suggests a reevaluation of 'elite expertise' (Spivak 2010: 37–38) in favour of 'differentiated structures of authority' (Chatterjee 1998: 274), so as to make space for the subaltern to speak and create anew. We must, therefore, '"bracket" the premises of modernity and the Enlightenment itself' (Nederveen Pieterse 1992: 23) to consider culture as an always-already political domain. At the same time, however, it is unhelpful to fuse culture with politics, divesting the former of its autonomous production – a move that would restore Raymond Williams' Gramscian divide between the city and the country uncritically.

I do not intend to reduce all responses of this mode to subaltern voices, but introduce instead the idea of lay expertise in a cosmological sense: what in the course of the world's multiple modernities was patronisingly cast as 'wisdom' or commoditised as 'exotic', survives tourist commoditisation and the reduction of lived-in land to consumption domains, only we must retrain ourselves to apprehend its tunes. To survive postcolonial post-Fordism, local wisdom was passed on to native experts moving in global networks of expertise, who now combine experience with scientific knowledge, but the results of this transposition vary. Herein I make connections between manufactured atmospheres in cinematic tourism, the atmospheric tonality of cosmological rootings and the possibility of restoring atmospheres of democracy, to quote Latour and Weibel's (2005) edited thesis. The fact that in postindustrial environments of cinematic tourism these three atmospheric forms occupy entirely separate domains of human action and perception (loosely connected to my three modes of response), is symptomatic of anthropocenic infestations on the holistic environment, where we should find orchestrations of action, affect and thought. In summary, in this section I explore various epistemic misalignments with preanthropocenic systems of thought (native holistic cosmologies). Incidentally, epistemic misalignment would limit Touraine's (1985) reflections on defensive conflicts to peaceful negotiations of the cultural and political spaces of mobility.

Mumbai, India

Asian spaces of misalignment tend to display strong aesthetic/somatosensory qualities – a rather neat response to former Western interpellations of the native subject as a *degenerate body* devoid of true intelligence (Law 2010). The misalignment leads to fixings in atmospheric mediations, proffering a critical response to occulocentrism, and through it, the Western ideology of consumerism. A rather famous local response to tourist intrusion in the slum of Dharavi, Mumbai, where *SM* was partly filmed, centred on the visitors' permission to use cameras in slum tours. Dharavi localities have been entertaining a healthy relationship with Reality Tours, the most successful slum tourist operator in the area since its founders and managers Krishnan Pujari and Chris Wray decided to permanently donate 80% of their profits to community projects and limit tour group sizes. This collaboration had an interesting clause: after resident accusations of voyeurism, Reality Tours agreed to forbid cameras during tours in the slum (Howard 21 March 2010; Swanson 16 May 2011), whereas visitors were also cautioned that it is disrespectful to block their nose when they enter the slum or 'flinch to touches' (Forster April 2009). For decades, but especially since the boom in slum tourism in the twenty-first century, Indian slums such as Dharavi have been represented in Western popular culture as spaces of death, disease and conflict. Hannam and Diekmann (2016) note that such representations are residues of the colonial imagination, which was built on binarisms separating European sanitary habits from those of dirty and malodorous colonised populations.

However, one must treat such representations as metaphors of intersectional inequalities within imperial complexes such as those of the British and French empires, which projected internal social problems of class, gender and sexuality onto colonial difference. Hence, the use of the discourse of 'European sanitation' in colonised areas metaphorised social problems (criminality, an impoverished working class, a growing underclass, and prostitution) encountered in slums in colonial metropoles (London and Paris). The phenomenon was constitutive of the ways reputed middle class activists (journalists and mostly women) became involved in the emergence of notions of welfarism in European metropolitan enclaves following industrialisation – a cosmogonic phenomenon, which brought the realities of waste closer to notions of moral and physical contamination (O'Brien 2008; Tzanelli 2015a). Such 'geographies of contamination' (McFarlane 2008) were linked in India particularly to the handling of human waste – a Hindu taboo assigned as a job to the 'untouchable' communities (the caste of the *dalit*) of the country (Tzanelli 2015a: 137; Jewitt 2011). It is small wonder that, after complaints in Dharavi about tourist behaviour, Reality Tour's website was populated with visual and textual narratives about the slum's propensity to strong family bonding, professional camaraderie, craftsmanship and a culinary style with which all visitors had to become familiar (Tzanelli 2015a: 153). Indeed, culinary skills were displayed both online and offline (during tours) for the benefit of *bon viveur* tourists, who were after a taste of native cuisine (Dharavi is the heart of local poppadum-making, a craft connected to village cuisine).

How could we approach these arrangements? We could follow Maoz's reflections on the local counter-gaze in India, which relays competitive encounters between hosts and guests, while also allowing the former to secretly construct the later as hedonistic, shallow, rude, 'badly educated and easily deceived' (Maoz 2006: 222–225). This would allow us to map the affective dimensions of the response in Dharavi (resentment), but not its synaesthetic dimensions, which reveal much about entrenched local-as-Indian style. First of all, the mode/response (blocking the vision) rejects the Western and European cosmological superframe of philosophy-science (Mignolo 2009: 165), dictating instead that the two sides swap roles: now tourists and business are placed in the position of students of local etiquette. Second, it challenges the ideology of visualism, proffering instead a completely different structure of experience, based on what is natively known as *rasas* or flavours/moods. Built in the interface of religion (Hinduism) and popular culture (Bollywood film aesthetics), the *rasas* point to the creation of a distinctive flavour ('taste') that defies Aristotelian aesthetic unities of time and place – something translating into emphasis on stylistic moments endowed with the affect we find in film music and Bollywood musicals (Thomas 1985: 130). It is important to bypass the Hindu origins of the term. This is so because its streamlining into Indian popular culture diffused its use across religious communities: watching TV, which appeals to visual sensory practices, is an everyday ritual for Indian families (Banks 2001). By waging war against visualism, Dharavi's culinary *rasas* replaced 'insensitive' Western consumerism with family and community practices of *consomality*, the practice of sharing in food and love for those one cooks for. This trope of intimacy, which alludes to the sense of proximity even online, casts Alfred Schutz's 'consociateship' into epistemontological performances (see Errington 2011: 37). As they become unhooked from the spatiotemporal coordinates of Western modernity, Dharavi's *rasas* stage the slum as the space in which communities experience a spiritual and emotional rapture. In this rupture, the body as the other of Western modernity, simulates environmental perception for outsiders through taskscapes (cooking, eating together) that elevate livelihood rituals (cooking for tourists) into a utopian process. A combination of technical-performative modifications (online) of all the unpleasant (for tourists) aspects of the slum environment (bad odours, mud, and dirt) and a written etiquette of tourist behaviour blocking negative sensory engagement, produce Dharavi's very own simulated stage.

Resorting to fabricated intimate domains, where communities instead of individuals appeal for privacy vis-à-vis touristification, increasingly finds extensions in the cybersphere, which is supposed to be one of the new public spheres (Habermas 1989). As Seyla Benhabib (1992) notes, the rise of the citizen-consumer has been accompanied by the growth of the society of surveillance *à la* Foucault and the colonisation of the lifeworld, *à la* Habermas; both analytical perspectives define contemporary online activity. Therefore, online community responses to touristification conform to contemporary transformations of public life preying on privacy (Sheller and Urry 2005: 118): campaigners such as those of Dharavi resort to a politics of confessional intimacy or shaming to arbitrate collective interests (Bauman 2000; Berlant 1997). One of the starkest paradoxes of this action is, as we saw in Dharavi's case, the mobilisation of intimacy as private space/life/sphere, which is symbolically demarcated by sociospatial arrangements associated with domesticity, bodily presence and the familial (Sennett 1977; Berlant 2011). Of course, such perceptions of privacy project utopian solidarities where, in reality, there are conflicting interests and agendas (Walby 1990; Williams 2004), so we should view them as aspects of the communal response/activism's design. By the same token, we must heed how the response/design mirrors traditional Western and European family structures (white, middle class and heterosexual), which are not shared across the world, but are considered a reputable paradigm.

Rio de Janeiro, Brazil

Another example is provided by the *CoG favela* tourism, which adheres to adaptive postcolonial patterns of mobility of emotive content. The widespread frustration at the reductive representation of *favela* life as crime-driven and dangerous in Meirelles and Lundt's film did not lead to open local protests at the time. However, 15 years after its release, it triggered activist responses, with a view to alter such negative portrayals of *favelas* such as Rocinha.

Nationally-based and American-networked NGO Rio on Watch commissioned interviews with 21 European and North American tourists before entering a *favela* and after attending a *favela* tour. With extensive quotations in an online article published on the NGO's official website, it was proven that tourists, affected by widespread negative media coverage, entered the *favela* fearing for their life, expecting police invasions and shootings, and experiencing an adrenaline rush one does not usually associate with a relaxing holiday. Contrariwise, after their visit, they commented on their surprising discovery of a 'proper system in place', which facilitates a 'strong sense of community' (van Rompu 6 May 2017). Activist critique was also recently prompted by academic activism and UK NGO *Tourism Concern*'s discussions of the rise of 'poorism', which only allegedly helps local communities (Cheded 17 January 2018).

Such interventions filter local sentiment, but do less in letting localities speak for themselves. At the same time, onsite activist work provides an alternative epistemontology of hospitality we should not dismiss as unhelpful or irrelevant for this study. Notably, *Tourism Concern* describes *favela* dwellers as feeling exploited by slum tour operators, 'who use the *favela* as a profit-making means without putting any money back in to the *favela* (whether through employing local guides, promoting local vendors or funding community projects)' (ibid.). Local mistrust of such 'untidy guests' is extended to film studios and filmmakers (Veijola *et al.* 2014), who, as was the case with Danny Boyle and his colleagues, try to establish local sustainability schemes for the benefit of the community, but may generate further controversies and local antagonisms instead (Tzanelli 2015a: Chapter 9) is understandable. Where charitable giving directed to individuals yields no positive results for the community (as was the case with *SM* charitable giving), practical action appeals to a relational ontology of giving, which creates the hope of collective autonomy. The *CoG* makers set up 'Cinema Nosso', a film school that works with schools local to the filmed *favela* to offer practical and theoretical workshops on subjects like animation and human rights. With 3,500 students, over 150 workshops, and over 150 short movies, the initiative strived to generate positive local legacies (Cheded 17 January 2018).

The fact that NGOs are still critical of the project exceeds my focus. What matters is the introduction of a modern (Western) technology that facilitates expressions of experience into a kinesphere favouring holistic productions of subjectivity – what we know as '*carioca* character' (Tzanelli 2017a: 18). Such classifications of Brazilian 'nature' communicate to international guests a highly complex assemblage of non-human and human qualities, which come together at an emotional/cognitive and somatosensory junction (Tzanelli 2015b). The assemblage is recognised by Rio's citizens as heritage, which is constantly revised through encounters with other foreign cultural systems. Rio's particular self-presentations thus emerge as postindustrial constructs, which are both stereotypical and real (in terms of self-perception). Such constructions of reality stress the local production of a glue (*goma*) that binds borrowed characteristics into a uniform character in such a unique way (Moehn 2008: 167; Tzanelli

2017a: 128), so the act of borrowing from foreign systems is not considered a copyright violation. The fact that 'Cinema Nosso' has survived in the *favela* for a while now, suggests the successful hybridisation of *carioca*-Western atmospheres into a mute amalgam of mediated civility – what international tourists may expect to find. It may be wrong to consider this adaptation as submission to the Western canon: now directed by the trained local body, the cinematic gaze relays atmospheric schemata that appeal to local concerns about Rocinha's place in the world. Whatever *ressentiment* activists perceived and relayed while relating with locals, it has now being transformed into a noble stylistics – a recurring process in global histories of sports and artistic production as a form of civilising process (Wenning 2009).

This stylistic seems to blend native love for dance and music as manifestations of *felicidade* (joy) and *giambarra* (resilience), with Western audiovisual variations of light and darkness to produce an atmosphere of compassionate connectivity – how else would local students be involved in moviemaking activities enhancing communal agendas? Such evident fusions of embodied technics with audiovisual technology are orientated towards the construction of a new reputable kinesphere. Compatible with UNESCO's policy of 'heritage kinesthetics', which advocates the preservation of Brazilian music and dance as living heritage in *favelas* through artistic projects (Dimitrova Savova 2009), such atmospheric hybrids modify the community's original transmodal *Gestalt*, so to speak (Griffero 2014: 26). Otherwise put, the mute and non-represented cultures of contempt have assumed an image, which, ironically, schematises the non-representational aspects of *carioca* slum identity through filmmaking performance.

Krabi, Thailand

It becomes increasingly more difficult to differentiate between communal and Western or international design of responses in the cybersphere. The case of *The Beach*, which is mostly discussed as an instance of hostipitality later in the chapter, also merits a mention here, because its *online activist presence* displays trace-forms of epistemic misalignment. Although the website was allegedly set up and maintained by Thai students, on closer inspection we find out that its actual developer was Richard Barrow, a Western teacher at Sriwittayapaknam public school in Samut Prakarn. The young pupils of the *secondary* school in which he was teaching at the time appeared in many photographs online as a façade. In reality, the website acted as advertising for Thai tourism, with hyperlinks to Phi islands' hotels, scuba diving courses, and reviews of Phuket holidays, as well as recommendations of Alex Garland's book from which the film was adapted, the film, and the soundtrack, rather than a critical and fair assessment of the controversy (Thai Students.com 2000 in Tzanelli 2007: 50–51). Nevertheless, the design of this digital response was beneficial for the regional cause: not only did it endow the environmental core of the petition (to keep 'the beach' pristine and thus local ecosystems intact) with the value of instantly recognisable social bonds (young generations fighting for their future), it redirected Western patronising discourses of progress and education to their source (young Thais teaching Westerners to be sensitive and open to the needs of the erstwhile colonised others).

Undoubtedly, the content of the response validates scholarly suggestions that the internet facilitates antiglobalisation movements favourable to centripetal conservative nativism (van Aelst and Walgrave 2004). Contrary to the aforementioned example's hidden commercialism, in other cases, nonviolent digital mediations of protest helped create 'an atmosphere of consensus, emotion and togetherness' (Walgrave and Massens 2000: 235), which neutralised journalistic commercialisation trends that reduce activist power (Kielbowicz and Scherer 1986).

Johannesburg, South Africa

Antiglobalist articulations of epistemic misalignment in the cybersphere may have a short life in already highly commoditised cultural contexts, especially when terrestrially embedded communities give way to disorganised networks of response. One such example, which never developed into fully-blown hostipital protest, partly because of its spacial disembeddedness, is that of *D9*. Admittedly, the filmed slums of Soweto in Johannesburg already had a global international tourist clientele long before the film, especially, but not exclusively, from African expatriate communities. In addition, the film's notoriety helped little in developing sustainable cinematic tourism, despite the emergence of relevant digital advertising (Tzanelli 2016b: 139–144). Controversies erupted mainly because of cinematic representations of Nigerian slum groups as gangsters, drug-dealers and cannibals, but also the allegedly demeaning representation of the protagonist as a racist bureaucrat. A Facebook group ('District 9 Hates Nigerians') was formed, urging people to sign a petition to demand an apology from the filmmakers (Onagua, 8 September 2009). There was additional digital activity, which was, however, equally disembedded from the filmed sites' localities. Finally, debates on representations of Nigerian migrants attained a generalised Pan-African dimension, which should not be dismissed. Blogger Nicole Stamp, for example wrote 'That's Hollywood's Africa, isn't it. Black Africans shown as degenerate savages who'll have sex with non-humans and are pretty damn eager to eat people. Disgusting.' Nigerian-born British actor Hakeem Kae-Kazim told South African *Beeld* that '[the country's] problems can't be ascribed only to a small group of people', and wrote on Facebook: 'If the African continent truly wants to be liberated, we cannot sit back and allow this depiction of a "few rotten apples" to be spread across the world' (Smith, 2 September 2009). This widely publicised, but unspotted deviation from national or regional trace-forms, scrutinises the filmmakers' 'jump-cut urbanism' (Halprin 1963 in Jensen 2014: 32) to 'expose' how their staging is full of vicious intentions: to tarnish a generic group of 'black African people'. What is concealed from global publics is, again, the ways indigenous intimate practices (of sorcery – the film's satirical focus), which in today's cosmopolitan environment often figure as relics of a bygone era, can be essentially destructive of communal wellbeing.

Jump-cut urbanism refers to the cinematographic technique of montage. It involves the placement of the director in the role of a car driver, who plausibly arranges shots by looking at both his/her rear and front windows, hence both backwards and forwards. This arrangement, which is simultaneously spatial and temporal, thrives now in digital videostagings of the urban street (Ingersol 2006). Thus, despite the exposure of corrupt filmmaking practices, it is commonplace technique of apprehending reality in African urban kinespheres, which are now organised on the principles of 'public domography' (streets and buildings as facets of public life), both on and offline. Public domography adheres to the principles of surveillance, which, in the case of Soweto, are used by privileged native groups to sort human populations. Unsurprisingly, the Facebook rebels' jump-cut urbanism failed to acknowledge the source of 'Africa's' self-declared environmental pollution: a rapidly disintegrating rural life, after successive migrations of destitute peasants to inhospitable urban slums (*D9*'s uncivil Nigerian cannibals/criminals are Soweto's ganglords). Such dark aesthetics appear to clash with African notions of beauty we find across Côte d' Ivoire, Congo, Nigeria and Sierra Leone (Vogel and Carrieri 1986), but, in reality, their strong performative and spiritual-visual nature aims to enable their holders to perceive the environment in a particular style. This style brings together romanticised traditions (derided in *D9*) with a sterilised urban modernity (critiqued in it as incomplete, corrupt and imposed from outside). In African aesthetic traditions vision is not what Westerners perceive as a single sense, but a metaphysical experience emanating from synaesthetic visual, verbal, and musical *performances* associated with the ability *to amaze* (like a con artist) and thus be unique and inimitable in a traditional framework (Tzanelli 2016b: 103).

Unfortunately, the ability to amaze is often connected to drugs, which in actually existing cannibalistic practices are administered by hired witchdoctors to targets before their mutilation. There is a lucrative trade in body parts across African regions and countries for a ritual called *muti/muthi*, in which all participants have to be members of a clan or family, of high socio-economic standing and nominated as business partners in it (Nel 2012). The short-lived protest/response on Facebook excelled in the discursive uses of this performance: on the one hand, it interpellated *D9*'s director Neill Blomkamp, a South African migrant to the West as a digital witchdoctor, who conned 'African people' out of their riches to traffic them in the West. On the other hand, the petition's supporters engaged in a jump-cut activist style, wherein all good parts of African cinematic urbanism were allowed to travel the world, while all its international sociocultural contradictions were either erased or modified to amaze Western spectators.

Kuki, Japan

There are, therefore, plausible connections to be made between capitalist development and visual marketing, to which localities and different communities are not uninitiated. However, this should not be identified with the suggestion that economic globalisation 'flattens out' the world and its field-worlds (Friedman 2005). Another comparable instance of atmospheric misalignment to discuss along the same lines comes from Japan. The 'flattening' argument could hastily link local reactions to film tourism to resentful affect, because of the troubled relationship of the country with its historic dominator, the United States. However, more careful analysis, which looks at local responses to tourist development induced by the success of *LS* (see also Chapter 4), casts doubts on this haste. First, although much was said about the role of *ressentiment* in geopolitical approaches to nationalism (e.g. Greenfeld 1992), the scope of research was mostly kept within the European space, so more contextual research is necessary (but see Tzanelli 2017: Chapter 6 on Japan). Second, whereas Chatterjee's (1998) 'modernity in two languages' (one rational/scientific/public and the other effective/spiritual/intimate) is a useful starting point to comprehend the potential nationalistic subtext of such shadow-forms in tourism (see also Chapter 3), when scaling down our focus to the production of atmospheres, we find that different tools of investigation are needed.

Yamamura (2015) provides a compelling account of community responses to tourism development in the Washimiya district of Kuki city, Saitama prefecture, where the anime TV series was filmed. Nevertheless, because he is interested in outlining the collaborative model fostered between business and community, he does not think outside the adaptive cultural style in which Japanese mobilities and globalisation happen (see Chapter 1). This adaptive style, which dominated in the post-1980s Japanese economic deceleration, was based on Takeshi Murakami's recipe of 'knowing your own identity', recognising the Western gaze at Japan and 'playing along with it for all its worth' to hone Japanese *gaisen kouen* (triumphal return performance) (Favell 2011: 50–51). Not thinking outside this mode helps to gloss over any dark spots in this collaboration – although, it must be stressed that he mentions instances where such community-business collaboration did not work. These include *Silver Spoon* (2013) contents tourism in the agricultural facility in the Tokachi-Obihiro region of Hokkaido, which induced local fears that fans would spread diseases in livestock, and *Ichigo Mashimaro* (2005) tourism in the filmed residential area of Hamamatsu city, Shizuoka prefecture, in which police 'questioned a fan acting suspiciously in the vicinity of a school that appeared in the story' (Yamamura 2015: 75–76). The two cases nicely combine concerns over crime and contamination, the source of which localities tend to attribute to exogenous sources also in other contexts (Tzanelli 2008b, 2011). As explained in the previous chapter, much like Zhangjiajie's Southern Sky in China after *Avatar* (Tzanelli 2015b), *LS* helped the town develop both a domestic and foreign tourist clientele, where it previously hardly had any (see Seaton *et al.* 2016: Chapter 4). But less than a year after the anime's airing, a self-published magazine dedicated to *LS* and featuring the first location map for fans, including Washimiya, raised concerns over unregulated contents overtourism (Yamamura 2015: 65). Similar fears were expressed locally about the dramatic rise in fan visitations to Washinomiya temple due to the anime series, although the regional Commerce and Industry Association downplayed them in their official accounts (ibid.: 72).

It is not surprising that the locality did not complain about the generation of *kontentsu tsūrizumu* because of the movie, and expressed concerns over 'safety' due to overtourism only in the early stages of its engagement with business and regional tourism authorities. On the one hand, what seemed to be at stake at this early stage was the type of *kontentsu tsūrizumu* the locality had to cater for, which refashioned religious pilgrimage into a secular practice (Okamoto 2015). The locality's trace-form, which significantly matched that of the other two aforementioned examples of cinematic touristifiction, appealed to a particular Western understanding of 'design' known as 'façadism' or 'camouflage' (Böhme 2017: 99–100). On the one hand, it endorsed the tourist market's replacement of the native religious content with Westernised popular mobilities. On the other, it secretly rejected this scientised illumination of local culture (*lumen*) that does not coordinate with a holistic environmental light (*shikai* as lux) cast on the world (*sekai*). The camouflaging of fear that this light is 'put out' under civil concerns over host and visitor safety employed the Western language of securitisation to this end (Bauman and Lyon 2013). Beneath this language there lay another discourse appealing to a *control of one's environment*, threatened by the rise of dedifferentiated zones of consumption, excess and waste (Urry 2010: 191–192). Modifying Chatterjee's (1998: 274) remark on careless applications of Kantian aesthetics and Herzfeld's analysis of public embarrassment (2005), we may conclude that, for the locality, the public sphere was not regarded as the sphere of discursive freedom in this instance: only in private could the locality express any dissatisfaction with tourist development. Thus, Washimiya's response to touristification displayed all the characteristics of what Nederveen Pieterse (2006) calls 'cosmetic cosmopolitanism', which involves the education of desire to join the game of global players in the market, by attending to surfaces and civil etiquette.

Whangara, Gisborne, New Zealand

Clearly, then, the compromise between preserving one's heritage and memory vaults in ancestral lands and making ends meet in a glocalised now neoliberal environment emerges as a form of adaptive agency for those truly disempowered in political, cultural and/or economic terms (also see Robertson 1992 on the origins of the debate). As already explained in previous chapters, regardless of their suspect nature, strategies of adaptation appeal to Western tropes of postcolonial community development. But there are also examples of nihilistic strategy in film tourism, in which development as such is blocked, or limited to such an extent, that is barely felt in economic or sociocultural terms. We need only look at representations and policies that framed *Whale Rider* (director Niki Carro 2002 – *WR*), a film based on the novel by Witi Ihimaera, to consider how conservative discourses on local ecosystems become solidified even in mobility environments. Today, those New Zealanders, who pride themselves on their versatility and entrepreneurialism (Perkins and Thorns 2001: 198), mimic European discourse while simultaneously erasing internal social divisions between Māori (native tribes) and Pākehā (white and colonial) settlers, with the latter being the socially privileged groups (Amoamo and Thompson 2010: 37). Textually, *WR* conveys such policy concerns through intergenerational conflict, by gendering Māori 'heritage' through the protagonists' contested visions: old community leader Koro's obsession with identifying a male successor to whom he can hand over his talisman (*reiputa*) and his granddaughter's (Paikea) determination to change his mind (as the 'whale rider' she feels that she embodies heritage). Such scripts debate the power of colonial legacies over interactions even within indigenous communities (Sinclair 1992). Regardless of their aquatic connection, *WR*'s characters acknowledge that they are born of the sea and will return to it, thus emphasising the spiritual value of 'land' and its naming as the basis of tribal identity (Thompson-Carr 2012: 39). Koro's *reiputa* (a whale ivory pendant, which populates today ethnological museums around the world) is also his honour (only the chosen successor can retrieve it from the bottom of the sea). The unexpected union of the pendant with Paikea reinstates the order of intergenerational transaction: the girl serves as a mobility instrument, a *hau* asserting the system of giving that Mauss explained in his anthropology of gift and giving. Contextually, the film is situated in a 'first people' countermovement that promotes films 'made by Māori and set in the Māori community' (Barclay 2003: 8), thus fostering tighter links between landscape, land and human capital (Turner 2002). This movement would adhere to visions of the seashore as a magical place and a livelihood factory rather than a Pākehā space of leisure.

Notably, proponents of 'cultural imperialism' in media studies were infuriated by filmmaking itself as a practice of worldmapping that adheres to the Western gaze. For Hokowhitu (2007: 24, 26), Caro's Pākehā/settler film perspective presents a

> self-determining Maori community coming to terms with the suppression of their people by their own primitive traditions [something which] serves to mask the actual oppressor: colonial imperialism. In this imagined community, a traditional Maori nation is reinvented and enlightened through a neo-colonial gaze.

However, the alternative of sociocultural and economic isolation is as grim, if not worse. It is otherwise understandable why the film was initially inserted into global flows that made the Whangara community of the filmed sites a tourist

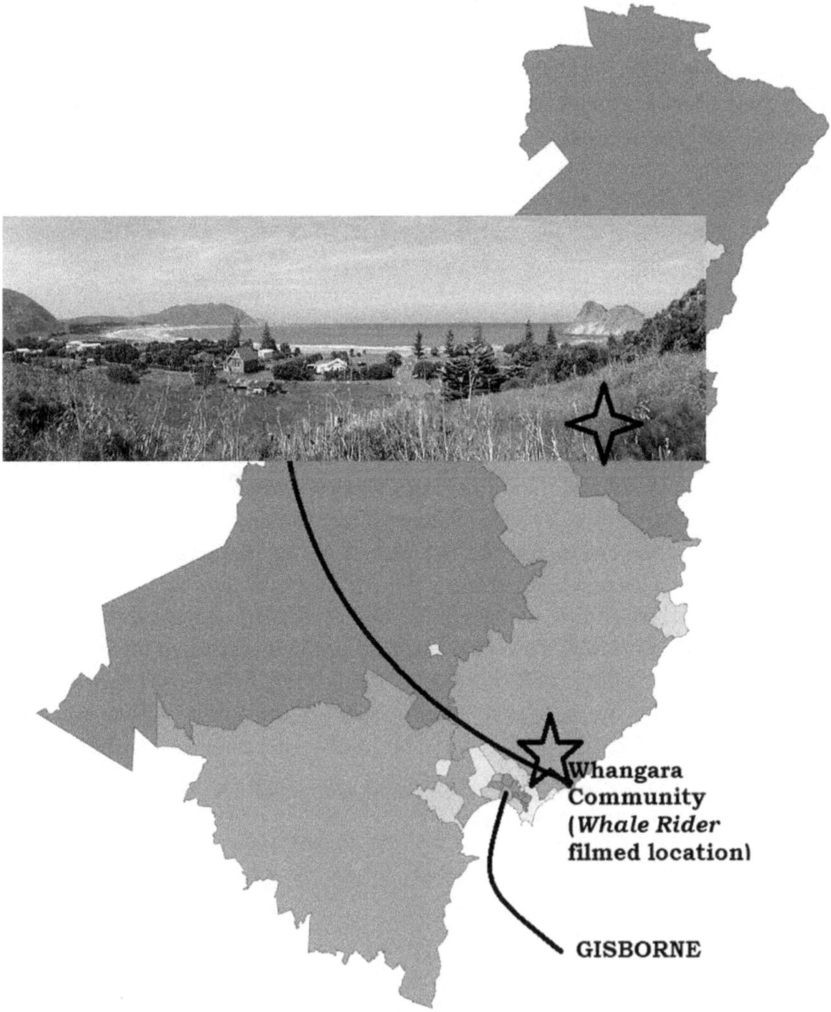

Figure 5.2 Whangara response to popcultural 'intrusion': blocking public access to the *WR* beach.

Map credit: Vardion, Wikimedia Creative Commons Attribution-Share Alike 3.0 Unported Licensing (retouched with arrows, signs and location names by Rodanthi Tzanelli); *embedded photograph credit*: Avenue, Wikimedia Creative Commons Attribution-Share Alike 3.0 Unported Licensing.

destination (Leotta 2012: 118–120). Experiencing landscapes from within would be communicated to cinematic tourists, strangers 'from without' with interest in the exotic. Back in 2003 and during filming, the small settlement, which is located 29 km north of Gisborne and 5 km off the main highway, was already attracting a few European and American tourists, who wanted to see the filmed locations, despite Whangara's lack of tourist facilities. The tourists' walking into the local *marae* (meeting grounds), which is the focal point of Māori communities that usually belongs to a particular *iwi* (tribe), *hapū* (sub tribe) or *whānau* (family), made the community put up a sign of 'No Trespassing', whereas the film's cultural adviser, Hone Taumaunu, who also lives at Whangara, supported the implementation of regulations on cinematic tourist traffic (*The New Zealand Herald* 8 March 2003).

In 2009, the landlords of a locked gate blocking public access to the beach made famous by *WR* were told by the region's administration to make the route accessible to the public. By that time, Tipuna Tours, one of few tour operators allowed to take visitors to the village and its marae, where some of the film props were kept, including four fibreglass whales, had made an unsigned agreement with the community to avoid fancrowding. The tour operator admitted that until the movie was made, the locals 'had a quiet, uninterrupted life', but 'since the film they've had people roaming in and out and they've got a bit toey ['edgy'] about it' (Stuff 31 January 2009). Although compatible with the national campaign '100% Pure New Zealand', which picked up after the international success of the *LOTR* (Frew and White 2011: 61–62), the management of *WR*'s locations by a largely marginalised ethnic group within the New Zealand nation, fostered an atmospheric 'enfolding' not dissimilar to that we find in self-destructive cultures of *ressentiment* and spite (Diken 2009). In the absence of an enlarged caring imagined community, this enfolding led Whangara's *iwi* to withdraw communication with the tourist world – a point enforced by limiting fans in the area, allowing them to photograph the magnificent filmed landscapes only from afar.

Conclusion

All in all, despite its emphasis on cultural differences emanating from the development of particular environmental technics (tools) and techniques (practices), epistemic misalignment does not entail lack of native/regional/national comprehension of, or ability to communicate with creative postindustrial Western processes. This observation dispels any suggestions that Western postindustrial creativity encounters 'captive minds' (Alatas 2004) that cannot devise their own innovative arguments, but also notes that, on its own, this does not constitute good analysis in decolonial or cultural economic terms. The actual focus of disagreement in epistemic misalignments is rooted in the contemporary global marriage between the ideologies of visualism and consumerism, and the ensuing fear of losing cultural, economic and/or political sovereignty – the governance source of cinematic tourist mobilities in short (Bærenholdt 2013). In this respect, I conclude that epistemic misalignments can serve both as honest expressions of disempowerment in international political contexts and performative tools that allow for the design of sustainable 'native' market strategies. Indeed, we may even be dealing with a replacement of tropes of sustainability with those of degrowth, as the decoupling of economic growth from wellbeing and tourist/guest wellbeing (D'Alisa *et al.* 2015; Andriotis 2018). In the following section I explore more tense or violent responses to cinematic tourist development. Although the styles of response can be as disconnected or disorganised as the ones I outlined in this section (or form an escalation), their media relaying provides stronger connections between humans, heritage artefacts and natural environments.

Hostipitality

The mode of hostipitality is based on Jacques Derrida's (2000) observation that hospitality and hostility form challenging blends in environments guided by legal regulations of human mobility, alliance, and communication. To clarify its significance, I stress that cinematic tourism maintains all the characteristics relating to the objectivisation of strangerhood. This status, which in ethnonational environments can also transmute into an identity badge, involves a coexistence of distance and disinterest on the one hand, and proximity and engagement on the other (Friese 2004: 68). More specifically in our case, cinematic or contents tourists help institute infrastructural and habitual bonds between the business of travel and host communities, therefore they must be considered as strangers who arrive today but remain tomorrow, at least in the shadow-forms that they generate locally. It is unsurprising that hospitality traces its etymological origins in the 'ghost' (O'Gorman 2006; 2007), an epistemontological process whereby external actors/actants are brought to life and light/knowledge through the relationship they form with their hosts. To extend this observation to the developed cinematic tourist sites, we must remember that hospitality always positions strangers at the threshold of home, thus challenging guests to define its limits (Lawlor 2002: 213; Westmoreland 2008: 4). To extend this into sociopolitical ecologies, tourists/strangers make national subjects question symbolic and actual borders in the national territory they inhabit (Rumford 2006; 2008).

As becomes evident below, hostipitality emerges where there are more advanced bureaucratic systems to differentiate between insiders and outsiders, friends and enemies, citizens and non- or postcitizens (i.e. cosmopolitan tourists). This is not to say that such 'advancement' is beneficial to either party or conducive to justice and local sustainability of an environmental type or otherwise. Korstanje (2018b), who is interested in the increasing withdrawal of hospitality in the West towards outsiders/migrants, does not discuss adverse reactions towards privileged forms of strangerhood we find in tourism, but does stress the significant role technologies of surveillance play in such contexts (see also Korstanje 2016). Hostipitality can yield more destructive results in some postcolonial contexts, where surveillance has been incorporated into local governance, without eliminating earlier forms of identity-as-identification. On this I defer discussions of native or indigenous self-destructive reactions to establish a framework of analysis first – for, such 'inclinations' merit their own analysis. Even epistemic misalignments display an element of hostipitality, but they differ from the forms of open, and often organised hostility I place in this second mode/category.

Notably, where epistemic misalignments originate in mechanical notions of belonging to a sphere/environment (*à la* Durkheim), which blends tools, actants and humans, hostipitality is an anthropocentric phenomenon enacted on affective and emotional platforms. However, as I explain in the cases of New Zealand and Thailand, the occasional featuring of livelihood needs, natural environments and nonhumans in this mode may come under Western forms of activism. This validates Castro-Gómez's (2007: 441) argument that, at international policy level, the recognition of non-occidental knowledge and the promotion of the 'indigenous person' to the 'guardian of biodiversity' is pragmatic, rather than epistemic: local 'wisdom' is considered 'useful' for the conservation of the environment, but its recognition never enters the realm of science. There are hopeful activist examples to refute this, but their presence is scarce in this second type of response to touristification. This can also be attributed to the fact that hostipitality coexists with dark-as-heritage tourism, a form of tourism appealing to emotional connections to land, especially, but not exclusively, in European contexts (see Chapter 2 on dark tourism and heritage). Such connections serve political agendas of the nation-state, which always seeks ways to strengthen its presence in global neoliberal networks.

Callanish/Carloway District, Scotland

Hostipitality reporting in the news is often based on particular episodes of hatred or discontent. Such episodes, which are treated here as discursively real rather than fictitious, are important for the tripartite actor/actant classification of the section, so I begin with them. The classification of such episodes within Europe centres on the ability of humans to control their communal territory, so their rationale is anthropocentric. Local complaint can become implicated in the politics of international heritage, even when it appears to be a small local incident. Such is the case of resident activism in the Callanish and Carloway district of Lewis, who had to put up with an increasing visitor influx to the Callanish Stones, a site featuring prominently in *Brave*. The focus of the complaint was clearly localised, unlike that of Disney Lucasfilm's 'facility fee' – free use for *Star Wars VII* and *Star Wars VIII* shootings in Skellig Michael, a UNESCO World Heritage Site that required minor repair works afterwards. Notably, the use of the monument for filming was not approved by the Minister for Arts,

Heritage and the Gaeltacht Heather Humphreys under section 14 of the National Monuments Act, which relates to a range of potential impacts to a monument. In addition to Birdwatch Ireland, cinematographer Chris O'Dell and a group of archaeologists and academics, An Taisce Vice-Chair Attracta Uí Bhroin expressed concerns about the site's protected ecology and archaeology, stressing the lack of accountability and transparency in the decision-making process (Siggins 26 September 2015).

In organised meetings, the Callanish petitioners explored the possibility of buying the Carloway estate, where the Stones are located – a petition that brought them in direct conflict with the official caretaker of the Calanais site, the public agency Historic Scotland (BBC News 2012b). The community's activism was framed by a culturally situated rationale: the standing stones are supposed to be *fir bhrèige* or 'false men', hence a thanatourist site that should not be entrusted to Hollywood magicians or their touristic sorcery. Anthropocentric heritage discourse came to the fore when the site was included in the 70-day Olympic Torch's relay journey (BBC News 2012a). The result was the accommodation of a localised trace-form to expressions of nationalist sentiment ('the land/heritage belongs to us, not tourists') and, finally, in universalised European traditions of Olympism (the Flame as a sign of human unity) (Sinclair 2000; Tzanelli 2014).

Edinburgh, Scotland

Other instances, such as Edinburgh's *HP* overtourism, are more nuanced, but equally important for analysis of hostipitality. In a few years, in addition to the crowds wrought upon the city from organised *HP* tours, the old town became inundated with J.K. Rowling pubs, Harry Potter bars, witchcraft and souvenir shops, similarly themed luxury apartments, and an Elephant House permanently surrounded 'by awestruck Spanish tourists and screaming Edinburgh Uni students in Hogwarts house scarves' (Turbett 18 January 2018). Cosplay situations similar to those we associate with Japanese anime and manga-inspired contents tourism have become ubiquitous, clashing with the sort of heritage tourism that branded Edinburgh mobilities for a long time (King 21 January 2018; Wardrop 2011). Perhaps not as funny as its black humourist desecrator might have assumed, was the recently scrawled 'Sirius Black, 1953–1996' on a tomb in the city's Greyfriars Kirkyard, close to the resting place of Thomas Riddell, whose name echoed that of the wicked wizard Lord Voldemort ('Tom Riddle'), the primary antagonist of Harry Potter (Turbett 18 January 2018). Conceptions of 'desecration' matched perceptions of Edinburgh's urbanite environment as sacred: particularly, such complaints were not backed by residents but famous novelists such as Alexander McCall Smith and Liam Turbett, also author of a lead article on the question, possibly in an attempt to amplify local involvement.

Advertising strategy aside, Edinburgh's status as sacred heritage terrain is implicated in European artistic and aesthetics hierarchies, which would place literary above digital-cinematic creations, so the two prominent novelists' indignation about the city's cinematic overtourism are implicated in cultural political agendas. Second, such responses are connected to the politics of heritage conservation, pointing to issues of custodianship and policing of sacred heritage landscapes. Not only did Edinburgh served as the first UNESCO World City of Literature, its historical city centre was registered on the list of UNESCO World Heritage Sites a long time ago (Eghbali *et al.* 2015: 720). With an increase of visitors between 2012 and 2017 to 3.85 million, a boost of visitor spending from £1.01 billion to £1.31 billion, and an impending Brexit that may find the city outside the European Union, from which it receives such tourists, economic returns from heritage tourism cannot be discounted. If we look at the general fall of migrant labour in the UK following the activation of Article 50 (Malik 25 February 2018), there may be additional problems to address: in a market of 30,000-strong tourism workers, worth around £400 million each year, in a city with tourism growing faster than the rate in both Scotland and the UK, and 'with a 33 per cent rise in domestic visitors and a 27 per cent increase from foreign tourists in five years', in less than two years, shortage of hands to cater for tourists becomes a dead certainty (Ferguson 12 July 2017).

Additionally, as a systemic complex in its own right, local tourism displays stakeholder conflicts that are not easy to resolve: the Edinburgh Tourism Action Group (ETAG) wants to boost profits from Chinese visitors by £400 million, whereas Edinburgh World Heritage (EWH) is concerned that development puts residents' needs last; the local council wishes to implement a sustainable plan with EWH and Historic Environment Scotland's (HES) input; finally, VisitScotland's regional director seems to be preoccupied with visitor sustainability more than labour or conservation issues. Such conflicting prioritisations and interpretations of what constitutes sustainable development regard the city itself as an attractor of human mobilities that can be treated separately from issues addressing environmental stability (Robinson 2004). It is significant that, less than a year before the Harry Potter incident, heritage watchdogs warned that Edinburgh is at risk of being overrun with tourists and suggested a change in the way its relevant mobilities are regulated, so that it does not end up a 'hollow city-museum shell' like Venice (Ferguson 12 July 2017). For the first time, the suggested planning addressed a few anthropocenic problems beckoning all of us. Pointing to additional European examples, such as Berlin, Barcelona, Amsterdam and Rome, heritage watchdogs proposed to the city council a sustainable plan that included stringent licensing controls, policing of street noise late at night, better waste management and the provision of more affordable housing. This concise plan effectively introduces the importance of both synaesthetics (noise) and environmental issues (waste management) in a Western European style of policy-making. This addresses notions of 'spatial cleansing' in ways that appeal both to Western notions of spatial ordering and symmetry, and internationalised understandings of justice (see for problematic implementations of similar policies outside Europe Herzfeld 2006, 2016).

If we now place the original celebrity-backed plea against overtourism within this stakeholder complexity, we retrieve two conflicting shadow forms: one speaks of nostalgic love for a structural utopia (heritage architecture), which resembles the affects induced by cinematic architectonic design (Bruno 2002: 49). The other is ubiquitous in European contexts, and reveals *ressentiment* towards both internal (filmmakers as the wizardly usurpers of literary heritage) and external enemies (foreign visitors polluting the place physically and symbolically – Douglas 1993: 132; Douglas and Wildavsky 1982), thus reiterating borders within the urban kinesphere (see also Chapter 3). A merging of the two shadow forms, which also manifests in other examples of hostipitality, generates an additional paradox standing at the heart of the separation of medieval theology from Enlightenment modernity: the uncompromising attack against the 'sorcery of capitalism' (Pignarre and Stengers 2011), which alienated humans from their unspoiled original home, also signals a regression to discourses of danger, when today we live in global risk environments (Beck 2006, 2007, 2009). The merger, which is not conducive to peaceful international relations, mobilises Christian religious values in the name of particular human interests. In such instances, which I present below, nature assumes the anthropomorphic characteristics of corruption, excess and greed thus reiterating biblical scriptures.

Skiathos and Skopelos, Greece

The strategy of making a politically correct Christian movie, so to speak, is prevalent in places accommodating lucrative heritage sites for the benefit of a Church establishment. On the Greek island of Skiathos, which served together with the neighbouring Skopelos as the stage for the first *MM* musical, nestles the Monastery of *Evangelístria* ('Annunciation'). This old religious building, which is still functional, once served as the centre of regional Christianity and the birthplace of the first Greek flag (1807), on which militia fighting for Greek independence from Ottoman Turks took the sacred oath of self-sacrifice for the nation-to-be (Tzanelli 2011: 52). Its presence in heritage tourism is significant for domestic entrepreneurs and visitors, but its involvement in other commoditisation domains is also telling: the monks run a souvenir, local wine and olive oil shop, but steer clear from anything that has to do with *MM* tourism mobilities.

Equally important is that, back in 2009, a banner was hung on the Monastery's entrance, depicting the Greek and the Byzantine flags, suggesting that they stood for a continuity in Greek imperial-nationalist ambitions ('Byzantium, the empire the Ottomans destroyed is Greek and we will get it back one day' – see Herzfeld 1982). When matched with the selection of Agios Ioannis to stage popular pilgrimages after the success of the film (for an analysis see Chapter 4), an affective geography of *ressentiment* formed in the region (Thrift 2007: 221; Tzanelli 2017b). The affective separation of field-worlds for play (Skopelos) and religious devotion (Skiathos) ended up enclosing each island's particular areas into separate kinespheres, even though both their histories and futures are closely linked. Skiathos' privileged connection to national histories and Skopelos' privileged connection to international popular cultural networks (it was the main filming ground for the musical), generated potential competition for national administrative, tourist or business clientele. Local administration did not necessarily share in this religious spatialisation of hostipitality, but had to both negotiate the island's branding as a cultural/literary destination and the Christian Orthodox Church's sensibilities, so the original split never went away. Thus, although all international tourists are welcome to the Monastery's grounds, narratives of its sacred history are addressed in a particular cultural grammar addressed to Greek visitors, leaving only its commercial areas 'grammatologically' (*à la* Derrida 1997) open to strangers.

Paris, France

Connections between literature (*belles lettrés*), high art (*belles arts*) and religious heritage persist across Europe to date, marking various sites as inhospitable grounds for tourists and non-believers, while achieving the maintenance of boundaries between 'real art' and 'pop fiction' (McRobbie 2006: 527; Hall 1992). We may heed Bruno Latour's (2002: 17) thesis to preamble the next hostipital discussion, that:

> We are digging for the origin of an absolute – not a relative – distinction between truth and falsity, between a pure world, absolutely emptied of human-made intermediaries and a disgusting world composed of impure but fascinating human-made mediators. 'If only, some say, we could do without any image. How so much better, purer, faster our access to God, to Nature, to Truth, to Science could be.' To which other voices (or sometimes the same) answer: 'Alas (or fortunately), we cannot do without images, intermediaries, mediators of all shapes and forms, because this is the only way to access God, Nature, Truth and Science.' It is this quandary that we want to document, to fathom and, maybe, to overcome. In the strong summary that Marie-José Mondzain proposed of the Byzantine quarrel over images, 'La vérité est image mais il n'y a pas d'image de la vérité [Truth is image, but there is no image of truth].'

The elusive truth of God and Art Proper certainly stood centre-stage in the *DVC* wars over images, especially when Dan Brown's novel was released as a film and tourists started gathering across different filmed sites in Europe. The real furore, which informed one of the strongest Church-led hostipitality responses to cinematic touristification, had as its epicentre religious and art heritage sites in France and Italy that we explored in the previous chapter. At first, artistic and religious responses were sporadic: a parishioner at the Church of Saint-Sulpice in Paris reportedly said to the press that the whole *DVC* story was wrong – 'The description of the artwork, the architecture, the documents in this church …

[the] secret rituals – I don't know, because we never had any secret rituals in the church' (CBS News 12 November 2004). The same parishioner proceeded to put on the wall next to the obelisk a notice when there was still not a movie but the novel had caused tourist ripples: 'Contrary to fanciful allegations in a recent best-selling novel, this is not a vestige of a pagan temple. No such temple existed in this place. It was never called a Rose Line. It does not coincide with the meridian' (Sacred Destinations undated). Over the same period, it was also reported that a staffer at the Louvre's information desk under Pei's glass Pyramid (the alleged tomb of Magdalene), retorted to a reporter that he 'has no advice for the daily trickle of curious fans. "After all", he sniffs, "the book is fiction"' (Bly 21 October 2004). Four years later, when *Angels & Demons* (director Ron Howard 2008 – *AD*) premiered internationally, priests were still unhappy, but less openly hostile. A tour guide was reported by CBS News to say:

> You never get a priest coming up and yelling at you 'get out you heretics'. Sometimes they might be a little bit edgy because they know it's 'Angels & Demons' but at the same time I think they are aware that it's, you know, a work of fiction and that it's bringing people into their churches.
>
> (CBS 19 June 2008)

Nevertheless, by then, the natural world had given way to dangerous human simulacra social scientists normally examine under the rubric of political ecology, with international dimensions: first, the *DVC* controversy had coerced the Vatican to appoint an official debunker of its scandalising content. Later, the Samoan government censor banned the film from cinemas and all local television stations, with the support of the Samoan Catholic Archbishop, prompting, by turn, Magik cinema owner Maposua Rudolf Keil to accuse both of violation of 'people's fundamental rights'. This had little effect, because, apparently, Samoa's principal censor also proceeded to ban *AD* from the cinemas a few years later (Tzanelli 2013: 66–68). Thereafter, the *DVC* would go all the way back to Italy, where Cardinal Tarcisio Bertone, the Vatican's secretary of state, would confirm that 'Boycotting this film is the least we can do', whereas during the making of *AD* Franco Zeffirelli, director of *Jesus of Nazareth* (1977 – *JoN*), would relay to Corriere della Sera: 'Dan Brown is a rapscallion. The Vicariate has done well to deny them access [to sacred sites for filming]' (*Telegraph* 17 June 2008).

We must put a brake on examples of hostipitality and examine their nature. All variations of the tensions between the Catholic Church, the international filmworld and tourist business appear to exemplify Beck's (2002: 27) 'cosmopolitan crisis', which commences from an ideological twister (France as an artistic heritage destination), and moves on to enmesh theological cannon (the Vatican responding to the novel/film's 'blasphemous' content) and representational propriety in the filmworld (Zeffireli's intervention), thus questioning the limits of human freedom in creativity at large, and, consequently, how we are granted with cultural citizenship. In other words, the cosmopolitan crisis delineates a postnational '*icono*-crisis', which, every time commences as a hunt for the original paradisiac condition, and every time concludes in merciless witch-hunting, a precondition for exclusion from a group (Latour 2002). In case it is still unclear, this witch-hunting affirms commitment to the darkness of material and intangible heritage, for which the Church wants to act as the sole custodian – a peculiar confirmation of 'zombie environmentalism' devouring human play as 'too shallow' to have any spiritual life (Phillips 2015: 59). Hence, the disgruntled parishioner's mourning *DVC*'s international fame that led to the alleged overcrowdings of the temple of God was expressing concern over the tourists' interest in celebrating the joyful and life-affirming qualities of a false Goddess instead: *eudaimonía* or the good life. The response is nothing short of a shambolic witch-burning ritual, which links medieval and early modern 'campaigns of terror against women', whose transgressive wisdom stood as one of the primary sources of resistance of European peasantry to state and gentry privatisation (Federici 2005: 165), as well as capitalist ontologies of insecurity and private securitisation (Bauman and Lyon 2013). Peculiarly then, the priest's attack upon the emergence of a secular commons was inviting neoliberal privatisation ('Zeffireli style') to interfere into Church business, hoping that together they could exorcise the threat of playful creativity in touristified contexts (Kirwan *et al.* 2015).

Dubrovnik, Croatia

The overall shift from 'fetishes' to 'factishes' for those who broke artistic idols by beginning to interpret them (Latour 1998, 1999) begins to assert itself in this peculiar interface between religious conviction, artistic cosmopolitanism and heritage conservation. Then custodians have to demonstrate that they can cure the decay of time while also shooing successfully the decadent 'pop tourists'. Such campaigns for decency, religious or not, may also be overtaken by campaigns for conservation, which maintain material forms of decency in the market. In 2014, it was reported that the *GoT* production team was prohibited by the Dubrovnik Film Commission from shooting a crucial topless scene at its planned location (Cercei Lanister's 'walk of shame' from a church through the streets of King's Landing). Although today the Jesuit Stairs off St. Dominca Street are visited by *GoT* fans as part of their Dubrovnik film tour, it is worth noting that the scene almost did not happen (Taylor 13 August 2017).The earmarked temple for the scene is deemed to be of local importance, so the pressure to ban shooting came in fact from Dubrovnik's Catholic Church of St Nicholas, 'which takes a hardline stance against public nudity, acts of sexuality and "immorality"' (Hawkes 26 August 2014). This *icono*-crisis, which, again, buries its non-representational basis underneath a moralising theological polemics, is only the smallest part of Dubrovnik's problems. Hollywood's discovery of Dubrovnik is rumoured to have had a

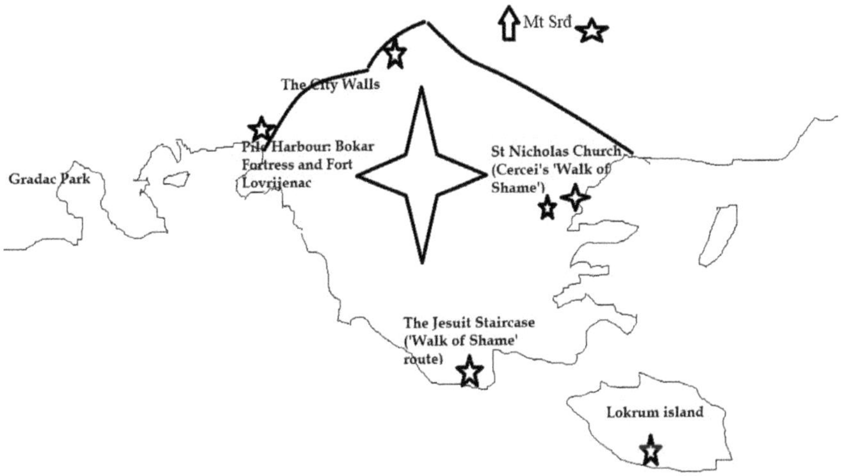

Figure 5.3 Map of responses to *GoT* touristification presenting the complexity of resident, institutional (Church and UNESCO), and cinematic tourist mobility interests.

Map credit: Rodanthi Tzanelli.

deleterious effect on its natural and cultural beauty: recently, the cinematic machine selected it to film parts of *The Last Jedi*, the eighth episode in the *Star Wars* series, a new *Robin Hood* film produced by Leonard DiCaprio and the twenty-fifth *JB* film. No other franchise has besieged the city more than *GoT*, and since the show's 2011 HBO premier, tourism has seen an increase of 9 to 12% annually, according to the Dubrovnik Tourist Board.

UNESCO has warned that the Old Town of Dubrovnik, a World Heritage Site since 1979, cannot accommodate the massive influx of cinematic fans (Capps 11 December 2011). A report pushed jointly by UNESCO and the ICOMOS in 2015, which monitored cruise ship and urban development (the building of a golf club, a recreation park and apartments overlooking the old town), expressed concerns that the plan would 'eradicate the clear distinction that has historically existed between the urban complex of Dubrovnik, as a unique creation of medieval architecture and town planning, its landscape and rural environment setting' (ICOMOS 2015: 6). On the same issue, many NGOs criticised the lack of transparency and stakeholder involvement in the decision-making process (ibid.: 13–14). Before leaving the heritage grounds in 2015, the UNESCO/ICOMOS mission proposed that the state considers the development and submission to the World Heritage Centre of a minor boundary modification proposal for an extension of the buffer zone to include 'the west facing slopes of Mt Srđ, the sea area around the Island of Lokrum and the fortress landscape of the Srđ plateau' (ibid.: 20).

The local residents also seem to have ambivalent feelings towards crammed cruise arrivals and on-foot pilgrimages of all sorts. The 2017 census, which put the population of Old Town at 1,557 people, down almost 30% from 2011, matches many households' decision to list their properties all year long on Airbnb, and the city's central planning guidelines ('General Urban Plan') to build more and more unwanted commercial buildings in the area (Capps 11 December 2011) on one thing: residents want to have a break from home. If anything, we deal with competing worldmappings, in which 'worlds' are moving lifescapes, enclosing, separating and controlling identities, practices and processes (see Cresswell 2014 on the case of the Israeli separation wall). Such segmentations do not eradicate the interpenetrations of molar and molecular movements, which stay as affectively porous and politically potent as ever (Merriman 2018: 9–10, 14).

There is, therefore, an issue of ecosystemic sustainability, including humans, architectural landscape and natural beauty transcending religious codes of conduct at play, which Dubrovnik mayor, Mato Franković, plans to address by capping the number of visitors mounting the city's medieval walls at 4,000 a day – just half of the number suggested by UNESCO (Rigby 16 August 2017). At the moment, the venture's success is unclear, but we can safely conclude that it displays traces similar to the *DVC*'s and *Brave*'s affective geographies of hostipitality. Notably, Dubrovnik is one of the many instances of *GoT* overtourism, which becomes specifically focused on environmental sustainability issues in other filmed locations, inviting local and national policy-makers to take drastic measures. One such case is the tunnel of beech trees on the Bregagh Road, near Armoy ('Kingsroad' in the TV series), which has become a major international tourist attraction. Stormont's Department for Infrastructure introduced a ban on cars using the road from 30 October 2017. Not all of the 'Dark Hedges', which were planted more than 200 years ago by the Stuart family stand intact today. Storm Gertrude ripped up two of them in January 2016, whereas later in that year a large rotten branch broke off another tree and fell across the road. A warning by conservationists that constant traffic damages the trees' roots, and constant media criticism that the 'national treasure' is being killed by pollution, convinced the Department to issue a ban on traffic, after consultation with Causeway Coast and Glens Borough Council, curbing at the same time *GoT* fans' automobile trips in the area (BBC 10 October 2017). Clearly, where citizen and administrative concern focus exclusively on environmental sustainability, agendas on low-carbon policy to address climate change come to the fore (Urry 2004: 26, 2011: 164–165; Sheller 2014: 5–9).

I commenced this section by noting that hostipital responses to touristification are connected to Western and European connections with dark-as-heritage tourism. In the remaining space I wish to draw attention to two non-European cases, each with its own complexities: an Indian one, which takes us back to debates on religious fundamentalism, and a Thai one, which brings together questions of human and natural ecosystemic resilience. Both share in the ways feelings of hostility towards strangers blend internal and external targets, although at the same time, their mode exceeds this hostility. The fundamentalist problems concerning a rise in Islamophobia and Jihadism in Europe and the United States (Sayyid 2015; Sayyid and Vakil (eds) 2010) find dangerous homologues in postcolonial contexts, in which cultural adaptation to foreign needs facilitate global political connectivity. We can imagine such phobic eruptions as adjustments of the system to its original precolonial status, or, better, an unwanted feedback loop to a broader global phobic system to which countries such as India belong.

Mumbai and Rajasthan, India

India hosts complex hybrids of fear, to which we can safely add tourismophobia. The Indian fear of tourists, which is essentially one of privileged stranger traffic with roots in Europe (Spode 2009), interacts with notions of religious propriety: the tool of political demagogy. Endemic corruption in the Indian public sector suggests that underhand dealings failing to yield desired results are supplemented with manipulations of public opinion regarding religious conviction (Davis 2004; Charron 2010). Tourismophobic surges connecting to cinematic tourism were present in the political mobilisation of slum residents in the case of *SM*. In line with accusations that the film peddles 'poverty porn', a Dharavi slumdweller welfare group filed a defamation lawsuit against film music composer A.R. Rahman and actor Anil Kapoor, alleging human rights violations (AFP Google News 22 January 2009). However, such 'human rights' agendas were soon streamlined into religious ones: Hindu organisations Janajagruti Samiti and Shiv Sena protested against the film's portrayal of the Hindu god Rama, arguing that it hurt the sentiments of Hindus (*The Times of India* 22 January 2009). Such allegations were expanded on in an article in the conservative *Daily Pioneer* on *SM* depictions of Hindus as 'rapacious monsters ... structured ... within the matrix of Western lib-left perceptions of the Indian "reality" ' which have little or nothing in common with the real India in which we live' (Tzanelli 2015a: 167). This localised response was repeated across other parts of the country, including Patna in Bihar, where posters of the movie were torn down by protesters (Weaver 27 January 2009), and Goa, where again Janjagruti Samiti demanded a ban on the release of the film for depicting the Indian god Rama in a denigrating way (*New York Times* 20 February 2009).

This example connects to business mobilities with tourist extensions, so I provide another now that is about direct expulsion of tourists from visiting sites. It concerns *Padmaavat* (director Sanjay Leela Bhansali 2018), the most expensive period drama ever made by Bollywood, loosely based on a Sufi epic poem. The film was initially scheduled for release on 1 December 2017, but violent protests, followed by a bounty on actress Deepika Padukone and the director that was doubled by the leader of the ruling Bharatiya Janata Party (BJP), Suraj Pal

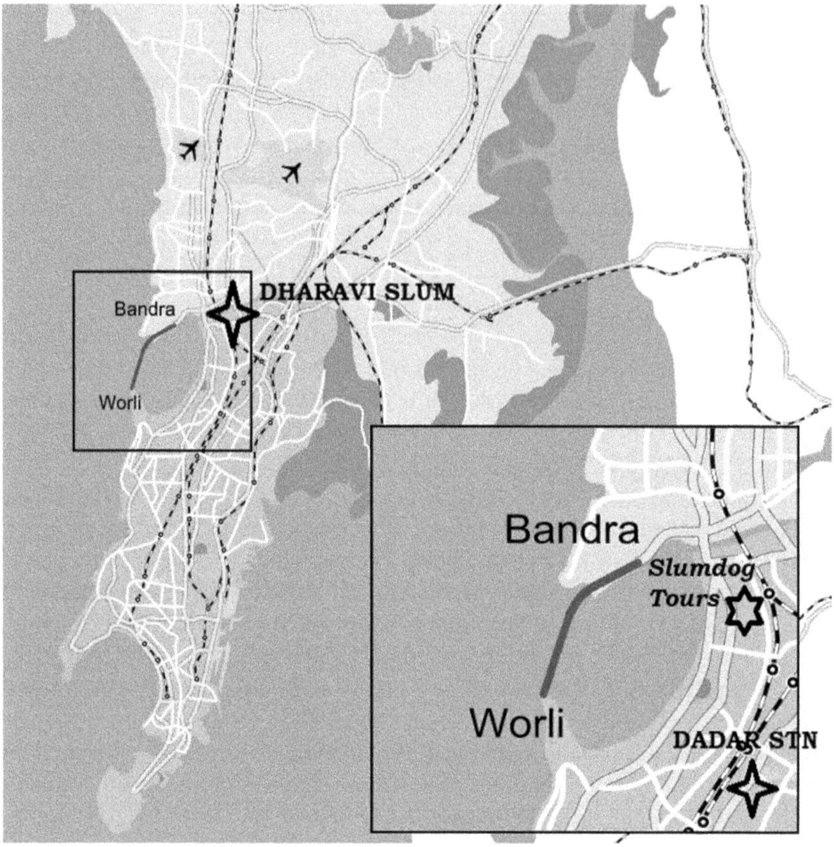

Figure 5.4 Map of Dharavi area in Mumbai including protest hotspot for the banning of *SM*, as well as local World Heritage sites and tourist business.

Map credit: Planemad (original author of retouched image – retouched again with arrows, signs and location names by Rodanthi Tzanelli), Wikimedia Creative Commons Attribution-Share Alike 2.5 Generic, 2.0 Generic and 1.0 Generic Licensing.

Amu, led to further delays (Ray 17 November 2017). The Central Board of Film Certification approved the film with a few changes, including the addition of multiple disclaimers and a change in the title. The film's production phase was marked by a series of activist incidents, including some led by Rajput caste organisations, which vandalised film sets claiming that the film portrays Padmavati, a Rajput Sinhala queen, in a bad light (*The Times of India* 19 January 2017), and some by BJP members and Muslim leaders, who alleged misrepresentation of Ala-ud-din Khilji and called for a ban (*Hindustan Times* 2 January 2018). All these responses exemplify India's postcolonial political ecologies that, while

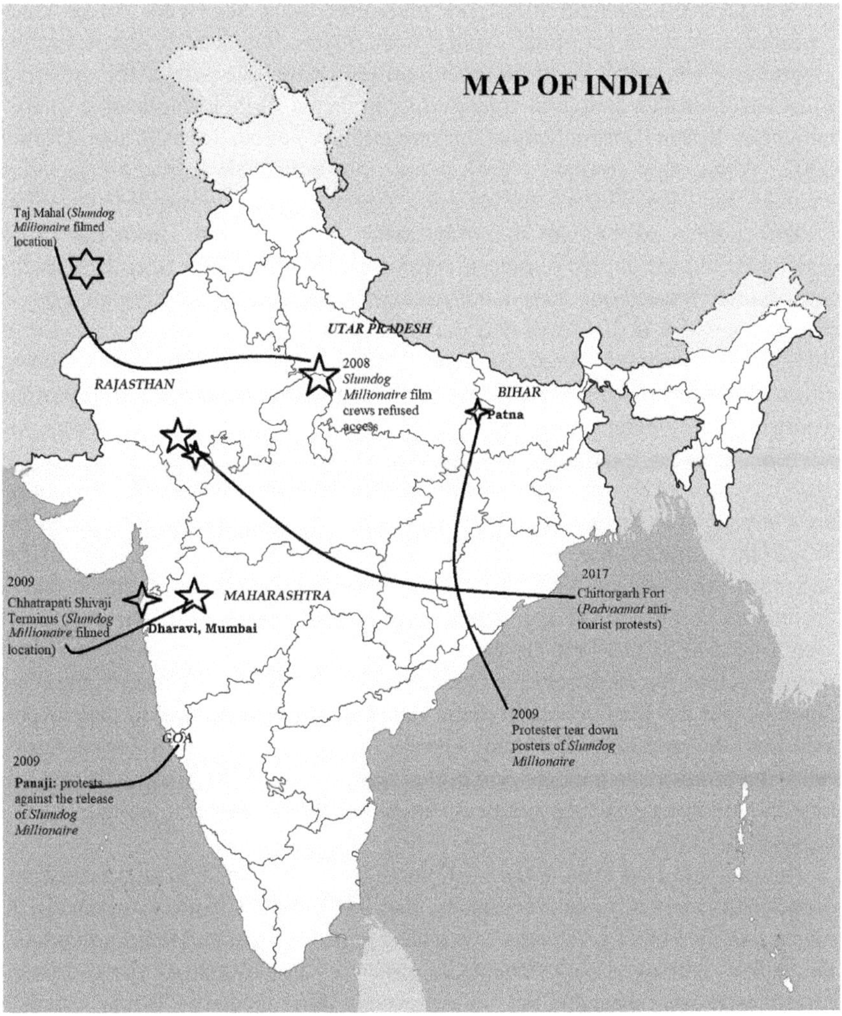

Figure 5.5 Country-wide perspective of recent religiously-induced riots and negative reactions against cinematic touristification.

Map credit: Nichalp (retouched with arrows, signs and location names by Rodanthi Tzanelli), Wikimedia Creative Commons Attribution-Share Alike 3.0 Unported, 2.5 Generic, 2.0 Generic and 1.0 Generic Licensing.

they enmesh all types of environmental racism and ethnoreligious sectarianism, in principle adhere to the utopic ideology of a peaceful bright world.

In fact, this world(-view), is both technologically (via cinema, tourism and general urban advertising) and ideologically mediated (political demagogy) in a concise 'Shining India' programme of development for the tourist gaze (in place since BJP's use of the term in the 2004 national elections – on 'Shining India' see Vanaik 2004; Tzanelli 2015a; on 'Incredible India' see Geary 2013), which reproduces Western scriptural ecologies of *lumen*, but fails to secure healthy kinespheric environments (how communities really live across the country). Most agents in this scriptural ecology live in denial of their implication in contemporary Indian constructions of the zero point of human hubris (Castro-Gómez 2007), which they constantly project not only onto their immediate sectarian enemies, but also Western consumption systems, firmly embedded in various Indian cultures of tourism and pilgrimage (Hannam and Diekmann 2010: 104–111). Indeed, in 2017 some of *Padvaamat*'s iconoclasts (members of the Sarv Samaj Sangathan) lashed out at tourist pilgrims to Chittorgarh Fort in Rajasthan, which in 2013 was declared by UNESCO a world heritage site for its 'eclectic architecture' (Singh 22 June 2013). A ban was imposed on tourist entries to the site by protesters, which nevertheless did not affect Rajasthan Tourism Development Corporation's (RTDC) operations of the 'Palace on Wheels', a luxury train going to Chittorgarh (*The Indian Express* 17 November 2017). By way of comparison, one may note that a decade before, the *SM* touring crew encountered similar hostility when attempting to complete the scenes of the Taj Mahal, which was recorded in the American press (Tzanelli 2015a: 135–136). The city of Agra, where the mausoleum exists, is a major tourist destination because of the Taj Mahal, Agra Fort and Fatehpu-r Sikrı, all three of which are UNESCO World Heritage Sites (Edensor 1998). Though by no means openly violent, the clash between Danny Boyle and his crew's casual filmmaking manners and the sites' iconic heritage status was enough to lead to their expulsion from the premises without any apparent religious altercations. Given Agra's left-wing politics, the incident proves that hostile responses to cinematic touristification transcend particular political viewpoints to focus on ethnoreligious ideologies of heritage.

Hannam and Diekmann (2010: 107) note that politicised Hindu organisations orchestrate *yatras* or large processions 'that traverse the country symbolically to map a specific Hindu geography'. Outside a narrow tourist and religious context, this defines embodied performances of protest of all kinds. In all the aforementioned instances, especially, but not exclusively those incited by Hindu organisations, *yatras* or marches with photos and slogans produce the psychogeography of activism against postindustrial development, which is set to replace theological with technological and scientific scripts in the country – only it does not. Significantly, whereas originally connected to histories of Bengali drama and the life of Krishna (Guha-Thakurta 2013: 18–19), *yatras* were never confined to a particular caste in Bengal, thus allowing for their democratisation across the country. Hence, the recent inclusion of *yatras* in demagogic contexts of political mobilisation introduces performative theatricality into the cause, to allow campaigners to take hold of space (see also Adey 2017: 157 on Debord). Unlike NSM contexts, where 'taking hold of space' facilitates the opportunity to change the status quo, *yatras* holders adhere to regressive psychogeographic situations of hatred against alternative viewpoints, thus paradoxically contrasting with the Hindu virtue (*dharma*) of harmlessness. All in all, however, their hostipital intentionality differs little from that displayed in other instances of cinematic touristification, such as the *DVC*.

Krabi, Thailand

The Thai case of hostipital resurgence is different from India's, in that it encloses interventions and contributions from outside the country's field-worlds. A different type of zero point was reached in 2000, when Thai regional and international organisations orchestrated a protest against the 'untidy guests' of Hollywood filmmaking in the region of Phuket (Veijola *et al.* 2014: 2). I have already discussed the case of *The Beach* in the previous section briefly, as a covert response to impeding cinematic touristification. However, I abstained from outlining the ecosystemic nuances and affective geographies of the transnational activist network within which we should place it, which, as I explain below, spoke three distinctive languages of action. Highlighting the network's cacophonous and melodic moments helps me outline the ways regional matters become ensnared into ecosystemic complexities extending beyond national borders. The network began to come to life when in 1998 Hollywood production giant Fox elected to film the story of *The Beach* in the Phi Leh island of the Krabi complex, and proceeded to bulldoze a few coconut trees and dunes on Maya Bay in the island of Phi Leh off Phuket, in preparation for some shooting. For this, Fox needed official permission, because Phi Phi Leh belongs to a national park and is protected by Thai laws.

When in November of the same year the Thai government, in expectation of tourism development from the film, gave its consent to the project, things turned sour. Fox's additional payment of four million baht (US$111,000) to the Royal Forestry Department of Thailand, which is responsible for conservation issues, a deposit of five million baht (US$135,000) as guarantee against damages at Maya Bay and an implicit promise to spend about $10 million on the site, were read as bribes by Thai and international environmentalist groups (*The Nation* 2000). The activist network, which openly displayed hostipital tendencies toward film crews and actors and was dispersed once by the police and militia (Third World Network 2000), comprised an interesting range of groups, including villagers and local representatives of civic groups from all over Thailand, Greenpeace, the Wildlife Fund Thailand, the Confederation of Inshore Fishermen and the Phuket Environment Protection Association (*International Herald Tribune* 2000). The case, which involved a lawsuit in 1999 against Fox and Thai government officials for encroachment upon Thai natural resources, was moved to the Civil Court of Law by residents and assemblies from the Krabi province, but additional protests erupted in other parts of the country serving as potential filming grounds and additional lawsuits were filed against Fox (*Guardian* 29 October 1999).

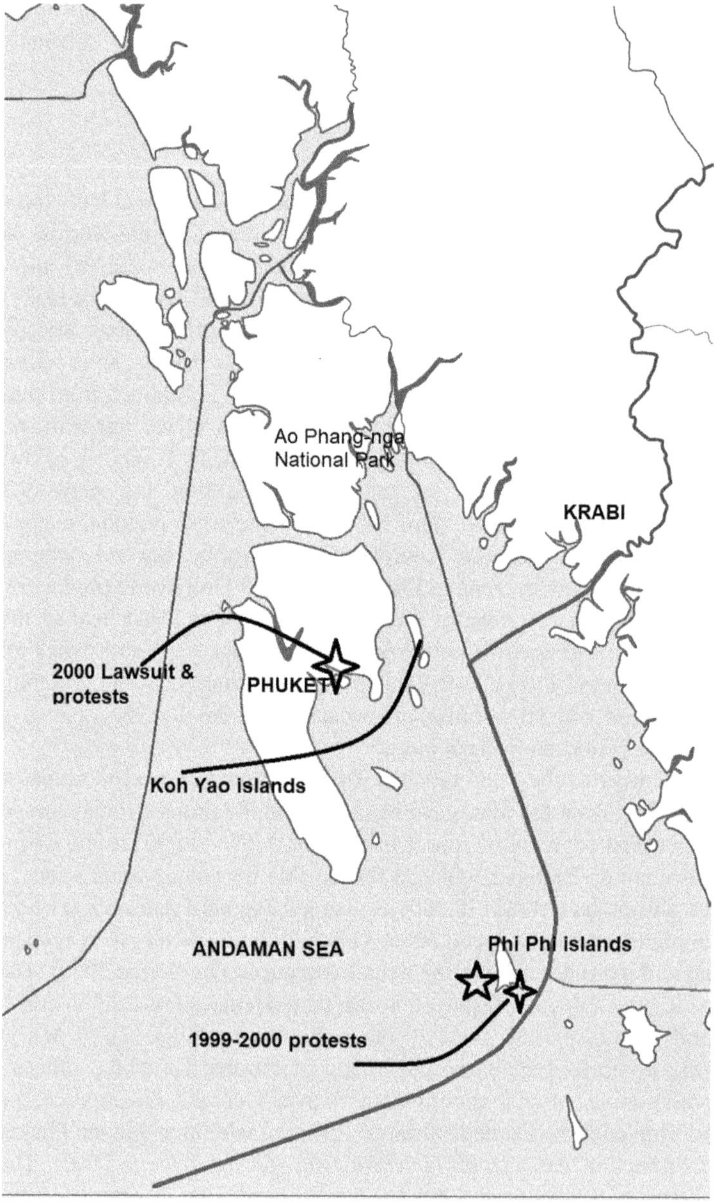

Figure 5.6 Eighteen years on: map of protests against the filming of *The Beach* and film-inspired tourist development, as well as threatened areas of local significance.

Map credit: Ahoerstemeier (retouched with arrows, signs and location names by Rodanthi Tzanelli), Wikimedia Creative Commons Attribution-Share Alike 3.0 Unported Licensing.

The climate of hostility, which was fuelled by a pathos we associate with experiencing injustice, exceeds traditional takes on *ressentiment*. As an affective situation, anger or frustration over the lack of regional and local involvement in decisions that may affect the everyday life of local communities (Prudishan and Maneerat 1997; Herzfeld 2003), including in our case ubiquitous Thai violations of environmental laws, could lead to fully-blossomed grievance. According to the conservative British newspaper the *Telegraph*, locals 'were glad of the income tourism has brought but regretted the arrival of strip joints, drug-fuelled

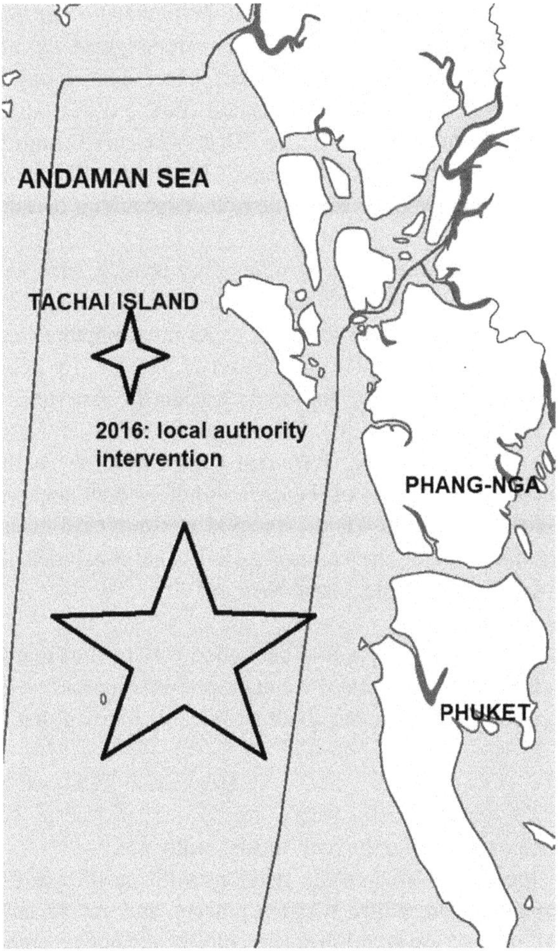

Figure 5.7 Protecting Andaman ecosystemic heritage: official Thai interventions in overtouristified islands.

Map credit: Ahoerstemeier (retouched by cropping and with arrows, signs and location names by Rodanthi Tzanelli), Wikimedia Creative Commons Attribution-Share Alike 3.0 Unported Licensing.

beach parties and cheap sex tourism, which had damaged their conservative, mostly Buddhist culture' (Chan 19 February 2010). In reality, all these transgressive cultures existed long before Fox's filmmaking, so we need to examine why they were associated with it so specifically. Indeed, the term *grievance*, which merges atmospheres of grief over an important loss with situations of political conflict (Torres and García-Hernández 2016: 208–209; Butler 2009), nicely outlines hostipitality's international foundations on law (Derrida 2000). But I endeavour to explain why, although in *The Beach* controversy accusations eventually turned to the general Thai tourist industry the authoritarian state wanted to bolster at the time, the named targets were particular foreign professionals and groups collaborating with such diverse actors/agents as Lonely Planet, EcoLert (an American tourism organisation), Reef Check (an international conservation group) and even the UN (Tzanelli 2007: 51–52). To do so, it is worth taking a journey forward in time, to 2018, when Thai authorities announced the closure of Maya Bay during the island's low season (from June to September), to allow its dilapidated coral reef time to recover after a decade and a half of overtourist pollution.

The decision followed similar measures on other Thai islands, such as Koh Tachai, which local authorities had closed to tourists in 2016 (Coldwell 14 February 2018) and the banning of smoking on some of its most popular beaches along the Andaman Coast and the Gulf of Thailand (Delahaye 15 February 2018). This time, the voice of protest was amplified by scientific expertise: Thon Thamrongnawasawat, Deputy Dean of the Faculty of Fisheries at Kasetsart University in Bangkok, said to *Deutsche Welle* that almost 80% of Thailand's coral reefs have been destroyed, because of 'beachfront hotels, boat anchors and plastic waste being dumped in the sea' (ibid.). In spite of some hard economic facts (tourism accounts for 18% of the country's GDP), he concluded in the same tone Greenpeace and local protesters used back in 1999:

> this [closure of beaches to tourists] would be a good way to start managing our tourist destinations.... It's important we manage our resources well. It's not about more numbers of tourists but about sustainable tourism that benefits locals as well.
>
> (MacGrath 29 March 2018)

However, even now it is not clear who the real 'locals' really are.

Thailand's place in the world affects state relations with its lifeworlds: the country was never formally colonised by Western powers, and yet, its submissive epistemontological attitude towards European cultures cannot be contested to date. Its lingering 'crypto-colonial' status (Herzfeld 2002) as a not-yet civilised ('Westernised' or 'Europeanised') backwater of Asia, an actual American militourist outpost after Vietnam, an overtouristified country for Western hippy backpackers, and an aggregate sociocultural formation refusing to grant all its ethnoreligious communities equal civic and human rights, cast fresh light on *The*

Beach incidents' ecological rationale from a holistic perspective. The involvement of international activist groups, such as Greenpeace, certainly added kudos to the legal case, but the charity's limitations were exposed by its failure to connect environmental devastation to ecosystemic racism. Claims by J. Ginsberg of the Wildlife Conservation Society's program (WCS) (Tzanelli 2007: 53) that the two filmed islands, Leh and Don, were 'empty grounds', pointed precisely in this direction – for, Koh Phi Phi Don was, at the time, already populated, mainly by Muslim groups from the south, who started moving into the area from the 1950s and were supposed to achieve full citizenship by law in the 1990s (Herzfeld 2002: 904–905). Today, Koh Phi Phi Leh is also populated by Buddhists, who work in the tourist and a fishing industry threatened with banning amidst an environmental controversy.

Mapping such complex overlaps of human demographics, ethnoreligious belief and livelihood, suggests that we can only touch the tip of a very deep and solid political iceberg. To follow Forsyth's argument (2002), the environmental angle of Thai activist discourse in 1999 was 'epiphenomenal', because it overlaid (*epí*) pre-existing problems concerning the (anti-multicultural) nature of the Thai nation-state, its policies and its place in the international political arena (*phenómena*). In Greenpeace's favour, a final note on this complex case has to be added: the involvement of regional organisations, which focused in the activist network on livelihood resources (fishing and agriculture), muddied the waters of collaborative action in 1999. Despite the knowledge that racial discrimination and conflict affected their social opportunities, Thai locals did not – perhaps could not – discuss their true source of grief (see Sheller 2009 on a similar case of touristification versus human rights). By concentrating on resolving a grievance, they consigned a question of holistic (human/non-human/environmental) rights to the same 'parasitological' condition they constantly endured at home (on guests as parasites, and hence outsiders, see Veijola *et al.* 2014: 43). Such phenomenologies of homeliness and homelessness certainly interact with labour conditions in post-Fordist contexts of touristification around the world – a theme that frames the final mode of response in the next section.

Reykjavík, Iceland and Flakstad, Norway

It is worth highlighting that, although parasitologies of hostipitality follow ethnonational controversies, they may also emerge independently in contexts of overtourism. The metaphor of the 'parasite' (something that *ístatai* (stands, exists) nearby, in the neighbourly environment (*para*)), which experts have to eliminate by employing rational means (*lógos*), fits nicely into the analytical foundation of the tourist gaze as the Western practice of producing pristine place and culture, free of what are perceived of as structural anomalies: transgressive identities and confusing alien lifestyles, among other things (see also Korstanje 2018a: 13–14 on the withdrawal of hospitality in the West). The *GoT* tourist boom in Iceland is instructive: a 124% increase in Airbnb rentals in one year, with more than 100 flats available on the Icelandic capital's main street alone, a dramatic increase in house prices in central Reykjavík, and a paucity of long-term rentals after the eruption of *GoT* tourism, prompted legislative changes to secure native human and environmental sustainability. Inadequate infrastructures and local media complaints that '"puffin shops" – those aimed at tourists – and Viking-themed enterprises were taking over in downtown Reykjavík' suggests that local hospitable behaviour may not last for long (Davies 30 May 2016). From a resident – and apparently, also a local administrative – perspective, such material manifestations of hospitality and their recipients/buyers stand (*ístantai*) in a space of those neighbours' local lifeworlds, and their mobile nature can only pollute them with sociocultural inconsistencies.

The case of *Frozen* is also relevant: although it made the remote Lofoten Islands in the Arctic Circle globally famous (a trend more generally associated with their use as backdrops in other Hollywood films), locals are reportedly fed up by the tourism boom, which led to traffic congestion, regular use of a forest as a public toilet and tourist-camping in cemeteries. Home to just over 250,000 people, in 2016 the picture-postcard islands were expected to attract over one million tourists. Fears that such 'overtourism' will lead to 'erosion on trails and paths to coastal beauty spots' and the renaming of a popular hiking trail at Reinebringen mountain as 'forest of s***' (Kitching 10 August 2016), even convinced the tourist board for Western Norway, the site of the country's most magnificent fjords, to slash its promotion budget for the following summer. Nevertheless, even in Norway's case, there is an interesting 'catch': the alleged cinematic overtourism is set to be tackled especially in Geiranger and Flåm, villages in the region's two UNESCO-listed fjords, Geirangerfjord and Aurlandsfjord. Significantly, Geiranger which has just 215 permanent inhabitants, is visited by about 700,000 tourists a year, according to Ove Skylstad, general manager for Tourism Geiranger. '"They're more-or-less 100 percent booked," he said of the village's four hotels. "I think the Hotel Union had only two rooms available for the whole of July"' (Orange 10 September 2016).

I want to make a realist and a phenomenological observation, which contributes to the cultural-political background of hostipitality. Practically and realistically, curbing tourism mobilities in an archipelago, in which tourism rose by 20% after the release of a movie, and public facilities were exhausted, with problems plaguing local waste disposal, public toilets and car parking, is sound policy (McMah 11 August 2016). The phenomenology of native experience sheds light on a different angle of overwhelmingly conservative press reports. This was not the first time these areas were used in cinematically successful films: parts of *LOTR* and *GoT* had been filmed there, giving the beautiful locations a headstart in film branding (Baart 28 August 2016). In 2016, the same locations were visited again by Hollywood for the filming of *Downsizing* (director Alexander Payne 2017). However, phenomenologically, there is a hidden atmospheric conflict between the cinematic and local staging of these places, which draws on synaesthetic scripts, also present in the ways Norwegian tourist operators think and act. In such scripts, touring local lifeworlds and nature become pilgrimage with the help of a sensory engagement with them, which follows the seasonal, rather the tourist business cycle. Böhme (1993) identifies in language a spatial and bodily artform with atmospheric qualities (Chandler 2011: 561): the ways perceptions of the environment are articulated are constitutive of the ways they are experienced. Likewise, dance philosopher Erin Manning sees sensations, materialities and worlds in embodied terms as emerging from types of movement, from minor gestures (Manning 2009) to collective affective and bodily mobilities that produce relationscapes (Manning 2016). Bodily functions and their linguistic atmospheres are central to the creation of a resurgent Lofoten spirit of antitourism. The local nomination of Reinebringen mountain as a 'forest of s***' is an olfactory statement of parasitological signification: much like *GoT* tourists, *Frozen* tourists pollute Lofoten's natural heritage. The replacement of this negative 'image' of Hollywood-induced tourists 'taking selfies like crazy', with an organic one of seasonal bliss (May), when fjords see flowers bloom and waterfalls 'swollen with melting snow', according to local tourism operators (Orange 16 September 2016), fosters an actor-network counterworld of heritage the tourist machine threatens with extinction. We are then back to a hostipital discourse of belonging that draws its power from notions of a pure lifeline: the blood of fjord peoples and nature.

Waiheke, New Zealand

Thanks to the *LOTR* cinematic trilogy, New Zealand has achieved celebrity status of such proportions that today its place in global tourist industries is recognised by powerful political players around the world. However, this speedy climb up the global ladder of major tourist destinations created a variety of problems, placing notions of 'cinematic tourist sustainability' under intense scrutiny. In recent years, mobilising the natural beauty of *LOTR*-filmed glacier-fed rivers, forests and mountainous areas contributed to overtourism, raised for the first time grave questions of environmental degradation, and brewed hostipital emotions in localities that used to welcome global visitors for bringing economic capital and an affirmation that the country is valued for its natural and cultural heritage. The emergence of a trend of littering 'freedom campers' in rented vans, speedboat cinematic tourists seeking Isengard, helicopter travellers over New Zealand's Peter Jackson-filmed glaciers, and popcultural die-hards, who now have to be rescued during their haphazard barefoot 'pilgrimage' to Mount Doom (Mount Ngauruhoe), has altered local perspectives on global mobility and connectivity (Pannett 22 May 2018). Such situations certainly bring to the fore the ways complex adaptive systems with human and non-human components achieve a form of ordering 'on the edge of chaos' that is primarily affective and emotional (Thrift 1999; Maasen and Weingart 2000; Urry 2005b). More correctly, we may have to acknowledge that structures of policy-making may have to be informed in such cases not just by established scientific facts pertaining to ecosystemic risks, but by 'structures of feeling' (Urry 2005b: 1–2), from a non-representational world informing lay social action.

This coexistence of the precognitive with the scientific in the 'mangle of practice' (Pickering 1995) may even lead to substitutions of the 'public sphere', or 'spheres' (Habermas 1989) by a '"public screen", visible everywhere linked to global networks' (Sheller and Urry 2003: 118). However, much like Mumbai's figurative slum feast for the digital tourist gaze, New Zealand's public screens are created by blends of local and global activist assemblages, striving to instil into non-representational worlds an audiovisual grammar that is managed by the 'people'. Interestingly, in contexts of overtourism, such initiatives establish (unacknowledged) continuums between formal and informal, public and private, unofficial and official action: nothing beats such ambiguities, when worldmaking authorities run out of solutions. Note, for example, that not only do officials reconsider raising taxes to control camper-van mobilities around Queenstown (a 'Ring'-site gateway, which has reached 120 tourists a year for every taxpayer), a particular town in the area considered shutting down Wi-Fi at night to deter campers (Pannett 22 May 2018). Despite the 2017 tourismophobic protests in Europe, several complaints filed by Federated Mountain Clubs to the country's Conservation Department about tour bus congestion around Fiordland, as well as accidents involving overseas drivers, and a worrying countrywide rise in taxpayer dissatisfaction with visitors, Tourism Industry Aotearoa and Conservation officials continue to make allowances for tourism mobilities. As a result, recent attempts at public consultation by the government's Conservation Department over nominations of new areas for development have been unsuccessful (ibid.). This is hardly surprising, given that today, the Department of Conservation operates its own commercial business unit, set to generate more profit from protected areas, providing GPS coordinates of *LOTR* locations. With a clear worldwide rise in Chinese middle-class tourism since 2008 (accounting for about 80% of global growth in dollar terms) and the strengthening of New Zealand-Chinese tourist bonds, problems will multiply.

A small protest, but one indicative of the general climate, took place in 2017 on Waiheke Island, off Auckland, when a group of 60 tried to stop double-decker buses with tourists from entering the town. Attempting to send the tourists back to the mainland, the group, led by Greenpeace founder Suzanne Newborn, made speeches and recreated the Abbey Rd album cover on the ferry zebra crossing, while singing a version of 'The Wheels on the Bus' but 'with modified lyrics ("It squeezes down the narrow roads, narrow roads, narrow roads")' (Greive 9 April 2017). Although married *in situ* with the green agenda of an international charity, the apparently 'traditional Waiheke' hostility against 'big business, the big nearby city, [and] lack of respect for the natural environment' (ibid.) constructed an embodied, vocal choreutics of social action that in fact spoke the language of communitarianism (Delanty 2013). Otherwise put, the small group's claims to privacy ('tourists go home!') collapsed into a socio-spatial relationship ('Double Decker, Island Wrecker!' claim protest banners)

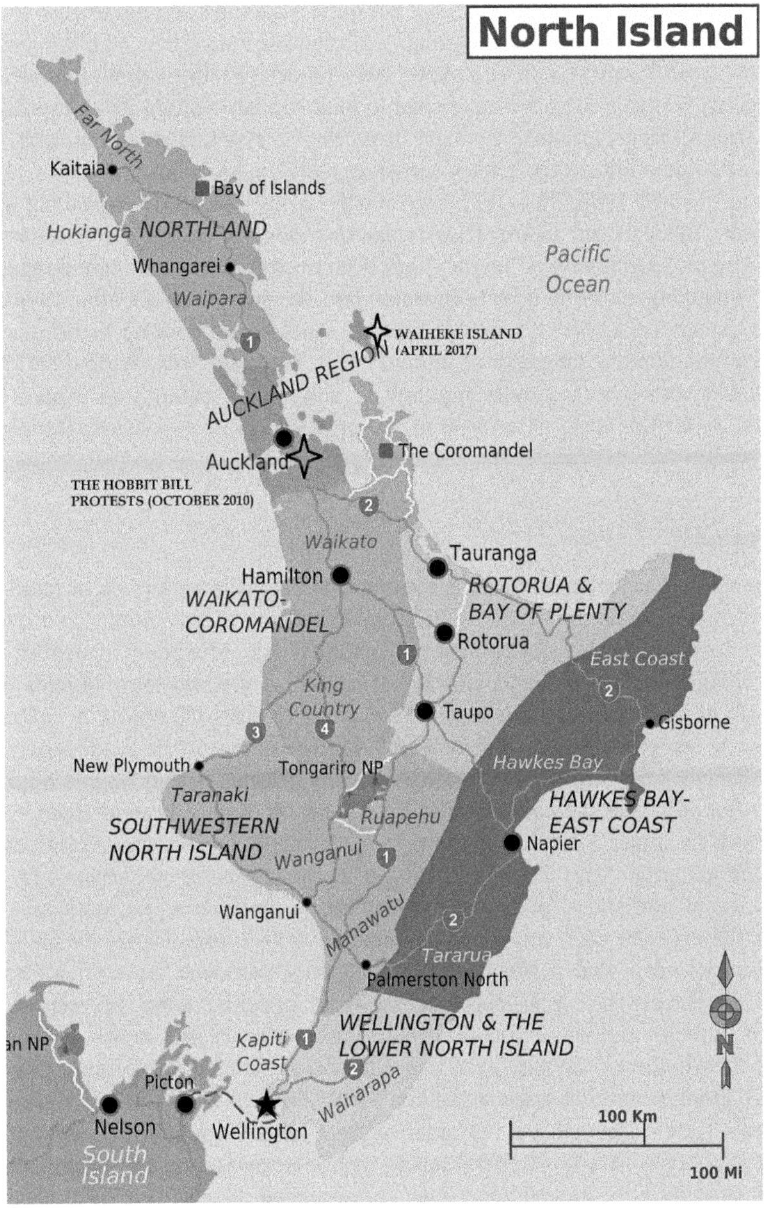

Figure 5.8 Between hostipitality and ecosystemic decline prevention: Waiheke Island protests against *LOTR* overtouristification.

Map credit: WT-shared Shaund (retouched with arrows, signs and location names by Rodanthi Tzanelli), Wikimedia Creative Commons Attribution-Share Alike 3.0 Unported Licensing.

marked off from the public spaces of the streets and parks (Weintraub 1997). In reality, the meaning of such protests did not quite match the petition to curb the wear and tear on local roads or the pruning of roadside native trees to allow bus operators to work safely (Greive 9 April 2017 on details). Instead, it attempted to retrieve a Weiheke's marine utopia lost to wine tourists visiting its vineyards, *LOTR* fans visiting the island by ferry from the overpopulated capital, and a system of automobility (cars, ferries, airplanes, helicopters, roads and their CO_2 emissions – Thrift 1996: 282–283; Urry 2004b: 26–27) endlessly expanding at the expense of locals and nature. Thus, reclaiming utopia as a sociospatial organisation also targeted the ways 'privacy' has been overtaken by institutional regulations, including those of private business and the state itself (Walby 1990), with headquarters in the very eye of Sauron: Auckland. Speaking a distorted version of the feminist language of intimacy (e.g. Pateman 1998; Walby 2011), the event nevertheless truthfully highlighted how *LOTR* cultures of mobility managed to displace local citizenship in favour of economic expansion (Berlant 1997).

Conclusion

Tourismophobic reactions in hostipitable contexts may develop *in lieu* of familiar problematic practices, including the romanticisation of community and the inability to acknowledge entrenched sociocultural and economic inequalities within village utopias (Williams [1973] 2016: 147). Given that more organised variations of hostipitality in the form of social movements take place in urban settings, or are controlled by the movement's networked urban headquarters, such stereotypes persist, at the expense of actually affected lifeworlds and fieldworlds. Not only does the ubiquitous archival function of the city in productions of memory or amnesia come to the fore in such highly tense settings (Gilloch 2007; Hetherington 2013; Tzanelli 2016b), it reinforces centripetal heritage discourses about touristified places of ethnonational significance (i.e. nationalist hatred). To separate such modes of hostipitality from postindustrial disobedience, I stress again that heritage battles eventually transcend the rationale of labour movements and transgressions, so as to prioritise ways of securing 'network capital', regional and global connectivity, prestige and capital generation for their holders, who may even be connected to the interests of regional or national administration (Larsen and Urry 2008; Tzanelli 2013, 2017). Hence, Saarinen's (2013: 10) call that 'in order to have tools for setting the limits to growth in tourism in a local-global nexus with less tourism-centric evaluation criteria, stronger governmental and inter-governmental policies and regulations are most probably needed' may not be the panacea. In short, consideration should be given to whether even fully-blown cinematic tourismophobic movements of hostipitable content emphasise structure or agency, reflexivity and self-limiting radicalism, as is the case with the NSM paradigm (Touraine 1981; Melucci 1989). The answer is usually found in context.

Postindustrial disobedience

Postindustrial disobedience refers to action or activism taken up by groups in creative markets, which seek to adjust the conditions under which they provide immaterial forms of labour. The mode emerges in post-Fordist environments of flexible capital accumulation, which involve postnational conglomerates or contingent strategic alliances between different postindustrial organisations, such as film and tourism (Piore and Sabel 1984; Esping-Andersen 1994; Lash and Urry 1994). The immateriality of the products that circulate in international markets by these new postindustrial formations has a particular aesthetic patina (hence Böhme's (2017) coining of the term 'aesthetic capitalism'), which makes them adaptable to the desires of an international clientele. The patina's adaptability is based on the maker's (immaterial/creative worker) ability to create open-ended ideas/products, 'signs' that can assume different meanings upon consumption (Lazzarato 2004; 2011). Previously I explored postindustrial collaborations between film and tourist industries under what I called 'global sign industries': '*industries* that trade in images and ideas, the intangible aspects of culture … [which] are *global*, because they thrive on their economic and political interconnections … [and] generate, manipulate and market cultural signs' (Tzanelli 2007: 9). Here I observe by example how these signs are also (re-) mobilised during antitourist and antivisitor campaigns by petitioning groups (creative/aesthetic labour or even localities), thus completing a second production-consumption cycle (the first being the one catering for tourist and film audience interpretations and the second controlled by resurgent activists – see Baudrillard 1975, 1994).

However, an economic or political sociological approach will not suffice for this chapter's analytical needs. First, we must devise a way to track down affective pulsations during this lay interpretative process [to understand and feel performances as what *they are made to be* – 'a simulation of the social matrix, the involved system of cross-cutting, overlapping, highly corporate groups … in which its devotees live' (Geertz in Warnke 2011: 46)], thus also accounting for atmospheric fluctuations in protests (Adey 2017: 201–202). Second, we must register such atmospheres materially (e.g. in embodied performances and onto architectural matrixes – Malbon 1999: 74; Stewart 2007). Third, we must identify the temporal depth of such fluctuations, because this is what grants them an epistemontological presence in the activist field-world. Therefore, it is not surprising that the mode of postindustrial disobedience shares trace-forms with lay enactments of epistemic disobedience. All the same, this occurs tangentially or circumstantially, so we should not confuse the two modes of response. Unqualified conflations of the two modes are often detected in polemical analyses on 'cultural imperialism' and framed with a pessimist Marxist discourse (e.g. workers' protests are read exclusively as symptoms of problematic postcolonial structuration of native economies), which assumes all class struggles are also racial struggles, driven by historical necessity so as to advance human/workers' rights. I wish to present a more complex picture of such responses, based on conflicting frameworks of sustainability, including those impacting on natural and built environments.

Kefalonia, Greece

I begin with an instance of postindustrial disobedience that, although it displays all the signs of capitalist complexity we find in postcolonial contexts, it does not really belong to them. I refer to cultures of protest connected to *CCM*, which, though largely localised in terms of demands, fed into national memory registers, as these were formed after the Second World War in Europe and specifically the south-eastern Mediterranean region. The example pointed to tourismophobic warnings before the filmed locations' extensive touristification, so it serves as an introduction to more straightforward instances of postindustrial disobedience on the same island (Kefalonia, Greece). The example's emotive geographical formations might be dissociated from local immaterial creativity for some. Another objection may come from the fact that local creativity was mainly based on individualised business initiative, so we cannot view it as a generalised trend. During filming, articles featuring local war veterans in the foreign press complaining about misrepresentations of Greek histories of the communist resistance in the film, followed by similar inflammatory leftwing Greek press publications, set the stage for a conflict. Louis de Bernières' (author of the adapted novel) work was extensively discussed for its alleged anti-communist plot, and Gerásimos Artelánis, mayor of Sámi, where *CCM* scenes were shot, stated that, if Hollywood turned the book into an anti-communist film, they would 'take the issue to the international court of justice at The Hague' (*Sunday Times* 4 June 2000 in Tzanelli 2007: 108).

When De Bernières stressed that Artelánis' protestations clashed with his willingness to participate in the film as an extra and invite the novelist as a special guest in Sami, while mourning how public opinion was manipulated by a group of 'leftwingers' (Clark 2001: 15), attitudes hardened further, and film director Madden threatened to move his crew to Greece's historical enemy, Turkey. Within Greece, local communist and central social responses splintered: on the one hand, business-orientated Dionísios Georgátos, elected Governor of Kefalonia and adherent of the Greek socialist party then in power (PA.SO.K.), proceeded to negotiate the terms under which Madden could shoot the film on the island (Papanikolátos 24 September 2000). On the other, communists followed up on previous actions, criticising Shawn Slovo's involvement in the making of *CCM*, because she is the daughter of murdered anti-apartheid activist Ruth First and former communist and African National Congress Leader Joe Slovo, and connecting their critique to that of other communist societies around the world that expressed a concern over the ways in which the media become sources of popular historical knowledge (see, for example, Praxis International 2000). Notably, all such responses asserted their aggressive non-representational tonality while trying to destroy a particular (novelist-come-cinematographic) representation of history. However, paradoxically, while doing so, they also restored an iconic version of historical factishness (Latour 2011).

Despite the film production company's reassurance that local sensibilities would not be offended, the subsequent remunerated participation of many locals in the filming of *CCM* and the rebranding of the island's resort industries (cafés, bars, travel agencies and restaurants) as Corelli and Pelagía's places in line with neoliberal protocols, Greek hospitality misdemeanours were bound to tarnish perceptions of native professional conduct. Herein we can detect modes of postindustrial disobedience: discussions in the British conservative press of Kefalonian complaints that 'the Corelli business' scared away 'the good people', who are 'afraid that [the island] will be swamped' by unwanted backpackers visiting the island to 'have one salad between them' (Tzanelli 2007: 109), formed a continuity with earlier observations on local storeowners' persistent demand of 'extortionate sums' from *CCM*'s producers for the use of their property as the film's stage (Papanikolátos 24 September 2000). In addition, a Kefalonian printing company took shots of the cinematic façades that represented old Argostóli (capital of Kefalonia) in filmed scenes in Sámi, because film fans began to photograph themselves in front of them. These shots were reproduced by the company as 'Old Argostóli' postcards for tourist consumption 'without bothering to explain that the images shown were of a film set that would only be there for a few weeks' (Clark 2001: 95).

Reminiscent of a rather distorted version of the so-called 'weapons of the weak' (Scott 1991) and the peasant cultures of resistance ('craft') that migrated to urban centres with industrialisation (Jacobs 1992), this disposition is known across Greece as *poniriá* or 'cleverness'. *Poniriá* as a thrifty and crafty attitude, was placed by anthropologists in the framework of the competitive relationship of locals with foreigners (Herzfeld 1985: 25). In terms of mobilities of affect, Kefalonian *poniriá* complied with the rules of nationalist *ressentiment*, for which leftwingers are notorious in Greece, while not in fact entirely dismissing the neoliberal spirit of competition (Tzanelli 2011). In terms of a choreutics of resistance, leftwing spatiotemporal segmentations and compartmentalisations of movement across different towns, but with Sámi as the protests' tectonic epicentre, resembled what Paul Routledge (1997) calls 'the pack': a fluid and elusive formation of small protest enclaves across (virtual and terrestrial) sites, resembling guerrilla warfare tactics, for which Greek communists were famous during the Greek Civil War (1944–1949).

Auckland and Wellington, New Zealand

The worship of factish Gods in postindustrial disobedience is by no means confined to European spaces of protest, where nationalist ideologies end up obscuring its economic nature as much as they deplete its cultural rationale in favour of pure politics (see Delanty and O'Mahony 2002 on European nationalism and economic structures). Another equally complex example of this mode of response, which was embroiled in nationalist and globalised networks of heritage governance, is that of *The Hobbit* (director Peter Jackson 2012) protests in 2010. To explore the controversy here, I take the *LOTR*'s institution of New Zealand as a cinematic, popular-cultural heritage destination – hence, its potentiality for the economically weak and politically isolated country in which the successful movies were filmed – as givens, as indeed they were for New Zealanders at the time. Events were set in motion in 2005, when special effects worker James Bryson who was made redundant, won his Supreme Court legal action against *LOTR* director Peter Jackson. Bryson, who was sacked by Jackson, claimed that he was an employee rather than a contractor (long-term workers in New Zealand are recognised as employees regardless of the type of contract they sign), so he could not be dismissed the way he was (Satherley 1: 29 October 2010). The conservative government of John Key tried to settle this issue with the introduction of the so-called 'Hobbit Amendment Act', by granting economic concessions to Warner Bros, which, for some jeopardised national interests, including taxing the studios accordingly and securing native labour employment opportunities (NZPA 1 November 2010). The so-called 'Hobbit Bill' was in fact secured when things had already taken a bad turn in terms of industrial action. New Zealanders had already organised protests in Auckland and Wellington against Warner Bros' threats to move the production elsewhere; and both Oscar-winning *LOTR* technician Richard Taylor and director Jackson had backed the action. Jackson in particular featured as producer of the protests' scriptural content, with BBC News reporting him saying: 'The created DNA is here; this is where Middle Earth was born and this is where it should stay' (Child 25 October 2010).

Designed to be openly confrontational towards the power of postindustrial media giant Warners, protests were 'swarm-like' in their style (Routledge 1997): they formed with stings targeting global media channels in the country's two largest cities, where both indigenous and popcultural museum heritage is stored (there is a *LOTR* museum in Auckland). Hence, protesters drew on the scenographic characters of New Zealand's two largest beautified cities to communicate an overall impression of the country's *Zeitgeist* or contemporary atmospheric ethos, replete with technological productions of native landscapes, which derived less from particular architectural details and more from a complex *Gestalt* (Hasse 2011: 49–50): an ecosystemic whole encompassing human cultures, native nature and imported technological mobilities. We can recall once more Ingold's observations on the significance of taskscapes for the organisation of social life and Laban's ([1966] 2011: 84–85) collapse of all principal traceforms in spiraloid DNA curves, to draw a lay, bee-like schematisation of New Zealand's new popular-cultural labour. As Labour Minister Kate Wilkinson claimed at the time: 'we were not prepared to see thousands of Kiwi jobs disappear and … the hard work of the many talented New Zealanders who built our film industry put at risk' (*Telegraph* 29 October 2010). Popular culture had

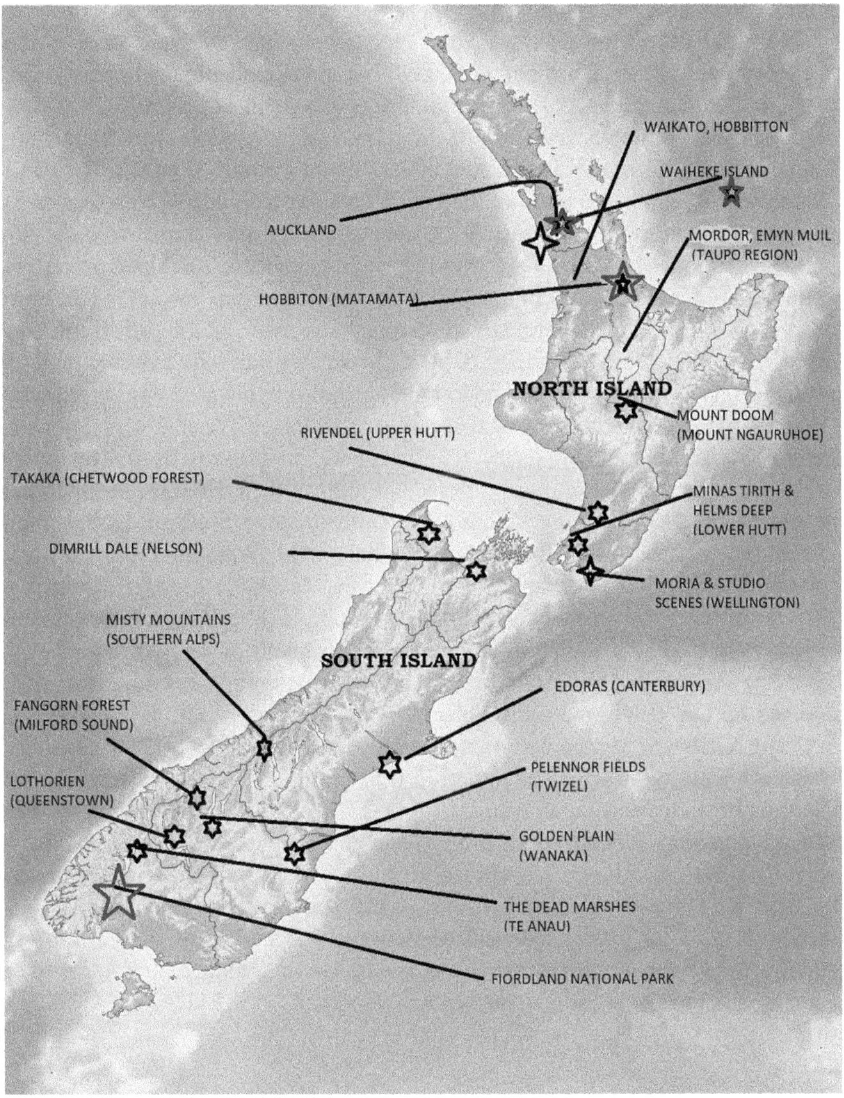

Figure 5.9 Two decades on: map of New Zealand's *LOTR* tourist development and the global/local responses to it. The map also marks areas that are considered 'national heritage' because of the cinematic trilogy.

Map credit: NordNordWest (retouched with arrows, signs and location names by Rodanthi Tzanelli), Wikimedia Creative Commons Attribution-Share Alike 3.0 Unported Licensing.

turned into national heritage, which, by turns, had formed the basis of the 'emotional labour' of national memory.

The original controversy was thus epiphenomenal, and, as other events proved, responses were not party-specific, but cultural-ideological through and through. Let us then also inspect the controversy's socialist discourse of nationalist factishity: ominously, in 2010, while *The Hobbit* protests were happening, Labour MP Trevor Mallard presented in Parliament a modified national flag with Warner Bros' logo in the place of the Union Jack and a note that 'New Zealand's sovereignty is finished' (Murray 29 October 2010). Further comparisons of this public performance of patriotism with the actual banners of Auckland protesters, which figured a Gollum pleading 'Please Save my Precious Home!' yield more observations on the idea that national memory was reconstituting itself relationally in global markets (Tzanelli 2013: 55). Notably, affective dispositions of protest enacted a performative contradiction, not unknown in market cultures (Bell 1976): whereas their nationalist rationale endorsed Western separations of natural from human field-worlds (Gollum stood in protests as the country's image-brand, a fully naturalised 'artefactual thing'), their affective atmospheres mobilised the *LOTR/Hobbit* scripts (the battle of good Smeagol-Hobbit New Zealanders versus the evil cinematic capitalism of Warners Dark Lord) as 'proof' that the films and their tourism are New Zealand's heritage. Thus, it is easy to decipher the presence of a homeless Gollum set against an inhospitable natural background, pleading to be freed from the spells of the evil ring of capitalist imperialism in *The Hobbit* protests. An outcast in the cinematic story condemned to live in swamps, the abject Hobbit creature, stood as the other of Western civility: needy but determined to reclaim the pureness of New Zealand's landscape identity, in which even native *Maoritanga* (of Māori origins) wisdom can pragmatically participate (Sinclair 1992). We may therefore conclude that '*The Hobbit* wars' displayed all the stylistic components of a movie, in which, although a national kinesphere was staged from the country's urban headquarters by both its lay and celebrity citizens, it claimed a rural utopian simulation. Indeed, at a closer glance, the tension between real and ideal sites of utopian struggle runs through most of the explored cases in this chapter, so it needs to be addressed in the last section's concluding remarks.

Conclusion

From these examples, it seems that postindustrial disobedience has an epiphenomenal content, facilitating overlaps with the previous two modes. At the same time, the resurgent groups' core petition brings postindustrial disobedience closer to the typical NSMs, which centre on formations of collective identity as *formations of postmodernity*. The slippage of actual social action from molecular to molar formations (i.e. from defence of labour rights to national identity) is also overlaid by shifts from barely perceptible affects to fully legible representations, modes of organisation and 'punctuality' (Deleuze and Guattari 1987:

215–217). The dynamism of the performative bodies involved in their orchestration/execution are constitutive of ad hoc stagings of a kinesphere – both in Laban's original definition, and mine, which is orientated more toward molar formations. In any case, it seems that, occasionally, their outwards (realist) orientation towards introducing a change in material conditions may ultimately clash with their inward-looking content, which aims to stabilise, fix the group's 'ideational' conditions of being in the world (of the nation or a territorially-bound ecosystem).

Islands of disorder and *choreosophies* of *potentia*

Let me begin with an observation that stands over and above this chapter's findings: though vital to my analysis of some examples across the gamut of responses, my practice of worldmapping was not discussed here. To claim that I ignored the visual stylistics of the Mercator (the spherological structuring of space) and Gall-Peter's (the emphasis on vastness) Projection of the world is only partially true, given my propensity to spatially illuminate events connected to particular responses (Mercator's philosophical connection to the world as a globe with particular regions illuminated/magnified better than others) and to stretch or contract distances in an almost 3D-fashion (Gall-Peter's scientific rationale of spatialisation). However, my principal aim in such 'worldmappings' as 'activist worldmakings' exceeds the epistemic properties of collective action, because my maps' design as such appeals to Bloch's 'sigillary signs', affects awaiting the usual nomination any institutional governmental machine – or, indeed, scholar – grants to them a posteriori. My propensity to approximate spatial formations of affect (e.g. nominate locations on the map) intentionally defied the accurate realist depictions of the world one finds in Gall-Peter's Projection – for, atmospheres are contagious and highly mobile formations that may even affect the researcher. As Ingold (2011: 233) notes, 'the vast majority of maps that have ever been produced in human societies ... have been improvised on the spot within a particular logic or storytelling context'. In this respect, trying to reform my previous chapter's ways and consider non-Western practices of pilgrimage, I followed a purpose that was not fully articulated, crafting instead my interpretative journey while on the move with my imagined interlocutors (Archer 2008). If, as Böhme (1993) contends, language is a spatial artform that makes atmospheres, then my epistemontological shift from mapping to narrative in this chapter never stood outside the atmospheric logic of my pilgrimage and that of my interlocutors. To clarify then: my mapping is embedded within ecologies and economies of interpretation, and does not exist outside them.

The 'strong programme' in cultural sociology stresses that in human lifeworlds we always deal with interplays of structures with agency, which we must place in context (Alexander 1988). When the anthroposcenic puzzle is scrutinised via structural hermeneutic methods, it must be extended to non-human actants, which form legitimate interlocutors in the environmental field.

Following this, I offer two sociological analyses of the findings: the first emphasises the structural aspects of the response or movement, whereas the second considers the resurgent quality of its agential components (see Urry (1978) on *ressentiment* and theories of revolution, Tzanelli (2011) *ditto* on theories of nationalism and Anderson (2009) on Marx's conception of atmosphere in relation to spaces of affect and emotion). Such agential moves, which are embedded in *the perspective of lay creativity* (Tzanelli 2008a), are often characterised by the imperceptibility of their affective qualities, and therefore commence their life in non-representational domains (Deleuze and Guattari 1987: 213; Merriman 2018: 7). Structurally, we must consider the globalised context in which the responses emerge, therefore we must 'uncover' the principal stressors in the particular movement, or group of movements under study. A spatialised distribution of tourismophobia points to cities which have been spectacularised with the help of filmmaking initiatives and are now reclaimed by their residents (see also Colomb and Novy 2016). This project of reclaiming, which is especially prominent within Europe, contests the substitution of residents with a new floating population of tourists. It often connects to a progressive gentrification of neighbourhoods (dubbed 'gentrification 2.0', when these are redesigned for tourists), so it has a strong element of class (Blanco-Romero *et al.* 2018). However, not all studied responses take place in urban settings, given that cinematic phantasmagorias and their resulting *faux* tourist counterworlds draw on the rural or marine idyllic and sublime, nor can we consider 'class' as a universally applicable social reality without appropriate modifications. At the same time, a 'superstressor' manifests across all studied responses, revealing their uniform 'deep play' and plot as 'mimetic [of larger structures] textual conjuring, which refers in turn to the real [political conditions] for validity, and then we find we have returned to our starting place' (Smith 2011: 26): at all times, 'petitioners' attack the tourist, the figure and ambassador of privileged mobility, who can cross borders easier than the migrant and can enjoy the journey's carefree feel more than a businessman (Korstanje 2018a). Soft and hard variations of tourismophobia end up attacking not just the appropriation of this mobility by cultural industries and experts (Urry 1990), but a whole ethos of being in the world associated with European cultures of cosmopolitanism and travel (Szerszynski and Urry 2006; Urry 2007; Andrews 2009; Blok and Farias 2016). The birthplace of modernity is set for demolition by those who crave to appropriate its mythopoetic origins (mobilities).

It is worth following this trope for a while, because it may lead to a more accurate understanding of tourismophobic variations in systemic contexts, which are both environmental and political. There is a homology between hierarchies of citizenship within the nation-state and in the global scene, with nationals/nationalised subjects occupying the former and cosmopolitan tourists the latter (see Habermas 1989 on system and lifeworld formations). If contemporary capitalist mutations have weakened (or altered, according to other arguments) the power of the nation-state, they worked wonders for transnational business networks that secure the tourists' 'cultural passport' (Stevenson 1997; 2003). Tourismophobia can even be regarded as a corollary or symptom of the end of a particular form of hospitality based on ethnocultural and naturalised bonds (consanguinity, blood, race), followed by its replacement with a supraprivileged form of belonging in the new Empire of capital (Hardt and Negri 2000; but see also Korstanje 2018b). Whether we agree with this thesis or not, it seems that the global migration crisis has found its sibling in the crisis of tourism mobilities, which yields an equally sinister face: now directing suspicion or hatred at both types of guests (migrants and tourist visitors – e.g. see Bianchi and Stephenson 2014), this new mobilities crisis threatens to close up the space of communication with others completely. The limited amount of responses to cinematic touristification that centre on postindustrial disputes confirms the presence of labour injustices as yet another epiphenomenal cause.

There can be a lot of speculation over the efficacy, or indeed positive radical potential of movements induced by fear: their articulation is often based on ad hoc 'events' and they can be radical, progressive or reactionary (Mouffe 1988; Hannam *et al.* 2016; Adey 2017). Nederveen Pieterse (1992: 9) stresses that definitions of emancipation as 'liberation of creative human potentialities from suffocating social structures', or as collective struggle on the part of an underprivileged group, do not distinguish between different types of collective action. This throws the baby (cross-cultural exchange, peaceful development and so forth – Blanchard and Higgins-Desbiolles 2013) and the tub (tourism) out of the window together with the filthy water (uneven development, environmental pollution and heritage eradication). Consider also how tourismophobic demands that the 'common people' have to acquire a voice in tourist development can degenerate into a neopopulist programme (Dahl 1970). From a neighbouring perspective, such 'movements' do little to change or problematise entrenched structures of power, including the very sources of heritage, which might be imposed onto localities by institutions they view as alien to their lifeworlds (i.e. UNESCO and/or the national centre). As Giesen (2011: 173) thoughtfully notes, people's calls for respect by power 'should not only command immaculate manners, but they also should conceive of and present themselves in terms of the classical heritage' – a realisation that locks localities into the existing system of conduct. At the same time, Nederveen Pieterse speculates that resistance may be cast as an art and a weapon of the weak, whereas emancipation is 'a project of the not-so-weak', who may truly attempt to change things, if only for themselves (Nederveen Pieterse 1992: 12). However, not only do such distinctions become blurred in contemporary societies affected by economic recessions, where even the disenfranchised middle classes may participate in the 'arts of resistance' (Scott 1991), traditional weapons of the weak (gossip, pilfering or sorcery) have entered the realm of aesthetic production (e.g. are being schematised in film and tourist advertising).

Bleak prognostications and dark potentialities should not make one discard the second interpretation centring on agency. There are many ways to approach agency, from which I select the one focusing on style because it connects tourist and film audience consumption of signs to immaterial labour, as well as political mobilisation of them in different post-Fordist contexts across world centres and peripheries. This encourages a contextual analysis of the ways collective subjectivities emerge not out of an oppositional, but *a relational imagination* (Harding 2000; Mahmood 2005; Braidotti 2008). This change of perspective calls for indepth investigation of any negative affective reactions or emotional residues as 'intimations' of a problem (Tzanelli 2008a), which can find a solution, if all sides sit at the negotiating table with an open mind. A non-Hegelian approach to such collective subjectivities can at least acknowledge that the subjects' ethical core 'is not their intentionality, but the effects of the relations of power' as both repressive (*potestas*) and positive/empowering (*potentia*) upon the world (Braidotti 2008: 15). This alternative perspective draws on a long tradition of postsecular feminism, stretching back to at least Audre Lorde (1984), Alice Walker (2005 [1984]) and Adrienne Rich (2001) in European, and bell hooks (1990), Vandana Shiva (1997) and Patricia Hill Collins (1991) in black feminist thought, which acknowledges the importance of the spiritual dimension in struggles for recognition and equality. At its creative end, it generates a new field we may call *neophenomenological aesthetics*, which is orientated towards the phenomenal potential of ethnic characters, and the impressions stemming out of them – hence, the ways atmospheres stand between intuition and irradiation. And whereas intuition allows resurgent collectivities to grasp their world and the worlds of their neighbours and tourist/visitors in an immediate and unitary fashion, irradiation consolidates in emotionally-rich interpretations of all these worlds in specific ways that end up governing the character of places and cultures. Such neophenomenologies turn physical bodies within which affects reside into 'felt-bodies', which occupy not geometrical space, but 'corporeal isles', non-anatomical zones standing between nature and culture (Griffero 2014: 23–28). Otherwise put, corporeal isles enable the production of characters (such as Orient and Occident, light and darkness and so forth) as *atmospheric situations* that reenchant worlds (turning them into a collection of field-worlds or spheres), by erasing their content of distance (the alleged reifying properties of globes).

My persistence to reconsider the genealogical roots of cinematic/contents tourism through a spiritual journey into the Japanese meaning of contents in Chapter 2 makes more sense now as a way of reaching to other worlds affected by capitalist and postcolonial restructuring. The *choreosophical* analysis of responses to development considers contexts, hence the specificity of cultural intimations with which we deal, as well as how each of them speaks to a different project of modernity (Eisenstadt 2000), with its own traditions of association between humans, land and other biospheres. To extend such observations to neovitalist analysis, I stress that all the recorded lay responses to cinematic touristification are addressed to impersonal technologies (of film, tourism and their governance), with more ease than to tourists as individuals, but eventually merge tourism and tourists with technologies of power (on this see also Urry's (1990) original thesis on the 'tourist gaze'). The inability or unwillingness of systems of production to distinguish sustainable tourism from sustainable tourism development facilitates capitalist development without addressing its consequences for human and native natural ecosystems (Scott *et al.* 2012; Korstanje and George 2015). Casting all intimations as a complaint that the all-consuming entropic energy of capitalism eats up the future (Flannery 1994; Braidotti 2008; Tzanelli 2016b), each style points towards what has to be respected, if it is not to damage the very future its enunciators wish to promote. Of course, it helps to remember that even the plea to preserve atmospheres can turn into a fundamentalist weapon for collectivities. With this note, I move past political sociological observations on the effects of *potestas* to deliberate on the futures of *potentia*: what can really be done at the minimum damage for all. This shift, which despite its sociological core prompts us to move our discussion into interdisciplinary planes, allows us to not just account for the ways effective mobilities and habitual materialities (e.g. sites or heritage) interact, but also see past them, and towards formations of cultures of native cosmopolitanism which can speak a very modern and global language (Appiah 2006). This theme is addressed in the last chapter.

Chapter 6

Crafting the impossible, meddling with the anthropocenic puzzle

Classroom experiments, lessons learned

I ran an undergraduate module on the sociology of tourism ('Tourism and Culture') for a few years at the University of Leeds. As is the case with most interdisciplinary pedagogical ventures, my aspiration to sociologise a subject that is inherently interdisciplinary, encountered some obstacles. An interesting one had to do with the ways students struggled to place themselves in roles other than those of the tourist. I personally struggled to make lucid some ideas that Higher Education students wrongly consider easy to grasp, without falling into Charles Wright Mill's proverbial trap of 'being condemned as a "mere literary man" or, worse still, "a mere journalist"' (Mills 1959: 239) – a condescending comment on another travelling profession. But I am stubborn, and I like interacting with journalism, which sometimes does clarify ideas scholars have to teach to those with little or no knowledge on a topic without compromising on their complexity. Borrowing from political satire and cultural analysis in this genre, I devised an exercise for my tourism seminar groups, who had to comprehend the complexity of film tourism in heritage locations. The decision turned me into an *I Ching* film director of sorts, who devises a problem and asks her audiences to seek solutions – with her help, of course. Regardless of whether you see me as a journalist, screenwriter, director, lecturer or seminar tutor, please read the story.

> WEEK 6: Cinematic Tourism ('The Greengrocer')
> The town of Yorkville was peaceful and uninteresting to strangers up until a Hollywood studio visited it in search for new scenic locations for its upcoming feature film *The Greengrocer* (directed by X X). The town has a budding agricultural co-op and a rather attractive little forest with old trees. The studio occupied all four of its B&Bs and hotels and, once the national and international press reported the first film shootings, all sorts of visitors flocked in to take snapshots of the stage, the film's protagonists and the scenic landscape.
>
> But Yorkville's forest includes a conservation park. It also includes an archaeological complex with an ancient Nordic tomb, a medieval Church

and a First World War cenotaph that was less well known to tourists until the story's 'greengrocer' (played by a famous actor), was filmed in its entrance kissing his cinematic sweetheart (played by a famous actress).

Thus commences cinematic tourism in Yorkville. The locality is upset because of the noise, but grateful for the capital inflow. The national centre (London) however worries for entirely different reasons: recently, the tomb and the cenotaph entered UNESCO's World Heritage list and acquired the status of a national treasure worthy of care and conservation. The forest is also protected by the National Trust, but constantly littered by young tourist couples that want to kiss and photograph where the story's protagonists got married in the film.

The townspeople are now angry. Too many '*******' invade their space, each with their own priorities.

In 'interest groups' discuss your policy planning for the place, taking into account your own priorities and the problems these may generate for yourselves and the other 'interest groups'. Would these suggested alliances last, or would they generate further problems (potential conflicts within the group)?

TEAM 1: London Conservation and UNESCO group, including Minister of Culture and Tourism.

TEAM 2: Town Council and the newly established local Tourism Office.

TEAM 3: Local greengrocers, the national co-op and local tourism labour (hotels and B&Bs).

TEAM 4: The Hollywood studio and its creative machine as well as the London film industry – the 'outsiders'.

I must add that the exercise was intentionally designed to (1) capture the moment a peaceful area is haphazardly turned into an international popcultural/tourist destination, and (2) make students think about conflicts of interest (hence my inclusion of stakeholders with almost definitely different priorities in the same group category). In addition, I wanted to see how much my students knew, or have thought about, policy regimes of heritage management independently from what they would learn from me and their weekly assigned reading.

I am confident that the groups learned something about who does what in nominations of specific monuments, areas and natural spots as 'World Heritage Sites'. I am not surprised that some students raised objections to my 'lumping together' of incompatible stakeholders, or that they simply felt unable to devise a viable policy: this helped highlight gaps in their knowledge, on which I could initiate a discussion. What struck me most was that our discussion problematised the practice of consuming protected landscapes very little, if at all, in the context of the Anthropocene. Another interesting lesson for me was that film/tourist 'development' was read as an inexcusable intrusion, whereas local modes of 'sticking to tradition' were not challenged. I regard my students as highly intelligent interlocutors and myself as a decently-read tutor – and yet, we all fell into this trap for a while.

In many respects, my fears (of being treated or acting like a 'common journalist') were misplaced. The problem was that even I had to take time to reflect on what it means to conserve, preserve, and protect material or immaterial heritage from the workings of the 'nefarious' cinematic witchcraft – hence, I remained too much of a scholar during the exercise (but too *a*ffective at that). The meaning of these activities (conservation, preservation or protection) can only be established after considerable elaboration over what constitutes the production (or alleged destruction) of location after cinematic touristification – a complex give-and-take between realist planning and the experiential provinces of host identity and identification. Heeding Böhme's (1993: 115) suggestion that artworks (films) can conjure up atmospheres as differential processes of signification, I should have concluded my classroom discussions with a double question: what can we include in a location's 'heritage'? Who decides on this? To conjure up is, after all, to summon a shadow or a ghost, like a magician, so even a film or its icons and atmospheres can be treated as products of some type of materiality next to monumental artforms or natural sites of aesthetic and ecological value. Why, therefore, do we tend to juxtapose films to 'heritage proper' on such occasions? Finally, is it actually right to consider heritage at all? I jump-cut to two answers to this question below.

Windows of darkness: degrowing and enfolding

Let me recapitulate first: this book explored ways that cinematic tourist development can construct, obstruct or unsettle different animate and inanimate systems, while often also unfurling native, translocal, national or globally networked pleas to not develop locations into cinematic tourist destinations. At times, it seemed to be an apolitical narrative of what I flagged from the outset as a politically charged discursive field, but first impressions lie. Proffering 'exploration' as a keyword, instead of the conventional 'critique' or 'criticism', is constitutive of my conviction that no entity, actant or agent in the discursive field we study knows who they are, what they want to be or what they become a priori, before their becoming (which is also processual). As an analytical statement, this observation works beyond inductivism or deductivism, because it facilitates 'abductive reasoning' to unfold the co-constitution of method, data and theory (Halford and Savage 2017: 1143). As a mobility method (multiple journeys by tourists, hosts and researchers), it helps us consolidate the centrality of ancient *mantras* in very modern social scientific investigations. A processual approach to subjectivity, identity and system-building is constitutive of epistemontologies that we associate with NRT and affective practice – both, by turn, constitutive of the creative process in the field.

However, such precognitive statuses alone cannot assist in the production of a social scientific journey, which also gestures toward a world of visualisation of results (Healy and Moody 2014). It is just that I, as the investigator/researcher, do not consider visualisation as a method that 'uncovers' facts. Thus, my task was neither to invalidate Benjamin's Arcadian dystopia of consumerism nor to exalt the wonders of postindustrial immaterial development. This would amount to the uncovering of a stable hidden truth, which only a privileged group holds at institutional, elite, intellectual or lay levels – a partition, which is fundamentally undemocratic (Ranciére 2006). Indeed, granting the trophy to either side would both endorse anthropocentrism and the belief that a good image of art, development or sedentary rural life is truthful only if it can be shattered (Latour 2011: 76–77). Incidentally, this casts tourismophobic reactions, protests and softer negative responses to development as the twin of image-breaking we associate with postindustrial growth: how could a pristine, filmed location develop into a tourist destination, if not by the destruction and reconstruction of its old way of life? Only, one may add, 'reconstruction' amounts to a chimera on the part of the image-breaking designer, who thinks that she or he knows 'what the act of breaking represents' (ibid.: 68).

My epistemontological framework had some solid narrative implications, because it was built into my scholarly practice as a form of performance. Michel Serres (1995, 2000) puts this succinctly when he notes that we live in a transitory state from the world of Atlas, who was condemned to carry the burden of earth on his shoulders, to that of Hermes, who grew wings to transport his messages to other worlds. Sociologists are manifestations of Hermes, travelling these days through intertwined informational spheres and terrestrial sites to relay the immersive affective and atmospheric forces both enclose. As is the case with peaceful sports competitions, such relaying illuminates how problems stem from bad articulations and behaviours, so the solution always lies in the formation of different values/attitudes (see Krippendorf 1999 on tourist behaviour). Given the enormity of my journey *on* the journeys of film and tourist designers, tourists and resurgent host communities, and heritage policy-makers, I could not reveal the importance of the qualitative and quantitative 'assessment' on all sides before the end: the study adds incrementally, chapter by chapter, observations on assemblages of things, people and natural or architectural habitats, and lets vitality processes speak for their viability (this is the 'messy narrative' Ingold (2000) modestly discusses as both lay and expert practice). If being *in* the world is actualised only through being *with* the world, then, as scholars, we are faced with serious ethical dilemmas not dissimilar to those raised by Derrida's (2000; Derrida and Dufourmantelle 2000) musings on the ethics of hospitality. On the one hand, stranded between the ethical imperative to accept alterity and the practical question 'can we live together?' has never led anywhere; on the other, the 'most flexible revolutions' (Guattari 2000: 66) and the worst disasters have been the outcome of ad hoc decisions on the ways events *seem* to be or go. A constructive response can only assess what is possible (Rich 2001) – an art that never ceased to create its own Nemeses, but a necessary one. Where institutions and policies clone the past and mutate problems to seed our past into our present, there can always be voices that 'break silence', asking simultaneously: 'what kind of silence is being broken?' (ibid.: 150).

Let us then return to the voices and whispers of previous chapters. From the perspective of responses to postmodern trends of touristification we can listen two forms of tension: one prioritising environmental degradation, whereas the other suggests a particular misanthropic attitude targeting host groups in precarious positions (women, ethnic minorities and tourist labour). The first trend agrees with a widespread admonition that we deal with the 'intrusion' of a fearsome Gaia into our lives. This is not the caring Mother of global interconnectedness, who ensures the health and balance of earthly ecosystems (e.g. Lovelock 2007), but an unpredictable chaotic force that restructures biospheres at a heavy price for humans, amongst other species (Hird 2010; Stengers 2015). Blencowe suggests that this 'intrusion' evokes a pragmatist political spirituality of sorts, which she associates with her refashioning of Derrida's 'Pharmakon' as the art of creative assemblage, so as to consider 'courageous attitudes of genuine experimentation (the thirst for some novelty)' (2016: 35). Such assemblages include tourism professionals, scientists and activists joined by common people in an attempt to cultivate new 'economies of imagination' (Tzanelli 2017: 32–33), capable of transcending 'the capitalist sorcery of infernal alternatives' (Blencowe 2016: 35). Art can figure in this project as the activity that can name problems (Tzanelli 2017: Chapter 3), a process of healing us from a sense of not being able to articulate 'what is wrong, what matters, what is the real' (Blencowe 2016: 36; Read 2011). It helps to remember that 'mastering pitfalls', is a timeless hexagram in the teachings of Liu I-ming (the writer of the Taoist *I Ching*), which considers overcoming obstacles, dealing with dangers in the mind and the environment as a path to development (Cleary 1986: 22). Could it be, then, that some discursively framed obstacles to cinematic tourist development are just that? Or is it that, as broken silences, they help the host to claim their place in worldmakings managed by strangers with little understanding of local human needs and environmental particularities?

The second trend is decisively anthropocentric and tackles the political ecologies of touristified spaces. It reminds passing onlookers that development comes at a price for localities, when populations are interpellated against hierarchies of an abstracted humanity. The practice of distinguishing human beings from communities (nominating them in racialised, gendered, and classed terms so as to fit them into a system of tourist/host production) leads to, if not aims at, demoting them to second-class citizens or non-citizens at best. The political ecologies of developing filmed locations are capricious in this respect: they criticise the representatives of development from without, by tightening from within the punitive reigns they put on their very own minorities. At times, such capriciousness blurs the vision, blocks the ears and debilitates all the sensory and affective pathways of those who research such ecologies. In the grander, decolonial scheme of things, this is connected to our inability or unwillingness to recognise that colonialism survived its institutional withdrawal from previously occupied cultural territories and managed to restructure governmentally within contemporary capitalism. The consequence of such restructuring has been the eradication of epistemic plurality – an issue at which many lay responses to cinematic touristification appear to hint.

Note that I am walking you through an argument: for Castro-Gómez we do not inhabit a world where epistemological plurality can be recognised anymore, because the conditions generated by Empire persist in the present, eliminating any possibility for 'epistemical democracy' (2007: 444). Here there is no futural alternative, and no 'art' of performative, governmental or decorative fashion can help the disenfranchised. Castro-Gómez's certainty of the elimination of plurality provides an unhappy ending, with no reflections on what can be done for this, only how things can get worse. If this humanistic pessimism is extended to holistic environments, in which at least for Marxists capitalist and postcolonial restructuring fuse, our survival prospects as a race or a broader ecosystem look very grim. There is the fear that, by accepting such hypotheses as certainties, we join the hordes of zombie environmentalists who eat out the future to produce living-dead ecologies, robbed of their vital forces and agential properties. This is the point of no return, where the 'dark side of modernity' turns into dark tourism for narcissistic consumption purposes.

Windows of hope: from heritage to identity reinterpretation

This is the reason why scientific and activist assemblages are necessary to construct counterpoints to this definitive pessimism, enabling the formation of economies of imagination that move beyond traditional notions of intergenerational reciprocity. Activist worldmaking, the practice of drafting alternative positive scenarios for the future, always relies on practices of worldmapping. Such practices favour obvious (that is, openly recognised) collaborations of lay *choreosophía* with professional *choreología*, thus exorcising the ghost of *ressentiment*, which feeds into marginalisation or patronising developmental planning 'from above'. Jensen (2014), who speaks of design mobilities staged 'from above' but performed 'from below', just brushes past this suggestion, by putting design in practice in postmodern urban settings. Nederveen Pieterse's (2004) indication that, especially professional middle-class creative migrants, who are attuned to international market mobilities, can devise new hybrid cultural grammars provides another key component of this dialogic blend. Finally, Swain's (2009) suggestion that worldmaking intelligence can be transformed into a form of critical cosmopolitan theory (in the tradition of Delanty's (2009) dialogics) in which the enunciative potential of worldmaking can benefit living worlds, completes the programmatic statement on tourist futures. Isin's discussion of citizenship as a performance, which yields results every time 'people stage creative and transformative resistances and articulate claims against' realities (2017: 506), is a useful reminder of the ways *choreosophia* circulates between, within and across national borders and even social groups (Ong 2005; Germann Molz 2006; Burdett and Sudjic 2010; Sassen 1991). Unfortunately, the act of speculating upon alternatives by attuning simultaneously to local needs and the world has been lodged into structurally determined ways of apprehending the world that we associate with Western provinces of meaning. Different lifeworlds structure experience via different aesthetic and somatosensory pathways, so newcomers to them need to be retrained to understand such discrepancies as intruders, before demanding reciprocation in training by the host. Several of the examples of local complaints against touristification appeal to hidden forms of rhizomatically-born affective labour, which may eventually transmute into the most destructive force for fellow humans, the natural ecosystem and oneself. Here, scopic practices are not effective 'preventative' tools, because they reproduce the eye of hungry, consumptive power. Rather than submitting to the temptation of visualism, we may consider not only how professional counter-activism has to speak a language the resurgent perpetrator understands, but also that, when synaesthetic communication becomes a strategy, it should not damage native experience and perception. Acknowledging that assemblies of thinkers share 'moods of thinking', an emotional framework for affective logics, is also another attempt to rectify the denial of their potency, which is present in societies prone to irrational undercurrents on the collective level (Hesse 2011: 69–70).

Of course, this near-utopian suggestion can also crash on another, much bigger and steeper rock, which interacts with negative affective local/national cultures and professional expansion, often in equal stead: pollution and climate change. Where a designed combination of cinematic pilgrimage and dark tourism to valued heritage spots might answer pleas to respect *choreosophic* provinces of meaning to some extent, development insensitive to the environment and an enfolding of the host who needs the help of international monitors on climate change can contribute to the earth's (and humanity's) extinction. Locally and regionally, the orchestration of the development of cinematic tourist resorts by international governmobile apparatuses leads to the degradation of cultural and natural capital. When, on top of causing environmental pollution, Western capital kills social richness, supports privatisation and halts investment in open monumentality, such as gardens, squares and avenues (Davis and Monk 2007), directing instead all forces towards cinematic privatopias, localities are getting poorer.

However, we must also note that notions of heritage and the project of heritage conservation as such obey old Western European scripts of patrilineage and authority that do not necessarily make a better world in tourism or other cross-cultural activities (Tzanelli 2013). These days, heritage as the intergenerational transmission of riches interacts structurally with mutations of old imperialist designs via the privatisation of riches, especially those based on inheritance (Gudeman 2015: 77), so it is highly possible to find out that even localities favour popcultural development over, say, monument conservation and visitation. In other words, scholarly or policy assumptions that localities simply follow

Bibliography

Adam, B. (1998) *Timescapes of Modernity: The Environment and the Invisible Hazards.* London: Routledge.

Adey, P. (2008) 'Airports, mobility and the calculative architecture of affective control', *Geoforum*, 39 (1): 438–451.

Adey, P. (2010) *Mobility*, 1st edn. London: Routledge.

Adey, P. (2017) *Mobility*, 2nd edn. London: Routledge.

Adler, J. (1989) 'Travel as performed art', *American Journey of Sociology*, 94 (6): 1366–1391.

Adler, J. (1992) 'Mobility and the creation of the subject', *International Tourism: Between Tradition and Modernity Colloquium*. Nice: France.

Adler, J. (2002) 'The holy man as traveller and travel attraction: Early Christian asceticism and the moral problematic of modernity'. In W. Swatos Jr. and L. Tomasi (eds), *From Medieval Pilgrimage to Religious Tourism*. Westport, CT: Praeger, 25–50.

Adventures by Disney Tours (2013) 'Scotland: A brave adventure'. Available at: www.adventuresbydisney.com/europe/scotland-vacations/ (accessed 28 June 2018).

AFP Google News (22 January 2009) '"Slumdog" stars sued for "defaming" India's slum-dwellers'. Available at: www.google.com/hostednews/afp/article/ALeqM5hKQWmfCUcwj1P5o8cSIxGLwRBwaw (accessed 15 September 2013).

Agamben, G. (1998) *Homo Sacer*. Stanford: Stanford University Press.

Agarwal, A. (26 January 2010) 'Chinese want to rename peaks "Hallelujah Mountains" following Avatar success', *Real Bollywood.* Available at: www.realbollywood.com/2010/01/chinese-rename-peaks-hallelujah-mountains-avatar-success.html (accessed 28 June 2018).

Ahmed, S. (2014) 'Not in the mood', *New Formations: A Journal of Culture/Theory/Politics*, 82: 13–28.

Alaimo, S. (2012) 'Sustainable this, sustainable that: New materialisms, posthumanism, and unknown futures', *PMLA*, 127 (3): 558–564.

Alatas, S.H. (2004) 'The captive mind and creative development'. In P.N. Mukherji and C. Sengupta (eds), *Indigeneity and Universality in Social Science.* New Delhi: Sage, 83–95.

Aldred, R. and Jungnickel, K. (2012) 'Constructing mobile places between "leisure" and "transport": A case study of two group cycle rides', *Sociology*, 46 (3): 523–539.

Alexander, J.C. (1988) *Action and its Environments: Towards a New Synthesis.* New York: Columbia University Press.

the state canon of heritage development may be just that, with the actual core problem being their exclusion from decision-making. We are therefore back to phenomenological debates on lay affective and embodied designs, which are also constantly sidelined in scholarship on tourism, hospitality, and popular culture, when they should serve as starting points, even for critical realist analysis.

Having run a full circle in this analysis of cinematic tourist development, we may conclude that, these days, all discussions on sustainable atmospheric design, which appeals to the soul and the senses, while also struggling to save the natural world, reproduce *I Ching*'s bipolar cosmic design of darkness (a Western European take on heritage-as-inheritance) versus light (a technical take on heritage interpretation, wrongly considered exclusively Western or European). This cosmic clash wrongly casts heritage as a positive force at all times, feeding into scholarly efforts to define effective regenerative tourism and conservation programmes (Uzzell 1996) while also displacing film and its popcultural hospitality extensions to critiques of capitalist development without a spirit. Might 'heritage' as a definitional node be the shackle not of development, but *communal welfare*? Forgetting not the past, but the nomothetic basis on which it exists and halters the future, alters the rules under which we consider dark spots and problems in contemporary cultural-political ecologies of tourism and hospitality. A dystopian world is never the only possible one. Therefore, strategisations involved in the governance of touristified locations should consider how localities are involved in the process. A badly existing world is a world in which some forms of work are not being recognised as such or as valuable (Bloch [1986] 1995: 210). The challenge before us is to distinguish between what to discard and preserve from past and memory, so that it does not obstruct a viable and just way forward.

Alexander, J.C. (2011) 'Clifford Geertz and the strong program: Human sciences and cultural sociology'. In J.C. Alexander, P. Smith, and M. Norton (eds), *Interpreting Clifford Geertz: Cultural Investigation in the Social Sciences*. New York: Palgrave Macmillan, 55–64.
Amoamo, M. and Thompson, A. (2010) '(Re)imagining Maori tourism: Representation and cultural hybridity in postcolonial New Zealand', *Tourist Studies*, 10 (1): 35–55.
Anders, C.J. (14 January 2010) 'Avatar's designers speak: Floating mountains, AMP suits 12 and the dragon', IO9.com. Available at: https://io9.gizmodo.com/5444960/avatars-designers-speak-floating-mountains-amp-suits-and-the-dragon (accessed 28 June 2018).
Anderson, B. (2006) *Imagined Communities*, 2nd edn. London: Verso.
Anderson, B. (2009) 'Affective atmospheres', *Emotion, Space and Society*, 2: 77–81.
Anderson, B. (2014) *Encountering Affect: Capacities, Apparatuses, Conditions*. Farnham, UK: Ashgate.
Anderson, B., Kearnes, M., McFarlane, C., and Swanton, D. (2012) 'Materialism and the politics of assemblage', *Dialogues in Human Geography*, 2 (2): 212–215.
Andrews, H. (2009) 'Tourism as a moment of being', *Suomen Anthropologi*, 34 (2): 5–21.
Andriotis, K. (2014) 'Tourism development and the degrowth paradigm', Middlesex University Business School UDC 338.48, 13: 37–45.
Andriotis, K. (2018) *Degrowth in Tourism: Conceptual, Theoretical and Philosophical Issues*. Wallingford: CABI.
Appadurai, A. (1986) 'Towards an anthropology of things'. In A. Appadurai (ed.), *The Social Life of Things: Commodities in Cultural Perspective*. Cambridge: Cambridge University Press, 3–63.
Appadurai, A. (1990) 'Disjuncture and difference in the global cultural economy', *Public Culture*, 2 (2): 1–24.
Appiah, K.A. (2006) *Cosmopolitanism*. New York: W.W. Norton & Co.
Archer, M. (1995) *Realist Social Theory*. Cambridge: Cambridge University Press.
Archer, M. (2000) *Being Human: The Problem of Agency*. Cambridge: Cambridge University Press.
Archer, M. (2008) *Structure, Agency and the Internal Conversation*. Cambridge: Cambridge University Press.
Arendt, H. (1958) *The Human Condition*. Chicago: University of Chicago Press.
Argyrou, V. (2005) *The Logic of Environmentalism*. Oxford: Berghahn.
Asad, T. (2009) *Genealogies of Religion: Discipline and Reasons of Power in Christianity and Islam*. Baltimore: Johns Hopkins University Press.
Ash, L. and Turner, J. (1975) *The Golden Hordes: International Tourism and Pleasure Periphery*. London: Constable.
Ashworth, G. and Page, D. (2011) 'Urban tourism research: Recent progress and current paradoxes', *Tourism Management*, 32 (1): 1–15.
Ateljevic, I. (2009) 'Transmodernity: Remaking our (tourism) world?'. In J. Tribe (ed.), *Philosophical Issues in Tourism*. Bristol and Toronto: Channel View Publications, 278–300.
Ateljevic, I. and Hall, D. (2007) 'Tourism embodiment of the macho gaze in the South Eastern Europe: Performing masculinity and femininity in Albania and Croatia'. In A. Pritchard, N. Morgan, and I. Ateljevic (eds), *Tourism and Gender: Essays on Embodiment, Sensuality and Experience*. Wallingford: CABI, 138–157.
Augé, M. (2008) *Non-Places: Introduction to an Anthropology of Supermodernity*. London and New York: Verso.
Baart, R. (28 August 2016) 'Disney causes tourism overload in Norway', Next Nature

Network. Available at: www.nextnature.net/2016/09/norway-tourist-overload/ (accessed 20 May 2018).
Bærenholdt, J.O. (2013) 'Governmobility: The powers of mobility', *Mobilities*, 8 (1): 20–34.
Bærenholdt, O., Haldrup, M., Larsen, J., and Urry, J. (2004) *Performing Tourist Places*. Aldershot: Ashgate.
Bakhtin M.M. (1984) *Problems of Dostoevski's Poetics*. Manchester: Manchester University Press.
Banks, M. (2001) *Visual Methods in Social Research*. London: Sage.
Barcelona Field Studies Centre (2018) 'Google maps projection'. Available at: https://setcompass.com/GoogleMapsProjection.htm (accessed 20 June 2018).
Barclay, B. (2003) 'Exploring Fourth Cinema'. In *Reimagining Indigenous Cultures: The Pacific Islands*. Honolulu, Hawaii: Summer Institute.
Barnett, L. (29 August 2012) 'A Scottish historian on Brave', *Guardian*. Available at: www.theguardian.com/film/2012/aug/29/scottish-historian-view-brave (accessed 9 February 2014).
Barry, A. and Thrift, N. (2007) 'Gabriel Tarde: Imitation, invention and economy', *Economy and Society*, 36 (4): 509–525.
Barthes, R. (1993) *Mythologies*. London: Vintage.
Basu, K. (2012) 'Slum tourism: For the poor, by the poor'. In F. Frenzel, K. Koens, and M. Steinbrink (eds), *Slum Tourism: Poverty, Power and Ethics*. London: Routledge, 66–82.
Basu, P. (2000) 'Sites of memory – sources of identity: Landscape narratives of the Sutherland Clearances'. In J.A. Atkinson, I. Banks, and G. MacGregor (eds), *Townships to Farmsteads: Rural Settlement Studies in Scotland, England and Wales*. Oxford: BAR British Series 293, 225–236.
Basu, P. (2004) 'Route metaphors of 'roots-tourism' in the Scottish Highland Diaspora'. In S. Coleman and J. Eade (eds), *Reframing Pilgrimage*. London: Routledge, 150–174.
Bateson, G. (1973) *Steps to an Ecology of Mind: Collected Essays in Anthropology, Psychiatry, Evolution and Epistemology*. Chicago: University of Chicago Press.
Bateson, G. (1980) *Mind and Nature*. London: Fontana.
Baudrillard, J. (1973) *Toward a Critique of the Political Economy of the Sign*. St Louis, MO: Telos.
Baudrillard, J. (1975) *The Mirror of Production*. St Louis, MO: Telos.
Baudrillard, J. (1988) *America*. London: Verso.
Baudrillard, J. (1994) *Simulacra and Simulations*. Ann Arbor: University of Michigan Press.
Bauman, Z. (1996) *Tourists and Vagabonds*. Institut für Höhere Studien (IHS), Wien, Abt. Politikwissenschaft, 30: 7–15. Available at: http://nbn-resolving.de/urn:nbn:de:0168-ssoar-266870 (accessed 13 September 2016).
Bauman, Z. (2000) *Liquid Modernity*. Cambridge: Polity.
Bauman, Z. (2007) *Consuming Life*. Cambridge: Polity.
Bauman, Z. (2008) *Liquid Fear*. Cambridge: Polity.
Bauman, Z. (2016) *Retrotopia*. Cambridge: Polity.
Bauman, Z. and Lyon, D. (2013) *Liquid Surveillance*. Cambridge: Polity.
BBC News (23 October 2009) 'Medieval keep becomes film set'. Available at: http://news.bbc.co.uk/1/hi/scotland/tayside_and_central/8322843.stm (accessed 28 June 2018).
BBC News (26 January 2010) 'China renames "Avatar" mountain in honour of film'. Available at: http://news.bbc.co.uk/1/hi/8480954.stm (accessed 28 June 2018).
BBC News (11 June 2012) 'Olympic Torch: Flame completes longest relay journey'. Available at: www.bbc.co.uk/news/uk-18387026 (accessed 28 June 2018).

BBC – Scotland Business (18 June 2012) 'Alex Salmond attending US premiere of Disney film Brave'. Available at: www.bbc.co.uk/news/uk-scotland-scotland-business-18467968 (accessed 28 June 2018).

BBC News (28 June 2012) 'Stones that helped to inspired Disney-Pixar's Brave in buyout plan'. Available at: www.bbc.co.uk/news/uk-scotland-highlands-islands-18623672 (accessed 28 June 2018).

BBC News Ireland (10 October 2017) 'Game of Thrones: Traffic banned from Dark Hedges road'. Available at: www.bbc.co.uk/news/uk-northern-ireland-41561589 (accessed 4 April 2018).

BBC News (18 May 2018) 'Viking TV shows boost Denmark tourist attractions'. Available at: www.bbc.co.uk/news/blogs-news-from-elsewhere-36323270 (accessed 18 January 2018).

Beck, U. (2006) 'Living in the world risk society', *Economy and Society*, 35 (3): 329–345.

Beck, U. (2007) 'The cosmopolitan condition: Why methodological nationalism fails', *Theory, Culture & Society*, 24 (7–8): 286–290.

Beck, U. (2009) *World at Risk.* Cambridge: Polity.

Beeton, S. (2004) 'The more things change ... A legacy of film-induced tourism'. In W. Frost, G. Croy, and S. Beeton (eds), *International Tourism and Media Proceedings.* Latrobe University: ITAM, 4–14.

Beeton, S. (2005) *Film-Induced Tourism*, 1st edn. Toronto: Channel View.

Beeton, S. (2006) 'Understanding film-induced tourism', *Tourism Analysis*, 11 (3): 181–188.

Beeton, S. (2016) *Film-Induced Tourism*, 2nd edn. Toronto: Channel View.

Beijing International Travel Website (undated) 'Tujia going to cry before getting married'. Available at: http://china.citw2008.com/html/2006/1108/1361.shtml. (accessed 15 March 2014).

Bell, C. and Lyall, J. (2002) *The Accelerated Sublime: Landscape, Tourism, and Identity.* Westport: Praeger.

Bell, D. (1976) *The Cultural Contradictions of Capitalism.* New York: Basic Books.

Bell, D. and Valentine, G. (1995) *Mapping Desire.* London: Routledge.

Belting, H. (2011) *An Anthropology of Images.* Princeton, NJ: Princeton University Press.

Bendix, R. (2002) 'Capitalising on memories past, present and future', *Theoretical Anthropology*, 2 (4): 469–487.

Benhabib, S. (1992) *Situating the Self.* New York: Routledge.

Benjamin, W. (1983) *Charles Baudelaire.* London: Verso.

Benjamin, W. (2002) *The Arcades Project.* Cambridge, MA: Harvard University Press.

Benjamin, W. (2006) *The Writer of Modern Life.* Cambridge, MA: The Belknap Press.

Bennett, J. (2001) *The Enchantment of Modern Life: Attachments, Crossings and Ethics.* Princeton, NJ: Princeton University Press.

Berlant, L. (1997) *The Queen of American Goes to Washington City.* Durham, NC: Duke University Press.

Berlant, L. (2011) *Cruel Optimism.* Durham, NC: Duke University Press.

Berman, M. (2010) *All That is Solid Melts into Earth: The Experience of Modernity*, revised edn. London and New York: Verso.

Bhabha, H.K. (1994) *The Location of Culture.* London and New York: Routledge.

Bianchi, R. and Stephenson, M. (2014) *Tourism and Citizenship: Rights, Freedoms and Responsibilities in the Global Order.* Abingdon: Routledge.

Bille, M. (2013) 'Luminous atmospheres: Energy politics, climate technologies, and cosiness in Denmark', *Ambiances. International Journal of Sensory Environment, Architecture and Urban Space*. Available at: http://ambiances.revues.org/376 (accessed 3 May 2018).

Biran, A., Poria, Y. and Oren, G. (2011) 'Sought experience at dark heritage sites', *Annals of Tourism Research*, 38 (3): 820–841.

Bissell, D. (2009) 'Moving with others: The sociality of the railway journey'. In P. Vannini (ed.), *The Cultures of Alternative Mobilities: The Routes Less Travelled*. Farnham and Burlington, VT: Ashgate, 55–70.

Bissell, D. (2016) 'Micropolitics of mobility: Public transport commuting and everyday encounters with forces of enablement and constraint', *Annals of the Association of American Geographers*, 106 (2): 394–403.

Bissell, D. and Fuller, G. (2009) 'The revenge of the still', *M/C Journal* 12 (1). Available at: http://journal.media-culture.org.au/index.php/mcjournal/article/view/136%3E/0 (accessed 29 June 2018).

Bissell, D. and Fuller, G. (2011) *Stillness in a Mobile World*. London: Routledge.

Blanchard, L.A. and Higgins-Desbiolles, F. (2013) *Peace through Tourism: Promoting Human Security through International Citizenship*. Abingdon: Routledge.

Blanco-Romero, A., Blázquez-Salom, M., and Cànoves, G. (2018) 'Barcelona, housing rent bubble in a tourist city: Social responses and local policies', *Sustainability*, 10 (6): 20–43.

Blanton, R. (2011) 'Chronotopic landscapes and environmental racism', *Linguistic Anthropology*, 21 (1): 76–93.

Bleicher, J. (1980) *Contemporary Hermeneutics: Hermeneutics as Method, Philosophy and Critique*. London and New York: Routledge.

Blencowe, C. (2016) 'Ecological attunement in a theological key: Adventures in antifascist aesthetics', *GeoHumanities*, 2 (1): 24–41.

Bloch, E. ([1986] 1995) *The Principle of Hope*, vols. I–III. Cambridge, MA: MIT Press.

Bloch, E. (1990) *Heritage of our Times*. Berkeley: University of California Press.

Bloch, E. (2000) *The Spirit of Utopia*. Palo Alto, CA: Stanford University Press.

Bloch, E. (2006) *Traces*. Palo Alto, CA: Stanford University Press.

Blok, A. and Farias, I. (2016) *Urban Cosmopolitics: Agencements, Assemblies, Atmospheres*. London: Routledge.

Bly, L. (21 October 2004) 'Tourists get into "Da Vinci" mode', *USA Today*. Available at: www.usatoday.com/travel/destinations (accessed 10 October 2006).

Boano, C., Hunter, W., and Newton, C. (2013) *Contested Urbanism in Dharavi*. Berkeley: University of California Press.

Böhme, G. (1992) 'An aesthetic theory of nature: An interim report', *Thesis Eleven*, 32 (1): 90–102.

Böhme, G. (1993) 'Atmosphere as the fundamental concept of a new aesthetics', *Thesis Eleven*, 36 (1): 113–126.

Böhme, G. (1995) *Atmosphere*. Frankfurt: Suhrkamp.

Böhme, G. (2006) 'Atmosphere as the subject of architecture'. In P. Ursprung (ed.), *Herzog and Meuron: Natural History*. London: Lars Műller Publications, 398–407.

Böhme, G. (2008) *Invasive Technification: Critical Essays in the Philosophy of Technology*. London: Bloomsbury.

Böhme, G. (2010) 'On beauty', *Nordic Journal of Aesthetics*, 21 (39): 22–33.

Böhme, G. (2016) *The Aesthetics of Atmospheres*. London: Routledge.

Böhme, G. (2017) *Critique of Aesthetic Capitalism*. Berlin Mimesis International/ Suhrkamp Verlag.

Bolan, P. (2010) 'Film-induced tourism: motivation, authenticity and displacement', PhD Thesis, Business School: University of Ulster.

Borén, T. and Young, C. (2013) 'Getting creative with the "creative city"? Towards new perspectives on creativity in urban policy', *International Journal of Urban and Regional Research*, 37 (5): 1799–1815.

Bourdieu, P. (1977) *Outline of a Theory of Practice*. Cambridge: Polity Press.

Bourdieu, P. (1984) *Distinction*. Cambridge: Harvard University Press.

Bourdieu, P. (1993) *The Field of Cultural Production*. Cambridge: Polity.

Braidotti, R. (2008) 'In spite of the times: The postsecular turn in feminism', *Theory, Culture & Society*, 25 (1): 1–24.

Braidotti, R. (2013) *The Posthuman*. Cambridge: Polity.

Bramwell, B. and Lane, B. (1993) 'Interpretation and sustainable tourism: The potential and the pitfalls', *Journal of Sustainable Tourism*, 1 (2): 71–80.

Braun, B. (2006) 'Toward a new earth and a new humanity: Nature, ontology, politics'. In N. Castree and D. Gregory (eds), *David Harvey: A Critical Reader*. Oxford: Blackwell, 191–222.

Braun, B. (2008) 'Environmental issues: Inventive life', *Progress in Human Geography*, 32 (5): 667–679.

Bravietour (2018) 'Social project visit to City of God'. Available at: www.bravietour.com.br/social-project-visit-at-city-of-god (accessed 24 April 2018).

Brigstocke, J. and Noorani, T. (2016) 'Posthuman attunements: Aesthetics, authority and the arts of creative listening', *GeoHumanities*, 2 (1): 1–7.

Broswimmer, F.J. (2002) *Ecocide: A Short History of the Mass Extinction of Species*. London: Pluto Press.

Bruno, G. (2002) *Atlas of Emotion: Journeys in Art, Architecture, and Film*. New York: Verso.

Brunton, (1 May 2018) 'Venice poised to segregate tourists as city braces itself for May Day "invasion" ', *Guardian*. Available at: www.theguardian.com/travel/2018/may/01/venice-to-segregate-tourists-in-may-day-overcrowding (accessed 2 May 2018).

Bryant, W.C. (1817) 'Thanatopsis', *North American Review*, 5 (15): 338–341.

Burdett, D. and Sudjic, R. (2010) *The Endless City: The Urban Age Project*. London: London School of Economics and Deutsche Bank's Alfred Herrhausen Society.

Büscher, M. (2006) 'Vision in motion', *Environment and Planning A*, 38 (2): 281–299.

Büscher, M., and Urry, J. (2009) 'Mobile methods and the empirical', *European Journal of Social Theory*, 12 (1): 99–116.

Büscher, M., Urry, J., and Witchger, K. (2011) *Mobile Methods*. London: Routledge.

Butler, J. (2009) *Frames of War: When is Life Grievable?* London: Verso.

Butler, R.W. (2006) *The Tourism Area Life Cycle: Conceptual and Theoretical Issues*. Clevedon, UK: Channel View.

Byrne, D. and Callaghan, G. (2014) *Complexity Theory and the Social Sciences: The State of the Art*. London: Routledge.

Callon, M. and Law, J. (1995) 'Agency and the hybrid collectif', *South Atlantic Quarterly*, 94 (2): 481–507.

Campbell, A. (2005) 'Keeping the "Lady" safe: The regulation of femininity through crime prevention', *Critical Criminology*, 13 (2): 119–140.

Capps, K. (11 December 2017) '"Game of Thrones" tourists are besieging Dubrovnik'. City Lab. Available at www.citylab.com/design/2017/12/game-of-thrones-tourists-are-beseiging-dubrovnik/544967/ (accessed 4 April 2018).

Capra, F. (2002) *The Hidden Connections: A Science for Sustainable Living*. Anchor Books.

Capra, F. and Luisi, P.L. (2014) *The Systems View of Life: A Unifying Vision*. Cambridge: Cambridge University Press.

Capra, F. and Spretnak, C. (1984) *Green Politics*. New York: Dutton.

Capra, P. (1996) *The Web of Life*. London: Harper Collins.

Carlson, A. (2000) *Aesthetics and the Environment: An Appreciation of Nature, Art and Architecture*. London: Routledge.

Carlton, D. (1994) *Looking for Little Egypt*. Bloomington, IN: IDD Books.

Carrell, S. (3 June 2012) 'Scotland rallies behind Brave animation on hopes it will buoy tourism', *Guardian*. Available at: www.theguardian.com/uk/2012/jun/03/scotland-brave-tourism-animation-disney (accessed 29 June 2018).

Castro-Gómez, S. (2007) 'The missing chapter of empire: Postmodern re-organization of coloniality and post-Fordist capitalism', *Cultural Studies*, 21 (2–3): 428–448.

Castro-Gómez, S. and Martin, D.A. (2002) 'The social sciences, epistemic violence, and the problem of the "invention of the other"', *Views from South*, 3 (2): 269–285.

Cateridge, J. (2015) 'Deep mapping and screen tourism: The Oxford of Harry Potter and Inspector Morse', *Humanities*, 4 (3): 320–333.

CBS News (12 November 2004) '"Da Vinci Code" tourist letdowns'. Available at: www.cbsnews.com/2100-500174_162-652625.html (accessed 13 May 2012).

CBS News (19 June 2008) 'Fans line up for "Angels & Demons" tours'. Available at: www.cbsnews.com/stories/2008/06/19/earlyshow/leisure/boxoffice/main4193975.shtml (accessed 2 September 2008).

Chakrabarty, D. (2000) *Provincializing Europe*. Princeton: Princeton University Press.

Chan, M.J. (18 February 2010) 'Thailand: The Beach revisited', *Telegraph*. Available at: www.telegraph.co.uk/travel/bestbeaches/7270079/Thailand-The-Beach-revisited.html (accessed 13 May 2018).

Chandler, T. (2011) 'Reading atmospheres: The ecocritical potential of Gernot Böhme's aesthetic theory of nature', *Interdisciplinary Studies in Literature and Environment*, 18 (3): 553–568.

Charron, N. (2010) 'The correlates of corruption in India: Analysis and evidence from the states', *Asian Journal of Political Science*, 18 (2): 177–194.

Chatterjee, P. (1998) *A Possible India: Essays in Political Criticism*. Calcutta: Oxford University Press.

Cheded, F. (17 January 2018) 'The legacy of "City of God" on Brazil's favelas', FSR. Available at: https://filmschoolrejects.com/legacy-city-god-brazils-favelas/ (accessed 24 April 2018).

Child, B. (25 October 2010) 'The Hobbit relocation row sparks street protests in New Zealand', *Guardian*. Available at: www.theguardian.com/film/2010/oct/25/the-hobbit-protests-new-zealand (accessed 18 December 2010).

Child, B. (13 May 2013) 'Brave director criticises Disney's "sexualised" princess Merida redesign', *Guardian*. Available at: www.theguardian.com/film/2013/may/13/brave-director-criticises-sexualised-merida-redesign (accessed 29 June 2018).

Child, B. (16 May 2013) 'Disney retreats from princess Merida makeover after wide-spread criticism', *Guardian*. Accessed at: www.theguardian.com/film/2013/may/16/Disney-princess-merida-makeover (accessed 29 June 2018).

Chowdry, G. (2007) 'Edward Said and contrapuntal reading: Implications for critical interventions in international relations', *Millennium*, 36 (1): 101–116.

Clark, S. (2001) *Captain Corelli's Mandolin: The Illustrated Film Companion*. London: Headline.

Clavé, S.A. (2007) *The Global Theme Park Industry*. Oxford: CABI.

Cleary, T. (1986) *The Taoist I Ching*. Boston: Shamabhala.

Cleary, T. (1994) *The Buddhist I Ching*. Boston: Shamabhala.

Clifford, J. (1997) *Routes*. Cambridge, MA: Harvard University Press.

Clifford, J. (2013) *Returns*. Cambridge, MA: Harvard University Press.

Clover, C.J. (1994) 'The eye of horror'. In L. Williams (ed.), *Viewing Positions: Ways of Seeing Film*. Brunswick, NJ: Rutgers University Press, 184–230.

Cochrane, A. (2004) 'Cities of light: Place-making in the 24-hour city', *Urban Design Quarterly*, 89: 12–14.

Cocks, J. (1989) *The Oppositional Imagination*. London: Routledge.

Cohen, E. (1996) 'A phenomenology of tourist experiences'. In Y. Apostolopoulos, S. Leivadi, and A. Yannakis (eds), *The Sociology of Tourism*. London: Routledge, 90–114.

Cohen, E.H. (2011) 'Educational dark tourism in populo site: The Holocaust Museum in Jerusalem', *Annals of Tourism Research*, 38 (1): 193–209.

Coldwell, W. (14 February 2018) 'Thailand's Maya Bay, location for The Beach, to close to tourists', *Guardian*. Available at: www.theguardian.com/travel/2018/feb/14/thailand-maya-bay-the-beach-movie-close-to-tourists-leonardo-dicaprio (accessed 13 May 2018).

Coleman, S. and Eade, J. (2004) 'Reframing pilgrimage'. In S. Coleman and J. Eade (eds), *Reframing Pilgrimage*. London: Routledge, 1–26.

Colomb, C. and Novy, J. (eds) (2016) *Protest and Resistance in the Tourist City*. New York: Routledge.

Condé Nast Traveller (2018) 'Places in Norway that inspired Disney's "Frozen"'. Available at: www.cntraveler.com/galleries/2014-11-02/places-in-norway-that-inspired-disneys-frozen (accessed 21 May 2018).

Connell, J. (2006) 'Medical tourism: Sea, sun, sand and … surgery', *Tourism Management*, 27 (6): 1093–1100.

Connell, J. (2012) 'Film tourism: Evolution, progress and prospects', *Tourism Management*, 33 (5): 1007–1029.

Connell, J. and Meyer, D. (2009) 'Balamory revisited: An evaluation of the screen tourism destination-tourist nexus', *Tourism Management*, 30 (2): 194–207.

Connerton, P. (1989) *How Societies Remember*. Cambridge: Cambridge University Press.

Cornwell, T. (1 July 2011) 'Scotland's Pixar tale hits the right note', *The Scotsman*. Available at: www.scotsman.com/news/scotland-s-pixar-tale-hits-the-right-note-1-1714496 (accessed 29 June 2018).

Cosgrove, D. (1998) *Social Formation and Symbolic Landscape*. Madison, WI: University of Wisconsin Press.

Cosslett, R.C. (26 October 2015) 'Interactive map reveals James Bond's travel destinations', *Guardian*. Available at: www.theguardian.com/travel/2015/oct/26/james-bond-travel-destinations-interactive-map?CMP=share_btn_link (accessed 16 January 2018).

Couch, D., Jackson, R., and Thompson, F. (2005) 'Introduction: The media and the tourist imagination'. In D. Crouch, R. Jackson, and F. Thompson (eds), *The Media and the Tourist Imagination: Converging Cultures*. Abingdon: Routledge, 1–13.

Couldry, N. (2003a) 'Media meta-capital: Extending the range of Bourdieu's field theory', *Theory and Society*, 32 (5/6): 653–677.

Couldry, N. (2003b) *Media Rituals*. New York: Routledge.

Cowan, J. (1990) *Dance and the Body Politic in Northern Greece*. Princeton, NJ: Princeton University Press.

Crampton, J. (1994) 'Cartography's defining moment: The Peters projection controversy 1974–1990', *Cartographica*, 31 (4): 16–32.

Cresswell, T. (2006) *On the Move: Mobility in the Modern Western World*. London: Routledge.

Cresswell, T. (2010) 'Towards a politics of mobility', *Environment and Planning D*, 28 (1): 17–31.

Cresswell, T. (2011) 'The vagrant/vagabond: The curious career of a mobile subject'. In T. Cresswell and P. Merriman (eds), *Geographies of Mobilities: Practices, Spaces, Subjects*. Farnham and Burlington, VT: Ashgate, 239–254.

Cresswell, T. (2014) 'Mobilities III: Moving on', *Progress in Human Geography*, 38 (5): 712–721.

Cronin, A. (2010) *Advertising, Commercial Spaces and the Urban*. Basingstoke: Palgrave Macmillan.

Cronin, A. and Hetherington, K. (eds) (2008) *Consuming the Entrepreneurial City: Image, Memory, Spectacle*. Abingdon and New York: Routledge.

Crouch, D. (2009) 'The diverse dynamics of cultural studies and tourism'. In T. Jamal and M. Robinson (eds), *The SAGE Handbook of Tourism Studies*. London: Sage, 82–98.

Croy, G.W. (2010) 'Planning for film tourism: Active destination image management', *Tourism and Hospitality Planning & Development*, 7 (1): 21–30.

Croy, G.W. (2011) 'Film tourism: Sustained economic contributions to destinations', *Worldwide Hospitality and Tourism Themes*, 3 (2): 159–164.

Croy, G.W. and Smith, N. (2005) 'Presentation of dark tourism: Te Wairoa, the buried village'. In C. Ryan, S. Page, and M. Aicken (eds), *Taking Tourism to the Limits*. London: Elsevier, 199–231.

Croy, W.G. and Buchmann, A. (2009) 'Film-induced tourism in the high country: Recreation and tourism contest', *Tourism Review International*, 13 (2): 147–155.

Crystal Travel & Tour (2018) 'Viking Tour of Ireland | 8 Day Self-Drive'. Available at: www.crystal-travel.com/by-destination/ireland/viking-tour-of-ireland/ (accessed 23 May 2018).

Curtis, L.P. (1971) *Apes and Angels: The Irishman in Victorian Caricature*. New York: Smithsonian Institution Press.

D'Alisa, G., Kallis, G., and DeMaria, F. (2015) 'From austerity to *dépense*'. In G. D'Alisa, F. DeMaria, and G. Kallis (eds), *Degrowth*. New York: Routledge, 215–220.

D'Andrea, A. (2006) 'Neo-nomadism: A theory of post-identarian mobility in the global age', *Mobilities*, 1 (1): 95–119.

D'Sa, E. (1999) 'Wanted: Tourists with a social conscious', *International Journal of Contemporary Hospitality Management*, 11 (2/3): 64–68.

Dahl, R.A. (1970) *After the Revolution? Authority in a Good Society*. New Haven, CT: Yale University Press.

Daly, F. (2013) 'The zero-point: Encountering the dark emptiness of nothingness'. In P. Thompson and S. Žižek (eds), *The Privatization of Hope: Ernst Bloch and the Future of Utopia*. Durham, NC: Duke University Press, 164–202.

Dann, G.M.S. (1996) *The Language of Tourism*. Wallingford: CABI.

Dann, G.M.S. (2001) 'Slavery, contested heritage and thanatourism', *International Journal of Tourism Hospitality and Administration*, 2 (3/4): 1–29.

Davis, C. (30 May 2016) 'Iceland plans Airbnb restrictions amid tourism explosion', *Guardian*. Available at: www.theguardian.com/world/2016/may/30/iceland-plans-airbnb-restrictions-amid-tourism-explosion?CMP=fb_gu (accessed 22 May 2018).

Davis, J. (2004) 'Corruption in public service delivery: Experience from South Asia's water and sanitation sector', *World Development*, 32 (1): 53–71.

Davis, M. and Monk, D.M. (2007) *Evil Paradises*. New York: The New Press.

De Bernières, Louis (1997) *Captain Corelli's Mandolin*. London: Minerva.

De Sousa Santos, B. (1995) *Towards a New Common Sense*. London: Routledge.

De Sousa Santos, B. (1999) 'Towards a multicultural conception of human rights'. In M. Featherstone and S. Lash (eds), *Spaces of Culture*. London: Sage, 214–229.

De Sousa Santos, B. (2007) 'From an epistemology of blindness to an epistemology of seeing'. In B. de Sousa Santos (ed.), *Cognitive Justice in a Global World: Prudent Knowledges for a Decent Life*. Plymouth: Lexington Books, 407–439.

De Souza e Silva, A. and Frith, J. (2011) *Net-Locality: Why Location Matters in a Networked World*. Malden, MA and Oxford: Wiley-Blackwell.

De Souza e Silva, A. and Sheller, M. (2014) *Mobility and Locative Media: Mobile Communication in Hybrid Spaces*. London: Routledge.

De Souza e Silva, A. and Sutko, D. (eds) (2010) *Digital Cityscapes: Merging Digital and Urban Playspaces*. New York: Peter Lang.

Degen, M., Melhuish, C., and Rose, G. (2010) 'Producing place atmospheres digitally: Architecture, digital visualisation practices and the experience economy', *Journal of Consumer Culture*, 17 (1): 3–24.

Delahaye, J. (15 February 2018) 'Iconic Thailand beach from Leonardo Di Caprio film The Beach is being closed to tourists'. *The Mirror*. Available at: www.mirror.co.uk/travel/asia-middle-east/beach-film-leonardo-dicaprio-location-12030282 (accessed 13 May 2018).

Delanty, G. (2009) *The Cosmopolitan Imagination*. Cambridge: Cambridge University Press.

Delanty, G. (2013) *Community*. Abingdon: Routledge.

Delanty, G. (2015) 'Not all is lost in translation: World varieties of cosmopolitanism', *Cultural Sociology*, 8 (4): 374–391.

Delanty, G. and O'Mahony, P. (2002) *Nationalism and Social Theory: Modernity and the Recalcitrance of the Nation*. London: Sage.

Deleuze, G. (1988) *Spinoza: Practical Philosophy*. San Francisco: City Light.

Deleuze, G. (1995) *Negotiations, 1972–1990*. New York: Columbia University Press.

Deleuze, G. and Guattari, F. (1983) *Anti-Oedipus*. Minneapolis, MN: University of Minnesota Press.

Deleuze, G. and Guattari, F. (1987) *A Thousand Plateaus: Capitalism and Schizophrenia*. Minneapolis, MN: University of Minnesota Press.

Della Porta, D. and Diani, M. (2006) *Social Movements*, 2nd edn. Oxford: Blackwell.

Dennis, K. and Urry, J. (2009) *After the Car*. Cambridge: Polity.

Derrida, J. (1994) *Spectres of Marx*. New York: Routledge.

Derrida, J. (1997) *Writing and Difference*. London: Routledge.

Derrida, J. (2000) 'Hostipitality', *Angelaki*, 5 (3): 3–18.

Derrida, J. and Dufourmantelle, A. (2000) *Of Hospitality*. Stanford: Stanford University Press.

Diekmann, A. and Hannam, K. (2012) 'Touristic mobilities in India's slum places', *Annals of Tourism Research*, 39 (3): 1315–1336.

Diken, B. (2009) 'The (impossible) society of spite: Revisiting nihilism', *Theory, Culture & Society*, 26 (4): 97–116.

Diken, B. (2010) 'Fire as a metaphor of (im)mobility', *Mobilities*, 6 (1): 95–102.

Dillette, A.K., Douglas, A.C., and Andrzejewski, C. (2017) 'Yoga tourism – a catalyst for transformation?', *Annals of Leisure Research*, DOI: 10.1080/11745398.2018.1459195.

Dimitrova Savova, N. (2009) 'Heritage kinaesthetics: Local constructivism and UNESCO's intangible-tangible politics at a favela museum', *Anthropological Quarterly*, 82 (2): 547–585.

Discover Northern Ireland.com (2014) 'Game of Thrones Tours'. Available at: www.discovernorthernireland.com/gameofthrones/ (accessed 8 December 2014).

Douglas, M. (1993) *Purity and Danger: An Analysis of the Concepts of Pollution and Taboo*. London: Routledge.

Douglas, M. and Wildavsky, A. (1982) *Risk and Culture*. Berkeley: University of California Press.

Doward, J. (29 December 2015) 'Star Wars awakens new wave of film tourism as its fans seek out locations'. *Guardian*. Available at: www.theguardian.com/film/2015/dec/26/uk-tourism-star-wars-fans-feel-force-heroes-footsteps?CMP=share_btn_link (accessed 16 January 2018).

Duff, D. (2010) 'On the role of affect and practice in the production of place', *Environment and Planning D: Society and Space*, 28 (5): 881–895.

Duffy, E. (2009) *The Speed Handbook: Velocity, Pleasure, Modernism*. Durham, NC: Duke University Press.

Dufrenne, M. ([1953] 1973) *The Phenomenology of Aesthetic Experience*. Evanston: Northwestern University Press.

Duncan, J. (1999) 'Dis-orientation: On the shock of the familiar in a far-away place'. In J. Duncan and D. Gregory (eds), *Writes of Passage*. London: Routledge, 161–179.

Duncan, J., and Duncan, N. (1988) '(Re)reading the landscape', *Environment and Planning D*, 6 (2): 117—126.

Dussel, E. (1985) *Philosophy of Liberation*. New York: Orbis.

Dyson, P. (2012) 'Slum tourism: Representing and interpreting "reality" in Dharavi, Mumbai', *Tourism Geographies*, 14 (2): 254–274.

Eade, J. (1992) 'Pilgrimage and tourism in Lourdes, France', *Annals of Tourism Research*, 19 (1): 18–32.

Eames, A. (26 May 2016) 'On the Kurt Wallander trails in Ystad, Sweden'. *The Independent*. Available at: www.independent.co.uk/travel/europe/kurt-wallander-bbc-ystad-sweden-a7047801.html (accessed 19 April 2018).

Earl, B. (2008) 'Literary tourism: Constructions of value, celebrity and distinction', *International Journal of Cultural Studies*, 11 (4): 401–417.

Eco, U. (1987) *Travels in Hyperreality*. London: Picador.

Edensor, T. (1998) *Tourists at the Taj*. London: Routledge.

Edensor, T. (2001) 'Performing tourism, staging tourism: (Re)producing tourism space and practice', *Tourist Studies*, 1 (1): 59–81.

Edensor, T. (2002) *National Identity, Popular Culture and Everyday Life*. London: Berg.

Edensor, T. (2004) 'Automobility and national identity: Representation, geography and driving practice', *Theory, Culture & Society*, 21 (4/5): 101–120.

Edensor, T. (2005a) *Industrial Ruins*. London: Berg.

Edensor, T. (2005b) 'Mediating William Wallace: Audio-visual technologies in tourism'. In D. Crouch, R. Jackson, and F. Thompson (eds), *The Media and the Tourist Imagination: Converging Cultures*. New York: Routledge, 105–118.

Edensor, T. (2012) 'Illuminated atmospheres: Anticipating and reproducing the flow of affective experience in Blackpool', *Environment and Planning B: Society and Space*, 30 (6): 1103–1122.

Egberts, L. (2017) *Chosen Legacies: Heritage in Regional Identity*. New York: Routledge.

Eghbali, N., Harazmi, N.A., and Rahnama, M.R. (2015) 'Comparative study of global experiences related to urban branding process and presenting a solution for Mashhad Metropolis', *Cumhuriyet Science Journal*, 36 (6): 716–728.

Eisenstadt, S.N. (2000) 'Multiple modernities', *Daedalus*, 129 (1): 1–29.

Eliade, M. (1989) *The Myth of the Eternal Return, or Cosmos and History*. London: Arkana.

Elias, N. (1978) *The Civilising Process, Vol. I: The History of Manners*. Oxford: Blackwell.

Elias, N. (1982) *The Civilizing Process, Vol. II: State Formation and Civilization*. Oxford: Blackwell.

Elliott, A. and Urry, J. (2010) *Mobile Lives*. Abingdon: Routledge.

Ellul, J. (1964) *The Technological Society*. New York: Vintage.

English Zhangjiajie Tourism (24 December 2010). Zhangjiajie National Forest Park. Available at: http://english.zhangjiajie.gov.cn/?action/viewnews/itemid/7.html (accessed 29 June 2018).

Errington, J. (2011) 'On not doing social systems'. In J. Alexander, S. Smith, and M. Norton (eds), *Interpreting Clifford Geertz: Cultural Investigation in the Social Sciences*. New York: Palgrave Macmillan, 33–44.

Escobar, A. (1995) *Encountering Development*. Princeton, NJ: Princeton University Press.

Esping-Andersen, G. (1994) 'Welfare state and the economy'. In N.J. Smelser and R. Swedberg (eds), *The Handbook of Economic Sociology*. Princeton, NJ: Princeton University Press, 711–732.

Evers Rosander, E. (2004) 'Going and not going to Porokhane: Mourid women and pilgrimage in Senegal and Spain'. In S. Coleman and J. Eade (eds), *Reframing Pilgrimage*. London: Routledge, 69–70.

Fairclough, N. (1992) *Discourse and Social Change*. Cambridge: Polity.

Fandom Wikia (undated) '*Outlander* wiki'. Available at: http://outlander.wikia.com/wiki/Fraser_of_Lovat (accessed 7 May 2018).

Favell, A. (2011) *Before and After Superflat: A Short History of Japanese Art 1990–2011*. Hong Kong: Blue Kingfisher.

Favell, A., Feldblum, M. and Smith, M.P. (2007) 'The human face of global mobility: A research agenda', *Society*, 44 (2): 25–55.

Featherstone, M. (1991) *Consumer Culture and Postmodernism*. London: Sage.

Federici, S. (2005) *Caliban and the Witch: Women, Capitalism and Primitive Accumulation*. New York: Autonomedia.

Fennell, D. (2009) 'Ethics and tourism'. In J. Tribe (ed.), *Philosophical Issues in Tourism*. Bristol: Channel View Publications, 211–226.

Ferguson, B. (12 July 2017) 'Edinburgh in danger of "losing its soul" to tourism, claim experts'. *The Scotsman*. Available at: www.scotsman.com/news/edinburgh-in-danger-of-losing-its-soul-to-tourism-claim-experts-1-4501174 (accessed 2 April 2018).

Fincham, B. (2006) 'Bicycle messengers and the road to freedom', *Sociological Review*, 54 (1): 208–222.

Flannery, T. (1994) *The Future Eaters*. Sydney: Reed New Holland.

Forster, J. (April 2009) 'Slumdog Millionaire puts slum tourism in the spotlight'. *Development Asia*, 3. Available at: http://development.asia/issue03/feature-01.asp (accessed 1 September 2013).

Forsyth, T. (2002) 'What happened on "The Beach"? Social movements and government of tourism in Thailand', *International Journal of Sustainable Development*, 5 (3): 326–337.

Foucault, M. (1986) 'Of other spaces', *Diacritics*, 16 (1): 22–27.

Foucault, M. (1997) 'The birth of biopolitics'. In P. Rabinow (ed.), *Michel Foucault: Ethics*. New York: New Press.

Fraser, N. and Honneth, A. (2003) *Redistribution or Recognition?* London: Verso.

Fraser, M., Kember, S., and Lury, C. (2005) 'Inventive life: Approaches to the new vitalism', *Theory, Culture & Society*, 22 (1): 1–14.

Fray, N. (1998) *Pilgrim Stories: On and off the Road to Santiago*. Berkeley: University of California Press.

Freire Medeiros, B. (2011) '"I went to the City of God": Gringos, guns and the touristic favela', *Journal of Latin American Cultural Studies*, 20 (1): 21–34.

Freire Medeiros, B. (2012) *Touring Poverty*. Abingdon: Routledge.

Fremont, M. (10 December 2017) 'The *Outlander* family tree: A complete guide to the major characters'. *Vulture*. Available at: www.vulture.com/2017/12/outlander-family-tree-character-guide.html (accessed 7 May 2018).

Freudendal-Pedersen, M. (2015) 'Whose commons are mobilities spaces? – The case of Copenhagen's cyclists', *ACME*, 14 (2): 598–621.

Frew, E. and White, E. (2011) *Tourism and National Identities: An International Perspective*. London: Routledge.

Friedberg, A. (1995) 'Cinema and the postmodern condition'. In L. Williams (ed.), *Viewing Positions: Ways of Seeing Film*. Brunswick, NJ: Rutgers University Press, 59–86.

Friedman, T. (2005) *The World is Flat*. New York: Farrar, Straus and Giroux.

Friese, H. (2004) 'Spaces of hospitality', *Angelaki* 9 (2): 67–79.

Fryer, J. (31 July 2009) 'Mamma Mia! How the feelgood movie of 2008 has ruined the Greek paradise island of Skopelos'. *Daily Mail* Available at: www.dailymail.co.uk/femail/article-1203536/Mamma-Mia-How-feelgood-movie-2008-ruined-Greek-paradise-island-Skopelos.html (accessed 29 June 2018).

Fullagar, S., Wilson, E., and Markwell, K. (2012) 'Starting slow: Slow mobilities and experiences'. In S. Fullagar, K. Markwell, and E. Wilson (eds), *Slow Tourism: Experiences and Mobilities*. Bristol: Channel View, 1–11.

Fuller M. (2005) *Media Ecologies: Materialist Energies in Art and Technoculture*. Cambridge, MA: MIT Press.

Fuller, S. (2011) *Humanity 2.0*. London: Palgrave Macmillan.

Fuller, S. (2012) 'The art of being human: A project for general philosophy of science', *Journal for General Philosophy of Science*, 43: 113–123.

Furness, Z. (2010) *One Less Car: Bicycling and the Politics of Automobility*. Philadelphia: Temple University Press.

Furness, Z. (2014) 'Bicycles'. In P. Adey, D. Bissel, K. Hannam, P. Merriman, and M. Sheller (eds), *The Routledge Handbook of Mobilities*. London: Routledge, 316–325.

Fussell, P. (1980) *Abroad: British Literary Travelling between the Wars*. Oxford: Oxford University Press.

Game of Thrones Tours (2014) Available from www.gameofthronestours.com/ (accessed 10 December 2014).

Gardiner, M. (1992) *The Dialogics of Critique: M.M. Bakhtin and the Theory of Ideology*. London: Routledge.

Gassner, J. (2002) *The Reader's Encyclopedia of World Drama*. New York: Courier Dover Publications.

Geary, D. (2013) 'Incredible India in a global age: The cultural politics of image branding in tourism', *Tourist Studies*, 13 (1): 36–61.

Germann Molz, J. (2006) 'Getting a "flexible eye": Round-the-world travel and scales of cosmopolitan citizenship', *Citizenship Studies*, 9 (5): 517–531.

Germann Molz, J. (2007) 'Cosmopolitans on the couch: Mobile hospitality and the internet'. In J. Germann Molz and S. Gibson (eds), *Mobilizing Hospitality: The Ethics of Social Relations in a Mobile World*. Aldershot: Ashgate, 65–80.

Germann Molz, J. (2012) *Travel Connections*. London: Routledge.

Germann-Molz, J. and Gibson, S. (eds) (2007) *Mobilizing Hospitality: The Ethics of Social Relations in a Mobile World*. Aldershot: Ashgate.

Gibson, J.J. (1979) *The Ecological Approach to Visual Perception*. Boston: Houghton Mifflin.

Giddens, A. (1984) *The Constitution of Society*. Cambridge: Polity.

Giddens, A. (1987) *Social Theory and Modern Sociology*. Cambridge: Polity.

Giddens, A. (1990) *The Consequences of Modernity*. Cambridge: Polity.

Giddens, A. (1991) *Modernity and Self-Identity*. Cambridge: Polity.

Giesen, B. (2011) 'Ritual, power, and style: The implications of *Negara* for the sociology of power'. In J.C. Alexander, P. Smith, and M. Norton (eds), *Interpreting Clifford Geertz: Cultural Investigation in the Social Sciences*. New York: Palgrave Macmillan, 167–177.

Gilloch, G. (2007) 'Urban optics: Film, phantasmagoria and the city in Benjamin and Kracauer', *New Formations*, 61 (2): 115–131.

Glezos, S. (2012) *The Politics of Speed: Capitalism, The State and War in an Accelerating World*. London: Routledge.

Godfrey, K. (11 August 2017) 'Anti-tourism protests now hit Croatia – but how is your summer holiday affected?', *Express*. Available at www.express.co.uk/travel/articles/839544/anti-tourism-spain-barcelona-riots-croatia (accessed 17 March 2018).

Goffman, E. (1987) *The Presentation of Self in Everyday Life*. Harmondsworth: Penguin.

Goodman, N. (1978) *Ways of Worldmaking*. Indianapolis: Hackett.

Graburn, N.H.H. (1977) 'Tourism: The sacred journey'. In V. Smith (ed.), *Hosts and Guests: An Anthropology of Tourism*. Philadelphia: University of Pennsylvania Press, 17–31.

Graburn, N.H.H. (2001) 'Relocating the tourist', *International Sociology*, 16 (2): 147–158.

Graburn, N.H.H. (2012) 'The dark is on the inside: The *honne* of Japanese exploratory tourists'. In D. Picard and M. Robinson (eds), *Emotion in Motion: Tourism, Affect and Transformation*. Farnham: Ashgate, 49–71.

Graml, R. (2004) '(Re)mapping the nation: Sound of Music tourism and national identity in Austria, ca 2000', *Tourist Studies*, 4 (2): 137–159.

Gravari-Barbas, M. and Graburn, N. (2012) 'Tourist imaginaries', *Via@ – International Interdisciplinary Review of Tourism*, 1 (1). Available at: www.viatourismreview.net/Editorial1_EN.php (accessed: 1 December 2016).

Greenfeld, L. (1992) *Nationalism: Five Roads to Modernity*. Cambridge, MA: Harvard University Press.

Greive, D. (9 April 2017) 'Waiheke island hosts New Zealand's bougiest protest'. *The Spinoff*. Available at: https://thespinoff.co.nz/auckland/09-04-2017/this-is-a-fun-protest-waiheke-style/ (accessed 7 June 2018).

Gretzel, U., Werthner, H., Koo, C., and Lamsfus, C. (2015) 'Conceptual foundations for understanding smart tourism ecosystems', *Computers in Human Behavior*, 50: 558–563.

Griffero, T. (2014) *Atmospheres: Aesthetics of Emotional Spaces*. London: Routledge.

Guardian (29 October 1999) 'Beach from Leonardo DiCaprio film to temporarily close due to tourist damage'. Available at: www.theguardian.com/film/2018/mar/28/thailand-beach-leonardo-dicaprio-closing (accessed 4 April 2018).

Guattari, F. (2000) *Three Ecologies*. New Brunswick, NJ: Athlone.

Gudeman, S. (2015) 'Piketty and anthropology', *Anthropological Forum*, 25 (1): 66–83.

Guha-Thakurta, P. (2013) *The Bengali Drama: Its Origin and Development*. London: Routledge.

Gyimóthy, S., Lundberg, C., Lindström, K.N., Hexhagen, M., and Larson, M. (2015) 'Popculture tourism: A research manifesto'. In D. Chambers and T. Rakic (eds), *Tourism Research Frontiers: Beyond the Boundaries of Knowledge*. Bingley: Emerald, 13–26.

Habermas, J. (1989) *The Theory of Communicative Action, Vol. II: Lifeworld and System*. Boston, MA: Beacon Press.

Haldrup, M. and Larsen, J. (2003) 'The family gaze', *Tourist Studies*, 3 (1): 23–46.

Haldrup, M. and Larsen, J. (2010) *Tourism, Performance and the Everyday: Consuming the Orient*. Abingdon: Routledge.

Halford, S. and Savage, M. (2017) 'Speaking sociologically with big data: Symphonic social science and the future for big data research', *Sociology*, 51 (6): 1132–1148.

Hall, E.T. (1966) *The Hidden Dimension*. New York: Doubleday.

Hall, S. (1992) 'The question of cultural identity'. In S. Hall, D. Held, and D. McGrew (eds), *Modernity and its Futures*, Oxford: Polity, 273–327.

Hand, M. and Sandywell, B. (2002) 'E-topia as cosmopolis or citadel', *Theory, Culture & Society*, 19 (1/2) 197–225.

Hannam, K. and Diekmann, A. (2010) *Tourism Development in India: A Critical Introduction*. London: Routledge.

Hannam, K. and Diekmann, A. (2016) '"Absolutely not smelly": The political ecology of disengaged slum tours in Mumbai, India'. In M. Mostafanezhad, R. Norum, E.J. Shelton, and A. Thompson-Carr (eds), *Political Ecology of Tourism: Community, Power and the Environment*. Abingdon: Routledge, 270–283.

Hannam, K., Mostafanezhad, M., and Rickly, J. (2016) 'Introduction'. In K. Hannam, M. Mostafanezhad, and J. Rickly (eds), *Event Mobilities: Politics, Place and Performance*. London: Routledge, 1–14.

Hannam, K., Sheller, M., and Urry, J. (2006) 'Mobilities, immobilites and moorings', *Mobilities*, 1 (1): 1–22.

Hannigan, J. (1998) *Fantasy City*. London: Routledge.

Hannigan, J. (2007) 'From fantasy city to creative city'. In G. Richards and J. Wilson (eds), *Tourism, Creativity and Development*. London: Routledge, pp. 48–56.

Harding, S. (1992) 'Subjectivity, experience and knowledge: An epistemology of/from Rainbow Coalition Politics'. In J. Nederveen Pieterse (ed.), *Emancipations, Modern and Postmodern*. London: Sage, 175–194.
Harding, S. (2012) *Grow Small, Think Beautiful: Ideas for a Sustainable World from Schumacher College*. Edinburgh: Floris Books.
Hardt, M. and Negri, A. (2000) *Empire*. Cambridge, MA: Harvard University Press.
Hardt, M. and Negri, A. (2004) *Multitude*. New York: Penguin.
Harraway, D. (2008) *When Species Meets*. Minneapolis, MN: University of Minnesota Press.
Harris, O.J.T. and Sørensen, T.F. (2010) 'Re-thinking emotion and material culture', *Archaeological Dialogues*, 17 (2): 145–163.
Harrison, D. (2005) 'Contested narratives in the domain of world heritage'. In D. Harrison and M. Hitchcock (eds), *The Politics of World Heritage*. Clevedon: Channel View, 1–8.
Harrison, J. (18 October 2013) 'Great Tapestry goes on show at Cockenzie House', *Herald Scotland*. Available at: www.heraldscotland.com/mobile/news/great-tapestry-goes-on-show-at-cockenzie-house.22443497?_=2087f0e42bf8a7f9ce88944047c01e0 (accessed 29 July 2018).
Harvey, D. (1985) *Consciousness and the Urban Experience*. Baltimore, MD: Johns Hopkins University Press.
Harvey, D. (1989) 'From managerialism to entrepreneuralism: The transformation of urban governance in late capitalism', *Geografiska Annaler*, 71 (1): 3–17.
Harvey, D. (1999) *The Limits to Capital*. London: Verso.
Harvey, D. (2000) *Spaces of Hope*. Berkeley, CA: University of Berkeley Press.
Harvey, D. (2006) *Paris, Capital of Modernity*. New York: Routledge.
Hasse, J. (2011) 'Emotions in an urban environment: Embellishing the cities from the perspective of the humanities'. In H. Schmid, W.-D. Sahr, and J. Urry (eds), *Cities and Fascination: Beyond the Surplus of Meaning*. London: Routledge, 49–74.
Hawkes, R. (26 August 2014) 'Game of Thrones: Church bans topless Cersei'. *Telegraph*. Available at: www.telegraph.co.uk/culture/tvandradio/game-of-thrones/11056279/Game-of-Thrones-church-bans-topless-Cersei.html (accessed 4 April 2018).
Healy, K. and Moody, J. (2014) 'Data visualisation in sociology', *Annual Review of Sociology*, 40: 105–128.
Heidegger, M. (1962) *Being and Time*. New York: Harper & Row.
Heidegger, M. (1971) *Poetry, Language, Thought*. New York: Harper & Row.
Heilbroner, B.L. (1999) *The Worldly Philosopher: The Lives, Times and Ideas of the Great Economic Thinkers*, 7th edn. New York: Simon & Schuster.
Hemme, D. (2005) 'Landscape, fairies and identity: Experience on the backstage of the fairy tale route', *Journal of Tourism and Cultural Change*, 3 (2): 71–87.
Henning, C. (2002) 'Tourism: Enacting modern myths'. In G.M.S. Dann (ed.), *The Tourist as a Metaphor of the Social World*. Wallingford: CABI, 169–188.
Hepburn, R. ([1966] 2004) 'Contemporary aesthetics and the neglect of natural beauty'. In A. Carlson and A. Berleant (eds), *The Aesthetics of Natural Environments*. Ontario: Broadview Press, 197–213.
Hepburn, R. (1995) 'Trivial and serious in aesthetic appreciation of nature'. In S. Kemal and I. Gaskell (eds), *Landscape, Natural Beauty and the Arts*. Cambridge: Cambridge University Press, 65–80.
Herzfeld, M. (1982) *Ours Once More: Folklore, Ideology, and the Making of Modern Greece*. Austin, TX: University of Texas Press.

Herzfeld, M. (1985) *The Poetics of Manhood: Contest and Identity in a Cretan Mountain Village*. Princeton, NJ: Princeton University Press.

Herzfeld, M. (1987) '"As in your own house": Hospitality, ethnography, and the stereotype of Mediterranean society'. In D. Gilmore (ed.), *Honour and Shame and the Unity of the Mediterranean*. American Anthropological Association Special Publication 22: 75–89.

Herzfeld, M. (2001) *Anthropology: Theoretical Practice in Culture and Society*. Oxford: Blackwell.

Herzfeld, M. (2002) 'The absent presence: Discourses of crypto-colonialism', *South Atlantic Quarterly*, 101 (4): 899–926.

Herzfeld, M. (2003) 'Pom Mahakan: Humanity and order in the historic center of Bangkok', *Thailand Human Rights Journal*, 1 (1): 101–119.

Herzfeld, M. (2004) *The Body Impolitic: Artisan and Artifice in the Global Hierarchy of Value*. Chicago: University of Chicago Press.

Herzfeld, M. (2005) *Cultural Intimacy*, 2nd edn. New York: Routledge.

Herzfeld, M. (2006) 'Spatial cleansing: Monumental vacuity and the idea of the West', *Journal of Material Culture*, 1 (1–2): 127–149.

Herzfeld, M. (2016) *The Siege of Spirits: Community and Polity in Bangkok*. Chicago: University of Chicago Press.

Hetherington, K. (2013) 'Rhythm and noise: The city, memory and the archive', *The Sociological Review*, 61 (1): 17–33.

Higgins, A. (17 September 2015). 'Norway again embraces the Vikings, minus the violence'. *New York Times*. Available at: www.nytimes.com/2015/09/18/world/europe/norway-again-embraces-the-vikings-minus-the-violence.html (accessed 18 January 2018).

Higgins, H.B. (2009) *The Grid Book*. Cambridge, MA: MIT Press.

Hill Collins, P. (1991) *Black Feminist Thought: Knowledge, Consciousness and the Politics of Empowerment*. London: Routledge.

Hindustan Times (2 January 2018) 'After Rajputs, Muslims want ban on Padmavati for showing them in "negative light"'. Available at: www.hindustantimes.com/jaipur/now-padmavati-hurts-muslim-sentiments/story-t4nSqsLwkxMgBRiMjNFogL.html (accessed 5 April 2018).

Hird, M.J. (2010) 'Indifferent globality, Gaia, symbiosis and "other worldliness"', *Theory, Culture & Society*, 27 (2–3): 54–72.

Hjarvad, S. (2008) 'The mediation of society: A theory of the media as agents of cultural change', *Nordicom Review*, 29 (2): 105–132.

Hokowhitu, B. (2007) 'Understanding Whangara: 'Whale Rider' as Simulacrum', *New Zealand Journal of Media Studies*, 10 (2): 22–29.

Holdnak, A. and Holland, S.M. (1996) 'Edu-tourism: Vacationing to learn', *Parks and Recreation*, 31 (9): 72–75.

Holland, T. (24 March 2013) 'Game of Thrones is more brutally realistic than most historical novels'. *Guardian*. Available at: www.theguardian.com/tv-and-radio/2013/mar/24/game-of-thrones-realistic-history (accessed 28 November 2014).

Holliday, R. and Potts, T. (2012) *Kitsch! Cultural Politics and Taste*. Manchester: Manchester University Press.

Holliday, R., Bell, D., Jones, M., Hardy, K., Hunter, E., Proby, E., and Sanchez Taylor, J. (2015) 'Beautiful face, beautiful place: Relational geographies and gender in cosmetic surgery tourism websites', *Gender, Place & Culture*, 22 (1): 90–106.

Hollinshead, K. (1998) 'Disney and commodity aesthetics: A critique of Fjellman's analysis of "distory" and the "historicide" of the past', *Current Issues in Tourism*, 1 (1): 58–119.

Hollinshead, K. (2002) *Tourism and the Making of the World*. Miami: Florida International University.

Hollinshead, K. (2009a) '"Tourism state" cultural production: The re-making of Nova Scotia', *Tourism Geographies*, 11 (4): 526–545.

Hollinshead, K. (2009b) 'The "worldmaking" prodigy of tourism: The reach and power of tourism in the dynamics of change and transformation', *Tourism Analysis*, 14 (1): 139–152.

Hollinshead, K. and Suleman, R. (2018) 'The everyday instillations of worldmaking: New vistas of understanding on the declarative reach of tourism', *Tourism Analysis*, 23 (2): 201–213.

Hollinshead, K., Ateljevic, I., and Ali, N. (2009) 'Worldmaking agency-worldmaking authority: The sovereign constitutive role of tourism', *Tourism Geographies*, 11 (4): 427–443.

Holton, R. (2005) 'The inclusion of the non-European world in international society, 1870–1920: Evidence from global networks', *Global Networks*, 5 (3): 239–259.

Honneth, A. (1992) *The Struggle for Recognition*. Cambridge: Polity.

Honneth, A. (2007) *Disrespect*. Cambridge: Polity.

Hooked on Houses (undated) 'The inn from 'Nights in Rodanthe: Rescued and renovated'. Available at: https://hookedonhouses.net/2011/07/25/the-inn-from-nights-in-rodanthe-rescued-and-renovated/ (accessed 13 May 2018).

hooks, b. (1990) 'Postmodern blackness'. In b. hooks (ed.), *Yearning Race, Gender and Cultural Politics*. Toronto: Between the Lines.

Howard, C. (2012) 'Speeding up and slowing down: Pilgrimage and slow travel through time'. In S. Fullagar, K. Markwell, and E. Wilson (eds), *Slow Tourism: Experiences and Mobilities*. Bristol: Channel View, 11–24.

Howard, T. (21 March 2010) 'Slumdog Millionaire tours: Tourists now visit Mumbai slums during India vacations', *Christian Science Monitor*. Available at: www.csmonitoes.com/World/Global-News/2010/0321/Slumdog-Millionaire-tours-Tourists-now-visit-Mumbai-slums-during-India-vacations (accessed 1 September 2013).

Hubbard, P. (2008), 'Here, there, everywhere: The ubiquitous geographies of heteronormativity', *Geography Compass*, 2 (3): 640–658.

Huber, M.T. (2013) *Lifeblood: Oil, Freedom, and the Forces of Capital*. Minneapolis, MN: University of Minnesota Press.

Hudson, S., and Ritchie, J.R.B. (2006) 'Promoting destinations via film tourism: An empirical identification of initiatives', *Journal of Travel Research*, 44 (3): 387–396.

Huggan, G. (2001) *The Post-Colonial Exotic: Marketing the Margins*. London: Routledge.

Hume, D. (2013) *Tourism Art and Souvenirs: The Material Culture of Tourism*. Abingdon: Routledge.

Huyssen, A. (2000) 'Present pasts: Media, politics, amnesia', *Public Culture*, 12 (1): 21–38.

Huyssen, A. (2003) *Present Pasts*. Stanford: Stanford University Press.

Iceland Magazine (3 March 2017) 'Iceland to play a big role in fifth season of the history channel TV series Vikings'. Available at: http://icelandmag.is/article/iceland-play-a-big-role-fifth-season-history-channel-tv-series-vikings (accessed 22 May 2018).

Ingersol, R. (2006) *Sprawltown: Looking for the City on its Edge*. New York: Princeton Architectural.

Inglis, D. (2010) 'Mapping global consciousness: Portuguese imperialism and the forging of modern global sensibilities', *Globalizations*, 8 (5): 1–20.

Ingold, T. (1986) *The Appropriation of Nature: Essays on Human Ecology and Social Relations*. Manchester: Manchester University Press.

Ingold, T. (2000) *The Perception of the Environment: Essays on Livelihood, Dwelling and Skill*, 1st edn. London: Routledge.

Ingold, T. (2010), 'Ways of mind-walking: Reading, writing, painting', *Visual Studies*, 25:1, pp. 15–23.

Ingold, T. (2011) *The Perception of the Environment: Essays on Livelihood, Dwelling and Skill*, 2nd edn. London: Routledge.

Ingold, T. (2015) *The Life of Lines*. New York: Routledge.

International Council on Monuments and Sites (ICOMOS) (2015) Report on the UNESCO-ICOMOS Reactive Monitoring Mission to Old City of Dubrovnik. Dubrovnik: UNESCO/ICOMOS. Available at: https://whc.unesco.org/en/documents/141053/ (accessed 31 May 2018).

International Herald Tribune (8 February 2000) 'Tourism lobby in defence of "The Beach"'.

Isaac, R.K. and Platenkamp, V. (2018) 'Dionysus versus Apollo: An uncertain search for identity through dark tourism – Palestine as a case study'. In P. Stone, R. Hartmann, T. Seaton, R. Sharpley, and L. White (eds), *The Palgrave Handbook of Dark Tourism Studies*. London: Palgrave Macmillan, 211–225.

Isin, E.F. (2017) 'Performative citizenship'. In A. Shachar, R. Bauböck, I. Bloemraad, and M. Vink (eds), *The Oxford Handbook of Citizenship*. Oxford: Oxford University Press. 500–523.

Iwashita, C. (2006) 'Media representation of the UK as a destination for Japanese tourists: Popular culture and tourism', *Tourist Studies*, 6 (1): 59–67.

Jacobs, J. (1992) *The Death and Life of Great American Cities*. New York: Vintage.

Jaguaribe, B. and Hetherington, K. (2004) '*Favela* tours: Indistinct and maples representations'. In M. Sheller and J. Urry (eds), *Tourism Mobilities: Places to Play, Places in Play*. London: Routledge, 155–166.

Jameson, F. (1986) 'Third-world literature in the era of multinational capitalism', *Social Text*, 15 (autumn): 65–88.

Jasper, J. (1997) *The Art of Moral Protest: Culture, Biography and Creativity in Social Movements*. Chicago: University of Chicago Press.

Jay, M. (1993) *Downcast Eye: The Denigration of Vision in Twentieth-Century French Thought*. Berkeley: University of California Press.

Jaya Travel & Tours (2017) 'Visit places that inspired the story of "District 9"'. Available at: www.jayatravel.com/visit-places-inspired-story-district-9/ (accessed 14 May 2018).

Jensen, O.B. (2010) 'Negotiation in motion: Unpacking a geography of mobility', *Space and Culture*, 13 (4): 389–402.

Jensen, O.B. (2013) *Staging Mobilities*. London: Routledge.

Jensen, O.B. (2014) *Designing Mobilities*. Aalborg: Aalborg University Press.

Jewitt, S. (2011) 'Geographies of shit: Spatial and temporal variations in attitudes towards human waste', *Progress in Human Geography*, 35 (5): 608–626.

Jirón, P. (2011) 'On becoming la sombre/the shadow'. In M. Büscher, J. Urry, and K. Witchger (eds), *Mobile Methods*. London: Routledge, 36–53.

Jones, P. (2005) 'Performing the city: A body and a bicycle take on Birmingham, UK', *Social & Cultural Geography*, 6 (6): 813–830.

Josh, R. (1 April 2012) 'Where HBO's hit Game of Thrones was filmed'. *USA Today*. Available at: http://travel.usatoday.com/destinations/story/2012-04-01/Where-the-HBO-hit-Game-of-Thrones-was-filmed/53876876/1 (accessed 28 November 2014).

Kagan, S. (2010a) 'Aesthetics of sustainability for the ecological age: Towards a literacy of complexity arts'. In *Environment. Sustainability. A Collection of Visions*. Singapore: Asia-Europe Foundation, 17–18.

Kagan, S. (2010b) 'Cultures of sustainability and the aesthetics of the pattern that connects', *Futures*, 42 (10): 1094–1101.

Kagan, S. (2011) *Art and Sustainability: Connecting Patterns for a Culture of Complexity*. Bielefeld, Germany: Verlag.

Kahneman, D. (2011) *Thinking, Fast and Slow*. London: Penguin.

Kandinsky, W. (1979) *Point and Line to Plane*. New York: Dover Pubs.

Kaplan, C. (1993) *Questions of Travel*. Durham, NC: Duke University Press.

Kemper, S. and Zylinska, J. (2012) *Life After New Media: Mediation as a Vital Process*. Cambridge, MA: MIT.

Kielbowicz, R.B. and Scherer, C. (1986) 'The role of the press in the dynamics of social movements', *Research in Social Movements, Conflict and Change*, 9: 71–96.

King, D. (21 January 2018) 'Lifestyle magazine says Harry Potter tourism "ruining Edinburgh"'. *Edinburgh Evening News*. Available at: www.edinburghnews.scotsman.com/our-region/edinburgh/lifestyle-magazine-says-harry-potter-tourism-ruining-edinburgh-1-4667644 (accessed 2 April 2018).

Kirschenblatt-Gimblett, B. (1997) *Destination Culture*. Berkeley, CA: University of California Press.

Kirwan, S., Dawney, L., and Brigstocke, J. (2015) *Space, Power, and the Commons: The Struggle for Alternative Futures*. New York: Routledge.

Kitching, C. (10 August 2016) 'The Frozen effect: Tourists desperate to see the Norwegian islands that inspired the Disney'. *The Daily Mail*. Available at: www.dailymail.co.uk/travel/travel_news/article-3732825/Norwegian-islands-inspired-Frozen-overrun-tourists.html (accessed 20 May 2018).

Klein, N. (2007) *The Shock Doctrine*. London: Allen Lane.

Knopp, L. (2007) 'From lesbian to queer geographies: Pasts, prospects and possibilities'. In G. Brown, J. Lim, and K. Browne (eds), *Geographies of Sexualities*. Chichester: Ashgate, 163–172.

Knorr Cetina, K. (1999) *Epistemic Cultures: How the Sciences Make Knowledge*. Cambridge, MA: Harvard University Press.

Kobayashi, A., Preston, V., and Murnaghan, A. (2011) 'Place, affect and transnationalism through the voices of Hong Kong immigrants to Canada', *Social and Cultural Geography*, 12 (8): 871–888.

Korstanje, M. (2013) 'The sense, landscape and image. How the tourist destination is replicated in modernist times', *Pasos*, 11 (3): 55–65.

Korstanje, M.E. (2009) 'Sport and civilization: The role of education in Western societies', *Georgian Electronic Scientific Journal: Education Science and Psychology*, 15 (2): 52–62.

Korstanje, M.E. (2011) 'Event-management and tourism: The archetype of heroism', *Palermo Business Review*, 5: 49–66.

Korstanje, M.E. (2016) *The Rise of Thana-Capitalism and Tourism.* Abingdon: Routledge.

Korstanje, M.E. (2018a) *The Mobilities Paradox: A Critical Analysis.* Cheltenham: Edward Elgar.

Korstanje, M.E. (2018b) *Terrorism, Tourism and the End of Hospitality in the West.* New York: Springer.

Korstanje, M.E. and George, B. (2015) 'The imposible sustainability: Applications of relational perspective in tourism fields', *Geoforum*, 1 (6): 21–24.

Kracauer, S. ([1960] 1997) *Theory of Film: The Redemption of Physical Reality.* Princeton, NJ and West Sussex: Princeton University Press.

Krippendorf, J. (1999) *The Holidaymakers: Understanding the Impact of Leisure and Travel.* London: Routledge.

Kugelmass, J. (1992) 'The rites of the tribe: American Jewish tourism in Poland'. In I. Karp, C. Kreamer, S. Lavine, and A. Karp (eds), *Museums and Communities: The Politics of Public Culture*. Washington, DC: Smithsonian Institution, 382–427.

Kugelmass, J. (1996) 'Missions to the past: Poland in contemporary Jewish thought and deed'. In P. Antze and M. Lambek (eds), *Tense Past: Cultural Essays in Trauma and Memory.* New York: Routledge, 199–214.

Kuhn, T. (1970) *The Structure of Scientific Revolutions*, 2nd edn. Chicago: University of Chicago Press.

Laachir, K. (2007) 'Hospitality and the limitations of the national'. In J. Germann Molz and S. Gibson (eds), *Mobilizing Hospitality: The Ethics of Social Relations in a Mobile World.* Aldershot: Ashgate, 177–193.

Lacy, M. (2005) *Security and Climate Change.* London: Routledge.

Lai, C.L. (2004) 'Art exhibitions travel the world'. In M. Sheller and J. Urry (eds), *Tourism Mobilities: Places to Play, Places in Play.* London: Routledge, 90–102.

Lamsfus, C., Martín, D., Alzua-Sorzabal, A., and Torres-Manzanera, E. (2015) 'Smart tourism destinations: An extended conception of smart cities focusing on human mobility'. In *Information and Communication Technologies in Tourism 2015*. New York: Springer International Publishing, 363–375.

Langlois, G., Redden, J., and Elmer, G. (2015) *Compromised Data: From Social Media to Big Data.* London: Bloomsbury.

Larsen, J. (2001) 'Tourism mobilities and the travel glance: Experiences of being on the move', *Scandinavian Journal of Hospitality and Tourism*, 1 (2): 80–98.

Larsen, J. (2005) 'Families seen photographing: The performativity of tourist photography', *Space and Culture*, 8 (4): 416–434.

Larsen, J. and Urry, J. (2008) 'Networking in mobile societies'. In J.O. Bærenholdt, B. Granås, and S. Kesserling (eds), *Mobility and Place*. Aldershot: Ashgate, 89–101.

Larsen, J., Urry, J., and Axhausen, K.W. (2006) 'Networks and tourism: Mobile social life', *Annals of Tourism Research*, 34 (1): 244–462.

Lash, S. and Urry, J. (1987) *The End of Organized Capitalism*. Madison WI: University of Wisconsin Press.

Lash, S. and Urry, J. (1994) *Economies of Signs and Space*. London: Sage.

Lashley, C. and Morrison, A. (eds) (2000) *In Search of Hospitality: Theoretical Perspectives and Debates*. Oxford: Butterworth-Heinemann.

Lashley, C., Lynch, P., and Morrison, A. (eds) (2007) *Hospitality: A Social Lens*. Oxford: Elsevier.

Latour, B. (1987) *Science in Action: How to Follow Scientists and Engineers through Society*. Milton Keynes: Open University Press.

Latour, B. (1988) *Pasteurization of France*. Cambridge, MA: Harvard University Press.

Latour, B. (1993) *We Have Never Been Modern*. Cambridge, MA: Harvard University Press.

Latour, B. (1998) 'How to be iconophilic in art, science and religion?'. In C. Jones and P. Galison (eds), *Picturing Science Producing Art*. London: Routledge, 418–440.

Latour, B. (1999) *Pandora's Hope: Essays on the Reality of Science Studies*. Cambridge, MA: Harvard University Press.

Latour, B. (2002) 'What is iconoclash? Or is there a world beyond the image wars?', *Media Cultures Net*. Available at: http://mediacultures.net/xmlui/bitstream/handle/10002/599/84-ICONOCLASH-GB.pdf?sequence=1 (accessed 3 April 2018).

Latour, B. (2004) 'Never too late to read Tarde', *Domus*. Available at www.domusweb.it/en/issues/2004/874.html (accessed 8 May 2015).

Latour, B. (2005) *Reassembling the Social*. Oxford: Oxford University Press.

Latour, B. (2011) *On the Modern Cult of Factish Gods*. Durham, NC: Duke University Press.

Latour, B. and Weibel, P. (eds) (2005) *Making Things Public: Atmospheres of Democracy*. Cambridge, MA: MIT Press.

Laurendeau, J. (2008) 'Gendered risk regimes', *Sociology of Sport Journal*, 25 (3): 293–309.

Law, C.M. (2002) *Urban Tourism: The Visitor Economy and the Growth of Large Cities*, 2nd edn. London: Continuum.

Law, I. (2010) *Racism: A Global Approach*. Pearson Education.

Law, J. and Hassard, J. (eds) (1999) *Actor Network Theory and After*. Oxford: Blackwell.

Lawlor, L. (2002) *Derrida and Husserl*. Indianapolis: Indiana University Press.

Lazzarato, M. (2004) 'From capital-labor to capital-life', *Ephemera Theory Multitude*, 4 (3): 187–208.

Lazzarato, M. (2011) 'The misfortunes of the "artistic critique" and cultural employment'. In G. Raunig, G. Ray, and U. Wuggenig (eds), *Critique of Creativity*. London: MayFly Books, 41–56.

Lazzarato, M. (2013) 'Art, work and politics in disciplinary societies and societies of security'. In E. Alliez and P. Osborne (eds), *Spheres of Action*. London: Tate Publishing, 87–97.

Lee, J. (23 September 2013) *Frozen: Final Shooting Draft*. Available at: https://web.archive.org/web/20140401054119/http://waltdisneystudiosawards.com/downloads/frozen-screenplay.pdf (accessed 21 May 2018).

Lefebvre, H. ([1992] 2015) *Rhythmanalysis*. London: Bloomsbury.

Lennon, J. and Foley, M. (2000) *Dark Tourism*. London: Continuum.

Leotta, A. (2012) *Touring the Screen*. Chicago, IL and Bristol: Intellect.

Levitas, R. (2013a) 'Singing summons the existence of the fountain: Bloch, music and utopia'. In P. Thompson and S. Žižek (eds), *The Privatization of Hope: Ernst Bloch and the Future of Utopia*. Durham, NC: Duke University Press, 219–245.

Levitas, R. (2013b) *Utopia as Method: The Imaginary Constitution of Society*. London: Palgrave Macmillan.

Linnett, J.T. (2011) 'Money can't buy me hygge: Danish middle-class consumption, egalitarianism and the sanctity of inner space', *Social Analysis*, 55 (2): 21–44.

Lobo, J. (11 August 2013) 'The ticking e-bomb', DNA India. Available at: www.dnaindia.com/mumbai/1872813/report-the-ticking-e-bomb (accessed 1 September 2013).

Löfgren, O. (1999) *On Holiday*. Berkeley, CA: University of California Press.

Lois, J. (2001) 'Peaks and valleys: the gendered emotional culture of edgework', *Gender & Society*, 15 (3): 381–406.

Lois, J. (2005) 'Gender and emotion management in the stages of edgework'. In S. Lyng (ed.), *Edgework*. New York: Routledge, 17–152.

Lorde, A. (1984) *Sister Outsider*. Trumansberg, NY: Crossing Press.

Lovelock, J.E. (2007) *Why the Earth is Fighting Back – and How we Can Still Save Humanity*. London: Penguin.

Lovelock, J.E. and Margulis, L. (1974) 'Atmospheric homeostasis by and for the biosphere: The Gaia hypothesis', *Tellus*, 26 (1): 2–10.

Lundberg, C. and Ziakas, V. (2018) 'Fantrepreneurs in the sharing economy: Cocreating neotribal events', *Event Management*, 22 (2): 287–301.

Lundberg, C., Ziakas, V., and Morgan, N. (2017) 'Conceptualising on-screen tourism destination development', *Tourist Studies*, 18 (1): 83–104.

Luo, J., Zhang, X., Wu, Y., Shen, J., Shen, L., and Xing, X. (2017) 'Urban land expansion and the floating population in China: For production or for living?', *Cities*, 74: 219–228.

Lynch, P., Di Domenico, M.L., and Sweeny, M. (2007) 'Resident hosts and mobile strangers: Temporary exchanges within the topography of the commercial home'. In J. Germann Molz and S. Gibson (eds), *Mobilizing Hospitality: The Ethics of Social Relations in a Mobile World*. Aldershot: Ashgate, 121–144.

Lyng, S. (1990) 'Edgework: A social psychological analysis of voluntary risk taking', *American Journal of Sociology*, 95 (4): 851–886.

Lyng, S. (2005) *Edgework*. New York: Routledge.

Lyotard, F. (1984) *The Postmodern Condition*. Manchester: Manchester University Press.

Maasen, S. and Weingart, P. (2000) *Metaphors and the Dynamics of Knowledge*. London: Routledge.

MacCannell, D. (1973) 'Staged authenticity: Arrangements of social space in tourist settings, *American Journal of Sociology*, 79 (3): 589–603.

MacCannell, D. (1989) *The Tourist*. London: Macmillan.

MacCannell, D. (2001) 'Tourist agency', *Tourist Studies*, 1 (1): 23–37.

MacGrath, C. (29 March 2018) 'Thailand shuts down The Beach from Leonardo DiCaprio film – and this is why'. *Sunday Express*. Available at: www.express.co.uk/news/world/939006/thailand-the-beach-leonardo-dicaprio-maya-bay-closed (accessed 13 May 2018).

Mackenzie, A. (2002) *Transductions*. London: Continuum.

Mackenzie, A. (2003) 'Transduction: Invention, innovation and collective life'. Available at: www.lancaster.ac.uk/staff/mackenza/papers/transduction.pdf (accessed 25 September 2016).

Macnaughten, P. and Urry, J. (2000) 'Bodies in the woods', *Body and Society*, 6 (3/4): 203–216.

Mahmood, S. (2005) *Politics of Piety: The Islamic Revival and the Feminist Subject*. Princeton, NJ: Princeton University Press.

Mail Foreign Service (27 January 2010) 'Found! The stunning mountain that inspired Avatar's "floating peaks"'. *Daily Mail*. Available at: www.dailymail.co.uk/news/article-1246457/China-renames-mountain-Avatar-8movie-Avatar-Hallelujah-Mountain.html (accessed 1 July 2018).

Maitland, R. and Smith, A. (2009) 'Tourism and the aesthetics of the built environment'. In J. Tribe (ed.), *Philosophical Issues in Tourism*. Clevedon: Channel View, 171–190.
Malbon, B. (1999) *Clubbing*. London: Routledge.
Malik, K. (25 February 2018) 'It's time to separate EU migration fact from Brexit fantasy'. *Guardian*. Available at: www.theguardian.com/commentisfree/2018/feb/25/time-to-divide-eu-migration-fact-from-brexit-fantasy (accessed 11 April 2018).
Manning, E. (2009) *Relationscapes*. Cambridge: MIT Press.
Manning, E. (2016) *The Minor Gesture*. Durham, NC: Duke University Press.
Maoz, D. (2006) 'The mutual gaze', *Annals of Tourism Research*, 33 (1): 221–239.
Marcuse, H. (1955) *Eros and Civilization*. New York: Beacon Press.
Martell, L. (2017) *The Sociology of Globalization*, 2nd edn. Cambridge: Polity.
Martinez-Alier, J. (2015) 'Environmentalism, currents of'. In G. D'Alisa, F. DeMaria, and G. Kallis (eds), *Degrowth*. New York and London: Routledge, 37–40.
Martin-Jones, D. (2014) 'Film tourism as heritage tourism: Scotland, diaspora and The Da Vinci Code (2006)', *New Review of Film and Television Studies*, 12 (2): 156–172.
Massey, D. (1993) 'Power-geometry and a progressive sense of place'. In B. Curties, G. Robertson, and L. Tickner (eds), *Mapping the Futures*. New York: Routledge, 59–69.
Massey, D. (1994) *Space, Place and Gender*. Cambridge: Polity.
Massey, D. (2005) *For Space*. London: Sage.
Massumi, B. (2015) *Politics of Affect*. Cambridge: Polity.
Massumi, B. (2017) *The Principle of Unrest*. London: Open Humanities Press.
McCarthy, A.-M. (18 February 2016) 'Vacation like a Viking: Best places to recreate epic TV series'. *The Lonely Planet*. Available at: www.lonelyplanet.com/news/2016/02/18/vacation-like-a-viking-best-places-to-recreate-epic-tv-series/ (accessed 23 May 2018).
McCormack, D. (2008) 'Molecular affects in human geographies', *Environment and Planning A*, 39 (2): 359–377.
McCrone, D., Morris, A., and Kiely, R. (1995) *Scotland the Brand*. Edinburgh: Edinburgh University Press.
McFarlane, C. (2008) 'Governing the contaminated city: Infrastructure and sanitation in colonial and post-colonial Bombay', *International Journal of Urban and Regional Research*, 32 (2): 415–435.
McKee, R. (1999) *Story*. London: Methuen.
McKenzie, F. (1996) *Beyond the Suburbs: Population Change in the Major Exurban Regions of Australia*. Canberra: Department of Immigration and Multicultural Affairs.
McKenzie, S. (2 July 2012) 'Brave's Andrews and Sarafian "changed by Scotland"'. BBC Scotland Highlands and Islands. Available at: www.bbc.co.uk/news/uk-scotland-highlands-islands-18671427 (accessed 14 February 2014).
McKenzie, S. (9 September 2013) 'Pixar's Brave forecast to generate £120m in five years'. BBC Scotland Highlands and Islands. Available at: www.bbc.co.uk/news/uk-scotland-highlands-islands-24014661 (accessed 18 February 2014).
McKittrick, D. *et al.* (2007) *Lost Lives: The Stories of the Men, Women and Children who Died as a Result of the Northern Ireland Troubles*. Edinburgh: Mainstream.
McLean, P. (29 June 2012) 'Disney-Pixar's Brave: "One of the most lavish depictions of Scotland'. BBC – Edinburgh, Fife and East Scotland. Available at: www.bbc.co.uk/news/uk-scotland-edinburgh-east-fife-18649751 (accessed 9 February 2014).
McLuhan, M. (1964) *Understanding the Media*. New York: McGraw.

McMah, L. (11 August 2016) 'How "Frozen" tourism is driving Norway to breaking point', *New Zealand Herald.* Available at: www.nzherald.co.nz/travel/news/article.cfm?c_id=7&objectid=11691619 (accessed 20 May 2018).

McRobbie, A. (2006) 'Feminism, postmodernism and the real "me"'. In M.G. Durham and D. Kellner (eds), *Media and Cultural Studies*. Malden: Blackwell, 520–532.

Meadows, D.H. (2008) *Thinking in Systems: A Primer*. White River Junction, VT: Chelsea Green Publishers.

Meadows, D.H., Renders, J., and Behrens, W.W. (1972) *The Limits to Growth: A Report from the Club of Rome's Project on the Predicaments of Mankind*. New York: Universe Books.

Meethan, K. (2001) *Tourism in Global Society*. New York: Palgrave.

Melucci, A. (1989) *Nomads of the Present*. London: Hutchinson Radius.

Merleau-Ponty, M. (1962) *Phenomenology of Perception.* London: Routledge and Kegan Paul.

Merleau-Ponty, M. (1964) 'Eye and mind'. In J.M. Edie (ed.), *The Primacy of Perception and Other Essays on Phenomenological Psychology, the Philosophy of Art, History and Politics*. Evanston, IL: Northwestern University Press, 159–190.

Merleau-Ponty, M. (1965) *The Structure of Behaviour*. London: Methuen.

Merriman, P. (2012) *Mobility, Space and Culture*. London: Routledge.

Merriman, P. (2018) 'Molar and molecular mobilities: The politics of perceptible and imperceptible movements', *Environment and Planning D: Society and Space*. DOI: 10.1177/0263775818776976.

Merton, R. (1936) 'The unanticipated consequences of purposive action', *American Sociological Review*, 1 (6): 894–904.

Meschkank, J. (2011) 'Investigations into slum tourism in Mumbai: Poverty tourism and the tensions between different constructions of reality', *Geographical Journal*, 76 (1): 47–62.

Meschkank, J. (2012) 'Negotiating poverty: The interplay between Dharavi's production and consumption as a tourist destination'. In F. Frenzel, K. Koens, and M. Steinbrink (eds), *Slum Tourism: Poverty, Power and Ethics*. London: Routledge, 144–148.

Metcalf, S. (2002) *They Lie, We Lie: Getting on with Anthropology.* New York: Routledge.

Mignolo, W.D. (1999) 'I am where I think: Epistemology and the colonial difference', *Journal of Latin American Cultural Studies*, 8 (2): 235–245.

Mignolo, W.D. (2000) *Local Histories/Global Designs*. Princeton, NJ: Princeton University Press.

Mignolo, W.D. (2002) 'The enduring enchantment (or the epistemic privilege of modernity and where to go from here)', *The South Atlantic Quarterly*, 101 (4): 927–954.

Mignolo, W.D. (2009) 'Epistemic disobedience, independent thought and decolonial freedom', *Theory, Culture & Society*, 26 (7–8): 159–181.

Mignolo, W.D. (2011) *The Darker Side of Western Modernity: Global Futures, Decolonial Options*. Durham, NC: Duke University Press.

Milano, C. (2017) *Overtourism y Turismofobia: Tendencias Globales y Contextos Locales*. Barcelona: Ostelea School of Tourism & Hospitality.

Miller, F. (23 February 2018) 'Working with Vikings: "They just … kick a few heads in and shag off"'. *The Irish Times*. Available at: www.irishtimes.com/news/ireland/irish-news/working-with-vikings-they-just-kick-a-few-heads-in-and-shag-off-1.3402059 (accessed 23 May 2018).

Mills, C.W. (1959) *The Sociological Imagination.* New York: Oxford University Press.

Mitchell, T. (2008) 'Rethinking economy', *Geoforum*, 39 (3): 1116–1121.
Mitchell, T. (2011) *Carbon Democracy: Political Power in the Age of Oil*. London: Verso.
Mitchell, W.J.T. (1994) *Landscape and Power*. Chicago: University of Chicago Press.
Moehn, F. (2008) 'Music, mixing and modernity in Rio de Janeiro', *Ethnomusicology Forum*, 17 (2): 165–202.
Monmonier, M. (2004) *Rhumb Lines and Map Wars: A Social History of the Mercator Projection*. Chicago: University of Chicago Press.
Moore, V. (23 August 2013) 'India's Dharavi recycling Slumdog entrepreneurs'. Keepinitreal. Available at: http://keepinitrealevanston.wordpress.com/2013/08/23/indias-dharavi-recycling-slumdog-entrepreneurs/ (accessed 1 September 2013).
Morin, E. (2008) *On Complexity*. Cresskill, NJ: Hampton Press.
Morinis, E.A. (1992) 'The territory of the anthropology of pilgrimage'. In E.A. Morinis (ed.), *Sacred Journeys*. Westport, CT: Greenwood, 1–14.
Moscardo, G. and Ballantyne, R. (2008) 'Interpretation and attractions: New directions'. In A. Fyall, A. Leask, and S. Wanhill (eds), *Managing Visitor Attractions*. Oxford: Elsevier, 237–252.
Mouffe, C. (1988) 'Hegemony and new political subjects: Towards a new concept of democracy'. In C. Nelson and E. Grossberg (eds), *Marxism and the Interpretation of Culture*. Basingstoke: Palgrave, 89–104.
Murray, J. (29 October 2010) 'Mallard flags Hobbit dissent'. *3news.NZ*. Available at: www.3news.co.nz/Mallard-flags-Hobbit-dissent/tabid/419/articleID/183707/Default.aspx (accessed 9 December 2011).
Nederveen Pieterse, J. (1992) 'Emancipations, modern and postmodern'. In J. Nederveen Pieterse (ed.), *Emancipations, Modern and Postmodern*. London: Sage, 5–42.
Nederveen Pieterse, J. (1997) 'Globalization as hybridization'. In M. Featherstone, S. Lash, and R. Robertson (eds), *Global Modernities*. London: Sage, 45–68.
Nederveen Pieterse, J. (2004) *Globalization and Culture: Global Mélange*. Lanham: Rowman & Littlefield.
Nederveen Pieterse, J. (2006) 'Emancipatory cosmopolitanism: Towards an agenda', *Development and Change*, 37 (6): 1247–1257.
Nederveen Pieterse, J. (2009) 'Multipolarity means thinking plural: Modernities', *Protosociology*, 26 (1): 19–35.
Nederveen Pieterse, J. and Parekh, B. (1995) 'Shifting imaginaries: Decolonization, internal decolonization, postcoloniality'. In J. Nederveen Pieterse and B. Parekh (eds), *The Decolonization of Imagination*. London: Zed, 1–19.
Nel, A. (2012) 'The repugnant appeal of the abject: Cityscape and cinematic corporality in *District 9*', *Critical Arts: South-North Cultural and Media Studies*, 26 (4): 547–569.
Neurath, O. (1983) 'Sociology in the framework of physicalism'. In R.S. Cohen and M. Neurath (eds), *Philosophical Papers 1913–1946. Vienna Circle Collection, Vol 16*. Dordrecht: Springer, 58–90.
New York Times (20 February 2009) 'The real roots of the "Slumdog" protests'. Available at: https://roomfordebate.blogs.nytimes.com/2009/02/20/the-real-roots-of-the-slumdog-protests/ (accessed 5 May 2018).
Newmahr, S. (2011) 'Chaos, order and collaboration: Toward a feminist conceptualization of edgework', *Journal of Contemporary Ethnography*, 40 (6): 682–712.
Nikolaisen, B. (2004) 'Embedded motion: Sacred travel among Mevlevi dervishes'. In S. Coleman and J. Eade (eds), *Reframing Pilgrimage*. London: Routledge, 91–104.

Nochlin, L. (1991) *The Politics of Vision: Essays on Nineteenth-Century Art and Society*. London: Thames and Hudson.

Nora, P. (1989) 'Between memory and history: *Les lieux de mémoire*', *Representations*, 26 (2): 7–25.

Northern Ireland Tourist Board (18 August 2008) 'Giant's Causeway remains Northern Ireland's Top Attraction'. Available from www.nitb.com/ (accessed 10 December 2014).

Nünning, A. and Nünning, V. (2010) 'Ways of worldmaking as a model for the study of culture'. In V. Nünning and A. Nünning (eds), *Cultural Ways of Worldmaking: Media and Narratives*. Berlin: de Gruyter, 215–244.

NZPA (1 November 2010) 'Hobbit drama – Govt comes out on top'. *3news.NZ*. Available at: www.3news.co.nz/Hobbit-drama-Govt-comes-out-on-top/tabid/419/articleID/183996/Default.aspx (accessed 19 December 2012).

O'Brien, M. (2008) *A Crisis of Waste?* New York: Routledge.

O'Gorman, K. (2006) 'Jacques Derrida's philosophy of hospitality', *Hospitality Review* 8 (4): 50–57.

O'Gorman, K. (2007) 'Dimensions of hospitality: Exploring ancient and classical origins'. In C. Lashley, P. Lynch, and A. Morrison (eds), *Hospitality*. Oxford: Elsevier, 17–32.

O'Neill, J. (1999) 'Economy, equality and recognition'. In L. Ray and A. Sayer (eds), *Culture and Economy after the Cultural Turn*. London: Sage, 76–91.

O'Reilly, C.C. (2005) 'Tourist or traveller? Narrating backpacker identity'. In A. Jaworski and A. Pritchard (eds), *Discourse, Communication and Tourism*. Clevedon: Channel View Publications, 150–169.

Okamoto (2015) 'Otaku tourism and the anime pilgrimage phenomenon in Japan', *Japan Forum*, 27 (1): 12–36.

Olsberg, SPI (4 March 2015) *Quantifying Film and Television Tourism in England – Report for Creative England in Association with VisitEngland by Olsberg SPI*. Available at: http://applications.creativeengland.co.uk/assets/public/resource/140.pdf (accessed 29 May 2018).

Onagua, T. (8 September 2009) 'Why *District 9* isn't racist against Nigerians'. *Guardian*. Available at: www.theguardian.com/film/filmblog/2009/sep/08/district9racism (accessed 15 February 2015).

Ong, A. (2005) 'Mutations in citizenship', *Theory, Culture & Society* 23 (2–3): 499–505.

Orange, R. (16 September 2016) 'Norway slashes tourism adverts as it is overwhelmed thanks to "Frozen effect"'. *Telegraph*. Available at: www.telegraph.co.uk/news/2016/09/16/norway-stops-promoting-tourism-as-it-is-overwhelmed-thanks-to-fr/ (accessed 20 May 2018).

Otto, R. (1936) *The Idea of the Holy: An Inquiry into the Non-rational Factor in the Idea of the Divine and its Relation to the Natural*. Oxford: Oxford University Press.

Pannett, R. (22 May 2018) 'Anger over tourists swarming vacation hot spots sparks global backlash'. *The Wall Street Journal*. Available at: www.wsj.com/articles/anger-over-tourists-swarming-vacation-hot-spots-sparks-global-backlash-1527000130 (accessed 3 June 2018).

Paolucci, G. (1998) 'Time shattered: The postindustrial city and women's temporal experience', *Time & Society*, 7 (2–3): 265–281.

Papanikolátos, N. (2000) 'Captain Corelli, the contradictions of Greek resistance, Hollywood and Cephallonia'. *AIM*. Available at: www.aimpress.org/dyn/trae/archive/data.200009/00924-005-traeath.htm (accessed 25 January 2006).

Parikka J. (2011) 'Media ecologies and imaginary media: Transversal expansions, contractions, and foldings', *The Fibreculture Journal*, 17 (Unnatural ecologies). Available at: http://seventeen.fibreculturejournal.org/fcj-116-media-ecologies-and-imaginary-media-transversal-expansions-contractions-and-foldings/ (accessed 1 July 2018).

Pateman, C. (1998) 'The patriarchal welfare state'. In J. Landes (ed.), *Feminism, the Public and the Private*. Oxford: Oxford University Press.

Paulson, S. (2015) 'Political ecology'. In G. D'Alisa, F. DeMaria, and G. Kallis (eds), *Degrowth*. New York and London: Routledge, 45–48.

Peaslee, R.M. (2010) '"The man from New Line knocked on the door": Tourism, media power, and Hobbiton/Matamata as boundaried space', *Tourist Studies*, 10 (1): 57–73.

Peaslee, R.M. (2011) 'One ring, many circles: The Hobbiton tour experience and a spatial approach to media power', *Tourist Studies*, 11 (1): 37–53.

Peirce, C. (1992) *The Essential Peirce, Vol. I: 1867–1893*. Bloomington, IN: Indiana University Press.

Peirce, C. (1998) 'The Harvard lectures of pragmaticism'. In C. Peirce, *The Essential Peirce, Vol. II*. Bloomington, IN: Indiana University Press.

Pels, D. (2003) *Unhastening Science: Autonomy and Reflexivity in the Social Theory of Knowledge*. Liverpool: Liverpool University Press.

Perkins, H.C. and Thorns, D.C. (2001) 'Gazing or performing? Reflections on Urry's tourist gaze in the context of contemporary experience in the Antipodes', *International Sociology*, 16 (2): 185–204.

Phelan, J. (29 April 2014) 'The 7 kingdoms in "Game of Thrones" are actually these 5 real-world places'. *Global Post*. Available at: www.salon.com/2014/04/29/the_7_kingdoms_in_game_of_thrones_are_actually_these_5_real_world_places_partner/ (accessed 28 November 2014).

Phillips, P. (2015) 'Artistic practices and ecoaesthetics in post-sustainable worlds'. In C. Crouch, N. Kaye, and J. Crouch (eds), *An Introduction to Sustainability and Aesthetics: The Arts and Design for the Environment*. Boca Raton, Florida: Brown Walker Press, 55–68.

Pickering, A. (1995) *The Mangle of Practice: Time, Agency & Science*. Chicago: University of Chicago Press.

Pignarre, P. and Stengers, I. (2011) *Capitalist Sorcery*. Basingstoke: Palgrave Macmillan.

Pine, B.J. and Gilmore, J. (1999) *The Experience Economy*. Cambridge, MA: Harvard Business School.

Piore, M.J. and Sabel, C.F. (1984) *The Second Industrial Divide*. New York: Basic Books.

Poon, A. (2009) 'Prospects for the British market', *Tourism Industry Intelligence*, 16 (1): 1–4.

Praxis International (2000) Available at: http://praxisinternational.tripod.com/MediaHP.htm (accessed 10 October 2003).

Prideaux, B. (2002) 'The cybertourist'. In G.M.S. Dann (ed.), *The Tourist as a Metaphor of the Social World*. Wallingford: CABI, 317–339.

PRNewswire (21 May 2012), 'Sounds of the Highlands; Disney-Pixar's "Brave" transports moviegoers to ancient Scotland with Oscar-nominated composer Patrick Doyle'. Available at: www.prnewswire.com/news-releases/sounds-of-the-highlands-disney-pixars-brave-transports-moviegoers-to-ancient-scotland-with-oscar-nominated-composer-patrick-doyle-plus-performers-julie-fowlis-and-birdy-with-mumford-sons-152256415.html (accessed 16 February 2014).

Prudishan, J. and Maneerat, M. (1997) 'Non-governmental development organization: Empowerment and environment'. In K. Hewison (ed.), *Political Change in Thailand*, London and New York: Routledge, 195–216.

Quaglieri Domínguez, A. and Scarnato, A. (2017) 'The Barrio Chino as last frontier: The penetration of everyday tourism and the dodgy heart of the Raval'. In M. Gravari-Barbas and S. Guinand (eds), *Tourism and Gentrification in Contemporary Metropolises: International Perspectives*. Abingdon: Routledge, 107–133.

Renciére, J. (2006) *The Politics of Aesthetics*. London: Continuum.

Ray, S. (17 November 2017) Bounty placed on Bollywood actress' head after Hindu-Muslim film outrage'. *Telegraph*. Available at: www.telegraph.co.uk/news/2017/11/17/bounty-placed-bollywood-actress-head-hindu-muslim-film-outrage/ (accessed 5 April 2018).

Read, J. (2011) 'The production of subjectivity: From transindividuality to the commons', *New Formations*, 70 (1): 113–131.

Reality Tours (undated) 'Bicycle tour'. Available at: http://realitytoursandtravel.com (accessed 1 September 2013).

Reijnders, S. (2009) 'Watching the detectives. Inside the guilty landscapes of Inspector Morse, Baantjer and Wallander', *European Journal of Communication*, 24 (2): 165–181.

Reijnders, S. (2010a) 'On the trail of 007: Media pilgrimages into the world of James Bond', *Area*, 42 (3): 369–377.

Reijnders, S. (2010b) 'Places of the imagination: An ethnography of the TV detective tour', *Cultural Geographies*, 17 (1): 37–52.

Reijnders, S. (2011) *Places of the Imagination: Media, Tourism, Culture*. Aldershot: Ashgate.

Renjie, M. (24 December 2009). 'Stunning Avatar'. *Global Times*. Available at: www.globaltimes.cn/life/entertainment/2009-12/494242.html (accessed 2 July 2018).

Rich, A. (2001) *Arts of the Possible*. New York and London: W.W. Norton.

Richards, G. (2010) *Leisure in the Network Society*. Tilburg: Tilburg University Press. Available at: www.academia.edu/1271795/Leisure_in_the_Network_Society?auto=download (accessed 15 December 2016).

Richards, G. (2011) 'Creativity and tourism: The state of the art', *Annals of Tourism Research*, 38 (4): 1225–1253.

Richards, G. (2014) 'Creativity and tourism in the city', *Current Issues in Tourism*, 17 (2): 119–144.

Richards, G. and Wilson, J. (2006) 'Developing creativity in tourist experiences: A solution to the serial production of culture?', *Tourism Management*, 27 (6): 1209–1223.

Richardson, N. (22 January 2009) 'Slumdog Millionaire: On the trail of Mumbai's slumdogs'. *Telegraph*. Available at: www.telegraph.co.uk/travel/destinations/asia/india/4306996/Slumdog-Millionaire-on-the-trail-of-Mumbais-slumdogs.html (accessed 1 September 2013).

Rickly-Boyd, J. (2013) '"Dirtbags": Mobility, community and rick climbing as performative of identity'. In T. Duncan, S.A. Cohen, and M. Thulemark (eds), *Lifestyle Mobilities: Intersections of Travel. Leisure and Migration*. Surrey: Ashgate, 51–64.

Rigby, S. (16 August 2017) '"Game of Thrones" is a blessing and a curse for Dubrovnik in Croatia', *Quartz*. Available at: https://qz.com/1054123/game-of-thrones-is-a-blessing-and-a-curse-for-dubrovnik-in-croatia/ (accessed 4 April 2018).

Ritzer, G. (2006) 'Globalization and McDonaldization'. In G. Ritzer (ed.), *McDonaldization*. London: Sage.

Ritzer, G. and Liska, A. (1997) '"McDisneyization" and "post-tourism": Contemporary perspectives on contemporary tourism'. In C. Rojek and J. Urry (eds), *Touring Cultures: Transformations of Travel and Theory*. London and New York: Routledge, 96–112.

Roberts, L. (2012) *Film, Mobility and Urban Space: A Cinematic Geography of Liverpool*. Liverpool: Liverpool University Press.

Robertson, R. (1992) *Glocalization*. London: Sage.

Robinson, A.H. (1985) 'Arno Peters and his new cartography', *American Cartographer*, 12 (2): 103–112.

Robinson, J. (2004) 'Squaring the circle? Some thoughts on the idea of sustainable development', *Ecological Economics*, 48 (4): 369–384.

Rojek, C. (1993) *Ways of Escape*. London: Routledge.

Rojek, C. (2001) *Celebrity*. London: Reaktion.

Rosa, H. (2013) *Social Acceleration: A New Theory of Modernity*. New York: Columbia University Press.

Rose, G., Degen, M., and Basdas, B. (2010) 'More on "big things": Building events and feelings', *Transactions of the Institute of British Ethnographers*, 35: 334–349.

Rose, N. (1999) *Powers of Freedom: Reframing Political Thought*. Cambridge: Cambridge University Press.

Routledge, P. (1997) 'A spatiality of resistance: Theory and practice in Nepal's revolution of 1990'. In S. Pile and M. Keith (eds), *Geographies of Resistance*. London: Routledge, 68–86.

Rumford, C. (2006) 'Theorizing borders', *European Journal of Social Theory*, 9 (2): 155–570.

Rumford, C. (2008) 'Citizens and borderwork in Europe', *Space and Polity*, 12 (1): 1–12.

Saarinen, J. (2013) 'Critical sustainability: Setting the limits to growth and responsibility in tourism', *Sustainability*, 6 (1): 1–17.

Sacco, P.L. (2011) 'Culture 3.0: A new perspective for the EU 2014–2020 structural funds programming' OMC Working Group on Cultural and Creative Industries. Available at: www.interarts.net/descargas/interarts2577.pdf (accessed 18 April 2018).

Sacred Destinations (undated) 'St Sulpice-Paris'. Available at: www.sacred-destinations.com/france/paris-st-sulpice (accessed 4 September 2012).

Sacred Earth Journeys (2006) 'On the trail of the Da Vinci Code'. Available at: www.sacredearthjourneys.ca/TOURS/sacred-Davinci-des.htm (accessed 11 November 2006).

Sacred Sites Journeys (2018) Available at: www.sacredsitesjourneys.com/ (accessed 4 May 2018).

Said, E. (1978) *Orientalism*. London: Penguin.

Salazar, N.B. (2009) 'Imaged or imagined? Cultural representations and the "tourismification" of peoples and places', *Cashiers d'Études Africaines*, 49 (1–2): 49–71.

Salazar, N.B. (2010) *Envisioning Eden: Mobilising Imaginaries in Tourism and Beyond*. Oxford: Berghahn.

Salazar, N.B. (2012) 'Tourism imaginaries: A conceptual approach', *Annals of Tourism Research*, 39 (2): 863–882.

Salazar, N.B. (2013) 'The (im)mobility of tourism imaginaries'. In M. Smith and G. Richards (eds), *The Routledge Handbook of Cultural Tourism*. London: Routledge, 34–39.

Salazar, N.B. (2017) 'The cosmopolitanisation of tourism: An afterthought'. In R. Shepherd (ed.), *Cosmopolitanism and Tourism: Rethinking Theory and Practice*. London: Lexington Books, 187–194.

Salazar, N.B. and Graburn, N.H.H. (2016) 'Towards an anthropology of tourism imaginaries'. In N.B. Salazar and N.H.H. Graburn (eds), *Tourism Imaginaries*. Oxford: Berghahn, 1–30.

Sandvik, R. (24 July 2014) 'Explore the breathtaking places that inspired Disney's Frozen in Norway', *The Fairy Tale Traveler*. Available at: http://thefairytaletraveler.com/2014/07/24/frozen/ (accessed 21 May 2018).

Sandywell, B. (2011) *Dictionary of Visual Discourse*. Surrey: Ashgate.

Sassen, S. (1991) *The Global City: New York, London, Tokyo*. Princeton: Princeton University Press.

Satherley, D. (29 October 2010) 1: 'Hobbit bill becomes law'. *3news.NZ*. Available at: www.suite101.com/content/peter-jacksons-hobbit-movie-invokes-industrialprotestsa301440 (accessed 19 December 2010).

Satherley, D. (29 October 2010) 2: 'Labor MP slams Hobbit law change'. *3news.NZ*. Available at: www.3news.co.nz/Labour-MP-slams-Hobbit-law-change/tabid/423/articleID/183695/Default.aspx (accessed 19 December 2010).

Sather-Wagstaff, J. (2011) *Heritage That Hurts: Tourists in the Memoryscapes of September 11th*. Walnut Creek, CA: Left Coast Press.

Savas, K. (22 December 2012) 'Composer interview: Ramin Djawadi'. *F.F.M.* Available at: www.filmmusicmedia.com/interviews/composerinterviewramindjawadi-1 (accessed 28 November 2014).

Sayer, A. (2000), 'Moral economy and political economy', *Studies in Political Economy*, 61 (2): 79–103.

Sayer, A. (2003) '(De-)commodification, consumer culture and moral economy', *Environment and Planning D*, 21 (3): 341–357.

Sayyid, S. (2015) *A Fundamental Fear: Eurocentrism and the Rise of Islamism*, 2nd edn. London: Zed.

Sayyid, S. and Vakil, A.K. (2010) *Thinking through Islamophobia: Global Perspectives*. New York: Columbia University Press.

Schäfer, D. (2018) 'Editorial: Mobility studies, a transdisciplinary field', *Transfers*, 8 (1): vii-x.

Schafer, R.M. (1994) *The Soundscape*. Rochester: Destiny.

Schiller, F. (2004) *On the Aesthetic Education of Man*. New York: Dover.

Schiller, G. (2008) 'From kinesphere to kinesfield: Three choreographic interactive artworks', *Leonardo*, 41 (5): 431–437.

Schilling, C. (2003) *The Body and Social Theory*. London: Sage.

Schmid, H., Sahr, W.D., and Urry, J. (2011) 'Introduction'. In H. Schmid, W.-D. Sahr, and J. Urry (eds), *Cities and Fascination: Beyond the Surplus of Meaning*. London: Routledge, 1–16.

Schramm, K. (2004) 'Coming home to the Motherland: Pilgrimage tourism in Ghana'. In S. Coleman and J. Eade (eds), *Reframing Pilgrimage*. London: Routledge, 133–149.

Schumpeter, J. ([1942] 1975) *Capitalism, Socialism and Democracy*. New York: Harper.

Scott, D., Hall, C.M., and Gössling, S. (2012) *Tourism and Climate Change: Impacts, Adaptation and Mitigation*. London: Routledge.

Scott, J. (1991) *Domination and the Arts of Resistance: Hidden Transcripts*. New Haven, CT: Yale University Press.

Seaton, A.V. (1998) 'The history of tourism in Scotland: Approaches, sources and issues'. In R. MacLellan and R. Smith (eds), *Tourism in Scotland*. London: International Thompson Business Press, 209–239.

Seaton, P. and Yamamura, T. (2015) 'Japanese popular culture and contents tourism – Introduction', *Japan Forum*, 27 (1): 1–11.

Seaton, P., Yamamura, T., Sugawa-Shimada, A., and Kyungjae, J. (2016) *Contents Tourism in Japan: Pilgrimages to "Sacred Sites" of Popular Culture*. Amherst, NY: Cambria Press.

Seaton, T. (2012) 'The literary evolution of slumming'. In F. Frenzel, K. Koens, and M. Steinbrink (eds), *Slum Tourism: Poverty, Power and Ethics*. London: Routledge, 21–48.

Sennett, R. (1977) *The Fall of Public Man*. Boston, MA: Faber and Faber.

Serres, M. (1995) *Angels*. Paris and New York: Flammarion.

Serres, M. (2000) *Atlas*. USA: Editiones Catedras.

Sesser, S. (21 February 2009) '"Slumdog" tour guide'. *Asia News*. Available at: http://online.wsj.com/article/SB123517711344337609.html (accessed 5 September 2013).

Sheller, M. (2004) 'Demobilizing and remobilizing Caribbean paradise'. In M. Sheller and J. Urry (eds), *Tourism Mobilities: Places to Play, Places in Play*. London: Routledge, 13–21.

Sheller, M. (2009) 'The new Caribbean complexity: Mobility systems, tourism and spatial rescaling', *Singapore Journal of Tropical Geography*, 30 (2): 189–203.

Sheller, M. (2011) 'Mobility'. In sociopedia.isa. Madrid: ISA.

Sheller, M. (2012a) *Citizenship from Below: Erotic Agency and Caribbean Freedom*. Durham, NC: Duke University Press.

Sheller, M. (2012b) 'The islanding effect: Post-disaster mobility systems and humanitarian logistics in Haiti', *Cultural Geographies*, 20 (2): 185–204.

Sheller, M. (2014) *Aluminum Dreams: The Making of Light Modernity*. Cambridge, MA: MIT Press.

Sheller, M. and Urry, J. (2003) 'Mobile transformations of "public" and "private" life', *Theory, Culture & Society*, 20 (3): 107–125.

Sheller, M. and Urry, J. (2004) 'Places to play, places in play'. In M. Sheller and J. Urry (eds), *Tourism Mobilities: Places to Play, Places in Play*. London and New York: Routledge, 1–10.

Sheller, M. and Urry, J. (2006) 'The new mobilities paradigm', *Environment and Planning A*, 38 (2): 207–226.

Shields, R. (1991) *Places on the Margin: Geographies of Modernity*. London: Routledge.

Shiva, V. (1993) *Monocultures of the Mind: Perspectives on Biodiversity and Biotechnology*. London: Palgrave Macmillan.

Shiva, V. (1997) *Biopiracy: The Plunder of Nature and Knowledge*. Boston, MA: South End Press.

Shklovsky, V., Jakubinsky, L., Brik, O., Polivavov, Y., and Eikenbaum, B. (1919) *Poetics: Collections on the Theory of Poetic Language*. Petrograd: 18th State Printing House.

Siggins, L. (26 September 2015) 'Star Wars filming behind "incidents" on Skellig Michael'. *The Irish Times*. Available at: www.irishtimes.com/news/ireland/irish-news/star-wars-filming-behind-incidents-on-skellig-michael-1.2366928 (accessed 16 January 2018).

Simmel, G. ([1903] 1997) 'The metropolis and mental life'. In D. Frisby and M. Featherstone (eds), *Simmel on Culture*. London: Sage, 174–186.

Simus, J.B. (2008) 'Aesthetic implications of the new paradigm in ecology', *The Journal of Aesthetic Education*, 42 (1): 63–79.

Sinclair, D. (1992) 'Land: Maori view and European response'. In M. King (ed.), *Te Ao Hurihuri: Aspects of Maoritanga*. Auckland: Reed, 65–84.

Sinclair, J. (2000) 'More than an old flame: National symbolism and the media in the torch ceremony of the Olympics', *Media International Australia*, 97 (1): 35–46.

Singh, M.P. (22 June 2013) 'Unesco declares 6 Rajasthan forts World Heritage Sites', *The Hindu*. Available at: www.thehindu.com/news/national/other-states/unesco-declares-6-rajasthan-forts-world-heritage-sites/article4838107.ece (accessed 5 April 2018).

Singh, S. (2002) 'Managing the impact of tourism and pilgrim mobility in the Indian Himalayas', *Revue de Géographie Alpine*, 90 (1): 25–34.

Singh, S. (2009) 'Spirituality and tourism: An anthropologist's view', *Tourism Recreation Research*, 34 (2): 143–155.

Singh, S. (2012) 'Slow travel and Indian culture: Philosophical and practical aspects'. In S. Fullagar, K. Markwell, and E. Wilson (eds), *Slow Tourism: Experiences and Mobilities*. Bristol: Channel View, 214–226.

Skopelos Net (2018) 'Agios Ioannis Chapel'. Available at: www.skopelostravel.net/agios-ioannis/ (accessed 11 May 2018).

Skopelos Travel (2018) Available at: http://skopelos.travel/mammamia/ (accessed 10 May 2018).

Sloterdijk, P. (2009) 'Geometry in the colossal: The project of metaphysical globalization', *Environment and Planning D: Society and Space*, 27 (1): 29–40.

Smith, A.D. (1986) *The Ethnic Origins of Nations*. Oxford: Blackwell.

Smith, D. (2 September 2009) '*District 9* labelled xenophobic by Nigerians'. *Guardian*. Available at: www.theguardian.com/film/2009/sep/02/district9labelledxenophobicnigerians (accessed 14 February 2015).

Smith, P. (2011) 'The Balinese Cockfight decoded: Reflections on Geertz and structuralism'. In C. Alexander, P. Smith, and M. Norton (eds), *Interpreting Clifford Geertz: Cultural Investigation in the Social Sciences*. New York: Palgrave Macmillan, 17–32.

Smith-Nonini, S. (2017) 'Making complexity your friend: Reframing social theory for the Anthropocene', *Weather, Climate, and Society*. DOI: 10.1175/WCAS-D-16-0124.1.

Snyder, J.P. (1987) *Map Projections – A Working Manual. US Geological Survey Professional Paper 1395*. Washington, DC: United States Government Printing Office.

Snyder, J.P. (1997) *Flattening the Earth: Two Thousand Years of Map Projections*. Chicago: University of Chicago Press.

Soper, K. (2007) 'Re-thinking the "good life": The citizenship dimension of consumer disaffection with consumerism', *Journal of Consumer Culture*, 7 (2): 205–229.

Soper, K. (2008) 'Alternative hedonism, cultural theory and the role of aesthetic revisioning', *Cultural Studies*, 22 (5): 567–587.

Sørensen, N. and Haug, P.N. (eds) (2012) *Nordic Light: Interpretations in Architecture*. København, Dansk Center for Lys.

Sørensen, T.F. (2015) 'More than a feeling', *Emotions, Space and Society*, 15 (4): 64–73.

Şorman, A.H. (2015) 'Metabolism, societal'. In G. D'Alisa, F. DeMaria, and G. Kallis (eds), *Degrowth*. New York and London: Routledge, 41–44.

Sorokin, P. and Merton, R. (1937) 'Social time: A methodological and functional analysis', *American Journal of Sociology*, 42 (5): 615–629.

Spivak, G.C. (2010) 'Can the subaltern speak?'. In R.C. Morris (ed.), *Can the Subaltern Speak? Reflections on the History of an Idea*. New York: Columbia University Press, 21–80.

Spode, H. (2009) 'Tourism research and theory in German-speaking countries'. In G.M.S. Dann and G. Parrinello (eds), *The Sociology of Tourism*. Bingley: Emerald, 65–94.

Squires, N. (12 September 2016) 'Venetians brandish shopping trolleys and pushchairs in protest against mass tourism'. *Telegraph*. Available at: www.telegraph.co.uk/news/2016/09/12/venetians-brandish-shopping-trolleys-and-pushchairs-in-protest-a/ (accessed 2 May 2018).

Squires, N. (25 April 2018) 'Venice to segregate locals from tourists heading to popular landmarks as crowds descend on city, *Telegraph*'. Available at: www.telegraph.co.uk/news/2018/04/25/venice-segregate-tourist-walking-routes-city-ahead-weekend-onslaught/?WT.mc_id=tmg_share_fb (accessed 2 May 2018).

Starhawk (1999) *The Spiral Dance: A Rebirth of the Ancient Religion of the Great Goddess*, 20th anniversary edn. San Francisco, CA: HarperOne.

Stengers, I. (2012) 'Reclaiming animism', *e-flux*, 36. Available at: www.e-flux.com/journal/36/61245/reclaiming-animism/ (accessed 2 July 2018).

Stengers, I. (2015) *In Catastrophic Times: Resisting the Coming Barbarism*. Germany: Open Humanities Press/Meson Press.

Stevenson, N. (1997) 'Globalisation, national cultures and cultural citizenship', *Sociological Quarterly*, 38 (1): 41–66.

Stevenson, N. (2003) *Cultural Citizenship*. Maidenhead: Open University Press.

Stewart, K. (2007) *Ordinary Affects*. Durham, NC: Duke University Press.

Stiegler, B. (1998) *Technics and Time, Vol. I: The Fault of Epimetheus*. Stanford, CA: Stanford University Press.

Stiegler, B. (2011) *Technics and Time, Vol. III: Cinematic Time and the Question of Malaise*. Stanford, CA: Stanford University Press.

Stone, P. (2006) 'A dark tourism spectrum: Towards a typology of death and macabre-related tourist sites, attractions and exhibitions', *Tourism: An Interdisciplinary International Journal*, 52 (2): 145–160.

Stone, P. (2013) 'Dark tourism scholarship: A critical review', *Journal of Tourism, Culture and Hospitality Research*, 7 (3): 307–318.

Strain, E. (2003) *Public Places, Private Journeys: Ethnography, Entertainment and the Tourist Gaze*. New Jersey: Rutgers University Press.

Stuff (31 January 2009) 'Gate to Whale Rider beach padlocked'. Available at: www.stuff.co.nz/dominion-post/archive/national-news/576982/Gate-to-Whale-Rider-beach-padlocked (accessed 15 May 2018).

Style Me Pretty – Europe (2018) Available at: www.stylemepretty.com/europe-weddings/greece/ (accessed 11 May 2018).

Sun Reality (undated) 'Inn at Rodanthe – Hatteras island's most celebrated vacation rental'. Available at: www.sunrealtync.com/inn-rodanthe-hatteras-islands-most-celebrated-vacation-rental (accessed 13 May 2018).

Sutherland, T. (2013) 'Liquid networks and the metaphysics of flux: Ontologies of flow in an age of speed and mobility', *Theory, Culture & Society*, 30 (5): 3–23.

Sutherland, T. (2014) 'Intensive mobilities: Figurations of the nomad in contemporary life', *Environment and Planning D: Society & Space*, 32 (5): 935–950.

Swain, M. (2009) 'The cosmopolitan hope of tourism: Critical action and worldmaking vistas', *Tourism Geographies*, 11(4): 505–525.

Swanson, J. (16 May 2011) 'The pros and cons of slum tourism'. *CNN Travel*. Available at: http://travel.cnn.com/mumbai/play/pros-and-cons-slum-tourism-723332 (accessed 6 September 2013).

Szerszynski, B. and Urry, J. (2006) 'Visuality, mobility and the cosmopolitan: Inhabiting the world from afar', *British Journal of Sociology*, 57 (1): 113–131.

Szerszynski, B., Heim, W., and Waterton, C. (2003) *Nature Performed: Environment, Culture and Performance*. Minneapolis, MN: University of Minnesota Press.

Tamara (June 2017) 'Disney's Frozen scenery originates from the Norwegian nature'. Nordiva Tours. Available at: www.nordivatours.com/blog/frozen-scenery/ (accessed 20 May 2018).

Tarde, G. ([1890] 2001) *The Laws of Imitation.* New York: Henry Holt & Co.

Taylor, E. (13 August 2017) 'Jet-setting: A *Game of Thrones* travel guide to Dubrovnik, Croatia (aka King's Landing)', *Vogue.* Available at: www.vogue.com/article/game-of-thrones-travel-guide-to-dubrovnik-croatia (accessed 17 March 2018).

Telegraph (17 June 2008) 'Vatican bans "godless" Da Vinci Code sequel Angels & Demons from Rome churches'. Available at: www.telegraph.co.uk/news/2139472/Vatican-bans-%27godless%27-Da-Vinci-Code-sequel-Angels-andamp-Demons-from-Rome-churches.html (accessed 1 September 2008).

The Disney Wiki (2018) 'Arandelle'. Available at: http://disney.wikia.com/wiki/Arendelle (accessed 21 May 2018).

The Indian Express (17 November 2017) 'Padvamati protesters block tourist entry to Chittorgargh Fort'. Available at: http://indianexpress.com/article/india/padmavati-protesters-block-tourist-entry-to-chhittorgarh-fort-4941766/ (accessed 5 April 2018).

The Local (3 August 2016) 'Frozen effect bringing "too many tourists" to Norway'. Available at: www.thelocal.no/20160803/frozen-effect-brings-norway-too-many-tourists (accessed 20 May 2018).

The Location Guide (20 January 2015) 'Online map of Bollywood shoots in Scotland designed to boost film tourism'. Available at: www.thelocationguide.com/2015/01/ng-film-tourism-online-map-of-bollywood-shoots-in-scotland-designed-to-boost-film-tourism/# (accessed 7 May 2018).

The New Zealand Herald (8 March 2003) 'Whale Rider fans overwhelm Whangara'. Available at: www.nzherald.co.nz/nz/news/article.cfm?c_id=1&objectid=3199752 (accessed 15 May 2018).

The Times of India (22 January 2009) 'Hindu group demands ban on "Slumdog Millionaire"'. Available at: http://articles.timesofindia.indiatimes.com/2009-01-22/goa/28046633_1_hjs-slumdog-millionaire-hindu-janjagruti-samiti (accessed 15 September 2013).

The Times of India (29 January 2017) 'Sanjay Leela Bhansali assault: "Padmavati" actors Deepika Padukone, Ranveer Singh and Shahid Kapoor break their silence'. Available at: https://timesofindia.indiatimes.com/entertainment/hindi/bollywood/news/sanjay-leela-bhansali-assault-padmavati-deepika-padukone-breaks-her-silence/articleshow/56832864.cms (accessed 5 April 2018).

Thibaud, J.-P. (2011) 'The sensory fabric of urban ambiances', *The Senses and Society*, 6 (2): 203–215.

Thomas, R. (1985) 'Indian cinema: Pleasures and popularity', *Screen*, 26 (3–4): 116–131.

Thompson, C. (18 February 2016) '10 amazing Viking sites in Norway you must visit if you're a Vikings fan'. *The Fairy Tale Traveler*. Available at: http://thefairytaletraveler.com/2016/02/18/viking-sites-in-norway/ (accessed 18 January 2018).

Thompson, P. (2013) 'Religion, utopia, and the metaphysics of contingency'. In P. Thompson and S. Žižek (eds), *The Privatization of Hope: Ernst Bloch and the Future of Utopia.* Durham, NC: Duke University Press, 82–105.

Thompson-Carr, A. (2012) 'Aoraki/Mt Cook and the Mackenzie basin's transition from wilderness to tourist place', *Journal of Tourism Consumption and Practice*, 4 (1): 30–58.

ThorNews (5 December 2013) 'Disney's animated film "Frozen" inspired by Norway'. Available at: https://thornews.com/2013/12/05/disneys-animated-film-frozen-inspired-by-norway/ (18 January 2018).

Thorpe, V. (15 August 2017) 'Bergen, where Jo Nesbø's Snowman carried out his grisly work, refashions its image'. *Guardian*. Available at: www.theguardian.com/world/2017/oct/14/bergen-refashions-its-image-jo-nesbo-snowman-jeremy-deller (accessed 18 April 2018).

Thrift, N. (1996) *Spatial Formations*. London: Sage.

Thrift, N. (1999) 'The place of complexity', *Theory, Culture & Society*, 16 (3): 31–70.

Thrift, N. (2004a) 'Intensities of feeling: Towards a spatial politics of affect', *Geografika Annaler B*, 86 (1): 57–78.

Thrift, N. (2004b) 'Movement-space: The changing domain of thinking resulting from the development of new kinds of spatial awareness', *Economy and Society*, 33 (4): 582–604.

Thrift, N. (2007) *Non-Representational Theory: Space, Politics, Affect*. London: Routledge.

Thrift, N. (2009) 'Understanding the effective spaces of political performance'. In M. Smith, J. Davidson, and L. Bondi (eds), *Emotion, Place and Culture*. Aldershot: Ashgate, 75–95.

Todd, S.C. (2009) 'Nature, beauty and tourism'. In J. Tribe (ed.), *Philosophical Issues in Tourism*. Clevedon: Channel View, 154–170.

Todorova, M. (1997) *Imagining the Balkans*. New York and Oxford: Oxford University Press.

Tolia-Kelly, D.P. (2006) 'Affect – an ethnographic encounter? Exploring the "universalist" imperative of emotional/affectual geographies', *Area*, 38 (2): 213–217.

Tolia-Kelly, D.P. (2008) 'Motion/emotion: Picturing translocal landscapes in the nurturing ecologies research project', *Mobilities* 3 (1): 117–140.

Tolia-Kelly, D.P. (2010) *Landscape, Race and Memory: Material Ecologies of Home*. Farnham: Ashgate.

Torres, G. and García-Hernández, A.M. (2016) 'From violation to voice, from pain to protest: Healing, and transforming unjust loss through the use of rituals and memorials'. In D.L. Harris and T.C. Bordere (eds), *Handbook of Social Justice in Loss and Grief: Exploring Diversity, Equity, and Inclusion*. London: Routledge, 202–212.

Touraine, A. (1981) *The Voice and the Eye*. Cambridge: Cambridge University Press.

Touraine, A. (1985) 'An introduction to the study of social movements', *Social Research*, 52 (4): 749–788.

Tourism Intelligence Unit (10 October 2011) *Sustainable Tourism: A Review of Indicators*. Office for National Statistics. Available at: https://data.gov.uk/dataset/sustainable_tourism/resource/ebc4ed1b-055f-4395-95d5-63aad17b5518 (accessed 15 March 2018).

Tourism Ireland (2 April 2014) 'Game of Thrones to promote Northern Ireland overseas: Foster'. Available at: www.tourismireland.com/Home!/About-Us/Press-Releases/2014/Game-of-Thrones-to-Promote-Northern-Ireland-Overse.aspx (accessed 29 November 2014).

Tourism Ireland (2014) 'Fantasy blockbuster Game of Thrones chose Northern Ireland as One of its primary filming locations. Why? Find out …'. Available at: www.ireland.com/en-gb/articles/game-of-thrones/ (accessed 10 December 2014).

Tribe, J. (2009) 'Introduction: Philosophical issues in tourism'. In J. Tribe (ed.), *Philosophical Issues in Tourism*. Clevedon: Channel View, 3–24.

Trip Advisor (2018) 'Agios Ioannis sto Kastri'. Available at: www.tripadvisor.co.uk/Attraction_Review-g189501-d2283043-Reviews-Agios_Ioannis_Beach-Skopelos_Sporades.html (accessed 11 May 2018).

Trip Advisor (2018) 'Memorial Acqui Division'. Available at: www.tripadvisor.co.uk/Attraction_Review-g780715-d3561773-Reviews-Memorial_Acqui_Division-Argostolion_Cephalonia_Ionian_Islands.html (accessed 13 May 2018).

Turbett, L. (18 January 2018) 'Harry Potter tourism is ruining Edinburgh'. *Vice*. Available at www.vice.com/en_uk/article/zmqkp3/harry-potter-tourism-is-ruining-edinburgh (accessed 2 April 2018).

Turner, S. (2002) 'Cinema of justice', *Illusions*, 33 (autumn): 9–11.

Turner, V. (1974) 'Liminal to liminoid, play flow and ritual', *Rice University Studies*, 50: 53–92.

Tzanelli, R. (2004) 'Orient(alizz)ando l' "Italia". Identità italiana e industria culturale ne "Il mandolino del Capitano Corelli" ', *Studi Culturali*, 1 (1): 31–58.

Tzanelli, R. (2007) *The Cinematic Tourist: Explorations in Globalization, Culture and Resistance*. London: Routledge.

Tzanelli, R. (2008a) 'Cultural intimations and the commodification of culture: Sign industries as makers of the "public sphere" ', *The Global Studies Journal*, 1 (3): 1–10.

Tzanelli, R. (2008b) *Nation-Building and Identity in Europe: The Dialogics of Reciprocity*. Basingstoke: Palgrave Macmillan.

Tzanelli, R. (2011) *Cosmopolitan Memory in Europe's 'Backwaters': Rethinking Civility*. Abingdon: Routledge.

Tzanelli, R. (2013) *Heritage in the Digital Era: Cinematic Tourism and the Activist Cause*. London: Routledge.

Tzanelli, R. (2014) 'Heritage entropy and tourist pilgrimage in Brave's Scotland', *Hospitality & Society*, 4 (2): 155–177.

Tzanelli, R. (2015a) *Mobility, Modernity and the Slum: The Real and Virtual Journeys of Slumdog Millionaire*. Abingdon: Routledge.

Tzanelli, R. (2015b) 'On *Avatar's* (2009) touring semiotechnologies: From cinematic utopias to Chinese heritage tourism', *Tourism Analysis*, 20 (3): 269–282.

Tzanelli, R. (2015c) *Socio-Cultural Mobility and Mega-Events: Ethics and Aesthetics in Brazil 2014*. Abingdon: Routledge.

Tzanelli, R. (2016a) 'Dark tourism and digital gift economies: Some epistemological notes'. In M.E. Korstanje (ed.), *Terrorism in a Global Village*. New York: Nova Publishers, 105–134.

Tzanelli, R. (2016b) *Thanatourism and Cinematic Representations of Risk: Screening the End of Tourism*. Abingdon: Routledge.

Tzanelli, R. (2017a) *Mega-Events as Economies of the Imagination: Creating Atmospheres for Rio 2016 and Tokyo 2020*. Abingdon: Routledge.

Tzanelli, R. (2017b) 'Staging pilgrimage on Skopelos after *Mamma Mia*! (2008): Digital and terrestrial hospitality in cinematic tourism'. In M.E. Korstanje and B. Handayani (eds), *Gazing Death: Dark Tourism as an Emergent Field of Research*. New York: Nova Publishers, 131–160.

UNESCO (2012) *World Heritage: Spectacular Nature*. Brussels: UNESCO Publishing.
UNESCO List (undated) 'Wulingyuan scenic and historic interest area'. Available at: http://whc.unesco.org/en/list/640 (accessed 2 July 2018).
Urry, J. (1978) *Reference Groups and the Theory of Revolution*. London: Routledge.
Urry, J. (1990) *The Tourist Gaze*. London and New Delhi: Sage.
Urry, J. (1995) *Consuming Places*. London: Routledge.
Urry, J. (2002) 'The global complexities of September the 11th', *Theory, Culture & Society*, 19 (4): 57–69.
Urry, J. (2003) *Global Complexity*. Cambridge: Polity.
Urry, J. (2004a) 'Death in Venice'. In M. Sheller and J. Urry (eds), *Tourism Mobilities: Places to Play, Places in Play*. London and New York: Routledge, 205–215.
Urry, J. (2004b) 'The system of automobility', *Theory, Culture & Society*, 21 (4/5): 25–39.
Urry, J. (2005a) 'The complexities of the global', *Theory, Culture & Society*, 22 (5): 235–254.
Urry, J. (2005b) 'The complexity turn', *Theory, Culture & Society*, 22(5): 1–14.
Urry, J. (2007) *Mobilities*. Cambridge: Polity.
Urry, J. (2008) 'Climate change, travel and complex futures', *British Journal of Sociology*, 59 (2): 261–279.
Urry, J. (2010) 'Consuming the planet to excess', *Theory, Culture & Society*, 27 (2–3): 191–212.
Urry, J. (2011a) *Climate Change and Society*. Cambridge: Polity.
Urry, J. (2011b) 'Excess, fascination and climates'. In H. Schmid, W.-D. Sahr, and J. Urry (eds), *Cities and Fascination: Beyond the Surplus of Meaning*. London: Routledge, 209–224.
Urry, J. (2013) *Societies Beyond Oil*. London: Zed.
Urry, J. (2014) *Offshoring*. Cambridge: Polity.
Uzzell, D.L. (1996) 'Creating place identity through heritage Interpretation', *International Journal of Heritage Studies*, 4 (1): 219–228.
Uzzell, D.L. and Ballantyne, R. (1998) 'Heritage that hurts: interpretation in a post-modern world'. In D.L. Uzzell and R. Ballantyne (eds), *Contemporary Issues in Heritage and Environmental Interpretation*. London: Stationary Office, 152–171.
van Aelst, P. and Walgrave, S. (2004) 'New media, new movements? The role of the Internet in shaping the "anti-globalization" movement'. In W. van de Donk (ed.), *Cyberprotest*. London: Routledge, 97–122.
van Eaden, J. (2007) 'Theming mythical Africa at the Lost City'. In S.A. Lukas (ed.), *The Themed Space: Locating Culture, Nation, and Self*. Lanham: Rowman & Littlefield, 113–136.
van Rompu, R. (6 May 2017) 'Social constructions of the favela Part 4: Tourist perceptions before and after favela tours', *Rio on Watch*. Available at: www.rioonwatch.org/?p=35699 (accessed 24 April 2018).
Vanaik, A. (2004) 'Rendezvous at Mumbai', *New Left Review*, 26: 53–65.
Vannini, P., Hodson, J., and Vannini, A. (2009) 'Toward a technography of everyday life', *Cultural Studies – Critical Methodologies*, 9 (3): 462–476.
Veijola, S. and Jokinen, E. (1994) 'The body in tourism', *Theory and Society*, 11 (3): 125–151.
Veijola, S. and Valtonen, A. (2007) 'The body in tourism industry'. In A. Pritchard, N. Morgan, I. Ateljevic, and C. Harris, (eds), *Tourism and Gender: Embodiment, Sexuality and Experience*. Wallingford: CABI, 13–31.

Veijola, S., Germann Molz, J., Pyyhtinen, O., Hockert, E., Grit, A., and Höckert, E. (2014) *Disruptive Tourism and its Untidy Guests: Alternative Ontologies for Future Hospitalities*. Basingstoke: Palgrave Macmillan.

Viator (undated) 'Mumbai bicycle tour'. Available at: https://uk.viator.com/tours/Mumbai/Mumbai-Bike-Tour/d953-6283BOMBIKE (accessed 1 May 2018).

Virilio, P. (21 October 1984) 'Cyberwar, god and television' (interview with L. Wilson). C-Theory.

VisitBritain (February 2018) 'Film and TV locations as a driver of tourism'. Foresight, 160. Available at: www.visitbritain.org/sites/default/files/vb-corporate/Documents-Library/documents/foresight_160_-_film_and_tv_locations.pdf (accessed 29 May 2018).

VisitNorway (2018) 'New "Frozen" attraction takes shape at Disney World's Norway Pavilion'. Available at: www.visitnorway.com/media/news-from-norway/new-frozen-attraction-takes-shape-at-disney-worlds-norway-pavilion/ (accessed 21 May 2018).

VisitScotland (2012a) 'VisitScotland and Disney announce marketing campaign for upcoming Disney-Pixar film "Brave"'. Available at: www.visitscotland.org/media_centre/visitscotland_disney_partners.aspx. (accessed 14 February 2014).

VisitScotland (2012b) 'Itineraries'. Available at: www.visitscotland.com/brave/itinerary. (accessed 17 February 2014).

VisitScotland (2018) 'Walk in the footsteps of your ancestors'. Available at: www.visitscotland.com/see-do/research-your-ancestry/ (accessed 7 May 2018).

VisitScotland (6 August 2016) 'Who do you think you are?'. Available at: http://media-centre.visitscotland.org/pressreleases/who-do-you-think-you-are-1592584 (accessed 7 May 2018).

VisitSweden (undated) 'Inspector Wallander has made Ystad famous around the world'. Available at: https://visitsweden.com/wallanders-ystad/ (accessed 19 April 2018).

Vogel, S.M. and Carrieri, M. (1986) *African Aesthetics*. New York: Museum for African Art.

Vostal, F., Benda, L., and Virtová, T. (2018) 'Against reductionism: On the complexity of scientific temporality', *Time & Society*. DOI: 10.1177/0961463X17752281.

Walby, S. (1990) *Theorising Patriarchy*. Oxford: Blackwell.

Walby, S. (2011) *The Future of Feminism*. Cambridge: Polity.

Walgrave, S. and Massens, J. (2000) 'The making of the White March: The mass media as mobilizing alternative to movement organizations', *Mobilization*, 5 (2): 217–239.

Walker, A. (2005 [1984]) *In Search of Our Mother's Gardens*. London: W & N.

Wallrup, E. (2015) *Being Musically Attuned: The Act of Listening to Music*. Farnham: Ashgate.

Walter, T. (2009) 'Dark tourism: Mediating between the dead and the living'. In R. Sharpley and P.R. Stone (eds), *The Darker Side of Travel*. Bristol: Channel View Publications, 39–55.

Wang, N. (1999) 'Rethinking authenticity in tourist experience', *Annals of Tourism Research*, 26 (2): 349–370.

Wang, N. (2000) *Tourism and Modernity: A Sociological Analysis*. Oxford: Pergamon.

Wardrop, K. (2011) 'Edinburgh: Scotland's inspiring capital'. In K. Dinnie (ed.), *City Branding: Theory and Cases*. Palgrave Macmillan, 138–149.

Warnke, G. (2011) 'Geertzian irony'. In J.C Alexander, P. Smith, and M. Norton (eds), *Interpreting Clifford Geertz: Cultural Investigation in the Social Sciences*. New York: Palgrave Macmillan, 45–54.

Weaver, D. (2005) 'The distinctive dynamics of exurban tourism', *The International Journal of Tourism Research*, 7 (1): 23–33.

Weaver, M. (27 January 2009) 'Protests at Indian cinemas over Slumdog Millionaire'. *Guardian*. Available at: www.theguardian.com/world/2009/jan/27/riots-india-slumdog-millionaire (accessed 5 May 2018).

Weintraub, J. (1997) 'The theory and politics of the public/private distinction'. In J. Weintraub and K. Kumar (eds), *Public and Private in Thought and Practice: Perspectives on a Grand Dichotomy*. Chicago: University of Chicago Press.

Weldon (18 March 2012) 'Home of the Brave'. *The Herald Scotland*. Available at: www.heraldscotland.com/news/13050922.Home_of_the_Brave/ (accessed 7 March 2018).

Wenning, M. (2009) 'The return of rage', *Parrhesia*, 8: 89–99.

Westerhausen, K. (2002) *Beyond the Beach: An Ethnography of Modern Travellers in Asia*. Bangkok: Thai Lotus Press.

Westmoreland, M. (2008) 'Interruptions: Derrida and hospitality', *Kritike: An Online Journal of Philosophy*, 2 (1): 1–10.

Whatt, A. (2010) 'The global theme park industry', *Worldwide Hospitality and Tourism*, 2 (3): 220–237.

Wiggershaus, R. (1994) *The Frankfurt School*. Cambridge: Polity.

Williams, F. (2004) *Rethinking Families*. London: Calouste Gulbenkian Foundation.

Williams, R. ([1973] 2016) *The Country and the City*. London: Vintage.

Wodak, R. (2015) *Methods of Critical Discourse Studies*. London: Sage.

Wolff, J. (1993) 'On the road again: Metaphors of travel in cultural criticism', *Cultural Studies*, 7 (2): 224–239.

Wood, R. (1986) *Hollywood: From Vietnam to Reagan*. New York: Columbia University Press.

World Tourism Organization (2004) *Indicators of Sustainable Development for Tourism Destinations: A Guidebook*. Madrid, Spain: WTO. Available at: www.adriaticgreenet.org/icareforeurope/wp-content/uploads/2013/11/Indicators-of-Sustainable-Development-for-Tourism-Destinations-A-Guide-Book-by-UNWTO.pdf (accessed 15 Match 2018).

Yamamura, T. (2015) 'Contents tourism and local community response: Lucky star and collaborative anime-induced tourism in Washimiya', *Japan Forum*, 27 (1): 59–81.

Yang, Y. (undated) 'Embracing stereotypes, Scottish tourism banks on "Brave"'. *Latitude News*. Available at: www.latitudenews.com/story/brave-moviestereotypes-scottish/ (accessed 9 February 2014).

YouTube (17 August 2012) 'VisitScotland – Landscapes of Brave Scotland', *VisitScotland*. Available at: www.youtube.com/watch?v=duivlAHVRo4 (accessed 17 May 2018).

Ystads Commun 1 (undated) 'Wallander'. Available at: www.ystad.se/kultur/film-i-ystad/info-in-english/wallander-film-tourism/wallander/ (accessed 19 April 2018).

Ystads Commun 2 (undated) 'Walk of film'. Available at: www.ystad.se/kultur/film-i-ystad/info-in-english/wallander-film-tourism/walk-of-film/ (accessed 19 April 2018).

Yue, A. (2006) 'Cultural governance and creative industries in Singapore', *International Journal of Cultural Policy*, 12 (1): 7–23.

Zelinsky, S. (2006) *Deep Time of the Media: Toward an Archaeology of Hearing and Seeing by Technical Means*. Cambridge, MA: MIT.

Ziakas, V. (2016) 'Fostering the social utility of events: An integrative framework for the strategic use of events in community development', *Current Issues in Tourism*, 19 (11): 1136–1157.

Žižek, S. (2014) *Event: Philosophy in Transit*. London and New York: Penguin.

Zukin, S. (1995) *The Cultures of Cities*. Malden, MA: Blackwell.

Zukin, S. (2010) *Naked City*. Oxford: Oxford University Press.

Index

Page numbers in *italics* denote figures.

Taylor & Francis Group
an informa business

Taylor & Francis eBooks

www.taylorfrancis.com

A single destination for eBooks from Taylor & Francis with increased functionality and an improved user experience to meet the needs of our customers.

90,000+ eBooks of award-winning academic content in Humanities, Social Science, Science, Technology, Engineering, and Medical written by a global network of editors and authors.

TAYLOR & FRANCIS EBOOKS OFFERS:

- A streamlined experience for our library customers
- A single point of discovery for all of our eBook content
- Improved search and discovery of content at both book and chapter level

REQUEST A FREE TRIAL

support@taylorfrancis.com

Routledge
Taylor & Francis Group

CRC Press
Taylor & Francis Group

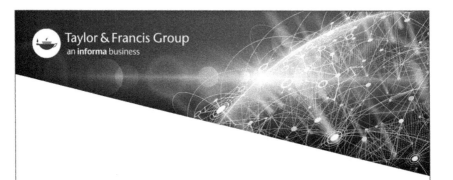

For Product Safety Concerns and Information please contact our EU
representative GPSR@taylorandfrancis.com
Taylor & Francis Verlag GmbH, Kaufingerstraße 24, 80331 München, Germany

www.ingramcontent.com/pod-product-compliance
Ingram Content Group UK Ltd.
Pitfield, Milton Keynes, MK11 3LW, UK
UKHW021031180425
457613UK00021B/1128

* 9 7 8 0 3 6 7 5 5 6 1 6 7 *